BOOKS BY GEORGE CROWDER

CLASSICAL ANARCHISM: THE POLITICAL THOUGHT
OF GODWIN, PROUDHON, BAKUNIN AND KROPOTKIN

LIBERALISM AND VALUE PLURALISM

ISAIAH BERLIN: LIBERTY AND PLURALISM

BOOKS BY ISAIAH BERLIN EDITED BY HENRY HARDY

RUSSIAN THINKERS
(co-edited with Aileen Kelly)

CONCEPTS AND CATEGORIES

AGAINST THE CURRENT

PERSONAL IMPRESSIONS

THE CROOKED TIMBER OF HUMANITY

THE SENSE OF REALITY

THE PROPER STUDY OF MANKIND
(co-edited with Roger Hausheer)

THE ROOTS OF ROMANTICISM

THE POWER OF IDEAS

THREE CRITICS OF THE ENLIGHTENMENT

FREEDOM AND ITS BETRAYAL

LIBERTY

THE SOVIET MIND

FLOURISHING: LETTERS 1928–1946
(published in the US as *Letters 1928–1946*)

POLITICAL IDEAS IN THE ROMANTIC AGE

For more information on Isaiah Berlin visit
http://berlin.wolf.ox.ac.uk/

The One and the Ma

The One and the Many

Reading
Isaiah Berlin

edited by

George Crowder & Henry Hardy

Prometheus Books
59 John Glenn Drive
Amherst, New York 14228-2197

Published 2007 by Prometheus Books

The One and the Many: Reading Isaiah Berlin. Selection and editorial matter © George Crowder and Henry Hardy 2007. Contributions © the respective contributors 2007 except as follows: 'Crooked Timber or Bent Twig? Berlin's Nationalism' © Political Studies Association 2005. 'Taking Pluralism Seriously' © Henry Hardy 1995, 2007. The moral right of George Crowder and Henry Hardy to be identified as the editors of this work has been asserted. All rights reserved. No part of this publication may be reproduced, stored in a retrieval system, or transmitted in any form or by any means, digital, electronic, mechanical, photocopying, recording, or otherwise, or conveyed via the Internet or a Web site without prior written permission of the publisher, except in the case of brief quotations embodied in critical articles and reviews.

Inquiries should be addressed to
Prometheus Books
59 John Glenn Drive
Amherst, New York 14228–2197
VOICE: 716–691–0133, ext. 207
FAX: 716–564–2711
WWW.PROMETHEUSBOOKS.COM

11 10 09 08 07   5 4 3 2 1

Library of Congress Cataloging-in-Publication Data

The one and the many : reading Isaiah Berlin / edited by George Crowder and Henry Hardy.
    p. cm.
Includes bibliographical references and index.
ISBN 978–1–59102–448–4 (alk. paper)
1. Berlin, Isaiah, Sir. I. Crowder, George. II. Hardy, Henry.

B1618.B454O54 2007
192—dc22

2006035313

Printed in the United States of America on acid-free paper

To the memory of Isaiah Berlin

[W]hat he sees is not the one, but always, with an ever-growing minuteness, in all its teeming individuality, with an obsessive, inescapable, incorruptible, all-penetrating lucidity which maddens him, the many.

The Hedgehog and the Fox (RT 74)

Contents

Preface

The plan to publish a book such as this one dates back over a decade. In the early 1990s, publications about Isaiah Berlin were snowballing, and it seemed increasingly desirable to collect the best of them into a single volume for the convenience of readers who wished to sample what had been written on the many aspects of his thought. But as the years went by this approach became decreasingly practical: the pace of publication of new work did not slow down, and the amount of first-rate writing rapidly outgrew the size of any manageable single volume. It became clear that a better option was to commission new pieces that would survey Berlin's contributions to the main fields in which he wrote, as well as the best work of his previous commentators.

This volume comprises the fruits of this initiative. Our aim has been to provide a systematic introduction to Berlin's work across its whole range. We approached established experts in the relevant areas, and asked them to describe Berlin's achievement, to evaluate the main (sometimes incompatible) interpretations which his work has enjoyed, refining or replacing these where necessary, and to suggest promising directions for innovative thinking on questions inspired or provoked by Berlin's ideas.

This brief makes this the first genuinely comprehensive collection of critical essays on Berlin. Previous multi-author volumes have been either Festschrifts, honouring Berlin but not necessarily focusing on his own work, or collections of studies of certain aspects of that work. Surveys of Berlin's work as a whole have been written by single authors; this new collection not only covers all the main departments of his thought, but also provides a multi-perspective examination that draws together many different interpretations.

All but two of the essays were written specially for this volume. The exceptions are David Miller's account of Berlin's views on nationalism (reprinted from *Political Studies*), which fitted our brief so well that it was not necessary to commission a new piece, and Henry Hardy's 'Taking Pluralism Seriously', which, however, has not appeared in print before, in its full version, in English.

There are certain debts of gratitude that we should record. First and foremost, we thank the contributors most warmly for writing for us in the midst of their many other commitments; we do not underestimate the disruption and sacrifice that this has sometimes entailed. In addition, each of us wishes to thank the other for his unfailing patience and support through all vicissitudes. Henry Hardy was helped at an early stage of planning by Ian Harris, whose command of the literature on Berlin is second to none. Both of us have benefited on a number of occasions from the sage counsel of Joshua Cherniss. And we gratefully acknowledge the permission given by Blackwell Publishing to reprint David Miller's 'Crooked Timber or Bent Twig? Isaiah Berlin's Nationalism' (in which a few small revisions have been made) from *Political Studies*.

Finally, perhaps it is worth saying explicitly what may in any case be self-evident: that the publication of this book reflects our belief that Berlin is a thinker of major importance and unique power with much to teach the twenty-first century; and that, despite the critical acclaim which has been widely (though by no means universally) accorded him, his work harbours a good deal of still untapped illumination and instruction.

G. C.
H. H.

Contributors

Jonathan Allen is Assistant Professor in the Department of Political Science, University of Illinois, Urbana-Champaign. He has broad interests in applied political theory and in contemporary and modern political thought, and is the author of several articles in these areas.

Shlomo Avineri is Emeritus Professor of Political Science at the Hebrew University of Jerusalem. He was Director-General of Israel's Ministry of Foreign Affairs from 1975 to 1977. His publications include *The Social and Political Thought of Karl Marx* (1968), *Hegel's Theory of the Modern State* (1972), *The Making of Modern Zionism* (1981) and *Moses Hess: Prophet of Communism and Zionism* (1985).

Terrell Carver is Professor of Political Theory, University of Bristol. His books include *Marx's Social Theory* (1982), *Engels* (1983), *The Postmodern Marx* (1998) and *Men in Political Theory* (2004). He is also the author of numerous articles, reference-book entries and chapters on Marx, Engels and Marxism.

Joshua L. Cherniss is the author of several articles on Berlin, including the introduction to Berlin's *Political Ideas in the Romantic Age* and (with Henry Hardy) the entry on Berlin in the online *Stanford Encyclopedia of Philosophy*. He is currently working on a study (which he is writing as a D.Phil. thesis in Modern History at Oxford) of the early development of Berlin's thought. He is also a graduate student in the Department of Government at Harvard University.

George Crowder is Associate Professor in the School of Political and International Studies, Flinders University, Adelaide, Australia. He is the author of *Classical Anarchism* (1991), *Liberalism and Value Pluralism* (2002), and *Isaiah Berlin: Liberty and Pluralism* (2004). He is currently working (with Ian Haddock) on *Theories of Multiculturalism.*

William A. Galston is Saul I. Stern Professor of Civic Engagement and Director, Institute for Philosophy and Public Policy, University of Maryland. He is the author of *Liberal Purposes* (1991), *Liberalism Pluralism* (2002) and *Liberal Pluralism in Theory and Practice* (2004). In the first two years of President Clinton's administration, Galston served as the Deputy Assistant to the President for Domestic Policy.

Graeme Garrard is Senior Lecturer in Political Theory and European Thought, School of European Studies, Cardiff University. He is the author of *Rousseau's Counter-Enlightenment* (2003) and *Counter-Enlightenments* (2005), and is currently working on a study of French political thought entitled *Anarchy and Authoritarianism.*

Ryan Patrick Hanley is Assistant Professor, Department of Political Science, Marquette University. His research focuses on the history of political philosophy, and on the Scottish Enlightenment in particular. He is co-editor, with the late Robert Wokler, of *The Enlightenment: Critical Concepts in History* (forthcoming), and is currently working on a book entitled *Adam Smith and the Character of Virtue.*

Henry Hardy, A Fellow of Wolfson College, Oxford, is one of Berlin's Literary Trustees. He has edited or co-edited sixteen volumes of Berlin's work (1978–2006), and is the compiler of *The Isaiah Berlin Virtual Library*, an online source of information on all aspects of Berlin's work. He is currently working with Jennifer Holmes on the second of three volumes of Berlin's letters.

Michael Jinkins is Academic Dean and Professor of Pastoral Theology, Austin Presbyterian Theological Seminary, Austin, Texas, and author of *Christianity, Tolerance and Pluralism: A Theological Engagement with Isaiah Berlin's Social Theory* (2004).

David Miller is Professor of Political Theory at the University of Oxford and an Official Fellow of Nuffield College. Among his books are *On Nationality* (1995), *Principles of Social Justice* (1999), *Citizenship and National Identity* (2000) and *Political Philosophy: A Very Short Introduction* (2003). He is currently finishing a book on *National Responsibility and Global Justice.*

Mario Ricciardi is Research Fellow in Jurisprudence at the University of Milan. He is co-editor, with Ian Carter, of *Freedom, Power and Political Morality* (2001), and the author of several articles on legal and political philosophy, including the thought of Isaiah Berlin.

Andrzej Walicki is O'Neill Family Professor Emeritus of History, University of Notre Dame. His many books include *A History of Russian Thought from the Enlightenment to Marxism* (1979), *Legal Philosophies of Russian Liberalism* (1987) and *Marxism and the Leap to the Kingdom of Freedom: The Rise and Fall of the Communist Utopia* (1995).

Abbreviations

The following abbreviations are used in this volume for the titles of books by and about Isaiah Berlin:

AC	*Against the Current* (1979)
CC	*Concepts and Categories* (1978)
CIB	Ramin Jahanbegloo, *Conversations with Isaiah Berlin* (1992)
CTH	*The Crooked Timber of Humanity* (1990)
FIB	*Freedom and Its Betrayal* (2002)
IBAC	Avishai Margalit and Edna Margalit (eds), *Isaiah Berlin: A Celebration* (1991)
IBCE	Joseph Mali and Robert Wokler (eds), *Isaiah Berlin's Counter-Enlightenment* (2003)
IBLP	George Crowder, *Isaiah Berlin: Liberty and Pluralism* (2004)
IBVL	*The Isaiah Berlin Virtual Library*, ed. Henry Hardy: <http://berlin.wolf.ox.ac.uk/>
JG	John Gray, *Isaiah Berlin* (1995)
KM	*Karl Marx* (edition-neutral reference)
KM1...KM4	*Karl Marx*: 1st edition (1939); 2nd edition (1948); 3rd edition (1963); 4th edition (1978)
L	*Liberty* (2002)

L1	[*Flourishing:*] *Letters 1928–1946* (2004)
LIB	Mark Lilla, Ronald Dworkin and Robert B. Silvers (eds), *The Legacy of Isaiah Berlin* (2001)
LVP	George Crowder, *Liberalism and Value Pluralism* (2002)
MI	Michael Ignatieff, *Isaiah Berlin: A Life*
MSB	Oxford, Bodleian Library, [shelfmark]/[folio(s)], e.g. MSB 232/1–3 = MS. Berlin 232, folios 1–3
OM	*The One and the Many*, ed. George Crowder and Henry Hardy (2007)
PI; PI2	*Personal Impressions* (1980); 2nd edition (1998)
PIRA	*Political Ideas in the Romantic Age* (2006)
POI	*The Power of Ideas* (2000)
PSM	*The Proper Study of Mankind* (1997)
RR	*The Roots of Romanticism* (1999)
RT	*Russian Thinkers* (1978)
SM	*The Soviet Mind* (2004)
SR	*The Sense of Reality* (1996)
TCE	*Three Critics of the Enlightenment* (2000)
UD	*Unfinished Dialogue* (with Beata Polanowska-Sygulska) (2006)

The main (arabic) pagination of all editions of these works, apart from the successive editions of KM and PI, is currently the same.[1] There is some variation, however, in roman pagination. This affects, in particular, Berlin's preface and Bernard Williams's introduction to CC, and (less importantly) the editorial prefaces to the collections of Berlin's essays. In these cases the pagination in the first UK edition (whose date appears in parentheses) is used unless otherwise specified.

Unpublished letters are cited by date, with the addition of an MSB reference where applicable. Such letters come from a number of sources, institutional and personal; copies of those cited only by date are currently held by Henry Hardy.

---

1. A forthcoming new edition of *Russian Thinkers* will be reset and therefore repaginated, but a concordance of the old and new page numbering will be provided, as in the case of *Four Essays on Liberty* and *Liberty* (the latter incorporating the former).

Introduction

THE ONE AND THE MANY

GEORGE CROWDER AND HENRY HARDY

> Pluralism, with the measure of 'negative' liberty that it entails, seems to me a truer and more humane ideal than the goals of those who seek in the great disciplined, authoritarian structures the ideal of 'positive' self-mastery by classes, or peoples, or the whole of mankind. (L 216)

These words come close to capturing the essence of Isaiah Berlin's political thought. They appear in the final section—'The One and the Many'—of his famous essay, 'Two Concepts of Liberty' (1958). Here he sets out his highly influential formulation of the distinction between negative and positive liberty, his liberal critique of distortions of positive liberty, his vision of what is now usually called 'value pluralism' (not his own term), and his association of this pluralism with liberalism. For this achievement alone Berlin arguably deserves a place as one of the most significant liberal political thinkers of the twentieth century. G. A. Cohen, for example, brackets Berlin and John Rawls as the two 'most celebrated twentieth-century Anglophone political philosophers' (2003, 6).[1]

Berlin's contribution to contemporary thought is by no means confined to

---

1. Similarly, Adam Swift writes that 'if Rawls's *A Theory of Justice* is the most influential book of contemporary political philosophy, Isaiah Berlin's "Two Concepts of Liberty" is the most influential single essay' (2001, 51).

moral and political philosophy. He also wrote illuminatingly on nineteenth-century Russian thinkers such as Belinsky, Herzen, Turgenev and Tolstoy; on 'Counter-Enlightenment' writers such as Vico, Hamann, Herder and Maistre; on the origins and development of the romantic movement; on the nature of explanation in history, philosophy and other human studies; and on the sources, history and resilience of nationalism.

Although his work in these fields might be seen as part of his broader defence of liberalism, many readers have been drawn to it for quite independent reasons. One of the most inspirational aspects of his legacy is his sheer enthusiasm for the history of ideas, together with his highly idiosyncratic approach to that field. His characteristic method was not the conventional analytical technique of constructing arguments and counter-arguments, but a historical approach that traced ideas to their origins in the work of key thinkers whose personalities were shown to be as important as their logic. His speciality was to step into the mental world of a thinker and to present that world on its own terms, for readers to make their own judgement. This 'inside view' was in keeping with his general approach to the explanation of human conduct, which opposed detached, impersonal methods based on the natural sciences (as championed, for example, by the logical positivists of the 1930s) in favour of an empathetic stress on the purposes, values and world-views of the actors themselves.

Berlin's work has attracted many different interpretations and evaluations. Is he primarily a liberal thinker or a value pluralist? Does his pluralism support his defence of liberal values such as negative liberty and personal autonomy, or does it in fact undermine any such defence? Is he right to pay so much attention to Counter-Enlightenment thinkers, or does he show them too much sympathy, and the Enlightenment too little? Is his work on nationalism a salutary correction to the cosmopolitanism dominant in the liberal outlook, or is it retrograde and confused? What bearing, if any, does his work have on concrete issues of public policy? What are the implications of his views for religious sensibilities: are these accommodated or excluded by his value pluralism? These are just a few of the questions debated by the contributors to this volume.

THREE TRADITIONS

Berlin came from a middle-class Russian-Jewish background. He was born in Riga, in what is now Latvia, then part of the Russian Empire; his father was a successful timber merchant. After moving to Petrograd, the Berlins were caught up in the revolutions of 1917. Isaiah was seven when he saw a tsarist policeman being dragged away by a crowd, apparently to his death—an image that remained with him for the rest of his life, crystallising his abiding fear of revolutionary violence and of political extremism in general.

The family left Russia in 1920, eventually settling in England in 1921. Berlin was educated at St Paul's School in London, before winning a scholarship to Oxford: he went up in 1928. As a philosopher, he was initially drawn to the vigorous empiricism of the logical positivists, led in Oxford by A. J. Ayer, but became frustrated by their abstract and ahistorical approach, and was increasingly attracted to the historically and culturally richer fields of the history of ideas and political theory. Researching his first book, *Karl Marx* (first edition 1939), he began to read the eighteenth- and nineteenth-century thinkers who preoccupied him later.

During the Second World War Berlin served as a British official, first at the Ministry of Information in New York, then at the British Embassy in Washington. In 1945 he was briefly transferred to the Soviet Union, where he came into contact with dissident Russian writers, most notably Anna Akhmatova and Boris Pasternak. These meetings brought home to him the plight of the creative individual under Soviet Communism, and sharpened his sense of his own Russian heritage.

After the war Berlin returned to Oxford, but soon acquired a more public profile as a leading commentator on the intellectual dimensions of the developing cold war. Throughout the early 1950s, he produced a steady stream of essays, lectures and radio broadcasts developing his central theme of the modern betrayal of freedom. He was knighted in 1957 after his election to the Chichele Professorship of Social and Political Theory at Oxford, a post he held until 1967, relinquishing it because of his appointment in 1966 as founding President of Wolfson College, Oxford. His inaugural lecture in 1958 was the famous 'Two Concepts of Liberty', which remains his most influential essay, and one of the most frequently cited works of twentieth-century political philosophy. By the time he retired he had become one of Britain's most prominent public intellectuals and a figure of international significance.

Towards the end of his life, Berlin reflected that he 'had been formed by three traditions—Russian, British and Jewish' (PI2 255). To take the British influence first, he confesses that his basic values express

> a pro-British bias. [...] I cannot judge English values impartially, for they are part of me: I count this as the greatest of intellectual and political good fortune. These values are the basis of what I believe: that decent respect for others and the toleration of dissent are better than pride and a sense of national mission; that liberty may be incompatible with, and better than, too much efficiency; that pluralism and untidiness are, to those who value freedom, better than the rigorous imposition of all-embracing systems, no matter how rational and disinter-

ested, or than the rule of majorities against which there is no appeal. All this is deeply and uniquely English, and I freely admit that I am steeped in it, and believe in it, and cannot breathe freely save in a society where these values are for the most part taken for granted. (PI2 257)

Berlin also attributes to his British education one of the fundamental starting points of his philosophy: his empiricism. At Oxford in the 1930s he found himself navigating between two opposed extremes. On the one hand there was the rich, historicist Hegelianism that had been influential, if not dominant, in the previous generation of British philosophers; on the other hand there was the logical positivism championed by younger thinkers such as A. J. Ayer. Berlin was impressed by the logical positivists' rejection of Hegelian speculation and obscurity, and by their insistence on grounding philosophy in experience. But he was also troubled by the narrowly scientistic version of empiricism they propounded, according to which no proposition had meaning unless it was verifiable by observation or deduction—essentially the claim that the only route to knowledge was through the natural sciences. What the Hegelian outlook had to recommend it, despite its excesses, was an appreciation of historical perspective and, more broadly, of the role of personal and cultural purposes in human conduct. To understand the actions of human beings, we should indeed follow the empiricist commitment to lived experience, but should also remember that access to that experience is available not through the natural sciences alone—indeed, they are distinctly insufficient in this respect—but rather through the 'inside view' of people's goals and values that requires the study of history and personality.

This broader approach to understanding informs Berlin's first book, *Karl Marx: His Life and Environment*, first published in 1939, and discussed in this volume by Terrell Carver. Because the book predates the cold war, Carver argues, it escapes the stultifying dogmatism of that era, and it is fortunate that Berlin was not tempted to tamper much with his text in the three subsequent editions. Although access to Marx's manuscripts since the 1930s has transformed our knowledge of his thought and led to several major reassessments, Berlin's balanced and humane biographical approach, and his understanding of Continental philosophy and politics, mean that this comparatively short work is still the best introduction in English. Moreover, Berlin unusually and presciently interpreted Marx, not in either of the orthodox ways (Marxist and anti-Marxist) of his time, but rather in a way that intuits the content of manuscripts to which he did not then have access. Carver draws on a new reconstruction of Berlin's original uncut manuscript to make observations on Berlin's thinking at the time of composition, and also to discuss the relationship of Berlin's thought at that point to his later work on value pluralism, liberty, intellectuals in politics and the Soviet experience.

The Russian dimension of Berlin's background is examined by Andrzej Walicki. What is the relation, Walicki asks, between Berlin's liberalism and his interest in the Russian thinkers of the nineteenth century? First, it was his favourite Russian thinkers—especially Belinsky and Herzen—who helped him analyse the anti-libertarian aspects of historical determinism. Their moral protest against Hegelianism inspired Berlin's criticism of 'historical inevitability' and enabled him to enlist them as allies in the struggle against Stalinist Marxism. Second, Berlin's value pluralism owed much to Turgenev's defence of those 'Hamlets' who perceive the plurality of truths and values and are consequently incapable of single-minded commitment. During the student revolts of 1968–70 Berlin explicitly identified himself with this 'liberal predicament'. Third, Berlin's response to the historical experience of the pre-Revolutionary Russian liberals serves as a corrective to one-sided interpretations of his analysis of negative and positive liberty, showing him to be much more sympathetic than is often assumed to links between liberty on the one hand and equality, education and justice on the other. Finally, Walicki points to some unexpected analogies between Berlin's secular liberalism and the revival of religious philosophy in Eastern Europe after perestroika.

The third strand of Berlin's identity, his Jewishness, is discussed by Shlomo Avineri. For Avineri, Berlin's writing on Jewish matters is remarkable in the way it 'starts from the outside'—that is, in universal principles that are subsequently applied to the Jewish experience rather than in the experience itself, about which he was personally ambivalent. Berlin's Zionism was always subordinate to his liberalism rather than the other way round. However, it is surely his Jewish identity that helped Berlin to grasp so strongly, as many liberals have not, the centrality to human well-being of the sense of belonging to a community—a sense so deeply disrupted by the Diaspora. Avineri traces Berlin's brilliant analyses of the various challenges faced by Jewish thinkers such as Disraeli and Marx in their efforts to feel at home with the people around them. Such case-studies, Berlin believes, show the failure of assimilation as an answer to 'the Jewish question'. Hence his Zionism. Berlin welcomed the creation of the State of Israel as at last enabling Jews to choose their own authentic identity, either becoming citizens of the new State or remaining outside, but in less discomfort. This latter option was preferred by Berlin himself, and defended by him on the universal ground of freedom of choice. Yet Avineri suggests that his choice in this matter also points to the complexity of Berlin's attitude to his Jewishness, revealed, for example, in the absence from his published writings and from his letters of any sustained discussion of the Holocaust.

THE BETRAYAL OF FREEDOM

The fact that Berlin never wrote directly on the Holocaust has been adduced as evidence that he ignored the central historical lesson of his time, the evil that people can do out of sheer wickedness (James 2004). Properly understood, however, Berlin's work is all about the Holocaust. His point is that much of the world's wickedness is not blankly inexplicable, but has its origins in our ideas. Ideas have enormous power. Moreover, in many cases the pernicious beliefs that have done the most damage originated in noble-sounding ideals propounded by the most high-minded of thinkers. Berlin's work covers a great range, but its dominant focus is a defence of liberal values against those currents of thought that had resulted in twentieth-century totalitarianism. The intellectual roots of modern totalitarianism can be found, he shows, at three principal levels in the history of Western ideas: in the 'betrayal of freedom', in the contest between the Enlightenment and its critics, and in the idea of ethical monism in contrast with value pluralism.

The 'betrayal of freedom' is the idea not of a simple rejection of political liberty but of a systematic distortion of what that freedom truly is. According to Berlin, the fundamental sense of liberty is 'negative': the absence of coercive human interference. This he contrasts with 'positive' liberty, the freedom of self-mastery, which comes into being when a person is ruled not by arbitrary desires but by the 'true' or authentic self. Although both negative and positive aspects of liberty are genuine and important, the positive idea leaves open the possibility that a person's authentic wishes may be identified with the commands of some external authority—for example, the State or the Party. Freedom can then be defined as obedience, and in effect twisted into its opposite. Berlin associates this kind of thinking with writers such as Rousseau, Fichte, Hegel and Marx. He does not reject positive liberty entirely, but sees negative liberty as the safer, and the primary, option politically.

In 'Berlin's Early Political Thought', Joshua L. Cherniss traces the origins of this analysis in Berlin's writings on politics before the composition of his famous lecture on 'Two Concepts of Liberty' in 1958. This body of work encompasses essays in both political theory and the history of ideas, as well as articles on world events and on Soviet politics and society. It includes the draft 'torso' on which Berlin drew in much of his later work, recently published as *Political Ideas in the Romantic Age* (PIRA), and the essays now collected in *The Soviet Mind* (SM). Cherniss demonstrates the influences on, and main characteristics of, Berlin's political thought, with particular emphasis on his understanding of liberty. In doing so, he both sets Berlin's political thought within its historical context, and provides a genealogy and analysis of the main conceptual claims of Berlin's political theory. A notable feature of Cherniss's discussion is his claim that Berlin's earlier work displays a higher valuation of the ideal of personal autonomy than he is often credited with by those who associate him only with the defence of negative liberty in 'Two Concepts of Liberty'.

This classic text is examined by Mario Ricciardi, who emphasises the essay's contribution to the case Berlin makes for the continued relevance of political philosophy. Berlin is responding not only to the political realities of the Cold War and decolonisation, but also, as Ricciardi points out, to the philosophical climate of the 1950s, in which political theory, conceived as a substantive enquiry into the nature of the good political society, had been reported dead. For Berlin, that report was thoroughly exaggerated, and he proceeded to demonstrate 'the power of ideas' in the political field, in this case ideas of liberty. These are distinctively 'philosophical' ideas, since the eponymous 'concepts' of liberty are among the 'concepts and categories', regulating our day-to-day understanding, that Berlin identifies as philosophy's peculiar bailiwick. The most famous theme of the essay is that a negative conception of liberty can be distinguished from a positive conception, and that the former is not as vulnerable as the latter to politically dangerous manipulation. Ricciardi traces Berlin's clarification of several aspects of the negative idea, including its relation to our desires, its potential for measurement, and its boundaries with other ideas, in particular notions of 'ability' or power, and of collective self-government. He ends by setting out Berlin's critique of positive liberty, connecting the conflict between the negative and positive ideals with the introduction, in the essay's last section, of the theme of value pluralism.

ENLIGHTENMENT, NATIONALISM AND HISTORY

At a second level, totalitarianism is traced by Berlin to the complex relationship between the Enlightenment on one side and the 'Counter-Enlightenment' and romanticism on the other. The legacy of both the Enlightenment and its critics is mixed, according to Berlin. As a liberal, he defends the faith of the French *philosophes* in reason, personal liberty and toleration. But he also argues that certain strains of Enlightenment thought take the claims of reason and science to utopian extremes, playing a significant part in the genesis of the totalitarianism of the left, which is Berlin's principal target. Soviet Communism can be traced back, through Marx, to the wildly optimistic scientism of well-meaning eighteenth-century philosophers such as Helvétius, Holbach, Condorcet and Saint-Simon. On the other hand, the Counter-Enlightenment, though a potent source of the anti-humanism and irrationalism that gave rise to Fascism, is also a source of opposition to the tyranny of scientism. Moreover, it is in Counter-Enlightenment thinkers such as Vico, Hamann and Herder that Berlin finds some of the earliest, tentative hints of value pluralism.

Still, most readers tend to see Berlin—as indeed he saw himself—as ultimately a man of the Enlightenment. Graeme Garrard takes issue with this orthodoxy, arguing that Berlin's treatment of the Enlightenment and its enemies amounts to a 'strange reversal' of standard liberal judgements—indeed, that Berlin's thought turns 'decisively' towards the Counter-Enlightenment.[2] The key point, according to Garrard, is that Berlin associates the Enlightenment as a whole with the ethical monism he opposes, and the Counter-Enlightenment with the value pluralism he supports. Garrard sees this view as one of Berlin's most original and least appreciated contributions to liberal thought—but also as one of his most contentious, since it ascribes a unity to the Enlightenment that overlooks a fundamental division within it between monists such as Holbach and pluralists such as Montesquieu. Rousseau, too, is no less a pluralist than Machiavelli, who provides (in a different context) one of Berlin's favourite examples of proto-pluralism. Berlin's judgement is surer, in Garrard's opinion, when it comes to the Counter-Enlightenment: this is as deeply pluralist in outlook as Berlin contends, but Berlin is also right to see only a 'contingent' relation between pluralism and liberalism.

Berlin's affinity for aspects of the Counter-Enlightenment is a key source for his critique of scientism and his endorsement of the inside view essential to historical understanding. This theme is explored by Ryan Hanley, who provides an overview of Berlin's approach to the study of history, with special emphasis on the history of ideas. Hanley begins by examining the critique of 'scientific history' presented in 'The Concept of Scientific History' and 'Historical Inevitability', locating this critique within Berlin's understanding of the quarrel between the humanities and the sciences. The dispassionately objective scientific method in history is contrasted by Berlin with an 'empathetic' approach, developed in particular in his writings on Vico. Hanley goes on to examine Berlin's notion of a historical 'sense of reality', an intuitive feel for the way particular observations and ideas fit within a plausible overall picture. The chapter concludes with a consideration of Berlin's influence on contemporary historiography. Hanley sees Berlin's abiding significance as consisting not in the founding of a 'Berlinian' school or doctrine, but in the transmission of a historical sensibility that sets ideas within their context but also looks beyond the immediate context to connect the past with the present. Vico's contextualism should be balanced by Voltaire's focus on the ideas that matter to us now.

Berlin also associates the Counter-Enlightenment, by way of romanticism, with the birth of modern nationalism. In 'Crooked Timber or Bent Twig?', David Miller examines Berlin's account of nationalism in general, and the relation

---

2. For a sustained recent identification of Berlin as a Counter-Enlightenment figure see Sternhell 2006.

between that account and contemporary liberal nationalism. According to Miller, Berlin gives conflicting definitions of nationalism in different places, and although he frequently contrasts more benign with more malign forms of nationalism, the terms in which he draws the contrast also vary. In Berlin's most explicit account, nationalist doctrine is presented as political, unitary, morally unrestricted and particularist, but these four dimensions are separate, and on each of them alternative nationalist positions are available. Berlin's account of the sources of nationalism is also inconsistent: his analysis of the Jewish condition in European societies and his support for Zionism contrast with his diagnosis of the origins of German nationalism. Comparing Berlin with later liberal nationalists, Miller argues that his liberalism prevents him from presenting a normative political theory in which liberal and nationalist commitments are successfully combined. Such a theory can indeed be developed, but the challenge that emerges from Berlin's writing is to explain how real-world nationalism can be kept within liberal limits.

VALUE PLURALISM AND ITS IMPLICATIONS

At a third level—the deepest—Berlin highlights the opposition between monist and pluralist conceptions of morality. The scientistic, utopian side of the Enlightenment is really a modern instance of a more deep-seated tendency in Western thought as a whole, which is to suppose that all genuine moral values must somehow fit together into a single formula capable of yielding a correct answer to any moral problem. This is ethical monism. Its political implication is utopian: the true moral system, once known, will make possible a perfect society in which there will be universal agreement on a single best way of life. Such a view, Berlin protests, is dangerous. To suppose that moral and political perfection is possible is to invite its pursuit by any means at whatever cost.

Moreover, moral monism is false to human experience, which teaches that we are frequently faced with choices among competing goods, choices to which no clear answers are forthcoming from simple rules. The truer and safer view of the deep nature of morality is 'value pluralism'. There are many human values, we can know objectively what these are, and some of them are universal—such as liberty and equality. But values are sometimes 'incommensurable': they are so distinct that each has its own character and force, untranslatable into the terms of any other. When incommensurable values come into conflict, the choices between them will be difficult, in part because in choosing one good we necessarily forgo another, and also because we will not be able to apply any simple rule that reduces the rival goods to a common denominator or that arranges them in a single hierarchy that applies in all cases.

Berlin finds hints of value pluralism in many writers—Machiavelli, Montesquieu, Vico, Hamann, Herder, Herzen, Turgenev—but his explicit formulation of the idea as a central theme of a whole political outlook is highly original.[3] The political system that fits best with pluralism, according to Berlin, is liberalism. However, the precise relation between pluralism and liberalism, both within Berlin's thought and more generally, has been energetically disputed. Berlin's views on the matter are not entirely clear, but he seems to have believed that pluralism supports liberalism. The inescapability of choice in human experience, he seems to say in 'Two Concepts of Liberty', implies an argument for freedom of choice. Also, the anti-utopian aspect of pluralism suggests a case for liberalism as a realistic, humane form of politics that seeks to contain and manage conflict rather than to transcend it.

The force of these pluralist arguments for liberalism has been questioned. If basic values are incommensurable, why should we privilege liberal values such as individual liberty and toleration over rival values or packages of values such as those of socialism or conservatism? Berlin's liberal reading of pluralism was subjected to an especially strong challenge in the 1990s, with John Gray's influential claim that liberal universalism is not even consistent with pluralism.[4] For Gray, the plurality of values means that many different rankings of basic goods are equally valid, and this rules out all but the 'thinnest' of universal value-systems. On this view, liberalism cannot possess universal moral authority, but only the 'agonistic' status of one locally valid ranking of goods among others. Berlin's link between pluralism and a more robust liberal project seems, on this interpretation, to have been broken.

More recently, however, Gray's position has been opposed by writers seeking to re-establish the coherence of liberal pluralism. William Galston, for example, has argued that value pluralism implies a generous form of multiculturalism that is best facilitated by an accommodating, tolerant form of liberalism (Galston 2002, 2005). A similar case has been advanced by George Crowder, although in terms rather less accommodating of cultural minorities that are hostile to personal autonomy (LVP, IBLP). In addition to individual autonomy, Crowder's case appeals to principles of value diversity and reasonable disagreement to link pluralism with liberalism. In his contribution to this volume, Crowder sets out his position, paying special attention to the extent to which it departs from Berlin's original suggestions as compared with the degree to which it builds on those suggestions.

---

3. The degree of originality of his formulation of value pluralism is contested, and he made no definite claims in this connection himself. For possible anticipations of the substance of Berlinian value pluralism see Stephen 1873, 93 ff., 118, 169, 172, 174, 180, 206, 225 and *passim*; Weber 1917, 17–18; Weber 1918a, 117, 126; and Weber 1918b, 147–8, 151–3; for anticipations of both substance and formulation see Lamprecht 1920, 1921 and Brogan 1931.

4. Gray 1993; JG; Gray 1995, 2000.

The practical implications of Berlinian value pluralism have so far received relatively little attention. Berlin himself said very little about concrete policy pre-scription, and he has been accused of neglecting this field unduly (Hitchens 1998). Even if this is true, however, it may also be true that the liberal-pluralist principles and insights inspired by Berlin have real and distinctive policy applications. Sug-gestions to this effect have been made in connection with issues such as distribu-tive justice, multiculturalism, democratic procedure and international ethics.[5]

To this developing literature Jonathan Allen contributes 'A Liberal-Pluralist Case for Truth Commissions'. The Truth and Reconciliation Commission in post-apartheid South Africa, Allen argues, presents an interesting example of a public institution struggling with a conflict between fundamental values—in this case, justice and social unity. But Allen makes the point that 'justice' and 'social unity' are themselves complex goods, with multiple aspects or forms. This com-plexity tells against the 'simple sacrifice' justification for the commissions, according to which 'justice' is flatly confronted by 'social unity', to which it must give way, *in toto*, in a one-for-one exchange. On the other hand, the pluralist out-look is also at odds with another justification for the commissions, the 'restorative justice' view, according to which there is really no conflict at all between justice and social unity once the former is suitably redefined. Between these extremes lies a middle way, Allen suggests, in a notion of 'complex compromise', under which social unity is sought in exchange for certain aspects of justice but not others. Allen's argument bears not only on the practice but also on the theory of value pluralism, since it takes issue with a common oversimplification according to which choices between incommensurables must be non-rational and either/or.

When it comes to assessing the implications of value pluralism, an area of special concern is religion. In 'Pluralism and Monotheism' William Galston addresses the worry that the idea of value pluralism may seem unacceptable to many religious believers—in particular, those who believe in a world created and governed by one God. If pluralism and monotheism were mutually exclusive, that would seem to place serious practical limitations on the extent to which a case for liberalism could appeal to pluralism in Berlin's sense: such a case could not be affirmed by many religiously minded citizens (Larmore 1996, chapter 7). Galston argues against the assumption that acceptance of Berlinian pluralism must be incompatible with the great monotheistic faiths. This is because the faiths in ques-tion—Judaism, Christianity, Islam—are actually pluralistic. Their core commit-ment, to 'right relations with God', involves in each case a 'minimal moral code' that can be interpreted in many different ways. That is shown by the fact that, over time, each of these beliefs has generated many distinct 'faith communities'. The

---

5. LVP chapter 9; IBLP chapter 8; Galston 2002, 2005; Ignatieff 2001, 2004.

world religions are thus capable of embracing such a range of different personal and social views that they are comfortably consistent with a pluralist outlook.

A similar position is adopted by Michael Jinkins. Religions, Jinkins acknowledges, frequently inspire among their adherents intolerance and exclusion rather than tolerance and inclusion, and they tend to do this in the name of God. Especially in the light of the flourishing of so many forms of religious fundamentalism, extremism and utopianism, and the religiously motivated violence these foment, one is bound to ask whether religion is not more a curse than a blessing. This chapter, written from the perspective of a specifically Christian theological response to Isaiah Berlin's pluralism, presents a possible alternative. Jinkins uses Berlin's social theory as the basis of an account of diversity that both possesses religious integrity and suggests how religious communities might move beyond the impasse of monism.

In 'Taking Pluralism Seriously', however, Henry Hardy takes a very different view from those of Galston and Jinkins. Drawing on Berlin's pluralist account of ultimate human values, an account whose radical unorthodoxy he emphasises, Hardy argues that value pluralists who are serious in their convictions cannot in consistency accept the intellectual credentials of any religious creed or political ideology that claims to espouse a uniquely valid view of the fundamental issues of human life. In the case of religious belief, Berlin did not draw this consequence of his pluralism explicitly. However, his endorsement of this essay (completed in 1995, but not previously published in English) adds usefully to the evidence available for the interpretation of his pluralist views.

PROTEUS VERSUS PROCRUSTES

In this Introduction we have presented Berlin's work both as many-sided and as unified by his underlying preoccupation with the intellectual roots of totalitarianism. This is one of a number of problematic dichotomies that can be grouped under the ancient Greek formula 'the one and the many', whose deployment by Berlin we noted at the outset. In this case it points to the need for a proper balance between, on the one hand, acknowledging the wide range of cultural and historical variety, and, on the other, seeking to understand and respond rationally to that variety on the basis of underlying patterns and principles.

Some readers familiar with Berlin's writing may protest that attributing even this degree of organisation to his work is an alien imposition. On this view, the real heart of Berlin's thought is an acute awareness of the irreducible, pullulating multiplicity of the world we encounter in our lives, of its vastly various contents and denizens, including ourselves. As Noel Annan has written of Berlin, 'He will always use two words where one will not do' (PI2 xxiii). In the same spirit, Berlin regularly prefers to recognise difference and idiosyncrasy where he finds it, rather than pretending, least of all in the service of some flattening ideology, that distinct phenomena are similar, still less identical. With occasional lapses, especially when characterising his opponents, he is the great non-simplifier, if not under-simplifier, of experience. He retains an almost childlike responsiveness to the 'great blooming, buzzing confusion' (James 1890, 1:488) of our pre-conceptualised sensory input—to what Louis MacNeice, in his poem 'Snow', called 'the drunkenness of things being various'. This seems to have been very much Berlin's own self-image, and a matter of temperament as well as conviction. As he put it in an interview, 'I don't want the universe to be too tidy' (UD 125).

An image that Berlin made famous in this connection is his contrast between the fox and the hedgehog. In his essay 'The Hedgehog and The Fox' (1953) he quotes the seventh-century-BCE Greek poet Archilochus, who wrote, 'The fox knows many things, but the hedgehog knows one big thing' (RT 22). Berlin develops this fragment into an account of two opposing kinds of intellectual disposition: that of the systematising hedgehogs, seeking to 'relate everything to a single vision' (Plato and Hegel, for example), and that of the unsystematic foxes, who celebrate 'a vast variety of experiences and objects for what they are in themselves' (for instance, Shakespeare and Montaigne). On the whole, Berlin seems to see himself as a fox, siding with vulpine receptive flexibility against the single-issue fanaticism of the bone-headed hedgehog.

Yet many commentators have noted that Berlin's defence of multiplicity and variety is itself paradoxically single-minded, and that his insistence on value pluralism is a persistent, if often implicit, theme underlying nearly everything he wrote. Moreover, between the hedgehogs and the foxes, Berlin sometimes identified awkward halfway cases of thinkers who consciously strove to fulfil hedgehog-like ambitions of monist systematisation, but were troubled and thwarted in this ambition by an innate foxlike sense of ineluctable plurality—this is his view of Tolstoy and J. S. Mill, for example. Might it be that Berlin was himself an anomalous case of the opposite kind: a hedgehog in fox's clothing?

The difficulty of pinning Berlin down on this point suggests a further pair of images, inspired by an article of Jonathan Allen's (1998).[6] Proteus and Procrustes are both figures from ancient Greek legend. Proteus is the old sage of the sea with the power to change his shape at high speed to escape those who wish to tap into his omniscience; Procrustes is the robber who forced his victims to lie on a bed and then either stretched their bodies if they were too short, or, if they were too

---

6. In this review of SR, Allen identifies Berlin's 'anti-Procrusteanism' as central to his thought (174), and also refers (separately) to 'the irreducibly protean character of human experience' (176). Berlin himself invoked Procrustes to analogous effect when still an undergraduate (Berlin 1930); and see Cherniss 2006, xliii–xlv.

long, cut their legs to fit. One must not of course be Procrustean in applying this analogy, but clearly there is much of Procrustes in the fanatical monists, the disciples of scientism and the ideologically driven totalitarians who people Berlin's demonology. Similarly, there is undeniably something protean about Berlin's vision: its lack of dogma, its fertility and its elusiveness—an elusiveness that troubles us even when it comes to determining the degree to which Berlin was a proponent of the many rather than the one.

To elicit Proteus' wisdom it was necessary to catch him when he was asleep and tie him fast: then he would be compelled to assume his true form and divulge what he knew. To judge by the continuing controversy stimulated by Isaiah Berlin's ideas, he may be a tougher nut to crack; but our hope is that this volume is a small step towards that objective.

1

Berlin's Karl Marx

TERRELL CARVER

erlin's relationship with Marx and Marxism was long and tortuous. It can never be said that he was a partisan of either. What people thought Marx and Marxism were, what the relationship between the two was or was supposed to be, and what the political implications were or might be of being for or against one or the other, changed a great deal during his lifetime. Marx and Marxism were thus both moving targets against a moving background. It can be readily discerned from my opening distinction that Marx's works and politics have never been the same thing as the diverse array of intellectual and political tendencies and movements that go under the name of Marxism, despite the very considerable efforts of intellectuals and politicians (both for and against) to merge the two.

My approach to this subject values complexity and open-endedness over reductionism and presumptions of certainty. While throughout his life Berlin made statements about Marx and Marxism that appear categorically critical, I am disinclined to present him as consistent in these views.[1] Nevertheless, I suggest that it would be inappropriate to tax him (at least unduly) with inconsistency in this regard. Moreover, there is real admiration and enthusiasm for many aspects of Marx in Berlin's writing, and it is important not to undervalue these at any

---

1. See the comments on Berlin as a 'cold war liberal' in Arblaster 1984, chapter 18; and on his relation as a liberal to Marx and Marxism in IBLP 21–7. See also the discussion of Berlin's views in the 1950s by John E. Toews, IBCE 169–70.

stage of his career, as I think some critics do. I am thus resisting the see-saw temptation amongst commentators to set Berlin's contrasting judgements against each
other as if this variety were itself a disadvantage, and as if the only other option
is to judge him wishy-washy or confused. My argument is rather that Berlin was
temperamentally in tune with complexity and open-endedness, and that this can
be a real scholarly and political virtue, especially in addressing Marx and
Marxism, precisely because the two have always been complex and open-ended
phenomena, and because readers can be well advised to treat them that way.

Moreover I argue that it is to Berlin's credit, and indeed another real benefit
to his readers, that he did not make his thought and work Marx- and Marxism-
centric, even for a time, as others were tempted to do (again, whether for or
against). And finally I contend that it is rather to the benefit of Marx and Marxism
to see them addressed and located differently as contexts change, and in fact to
see them, as Berlin does, within a diverse and fluid mainstream of intellectual and
political developments (both laudable and regrettable) in the West and beyond.
Overall I would say that this is a lasting achievement, pioneered by Berlin in his
very first work, *Karl Marx: His Life and Environment.*[2] Or rather, that when I first
read his short book in the mid-1960s, that is what I made of it, albeit subliminally.
Now, more than forty years later, that is what I see in it once again, but with much
more clarity, notwithstanding any particular changes Berlin made to his text over
time, nor because of them.

This chapter is not the story of how Berlin came to write the book, nor the
history of his views on Marx and Marxism. Rather it reviews the book (in its various stages) against political and intellectual orthodoxies that Berlin was characteristically keen to avoid. Berlin emerges as someone in favour of pursuing his
own lines of thought, even if they resembled no one else's exactly, and even if
they rippled the pond somewhat with his friends, and let his foes off rather lightly.
His method (for this reader) was thus one of critical and nuanced appreciation,
rather than of condemnation or hagiography driven by analytical dichotomies
and judgemental certainties. Marx was lucky when Berlin was sent his way,
because after Berlin he became less doctrinal and dogmatic, more open to multiple interpretations, and a more protean and stimulating intellectual for
enquiring minds to engage with.

---

2. Published by Thornton Butterworth in London in 1939. In his British Academy
memoir of Berlin, Alan Ryan makes a similar judgement, saying that KM was 'one of the
first works in English to treat Marx objectively—neither belittling the real intellectual
power of his work, nor descending into hagiography' (Ryan 2005, 7).

KARL MARX: HIS LIFE AND ENVIRONMENT

Berlin published his short intellectual biography *Karl Marx: His Life and Environment* in 1939 in the 'Home University Library of Modern Knowledge' (KM1 1). This first book was dedicated, as first books often are, to his parents. It was a modest but appropriate genesis for a classic work, though presumably few at the time thought that about Berlin's readable but serious little volume. As Michael Ignatieff remarks, 'Isaiah knew next to nothing about the subject', and the 'interesting question is why he did not turn it down' (MI 70). Certainly many more people never expected Marx himself to last, indeed quite the opposite: an enormous number of people in liberal democratic as well as right-wing circles (not to mention religious people of many faiths) positively wanted his thought, and all trace of him personally, expunged for ever. His reputation as a Communist and an atheist was for many people all that they needed to consider.

As an Oxford intellectual, Berlin was an unlikely choice to write the book.[3] In the late 1920s and during the 1930s liberals and democrats, even socialist-leaning ones, were on their guard against Marxism and Bolshevism. Fascism was of course an extreme form of anti-Marxism, mobilising many working-class people and intellectuals—precisely the ground where Marxists wanted to be—into violent opposition to Communism, socialism and liberalism—precisely the heritage of political ideas that Marxists claimed to fulfil. It is also the case that Berlin himself had no great personal stake in trying to portray Marx biographically as an intellectual figure, and indeed it seems odd in retrospect that he did so well with his subject and wrote such a sympathetic book. This is especially so since, as Berlin himself notes, it was 'a subject wholly outside the scope of my proper studies' (KM1 6; KM4 xviii), taken on during a fellowship at All Souls College, Oxford. Perhaps the likeliest explanation is that when he came to read Marx, he was impressed with his thought, and intrigued with his life and environment. After the commission in 1933, he spent some five years or so on the manuscript.[4] The fact that his initial draft of the book was much too long testifies to this. The manuscript material left behind contained extensive critical explanation of Marx's thought in detail (though no great surprises that I noticed), and Berlin was clearly

---

3. The papers (in the Bodleian Library, Oxford) of H. A. L. Fisher, Warden of New College, one of the editors of the Home University Library, reveal a list of rather more likely candidates who turned down the offer: Harold Laski, Sidney Webb (Lord Passfield) and Frank Pakenham (later Lord Longford), in that order; Berlin's own (sometimes creative) memory inserts an offer to G. D. H. Cole not borne out by the Fisher papers (L1 67). I owe this information to Henry Hardy.

4. MI 69–72, 90; Ryan 2005, 6–7.

stimulated by and involved with the ideas and theories that have since Marx's time come to be filed under 'sociology, economics and theory of history'.[5]

Berlin was also excited by the revolutionary side of nineteenth-century liberalism and nationalism. This was a long march of representative democracy, human rights, liberality and tolerance against repressive autocracies and authoritarian regimes, the stuffy selfishness and inequality of aristocratic privilege, and the hateful obscurantism of religious bigotry and censorship. Most liberal democrats in his day and ours would like to rest on their constitutional laurels, counsel caution and order, and warn their citizen-subjects against taking power back into their own hands, destabilising established legal structures and class-systems, and reinvoking the forgotten enthusiasms, mass politics and even violence through which representative democracy had itself arisen. Berlin was not like most liberals, though, and daringly, from the beginning of his career, he involved himself with the revolutionary romantics of the Continent, making them and their thoughts and philosophies, their emotions and tribulations, visible to an English-reading, Anglo-American public.[6] This was a public that had been defining itself in opposition to the French Revolution, the revolutions of the '48-ers' and the subsequent violence that was required to establish and maintain the constitutional regimes of the Continent against enemies on the left and right. These were the things that fascinated Berlin.

Over the long term, so persuasive was Berlin's achievement in this area that Anglo-American, English-reading liberalism has somewhat redefined itself to accommodate his Continental perspective and his invocation of mid-nineteenth-century mass politics, revolutionary thought and intellectual profundity. This is not to say that Berlin argued a triumph of Marx over Mill,[7] but rather that he made it possible for the debate to take place on something like equal terms. From the Bolshevik revolution of 1917 to the Fall of the Wall in 1989, it was easy enough in the West to demonise Marx, his thought and his motives. As with the devil generally, it is important not to make him too interesting, and to make sure that his evil is perpetrated with monotonous, monomaniacal uniformity in an almost inexplicable manner. There were plenty of accounts of Marx and Marxism that did just that, and indeed there is still a hint of danger and subversion today in reading the *Communist Manifesto*, even in the most of liberal of democracies. Conversely there are hagiographies of Marx that Marxists like to deploy, but again, in those accounts he cannot be too complex, conflicted or wrong.

---

5. The original typescript survives: MSB 413–14.

6. See the discussion by Toews, IBCE 172–5, which explains Berlin's 'romantic' Marx but sets out to resolve a contradiction with a deterministic 'Enlightenment' Marx.

7. An early and characteristic instance of this genre was Duncan 1973.

Engels began this genre, quite innocently and reasonably enough, when he reviewed Marx's *A Contribution to the Critique of Political Economy* on its publication in 1859, and Lenin repeated its terms in his own later effort in 1915, a brief life much republished along with catechistic accounts of 'scientific socialism', 'historical materialism' and 'materialist dialectics'.[8] These lives were of course those of a scientific saint and, in their way, just as monotone as their opposite. Whether saint or devil, in the Marxist frame of reference Marx had to be extraordinary, whereas for Anglo-American, English-reading liberal democrats in general, he was threatening or irrelevant. Berlin changed all that with his unassuming life of 'Karl Marx' (not just 'Marx'), but in the limited sense that he made it possible and indeed respectable to consider Marx in a different way. Although, astonishingly, Marx was voted 'the Greatest Philosopher of all time' in a recent BBC Radio 4 national poll,[9] I suspect that random interviews in the English-speaking world would produce a consensus, or at least significant minority view, that he was Russian.[10] There is still considerable struggle required even today to make Marx accessible and interesting, and not alien to the traditions of liberal and social democracy, and so neither mad and bad, nor inhumanly rational and scientific.

The recent substantial life by Francis Wheen (1999) won a number of awards and a large paperback sale, promising to 'humanise' Marx, though in my view this account veered toward trivialisation and cheap laughs. One reason that Wheen ('writer, broadcaster and journalist')[11] was able to do this is that he had access to enormous amounts of published material in English translation. Berlin did not have anything like this wealth of material in German, never mind English, or in any other published version. Nor did he have access to the archives available in Amsterdam and Moscow and various other scattered locations; in the 1930s these were inaccessible to anyone like Berlin, and virtually inaccessible anyway. At best the papers were boxed up and stored safe from Fascist attack, and Berlin was hardly at liberty to make the visits and write that sort of book under those conditions. None the less he produced a book that treated his subject with considerable and enduring humanity.

Besides the benefit of the published collections of Marx's writings and correspondence, where the text appears to the reader directly, rather than in some secondary account (such as Engels's canonical works), we have had since the later 1950s the benefit of popular publication of non-canonical works by Marx in all

---

8. Lenin 1915. For a textual study of Engels's review and its relation to Marx's thought, see Carver 1983, 96–117.

9. <http://www.bbc.co.uk/pressoffice/pressreleases/stories/2005/07_july/13/radio4.shtml> (accessed 21 January 2006).

10. He was in fact a German Jew born in 1818 in Trier in Rhenish Prussia.

11. Wheen 1999, half-title page.

the world's major languages. English translation (and German publication) has led the field in variety of items if not in sheer numbers of copies, compared with repeated editions in Russian and Chinese. This diversity of published work available in English and German included a very significant amount of correspondence and some further memoir material, but more importantly it included the publication of the 'early Marx' in the form of 'economic and philosophical manuscripts'.[12] Excerpts from these materials had been circulating in the West since the 1940s, when the German socialist archives (sent to Amsterdam during the Nazi rise to power) became available to scholars. Eventually the mountain of Marx manuscripts in print has come to include juvenilia and family correspondence, a gold mine for Wheen's 'humanisation' of a Great Man.

What Berlin had access to were biographies of Marx in German by Franz Mehring and by Boris Nicolaievsky and Otto Maenchen-Helfen, published in 1918 and 1933,[13] a few 'humanising' reminiscences from family and friends, and various editions of the then canonical works of the two.[14] The canon at the time was not all that promising for Berlin's approach, which was (at least nascently) that of value pluralism, human complexity, and grave suspicion of intellectual systems that simplify thought and brutalise people. The canonical works, as defined, republished and translated (initially under Engels's auspices) were generally limited to the *Communist Manifesto* (jointly written with Engels), *Wage-labour and Capital*, *The Eighteenth Brumaire of Louis Bonaparte*, the 1859 'Preface' to *A Contribution to the Critique of Political Economy*, *Capital* vol. 1, and *The Civil War in France* (written in English).

However, until well into the post-war period, the Marx canon was dominated by the works of Engels: *Anti-Dühring*, *Socialism: Utopian and Scientific*, *The Origin of the Family, Private Property and the State*, *Ludwig Feuerbach and the End of Classical German Philosophy* and, by the 1930s, the posthumously published *Dialectics of Nature*. These works, rather than Marx's, were the major source for the historical materialism and materialist dialectics of Plekhanov, Kautsky, Lenin, Stalin, Mao and even Trotsky, whose nuanced political and historical writing rather belied Engels's formulaic and inelegant system-building. Engels's exposition of 'Marx's outlook' set the terms through which the revisionist controversies of Western

---

12. Berlin later revised his text somewhat to take the manuscripts on 'alienation' into account; see 39–40 below, and note 19.

13. Ryan reviews this literature in his 'Introduction' to KM4, xii–xiii. Both German-language biographies appeared in English translation in 1936, midway through Berlin's work on his manuscript.

14. See Berlin's original bibliography in KM1, 251–2, where he specifically notes the 'competent translations published by Messrs Martin Lawrence (now Lawrence and Wishart)' (251).

Marxism were negotiated, beginning with Bernstein and Labriola at the turn of the twentieth century, and continuing through the Frankfurt and Austro-Marxist schools of the 1930s with which Berlin, in his life of Karl Marx at any rate, was comparatively unconcerned.[15]

The British Museum in London and the Bodleian Library in Oxford had copies of the very few volumes actually published (in the late 1920s and early 1930s) of the planned complete works of Marx and of Engels (with due attention to individual or joint authorship and to textual details and histories), set out in the original languages of composition. This first *Marx–Engels Gesamtausgabe* was cut short by Stalinist repression and the Nazi threat to the Soviet Union, as Berlin notes in his original bibliography (KM1 251). The first few volumes would not, however, have benefited Berlin very much, nor the Russian-language version which was running somewhat ahead of it, given his interest in a biographical overview balanced with intellectual contextualisation in relation to influences, forebears and parallel figures. It was not until the 1950s that a large-scale collected edition (the German-language Marx–Engels *Werke*, 41 volumes) began to appear, suitably framed with introductions reflecting the current orthodoxies of the East German and Soviet Russian Communist parties. This consortium and their house publisher Dietz Verlag sponsored the scholarly and archival work required to collect a large-scale selection of works, hitherto unpublished manuscripts and vast personal correspondence. In the 1970s the English-language *Collected Works* (now complete in 50 volumes from Lawrence and Wishart) began to appear, building on Communist Party scholarship and incorporating as it went along some of the materials and achievements of the newly revitalised *Marx–Engels Gesamtausgabe*. This was planned in the late 1960s to comprise about 150 double volumes, and from the 1970s onwards it made gradual progress. It continues today under the auspices of the Berlin-Brandenburg Academy of Sciences, somewhat reduced in scope.

However, in the 1930s there was no incentive from any perspective other than Berlin's to look into Marx's 'life and environment' in terms that were independent of Marxist orthodoxies and their mirror image in anti-Marxist critiques. Nor was there any incentive to look into Marx's works in a way that was largely independent of Engels's defining summaries, glosses and biographical and intellectual contextualisations. Indeed in retrospect it is hard to see why Berlin could have been so perverse, never mind how he was able to do it. To look at Marx from his perspective he not only had to want to avoid contaminating his study with orthodox hindsight, he had to set those orthodoxies to one side of his main focus and thus engage with them only as marginal to his enterprise, and presumably to

---

15. For a discussion of the Marx canon and its reception, see Thomas 1991.

his readers' real interests. As an authorial strategy toward Marx this is quite remarkable even now, much less in the 1930s when ideological strife was everywhere. To try to dodge it was surely an act of defiance, however cunningly disguised or even inadvertently executed.[16]

Later on, the *volte face* undertaken by liberal anti-Marxists as they allied with Soviet Russia in 1941 against the Axis Powers did not result in any widespread reassessment of Marxism, even in intellectual terms, let alone the terms of party politics. There were certainly some triumphs of social democracy after the Second World War, but none for Marxism as such, given the repression of Marxist parties and partisans in Europe from France to Greece, and the grim brutalities of Soviet occupation throughout Eastern Europe. While the latter was done in the name of Marxism, many Marxists had already distanced themselves from Stalin during the pre-war purges, and as the 1950s wore on many more came to see little resemblance between the satellite regimes, and even the Soviet Union itself, and Marx's communism. Anti-Marxists by contrast had a continuing stake in maintaining the link between Communist repression, Marxism and Marx's thought that politicians and intellectuals on both sides had striven to establish. Berlin, however, did not cast his original book or any of his subsequent revisions primarily in terms of Marxism—for or against—at all, as it would have been so easy, indeed seemingly obligatory, to do.[17]

Crucially today we have the benefit of the work done by David McLellan, a student of Berlin's, and a writer much more in line with his perspective and methods. McLellan was excited by the 'early Marx' as it filtered through the French Marxism and socialist radicalism of the early 1960s, and his successive works making Marx's manuscript thoughts accessible and interesting in English (and indeed in many other languages in translation) cannot be underestimated.[18] Like Berlin, McLellan had little if any investment in Marxist orthodoxies as they descended from Engels's canonical accounts, and, indeed, his careful contextualisation of the 'early Marx' required that he approach his subject in this way, as the

---

16. Ignatieff notes Berlin's 'playful' view of politics, and the way he was viewed as 'too detached and introspective' by some of his more politically engaged contemporaries (MI 72–3); Ryan comments that Berlin's book was 'decidedly lopsided' because 'Berlin never took any interest in Marx's economics' (2005, 7). However, this rather supports my point about Berlin's effective unorthodoxy in his approach, and Ryan thus undervalues Berlin's reading of *Capital*, vol. 1, as primarily an exercise in historical analysis and political criticism; see also 45–6 below, and note 28 there.

17. Lichtheim 1961 contrasts with Berlin's *Karl Marx* by tackling Marxism directly, but also contrasts with virtually all the other literature on Marxism of the era by exploring rather than assuming Marx's link with Marxism and twentieth-century Communism.

18. See McLellan 1969, 1970, 1971a, 1971b, 1973 and other works.

two—Marx and Engels—had not yet met in any significant way. Moreover the 'Young Hegelian' intellectual milieu in which the two were rather separately involved has a problematic relationship at best with the intellectual and political interests of the later 1850s and onwards. Indeed the idea that there should be an 'early Marx' of interest was itself highly controversial in orthodox Engelsian terms. Engels himself revisited the 1840s only late in life as part of his much later political and theoretical projects, and he did so with the full armour of hindsight, and without availing himself of Marx's manuscripts to any great extent. McLellan had available published versions of manuscript works Berlin had not dreamt of and, like Berlin, he eschewed hindsight and political axe-grinding.

McLellan's job was never to produce a reconciliation of the 'early' with the 'later' or 'late' Marx, but rather to recount, explore and appreciate the philosophical complexities and intellectual subtleties of Marx's 'humanism'. The term was itself a red rag to the materialisms of Marxist orthodoxies. McLellan's works virtually established the 'early Marx' as an object of study in its own right, without any need for the invocation of Engels's avuncular presence or of doctrinal Marxism as framing devices, much less of any rigid orthodoxies to which Marx's text must somehow be made to conform. By contrast certain Marxists, notably Louis Althusser and his school, were driven during the 1960s and early 1970s to look for a 'break' in Marx's texts which would thus self-validate the orthodoxies through which Marxism was itself defined and understood. As the 1960s and 1970s wore on, however, the chances of locating and defending such a 'break' receded, not least because those who had read McLellan, and had ready access to his translation (and others') of the 'early Marx', had plenty of textual ammunition with which to demolish it in its various guises. While this scholarly fracas has never produced a consensus on a 'seamless' Marx, it has certainly dealt a heavy blow to the previously settled view (for Marxists and anti-Marxists alike) that Engels was the sole way to Marx, and that close contact with the master's texts themselves was only for the initiated, who were destined to confirm the truths that orthodoxy had already established.

On the one hand all this would not have happened as smoothly as it did, had Berlin not published his modest volume in 1939; on the other hand, it is astonishing how Berlin managed to blaze such a trail, given the paucity of materials he had to work with and the absence of any models. Ignatieff notes that for 'all the political interest in Marxism, there was no one in Oxford who worked on Marxism as an intellectual speciality'; moreover 'the study of the history of ideas—let alone socialist ones—barely existed' there (MI 71). Writing in 1963 and again in 1977 Berlin notes in successive prefaces to new editions of his book that he had updated and corrected his text somewhat. This happened particularly in relation to a post-war (and decidedly non-orthodox) debate on 'the relation between the alienation and the freedom of men'.[19] Berlin notes quite accurately that he undertook no large-scale rewriting and revision of his text over the years, since a 'vast expansion of Marxist studies has taken place' (KM4 ix). What he fails to note, with characteristic modesty, is the role that his own little book played in making this possible. How exactly was this so?

BERLIN'S MARX, ORTHODOX OR OTHERWISE

Berlin himself says in 1977 that his 1939 text 'was perhaps too deeply influenced by the classical interpretations of Engels, Plekhanov and Mehring', which is possibly a further comment on his 1963 note that he had been adjusting his text to incorporate the non-classical concept of alienation. However, 1963 is quite early in the development of the literature in print on alienation; McLellan's *The Young Hegelians and Karl Marx* was not published until 1969, and John Plamenatz's *Karl Marx's Philosophy of Man*, where alienation was extensively discussed, did not appear till 1975. Alan Ryan argues that Berlin was wise to adjust his overt orthodoxy only slightly in the direction of 'humanism',[20] because the Hegelian obscurities of the 'alienation' debate had been wisely set aside by the later Marx, and indeed by later commentators of the 1970s, in favour of an empirical social science coincident (or at least coincident enough) with Marxist orthodoxies (KM4 xii). However, what Berlin actually acknowledges in 1963 is the defective character of works done by 'the first generation of [Marx's] disciples' (KM3 vi; KM4 xii). This is not in fact a retrospective endorsement of their orthodoxy in the first place. My view, contrary to Ryan's,[21] is that Berlin's first text was never very orthodox; instead he laid the groundwork for a new and different Marx, given that

---

19. KM4 xviii. Henry Hardy informs me that Berlin's main pre-KM4 additions on alienation (KM4 99–102, 104–5), prepared for a German translation published in 1959, were introduced in the fourth reprint (1960) of KM2, rather than in KM3, as Berlin states in his preface to the latter (see <http://berlin.wolf.ox.ac.uk/published_works/km/marx-concordance.html>). Note, however, that the manuscript material of Marx's that featured in the post-war controversy about 'alienation' had already been published in the pre-war *Gesamtausgabe* edition mentioned by Berlin (KM1 251).

20. Berlin did, however, make notable and sometimes extensive insertions in the text of later editions and impressions. Toews discusses some of these insertions at IBCE 170–72, though he understandably misdates the 1960 insertions to 1963 (see previous note).

21. Ryan says categorically that there 'was nothing in the work of apologists for the Soviet regime to make one think that Berlin's emphasis on the deterministic rigidity of Marx's vision of history was excessive, and nothing to make one think that Marx's materialism might have been less extreme than his disciples had suggested' (KM4 x).

there is more to an 'alternative', non-orthodox Marx than a focus on 'alienation', as Ryan seems to imply.

Berlin seems to have been rather unaware how unorthodox his Marx really was, both in 1939 and in retrospect, and, *pace* Ryan, I think that a contrast between a Hegelian 'philosophical' Marx and an orthodox 'empirical' Marx is a false dichotomy. Rather I argue that Berlin sensed a continuity in Marx's thought in which the conceptual and the empirical are linked experientially and politically, so surface shifts in his vocabulary (e.g. from frequent to infrequent use of 'alienation') are not necessarily all that important. In effect Berlin refused all along the line both the Punch-and-Judy political framing of Marxist/anti-Marxist caricature, and the temptation to give Marx an alternative 'ism' by focusing on some unfashionable (or alternately fashionable) aspect of his thought (e.g. materialism, humanism, determinism etc.). This is what enables his little book to survive political and scholarly vicissitudes and to remain continuously in print.

However, it is not that Berlin produced something bland and cowardly, far from it. Berlin's Karl Marx is interesting, accessible and exciting. This is what attracts readers, and however much the scholarly, interpretive and political world moves on, it is these features that are likely to shine through. Close reading and inspiring contextualisation constitute sufficient scholarly virtues for the enterprise. How then did Berlin make such a successful Marx?

Compared with the general run of Marxist and anti-Marxist accounts, or even with the best exemplars of both these genres, Berlin's historical perspective and analytical framework are strikingly unorthodox. His opening chapter gives an astonishing overview of Marx's character and thought, placing him firmly in the 'golden age of democratic nationalism' and distinguishing very carefully between his later, mostly posthumous reputation (mentioning both fame and notoriety) and what Marx and his thought were like in contemporary terms (KM1 9; KM4 1). By contrast Marxists from Engels onwards identified Marx with the history of socialism, and with the great philosophical and scientific intellects of all time (e.g. Hegel and Darwin). Their accounts rested on the view that there could be no space between his current reputation (correctly understood, of course) and what he was actually like in the past and what he was actually doing.[22] Anti-Marxists, as noted above, had little interest in deviating from the Marxist pattern, except in their overall and detailed evaluations. Many writers who apparently identified with neither camp in fact took the easy route (and still do), reproducing the simplicities of 'received truth'. Effortlessly, Berlin's portrait opens up questions about Marx and about Marxists who speak for him, and surreptitiously it contradicts their standard accounts in its methodology and substance. The last thing it does is reproduce commonplace views as a shortcut.

---

22. Hegel is discussed in this regard in Carver 1983, 102–6, and Darwin at 135–6.

Berlin nods to orthodoxy when he writes that Marx 'was convinced that human history is governed by laws which, like the laws which govern nature, cannot be altered by the mere intervention of individuals actuated by this or that ideal' (KM1 13; cf. KM4 4). His exposition of this, however, has none of Engels's clunky metaphysics or dogmatic circularity concerning these 'laws', and he wisely does not try to formulate Marx's thought in those terms. His rendering of Marx's account of class struggle, exploitation and social development in history derives instead from close and sympathetic reading of both the *Communist Manifesto* and the 1859 'Preface' to *A Contribution to the Critique of Political Economy*, not from Engels's potted versions and laboured defences. His drive to create a readable, sweeping and persuasive synthesis is methodologically opposite to the propositional reductionism of G. A. Cohen's much later 'defence' of Marx's 'theory of history', construed in what are said to be logically rigorous and empirically testable terms.[23] Berlin's concept of the relationship between Marx's thought, political action and empirical facts as evidence is deliberately loose and ambiguous, best summed up in a word he uses quite frequently: 'realism'.

Berlin's gift was to allow Marx a methodology that could be stated independently of the dichotomies of Berlin's time (and ours): metaphysics/science, idealism/empiricism, fact/value. 'Marx believed', he comments, 'that values could not be contemplated in isolation from facts, but necessarily depended on the manner in which the facts were viewed' (KM1 13–14; cf. KM4 4). Quite what Berlin meant by 'the manner in which the facts were viewed' is not stated, but he appears to be allowing Marx an opt-out from the (then current) fact/value controversy, as he simply moves on without comment.[24] While assigning to Marx a belief in 'laws of history' that are 'indeed eternal and immutable', he then declares that 'to grasp this fact a metaphysical intuition was required' (KM1 26; cf. KM4 14). This is not the way that Engels put it, nor would anyone else at the time have been tempted in this direction, except perhaps to denounce Marx for violating the rules of science. Berlin seems simply not to mind about such putative problems.

Rather similarly, Berlin then goes on to explain that Marx's 'laws' could be established 'only by the evidence of empirical facts', but is then simply not preoccupied with explaining how this works, nor with berating Marx for failing in this regard. Berlin says merely that Marx's 'intellectual system' was 'closed', yet grounded in 'observation and experience' (KM1 26; KM4 14). For a trained

---

23. Cohen 1978. Berlin was well known as a conspicuous admirer of Cohen's 'analytical' philosophical method; however, he seems to have felt no need to reject or modify his own very different approach.

24. Later in the book he locates this opt-out from the fact/value distinction in Hegel's work, but does not argue the issue to a conclusion either way (KM1 134–5; KM4 113).

philosopher to make that kind of statement, and then move swiftly on, is something of an achievement. In my view this is very positive, because it allows Berlin to pose an issue, rather than making it the commentator's job to close one down. In itself, this is a kind of unorthodoxy. Shockingly perhaps, Berlin recounts without comment Marx's view that 'conceptions of natural rights, and of conscience' are 'liberal illusions', thus confronting the reader with the idea that this might indeed be so (KM1 16–17; cf. KM4 7).

In his 1977 preface Berlin adds, tellingly, that it was not Marx's purpose 'to construct a single, all-embracing system of ideas in the sense in which this could be said to be the aim of such thinkers as Spinoza or Hegel or Comte' (KM4 xvi). Again, it is hard to imagine anything less Engelsian as a comment on Marx's intent and works, and it is no way inconsistent with his 1939 view of things. But in what sense did Berlin see Marx's thought as a 'system'?

On the one hand Berlin credits Marx with massive ambitions and ferocious thoroughness; on the other hand he conceives of his life's work as a well-defined project, far short of a universal system, which, as Engels put it, would employ a 'materialist dialectic' to account for 'nature, history and thought', thus setting foundational terms for Marxism (and its anti-Marxist counterpart).[25] Berlin's view was that Marx aimed to provide 'a complete account and explanation of the rise and imminent fall of the capitalist system' (KM1 24; KM4 13). Very deftly Berlin explained that this comprised 'a complete economic theory treated historically, and, less explicitly, a theory of history as determined by economic factors' (KM1 27; cf. KM4 15). Leaving aside any question of taking up the truth or falsity of this position, and thus encouraging the reader to take this as an open issue, Berlin praises 'the Marxist emphasis upon the primacy of economic factors in determining human behaviour' for encouraging 'an intensified study of economic history' (KM1 23; KM4 12).

It is as if Berlin had been asked to give Marx his best chance with the reader, talking him up at every turn, and forbearing to pronounce on his obviously controversial, and indeed, according to some Western commentators, damningly nonsensical and overtly dangerous views. At the same time his framing of Marx's thought was so different from the orthodoxies of historical and dialectical materialism that he could hardly be accused of parroting a Marxist line. Surely Western liberal democrats would find Berlin insufficiently critical of Marx, and dangerously lax in letting his assertions stand; surely Marxists would want more certainty and authority in his account of their Great Man, and the familiar ring of dialectics and scientific socialism. Berlin's 'Introduction' gives us a Marx who is engaged with the contemporary class struggle, and whose interest in facts and

---

25. Carver 1983, 96–117.

values, method and critique, derives pragmatically and eclectically from that. What Marx ended up with, according to Berlin, was a 'remarkable combination of simple fundamental principles with comprehensiveness, detail and realism', assuming an environment that 'actually corresponded to the personal, first-hand experience of the public to which it was addressed' (KM1 22; cf. KM4 11). Berlin's Marx was thus like no one else's.

There is a generosity here, namely an allowance that Marx should be allowed to express himself in something like his own words (just in better edited, more flowing prose), and that he was entitled to his claims even if they did not readily conform to later or even contemporary schemata of validation. While there is due respect allotted to the way that Marx's ideas apparently mobilised the masses (and considerable allowance here for the posthumous and misleading use of Marx as an icon), Berlin's real appreciation for Marx is as an intellectual. He gives Marx a lineage of precursors and contemporaries and congratulates him on helping himself to whatever ideas he fancied from any of them. Having produced all the evidence to convict Marx of unoriginality, if not plagiarism, Berlin then gives Marx full credit for an intellectually 'new and revolutionary method of historical writing'. He seems enthusiastic about Marx's rude iconoclasm and relentless critique, commenting that his work 'constitutes the most formidable, sustained and elaborate indictment ever delivered against an entire social order'.[26]

This sweeping judgement seems complicit with Marx's revolutionary attack on the exploitation of contemporary capitalism, and Berlin seems inclined to let it stand. Quite why he does not follow it up, even in later editions of the book, with further comment on the need to keep a pluralist political system in place, is rather a mystery. In other passages, Berlin clearly associates Marx's ideas with authoritarian movements and brutal political systems (KM1 25–6; KM4 13–14), and he could certainly have revised his text to produce a clearer judgement, defend himself from inconsistency, and indeed construct a consistent view. My comment is once again that Berlin's text sometimes challenges the reader to grasp nettles, rather merely react to an authoritative view, and that (for whatever reason or from whatever motivation or happenstance) as an authorial strategy this has its merits.

Berlin's account takes (perhaps inadvertently) too many covert pot-shots at orthodoxy to qualify as such, notwithstanding his occasional linking of Marx to Marxist doctrines; while rooted in the values of European liberal democracy and national liberation, he *includes* Marx in this heritage, despite his occasional comments on Marx's relentless single-mindedness and inability to tolerate dissenters

---

26. KM1 27; cf. KM4 15. Ignatieff sees Berlin's work on Marx branching swiftly off into a study of intellectual sources and contemporaries that provided the 'intellectual capital' for the rest of his career (MI 71); Ryan agrees (2005, 7), and cf. PIRA ix.

with any grace. This was a hugely radical move, given that Marxists since the time of Engels's 'On Authority' and Lenin's *What Is to Be Done?* were arguing openly for a degree of necessary authoritarianism, and anti-Marxists were only too eager to criticise them for it. Berlin may have been, or may still be, right or wrong on all these points, but it is a central feature of *Karl Marx* that he opens a plausible (if not comprehensively defended and textually argued) 'third way'.

This applies as well to the way he framed his account in rather lofty indifference not just to existing political orthodoxies but also to some of the principal terms through which critical, philosophical and moral judgements had supposedly to be formulated. While he certainly mentions Marxism and Engels, the strength and originality of his account, and its covert and possibly unconscious unorthodoxy, derive from his own contact, in the first instance and throughout his discussions, with *Marx's texts as such*, his words, his mind, his life and his environment, not with what he was supposed by others to have been, to have said, to have done and to have meant. Essentially Berlin was *Marx's* reader, and so left Engels and Marxism to look after themselves, on the whole, no matter how important they may have been to others, or how significant they may have been in other ways.

This is not to argue that Berlin intended his book to be an overt attack on Marxist (and anti-Marxist) orthodoxies, far from it. Rather the work displays his unusual interest in the history of socialist ideas (cast as part of the general European movement of national democratic struggles of the nineteenth century), and his enthusiasm for conveying this milieu to the reading public. He makes it clear that he regarded Engels and orthodoxy not so much as wrong or indefensible but as rather poor stuff, far below Marx's level in terms of literary and historical reference, political excitement and narrative sweep (KM1 235; KM4 196–7). Berlin is clearly captivated by Marx's approach to human history, relying not simply on the *Communist Manifesto* and the 1859 'Preface', texts to which orthodox writers from Engels onwards standardly turned, but also on *The German Ideology*, regarded by Marxists in the 1930s as non-canonical, obscure and unsystematic, in supposed contrast to later works.[27]

Berlin approaches *Capital*, vol. 1, in the same light, going very easy on the system-building, keeping the focus on the capitalist economic and political order, saying hardly anything substantial either way about the labour theory of value, itself the cornerstone of orthodox accounts of this 'difficult' work.[28] Instead he

---

27. Berlin comments dismissively on *The German Ideology* as a book (KM1 118, 125; KM4 90, 105–6) but is evidently using the text to explicate 'historical materialism' (e.g. KM1 123–5; KM4 97–8): extensive excerpts in English were first published by Lawrence and Wishart in 1938, based on the first complete edition (1932) of this manuscript work in the (unfinished) Marx–Engels Gesamtausgabe series.

28. Indeed Berlin makes the claim, still highly unusual and controversial, that—however one interprets the labour theory of value (a comment that in itself suggests it is

focuses on the linkage between Marx's exploratory salvos on the history of modern society, dating from the 1840s and early 1850s, and the way he used this rather unsystematic collection of hypotheses and insights in his historical and political analysis of the modern economic system in *Capital*, vol. 1.

BERLIN'S LEGACY

It would be hard to argue that everything, or most things, that Berlin says, are somehow at odds with Marxist orthodoxies; they are not. Rather I am suggesting that Berlin's approach was at least an implicit challenge to orthodoxy of his time and later, but also more productively an important marker and inspiration for future commentators on Marx and historians of ideas. After Berlin it was not only respectable to work on Marx as an important intellectual in a broad sense (rather than to pigeonhole him, for better or worse, as a 'scientific socialist'), it was also valid to approach Marx through his own texts, on his own terms, and to exercise one's critical faculties on that material as such, more or less in isolation from current political polarities and ideological framing (whether in a disparaging or motivating sense of the term 'ideological'). That Marx could be considered an important and indeed first-rate intellectual figure over and above the now dated controversies to do with Bolshevism, the cold war, the Iron Curtain and the Berlin Wall is really Berlin's achievement.

Karl Marx: His Life and Environment is not only eminently readable in its way, despite the fact that there are some very long passages where Berlin's tangents get the better of him and Marx almost disappears from view.[29] Berlin's little book is still remarkably fresh, not simply for his famously generous pluralism and his enthusiastic portrayal of the role of ideas in revolutionary change; it is also notable for the distinct pluralism that he created about Marx, by putting (with elegant understatement and decidedly faint praise) quite a lot of distance between his approach, judgement and scholarship and the orthodoxies of the Marxist tradition. Indeed the open-ended and challenging *inconsistencies* he attributed to Marx are a challenge to orthodoxies of any kind. Berlin thus created quite a lot of *uncertainty* about Marx, and we can all benefit from that.

---

relatively unimportant)—the theory of exploitation based on it 'remains comparatively unaffected' (KM1 212; KM4 176; see 38 above, note 16).

29. Chapter 3, 'The Philosophy of the Spirit', says almost nothing about Marx.

2

Berlin and the Russian Intelligentsia

Andrzej Walicki

At the end of his visit to the Soviet Union in the autumn of 1945, Berlin, then an official of the British Foreign Office, wrote a long memorandum, since published as 'The Arts in Russia under Stalin'. This extraordinary document does not resemble routine intelligence reports: it is a brilliant essay on the tragic fate of Russian culture under Stalin's totalitarian regime, carefully distinguishing between the 'Soviet aspects' and the 'Russian aspects' of Soviet Russia. It ends with an impressive declaration of faith in Russia's spiritual revival:

> The principal hope of a new flowering of the liberated Russian genius lies in the still unexhausted vitality, the omnivorous curiosity, the astonishingly undiminished moral and intellectual appetite of this most imaginative and least narrow of peoples, which in the long—perhaps very long—run, and despite the appalling damage done to it by the chains which bind it at present, still shows greater promise of gigantic achievement in the use of its vast material resources, and, by the same token, *pari passu*, in the arts and sciences, than any other contemporary society. (SM 27)

I fully shared this attitude and this faith. During my studies at the Warsaw Faculty of Russian Philology in the early 1950s I saw the pre-Revolutionary Russian writers and thinkers (especially Herzen) as my allies in resisting totalitarian indoctrination. I felt indignant that Russian culture was being kept in manacles and its past shamelessly falsified. During a visit to the Soviet Union at the end of 1956 I felt confirmed in my conviction that 'what is Soviet' and 'what is Russian' are two different things. I hoped that the 'thaw' of 1956 might prove to be the beginning of a gradual process of liberation which, in the final result, would overturn the edifice of totalitarian lies and create conditions for a regeneration and wonderful flowering of the best features of Russia's cultural heritage.

In my first conversation with Berlin, in January 1960, I shared these views with him, supporting my hopes with references to Belinsky and quotations from Pasternak's poems (which, as it turned out, both of us knew by heart: Walicki 2005, 6–7). That conversation was the foundation of the moral and intellectual bond that developed between us, resulting in Berlin's steady interest in my work, and in an exchange of letters that continued until his last years. This correspondence enables me to testify that, despite many disappointments, Berlin did not abandon his early hope for Russia's cultural regeneration. He remained faithful to his view, inspired by Turgenev, that Russia's place is in Europe, and faithful to his strongly felt conviction that Western culture and Russian culture should not be perceived as alien and mutually exclusive. In the face of fashionable attempts to derive Soviet Communism from traditions and ideologies specific to Russia, he strongly upheld the view that the main source of the disastrous Communist experiment in Russia was Marxism, and not an exotic 'Russianness' supposedly alien to Western culture. Because of this he believed that the West should acknowledge its share of responsibility for Soviet Communism, and that when the Soviet Union collapsed it would be inopportune 'to dance upon its grave'.[1]

THE RUSSIAN INTELLIGENTSIA
AND SOVIET TOTALITARIANISM

In his splendid essay 'The Birth of the Russian Intelligentsia' (1955), Isaiah Berlin endorsed the widespread view that the term 'intelligentsia' appeared for the first time (around 1860) in pre-Revolutionary Russia, as the name of a peculiarly Russian phenomenon. He added to this an important statement on the worldwide significance of this phenomenon: 'The phenomenon itself, with its historical and literally revolutionary consequences, is, I suppose, the largest single Russian contribution to social change in the world' (RT 116).

Formally speaking, it is not true that the birthplace of the term 'intelligentsia' was Russia; in fact this term had been used for the first time in Poland—by Karol Libelt, a philosopher from Poznań, who in 1844 developed a coherent theory of

---

1. Letter to Henry Hardy, quoted at SM xix–xx.

the intelligentsia's role in national life.[2] Nevertheless, Berlin was right to stress the unique features and peculiar importance of the Russian case. Pre-Revolutionary Russia created the most impressive and instructive model of the intelligentsia as a relatively autonomous group, a group united by common values and a sense of mission in the service of national and universal progress. Its specific contribution was the so-called 'normative' (or 'ethical') conception of the intelligentsia, as opposed to descriptive, sociological definitions.[3] According to this conception, a necessary condition of membership in the intelligentsia was an ethical commitment to the struggle for progress, conceived as the liberation of the people from political and socio-economic oppression. The importance of this Russian conception derived from the fact that it was not *exclusive* to Russia. Comparative studies in the field have shown that the intelligentsia in this sense is typical of backward, agrarian countries in a state of transition: countries that face the painful problems of modernisation but lack the leadership of an organic social class, with a vital interest in the required transformations. It can be argued, however, that the ethos of the classical Russian intelligentsia required an exceptionally strong commitment to progress, raised to the status of a secular religion of humankind, and that the Russian *intelligents* were, on average, more inclined towards social radicalism, revolutionary methods and utopian dreams than their counterparts elsewhere.

The notion of 'Russian thinkers' is not synonymous with the notion of 'thinkers of the Russian intelligentsia'. Berlin was acutely aware of this. In his conversations with Ramin Jahanbegloo, he explained that neither Tolstoy, perhaps his favourite Russian writer, nor Dostoevsky belonged to the intelligentsia in the Russian sense of the word: the first because of his rejection of the very concept of progress, the second because of his conservative political views (see CIB 184). The same exclusion from the intelligentsia applied to Pushkin (because of his defence of art for art's sake) and even to Chekhov (who was too 'apolitical' to meet the criteria of membership). Those thinkers who unquestionably belonged to the Russian intelligentsia were the representatives of the radical tradition: Vissarion Belinsky, Alexander Herzen, Nikolay Chernyshevsky, populists of the 1870s, and early Marxists. Ivan Turgenev, a left-wing liberal, could be admitted to the membership of the intelligentsia because of his deep respect for the intelligentsia's 'struggle for liberation' (*osvoboditel'noe dvizhenie*), vividly portrayed in his novels.

Berlin accepted the logic of these distinctions. He loved Tolstoy and devoted

---

2. Libelt used and defined the term 'intelligentsia' in his treatise *On the Love of the Fatherland* (1844, 61–2). Cf. Walicki 1982, 176–80.

3. Ivanov-Razumnik's classic *Istoriya russkoi obshchestvennoi mysli* (1907) provides a definition of the intelligentsia as an ethical concept (12) and uses it as a typological category, opposed to 'bourgeois conformism' (*meschchanstvo*).

to him one of his best-known essays,[4] but he was careful not to treat his writings as a part of the specific tradition of the intelligentsia.

Berlin's interpretation of the Russian intelligentsia emerged in opposition to an influential view—held by several distinguished scholars, including Berlin's friend Leonard Schapiro, Martin Malia[5] and (in a more extreme version) Richard Pipes—that the role of the intelligentsia in pre-Revolutionary Russian history proved to be fatal: its ideological fanaticism, irresponsible utopianism and uncompromising attitude towards the existing Russian State thwarted the plans of moderate liberal reformers and thus paved the way for the totalitarian Communist Revolution. Prophesies of such an outcome had already been formulated in Russia in 1909, in the symposium *Signposts* (Berdyaev and others 1909), whose authors—mostly Marxist philosophers who had evolved into religious idealists—subjected the tradition of the radical intelligentsia to wholesale criticism, accusing it of a nihilist attitude towards truth, law and cultural values. Leonard Schapiro recommended this book as an important explanation of the predictable defeat of the forces of moderation in Russia.

Berlin did not share Schapiro's views in this matter, and he saw the criticism of the intelligentsia by the contributors to *Signposts* as unfair and injurious. He did concede a connection between the Russian intelligentsia and Soviet totalitarianism, but interpreted it differently from the mainstream representatives of cold war liberalism, emphasising not the dogmatic narrow-mindedness and intolerant sectarianism of the intelligentsia, but rather the inevitably tragic, self-contradictory character of its total commitment to the pursuit of great and noble ideals. He stressed that the greatest thinkers of the intelligentsia were not uncritical believers in the 'religion of progress', in either its Hegelian or its socialist version, but rather boldly innovative critics of this modern idolatry, whose ideas remained fully relevant in the struggle against Stalinist totalitarianism. His most distinctive contribution to cold war liberalism (which he himself proudly acknowledged in his last years)[6] consisted

---

4. 'The Hedgehog and the Fox', in RT and PSM.

5. In one of his letters to me (of 2 March 1981) Berlin wrote: 'You and Malia are the only people I can talk to about the Russian intelligentsia—*a subject which still is closer to my heart than any other*—I can talk to you more easily than to Martin, because he is constantly thinking of the part these people played in bringing about what he regards as a major human disaster (he did not always think this).' Walicki 2005, 123 (my emphasis).

6. In chapter 18 of Arblaster 1984 Berlin is presented—along with Raymond Aron, Albert Camus, Karl Popper, Daniel Bell and Seymour Martin Lipset—as one of the main ideologists of cold war liberalism. In his response Berlin admitted that he was indeed a cold war warrior in the sense of calling the Western world to resist the Communist threat (see Galipeau 1994, 133 note 54). However, he was careful to be a cold war warrior *only* in this sense. When it became known—in 1967—that the magazine *Encounter*, together with about twenty other

in using the great thinkers of the Russian intelligentsia not as targets of criticism but as allies in the universal struggle for freedom; a struggle not only against totalitarianism in Soviet Russia, but also, and no less, against the totalitarian tendencies in some of the old and venerable currents of Western thought.

In an important article on his complex identity Berlin discussed the 'Russian strand' in his life, attributing to his Russian origins his 'lifelong interest in ideas'. Russia, he wrote, 'is a country whose modern history is an object lesson in the enormous power of abstract ideas, even when they are self-refuting' (PI2 255).

In a much earlier text on 'Soviet Russian Culture' (1957), Berlin developed this view of Russia in part-answer to the question of the responsibility of the Russian intelligentsia for the totalitarian outcome of the Russian Revolution.[7] He wrote there about the obsessive Russian propensity to elaborate integral visions of the world that would give deep meaning to individual and national life, demanding a total commitment to the pursuit of the ideal; not the modest aim of negative liberty in a decent society, but the lofty ideal of positive freedom, obliterating all frontiers between public and private life in a sustained effort to subordinate everything to the ultimate human purpose (SM 134).

This attitude, characteristic 'of the outlook of civilised Russians of all shades of political opinion' (SM 132), was most pronounced in the Russian intelligentsia, demanding from its members a total commitment to the cause of earthly salvation. The totalitarian features of these strivings were not something exclusive to Russia; they were a constitutive part of a number of influential Western doctrines, such as Hegelianism and socialism. What was specifically Russian was the tendency to strip these doctrines of common-sense qualifications and thus give them a more extreme form than in their countries of origin.

The most important among the pre-totalitarian doctrines of the West was, of course, Marxism. When it arrived in Russia, Marxism found 'an almost ideal soil for its seeds'. The Russian Marxists transformed Marxism into a secular theology, demanding that its believers sacrifice themselves on the altar of the Communist future (SM 134–5, 154). The noble idealism of the Russian intelligentsia—its attitude of total commitment and its readiness to sacrifice itself for a great universalist ideal—helped to give birth to totalitarian dictatorship, allowing itself to use the use the most brutal means for the realisation of the ultimate purpose of human history.

In a retrospective summary of his ideas, 'My Intellectual Path' (1996), Berlin

---

periodicals in other countries, was financed, through the Congress of Cultural Freedom, by the American Central Intelligence Agency, he saw this as a moral scandal and broke his relations with the journal. See Berlin's letter to me of 14 November 1975, Walicki 2005, 93.

7. See SM 130–65; the article was originally published in two parts (the second under a pseudonym) in *Foreign Affairs*.

expressed the view that 'some of the most frightful forms of oppression and enslave-ment in human history' derived from the authoritarian perversion of the positive notion of liberty (POI 18). There is no doubt that he meant above all the intellectual genesis of Russian totalitarianism. Russia was, in his eyes, the most important example of a country in which a perversion of the noble pursuit of the ideal of pos-itive freedom paved the way for a system of unprecedented totalitarian oppression.[8]

A telling confirmation of this diagnosis is Berlin's disagreement with Hannah Arendt's explanation of the origins of totalitarianism. In his conversations with Jahanbegloo, Berlin pointed out that Arendt was right about Nazism, but wrong about Russian Communism (CIB 82). She was right to look for the intellectual sources of Nazism in the doctrines of enslavement, such as anti-Semitism, racism and imperialism, but she failed to understand that Russian Communism emerged from a tragic perversion of the great humanistic ideal of positive freedom. In the practical functioning of the two totalitarianisms this difference of intellectual genesis was often quite unimportant. Berlin, however, saw it as fundamental for the moral and historical appraisal of the mainstream traditions of the Russian intelligentsia.

RUSSIAN THINKERS AND HISTORICAL INEVITABILITY

Berlin's great essay 'Historical Inevitability' (1954) was a powerful, although indi-rect, attack on the ideological legitimation of Stalinism—both in the Soviet Union and, even more, among Western Communists and fellow-travellers. The Stalinist 'revolution from above' put an end to the predominantly teleological legitimation of totalitarian practices, which justified their cruelty by constant invocation of the Great Final Goal of Communism. Stalin was acutely aware that utopian radicalism destabilised and undermined his State; hence he consciously modified the legitimation of his rule, shifting the emphasis from the great revolu-tionary goal to the 'objective laws of history', justifying Communist dictatorship in terms of inalterable historical necessity. This necessitarian legitimation of the Soviet Union was extremely attractive for the Western sympathisers of the 'first proletarian State': it enabled them to explain away all its cruelties and crimes as a necessary price for progress. Defending Stalinism in the name of the Hegelian cult of History seemed more convincing and sophisticated than doing so on the basis of utopianism.

---

8. For Berlin's view of the Enlightenment as a source of Communist totalitarianism see IBLP 46–51.

After the Moscow Trials, followed by the victory of the USSR in the war against Nazi Germany, the necessitarian explanations of Stalinism became widespread in the West. Arthur Koestler's *Darkness at Noon* (1947) showed that even the victims of Stalinism deeply believed in the necessity of their own death, as demanded by the cruel rationality of the Laws of History. The French philosopher Maurice Merleau-Ponty, in his book *Humanism and Terror* (1947), presented Stalinism as the embodiment of the Hegelian *Weltgeist*, praising Marxist philosophy as 'a theory of violence and justification of Terror'—a philosophy that 'brings reason out of unreason', distinguishing revolutionary violence from 'regressive forms of violence', and thus making possible belief in the rationality of history, the only remedy against nihilism and despair (1969, 98, 153). Similar rationalisations of Communist terror abound in the works of Jean-Paul Sartre. Czesław Miłosz in his *The Captive Mind* (1953) revolted against 'the monster of Historical Necessity' but still acknowledged it as the strongest pillar of the Stalinist indoctrination of writers in Poland (cf. Walicki 1990). In empirically minded Great Britain necessitarian metaphysics was much less visible, but even there justifications of the cruelties of the Soviet development in terms of historical inevitability became widely accepted; a good example of this was the famous historian of the Russian Revolution, E. H. Carr, whose views were subjected to criticism in Berlin's introduction to *Four Essays on Liberty*. On the whole, Berlin's friend Karl Popper was right in claiming—in his *Open Society and Its Enemies* (1945)—that Hegelianising historicism was then the main justification of the victorious Soviet totalitarianism and the main instrument of the moral intimidation of its opponents. On this point Berlin fully agreed with Popper.

In a series of articles entitled 'A Marvellous Decade', published in *Encounter* during the 1955–6 post-Stalinist 'thaw' (and included later as 'A Remarkable Decade' in his *Russian Thinkers*), Berlin achieved a truly remarkable feat—making Belinsky and Herzen his allies in his protest against the mythology of 'historical inevitability'. His account of their revolt against necessitarian justifications of despotism was a forceful attack on Soviet totalitarianism. He never said this outright, but the readers of *Encounter* needed no further clues to his intentions.

Belinsky's moral revolt against Hegelianism was preceded by a period of self-enforced 'reconciliation with reality'; a period in which he desperately tried to persuade himself that the post-Petrine Russian autocracy—as a modernising force that had brought Russia closer to Europe—represented an unpleasant but inherently rational historical necessity. His interpretation of the idea of 'rational necessity' was very similar to the views of the Hegelianising Marxists of the Stalinist epoch. In both cases philosophical belief in the (allegedly) objective laws of Historical Reason provided a justification for all the atrocities of history, for the rationalisation of human suffering as the unavoidable price for a happy resolution of history's dramas in the future. Thus, in both cases, a concept based on the universality and necessity of progress dwindled to a historiosophical[9] theodicy vindicating autocratic ruthlessness. For Belinsky, the embodiment of rational necessity was the imperial autocracy that brought Russia on to the broad avenue of universal European history. A century later such interpretations were eagerly applied to Stalin's totalitarian State, which was frequently perceived as the 'lantern' at history's forefront, illuminating humanity's road to a happy socialist future (see Furet 1995).

However, the period of 'reconciliation' was only a transitory episode in Belinsky's life. He failed to achieve a genuine identification with autocratic Russia, and finally found in himself the spiritual resources to rebel against Hegelian historiodicy in the name of the freedom and happiness of the individual. In a letter to V. Botkin of 1 March 1841 he expressed this 'revolt' in the following terms:

> I thank you most humbly, Egor Fedorovich [Hegel], I acknowledge your philosophical prowess, but with all due respect for your philosophical cap and gown I have the honour to inform you that even if I attained to the actual top of the ladder of human development, I should at that point still have to ask you to account for all the victims of life and history, all the victims of accident and superstition, of the Inquisition and Philip II, and so on and so forth; otherwise I would throw myself off head-downwards. I do not want happiness even as a gift, if I cannot be easy about the fate of all my brethren, my own flesh and blood. I am told that disharmony is a condition of harmony. This may be found agreeable by [...] musical persons, but is not quite so satisfactory from the point of view of those whose fate is to express in their lives the element of disharmony [...] What good is it for me to know that reason will ultimately be victorious and that the future will be beautiful, if I am forced by fate to witness the triumph of chance, irrationality and brute force?[10]

Berlin quoted these words in 'A Remarkable Decade' in the belief that they were relevant in his own time and required no comment. Of course, they were especially relevant in the countries under Communist rule.[11]

---

9. Historiosophy is speculative philosophy of history.

10. Quoted from RT 170. To the text quoted by Berlin I have added the beginning of the first sentence, one sentence (omitted by Berlin) in the middle, and the last sentence.

11. I am one of the witnesses of the relevance of the quoted passage. At the beginning of 1953 I was deeply impressed by the letter from Belinsky to Botkin quoted above, especially by his threat 'to throw himself off head-downwards' from the highest rung of the ladder of progress. I commented on these words as follows: 'This one sentence is worth remembering at the moment when we console ourselves with Marxism and its "historical

Equally relevant was Berlin's reconstruction of Herzen's philosophical views —especially of his brilliant critique of the Hegelian teleology of progress in *From the Other Shore* (1855). Berlin approvingly quoted Herzen's thesis that history was neither rational nor a route to goals, but a whirl of chance, a constant improvisation knocking at a thousand doors at once (cf. RT 92, 195–7); that the regularities it did display were a result of clashing blind forces that could—and should—be countered by the unhindered self-creation and moral self-determination of the individual personality; that universal and necessary progress was a Moloch 'who, as the toilers approach him, instead of rewarding them, only recedes, and as a consolation to the exhausted, doomed multitudes crying "morituri te salutant", can give back only the mocking answer that after their death all will be beautiful on earth';[12] that the death of an individual was just as absurd as the annihilation of the entire species; that rational individuals should, after losing their faith in a heavenly paradise, proceed to abandon their belief in the existence of a paradise on earth and concentrate on liberating their own selves instead of saving the world; that 'the submission of the individual to society, to the people, to humanity, to the Idea, is merely a continuation of human sacrifice, of the immolation of the lamb to pacify God, of the crucifixion of the innocent for the sake of the guilty'.[13] This merciless dismissal of all forms of historiosophical theodicy also applied to an ideology still very close to Herzen's heart—socialism. In the last chapter of the book—'Epilogue'—he wrote: 'Socialism will develop in all its phases until it reaches its own extremes and absurdities. Then once again a cry of denial will break from the titanic chest of the revolutionary minority and again a mortal struggle will begin, in which socialism will play the role of contemporary conservatism and will be overwhelmed in the subsequent revolution, as yet unknown to us.'[14]

In this manner Berlin employed quotations from Belinsky and Herzen—the two fathers of the Russian intelligentsia—to attack Stalinist Marxism, as well as all other attempts to justify Communist totalitarianism in the name of the ideological fiction of 'the necessary laws of history'. One of Berlin's commentators, Steven Lukes, paid due attention to this fact, treating it as one of the distinctive features of Berlin's liberal *Weltanschauung* (1994, 696). Aileen Kelly added that Berlin's use of the Russian radical thinkers in the struggle against Russian totalitarianism sharply contrasted with the dominant tendency of other cold war liberals who 'depicted the same people as fanatical, deluded utopians who prepared the ground for Bolshevik despotism'.[15]

---

inevitability"—because it is a sentence "born in pain", one of those which are as true as Pascal's thoughts.' Walicki 1993, 47–8.

12. Herzen 1855, 134–5, 36 (quoted at RT 92 in a different translation).
13. Herzen 1855, 134–5 (quoted at RT 89 in a different translation).
14. Herzen 1855, 147 (quoted at RT 98 in a different translation).
15. LIB 9. Cf. the elaboration of this idea in Kelly 1998, chapters 1–2.

THE RUSSIAN CONTROVERSY OVER
FATHERS AND CHILDREN AND
BERLIN'S VALUE PLURALISM

Of the two intellectual leaders of the 'remarkable decade', Vissarion Belinsky—regarded by Berlin as 'the father of the social criticism of literature, not only in Russia but perhaps even in Europe' (RT 152)—was more radical than Herzen, more ardent and aggressive in his moral preaching but, at the same time, somewhat provincial in his outlook and often one-sided in his judgments. In this respect (as Berlin has rightly noticed) Belinsky was a predecessor of the radical *raznochintsy* of 'the sixties'—that is, of the second generation of the Russian intelligentsia, the generation of the 'sons', typified by the 'nihilist' Bazarov in Turgenev's *Fathers and Children*.[16] Herzen, for his part, represented the best features of the generation of 'fathers': the generation of well-educated, morally sensitive and thoroughly Europeanised noblemen, alienated from the official Russia and, therefore, condemned to the status of 'superfluous men' (Turgenev's expression) in their own country (RT 187). As a revolutionary, however, he was not satisfied with the sort of freedom available to the personally liberated and materially secure élite within the system of glaring social injustice and political despotism; he felt close to the 'superfluous men' of the Nikolaevan period, defended them against attacks by the radicals of the 1860s, but, at the same time, criticised their painful doubts, scruples and Hamletic inability to choose in the name of a revolutionary 'philosophy of action'.

For the author of *Russian Thinkers*, Belinsky was an important, heroic figure, but Herzen was more than that. Berlin described Herzen as a 'moral preacher of genius', 'the most arresting Russian political writer in the nineteenth century' (RT 83, 186), and, above all, a great, original philosopher of freedom. He willingly acknowledged his own indebtedness to Herzen's ideas, treated him as his beloved teacher, and repeatedly pointed out the continuing and truly universal relevance of his thought.

Berlin's seminal essay 'Herzen and Bakunin on Individual Liberty' begins with a comparison between Herzen and his great friend, Giuseppe Mazzini. This comparison has two sides: it points out both a similarity and a contrast. 'What Mazzini did for the Italians', writes Berlin, 'Herzen did for his countrymen: he

---

16. RT 176. The term *raznochintsy* referred to people of mixed, non-noble background, who had to earn their living by their brains. Belinsky, the son of a provincial doctor, belonged to this category. In the 1860s (i.e. in the period of the so-called Great Reforms which began in Russia in 1855, after the enthronement of Alexander II) *raznochintsy* became dominant among the increasingly influential radical intelligentsia.

created, almost single-handed, the tradition and the "ideology" of systematic revolutionary agitation, and thereby founded the revolutionary movement in Russia' (RT 83). Elsewhere, however, Berlin emphasised a difference between the creator of 'Russian socialism' and the leader of the *Risorgimento*: Herzen, in his view, was unique in his adamant individualism, in his deep conviction that the individual can never be sacrificed for collective values. This was 'Herzen's answer to all those who, like Mazzini, or the socialists of his time, called for supreme sacrifices and sufferings for the sake of nationality, or human civilisation, or socialism, or justice, or humanity—if not in the present, then in the future' (RT 197).

Berlin's essays on Herzen concentrate on this second aspect of Herzen's legacy as a thinker. In Berlin's view Herzen's most original and lasting contribution to European thought was his philosophy of individual freedom, based upon the view of history as an eternal improvisation, without inner meaning, without a timetable and without a libretto. In fact Berlin, despite his declared intentions, failed to present Herzen as a counterpart to Mazzini—that is, as the creator of 'Russian socialism' and a philosopher of Russia's national identity and national destiny.[17] Instead, he portrayed Herzen as an existentialist philosopher of life's contingency, seen as a condition of freedom—which led him later to the discovery of an essential similarity between the author of *From the Other Shore* and Lev Shestov. None the less, he succeeded in showing that Herzen's thought could not be reduced to a single idea. It was always torn, as it were, between two opposing tendencies: individualism and egalitarian collectivism, libertarianism and communitarianism. The peculiarity of Berlin's interpretation of this inner tension in Herzen's thought was the conscious avoidance of attempts to show that in the final result Herzen had 'reconciled' the two tendencies in a harmonious synthesis. In Berlin's view the two sets of values in Herzen's thought remained not only unreconciled but even fundamentally incommensurable. Striking evidence for this interpretation is suggested by a chapter in *From the Other Shore* where Herzen feels so deeply divided within himself that he expresses his views in the form of a dialogue between the two persons, each of them representing a part of himself: a sceptical individualist, staunchly rejecting all historical consolations, and an unregenerate idealist, disillusioned with the West but trying to save his hopes by pinning them to the communitarian promises of 'Russian socialism'.[18]

It can hardly be denied that the discovery of the coexistence of incommensurable values in the views of his favourite thinker was one of the sources

---

17. Strangely enough, in his articles on Herzen (including his introduction to Herzen's *My Past and Thoughts*, reprinted in AC and PSM) Berlin does not mention the Polish question, which played an important part in Herzen's life and proved fatal for his revolutionary career.

18. See Herzen 1855, chapter 4, 70–98.

of Berlin's value pluralism (cf. Aileen Kelly, LIB 18–19). Bernard Williams has rightly observed that value pluralism is not merely a theory of the pluralism of values in social life: 'What above all concerns Berlin is the tension between conflicting values in *one* consciousness' (CC xvi). And this was exactly Herzen's case.

It is obvious that a thinker so deeply divided within himself, and endowed with such a capacity of understanding the mutually exclusive systems of values from within, had to clash with the monistically minded radicals of the younger generation. A typical representative of these dogmatically self-confident 'new men' was the literary critic Nikolay Dobrolyubov, described by Berlin as having a genuine 'Bolshevik temperament' (RT 275). Dobrolyubov's constant, unscrupulous attacks on the older generation of the oppositional intelligentsia, portrayed in Turgenev's novels as 'superfluous men', led to a conflict between Herzen and the Petersburg progressive journal *Sovremennik* (*The Contemporary*), edited by Dobrolyubov's older friend Nikolay Chernyshevsky.

The conflict between the new radicals and Turgenev—who, unlike Herzen, rejected revolutionary solutions in principle—proved to be even sharper and more intractable. Under the pressure of Dobrolyubov's arrogant intransigence, Turgenev was forced to sever his connections with *Sovremennik* (in 1860) and to publish his *Fathers and Children* in Katkov's *Russkii vestnik* (*Russian Messenger*). But he did not react to this conflict by condemning his radical critics. On the contrary: in his beautiful essay 'Hamlet and Don Quixote' (1860) he indirectly presented the conflict as an instance of an eternal opposition between the two human types—the many-sided, thoughtful Hamlets, capable of understanding the plurality of truths and values but, precisely because of this, unable to commit themselves to a resolute action, and the enthusiastically one-sided Don Quixotes, capable of strong commitments but deriving this strength from unreflective dogmatic faith. He severely criticised the Hamlets for their weakness of character, praising the Don Quixotes for their activism, necessary for human progress. At the same time, however, he pointed out the tragic price paid for this capacity to act: the price of simple-minded, narrow dogmatism, incompatible with critical self-consciousness, demanding total concentration on 'one sole point on the horizon'.[19]

Berlin experienced similar problems at the time of his own conflict with the radicals—the leaders of the 1968 student revolution and the activists of the emerging New Left. He was fully aware of this important similarity. In 1970 he gave an excellent public lecture entitled 'Fathers and Children', in which he argued that Turgenev's conflict with the generation of the Bazarovs, described in his *Fathers and*

---

19. Turgenev 1860, 26.

Children, was a typical, even paradigmatic, example of the moral dilemmas experienced by liberals in times of sharp divisions of opinion and political polarisation.[20]

However, Turgenev's attitude towards the radicals could not be reduced to this simple rule of 'political correctness'. In Berlin's view, it stemmed above all from Turgenev's exceptional capacity for empathetic understanding—'an ability to enter into beliefs, feelings and attitudes alien and at times acutely antipathetic to his own' (RT 263). Herzen, of course, also represented this capacity, but in his case the Hamletic desire to understand everything was limited by the imperative of active political involvement. Turgenev, for his part, as a follower of Schopenhauer's pessimistic philosophy,[21] did not believe in improving the world, and therefore remained a pure Hamlet; a Hamlet who admired the revolutionary Don Quixotes but was wholly unable to follow them. This was his weakness, but also his strength. His capacity for empathy paralysed his will, but at the same time enabled him to understand from within the irreducible pluralism of conflicting values. His pessimism about all dogmas was even more consistent than Herzen's, more consonant with Kant's famous dictum that 'Out of the crooked timber of humanity no straight thing was ever made.'[22] In this sense he was also an important predecessor of Berlin's value pluralism—a philosophy requiring empathy but excluding all utopias of earthly salvation.

In his portrait of the author of *Fathers and Children* Berlin presented, of course, his own features. But it was not easy for him to confess this openly. He wanted to remain faithful to his own ideal, and this ideal was Herzen, who saw Turgenev as 'an amiable old friend' but also as a feeble, unreliable ally and 'inveterate compromiser' (RT 293). Berlin was *psychologically* closer to Turgenev; Turgenev's 'Hamletism' was an essential component of his liberal stance. But he wanted to be much more than a Hamlet and, therefore, unhesitatingly proclaimed Herzen's superiority. Herzen represented for him an enviable model of combining the sceptical, all-embracing wisdom of the Hamlets, consistently rejecting all forms of the narrow dogmatism of the Don Quixotes, with heroic revolutionary commitment to changing the world. In Berlin's eyes this was morally admirable although unattainable in his own case. He was fully aware of his proximity to Turgenev but precisely because of this he had to be critical of him. Ide-

---

20. Cf. RT 303. While working on this lecture he wrote two important letters to me (25 March 1970 and 26 June 1970: Walicki 2005, 77–82) in which he drew an explicit parallel between Turgenev's outlook on radicals and his own attitude toward the New Left. In both cases genuine liberals had to combine an acute awareness of the perils of radicalism with careful avoidance of opposing radicals in an alliance with the right.

21. See Walicki 1962. This text was a lecture delivered, under Berlin's auspices, in Oxford on 23 January 1961.

22. This was Berlin's favourite quotation from Kant. On its source see CTH vii–viii.

alising Turgenev would involve idealising himself—an attitude deeply alien to the critical self-consciousness of a Hamlet. Hence when he was asked 'Who or what would you like to have been?' he answered: Alexander Herzen (1993a).

It was no coincidence that the Russian liberalism of Turgenev's day was so closely associated with Hamletism. This was the liberalism of Turgenev's 'super-fluous men'—alienated intellectuals, deprived of social roots, hence, despite their Anglophile feelings, fundamentally different from the bourgeois liberals of Victorian England. It was not an ideology of a well-established social class possessing its own economic *credo* and boldly striving for political power. The liberalism of the Russian Hamlets concentrated on non-economic and non-political personal freedom, that is, on the negative liberty of a thoughtful, morally sensitive and materially comfortable élite, endangered not only by unreflective traditionalism and political authoritarianism, but also—and no less—by revolutionary radicalism. It had to defend itself against extremes of both right and left—since the domination of either would have taken as its first victim the right to freedom of conscience, thought and speech, which existed among Russia's educated and affluent classes. Berlin transplanted this Turgenevian understanding of liberalism into British soil.

RUSSIAN THINKERS AND THE LIMITATIONS OF THE LIBERAL CONCEPTION OF FREEDOM

As we have seen, Berlin strongly identified himself with the first generation of the Russian intelligentsia—the generation of Turgenev's 'fathers'—for two reasons, both central to his moral and political philosophy: in Belinsky and Herzen he saw allies in his struggle against the intimidating fiction of historical inevitability; in Herzen and Turgenev he found important predecessors of his value pluralism. Thus he saw the ideas of these Russian thinkers as relevant to the most important task facing the defenders of freedom in his own time: undermining the necessitarian and monistic foundations of the 'great despotic visions' (RT 86)—above all (though not exclusively) Communist totalitarianism. The only negative exception among the founding fathers of the intelligentsia was, in his eyes, Mikhail Bakunin, whom he treated (not always with sufficient justification) as a simple-minded ideologist of revolutionary negation, a predecessor of the arrogant Dobrolyubov and a teacher of the fanatical Sergey Nechaev, who had played such a fatal role in the last year of Herzen's life.[23]

---

23. Cf. Berlin's 'Herzen and Bakunin on Individual Liberty', in RT, and his comparison between Bakunin and Herzen in 'Fathers and Children' (RT 299). On Nechaev's role in Herzen's life see Confino 1974 and Orlova 1982.

However, as we shall see, Berlin was also able to learn from Turgenev's 'sons'—the impatient radicals who saw Herzen as a moral prisoner of gentry liberals, that is people whom they castigated not only for their 'Hamletism' but, above all, for professing a false, fraudulent, class-bound conception of freedom. Their own conception, stressing above all the social dimension of freedom, was diametrically opposite to the liberal idea of negative individual freedom, which in Berlin's view constituted the core meaning of freedom as such.

Berlin's classic essay 'Two Concepts of Liberty' is often interpreted very one-sidedly. In fact Berlin never claimed that negative liberty—although defined by him as liberty in the strict sense—was a priority regardless of circumstance; neither did he say that the quest for freedom warranted contempt towards, much less the rejection of, such values as equality, security, education and, most of all, justice. On the contrary, he admitted that freedom was of no value to those who did not have the means to partake of it; that 'elementary needs come first: there are situations [...] in which boots are superior to the works of Shakespeare', and that 'individual freedom is not everybody's primary need' (L 171). The importance attributed by him to negative liberty was limited by the main tenet of his value pluralism, proclaiming that no single value should be made absolute and dominant over others. And—like a truly Russian *intelligent*—he was peculiarly insistent that individual freedom should not be pursued at the expense of social justice. In the key part of his reflections on negative freedom he even voiced the opinion that individual freedom requires moral justification, and that precisely this was the basic problem of contemporary Western liberalism. In an eloquent passage he writes:

> What troubles the consciences of Western liberals is not, I think, the belief that the freedom that men seek differs according to their social or economic conditions, but that the minority who possess it have gained it by exploiting, or, at least, averting their gaze from, the vast majority who do not [...] Equality of liberty; not to treat others as I should not wish them to treat me; repayment of my debt to those who alone have made possible my liberty or prosperity or enlightenment; justice in its simplest and most universal sense—these are the foundations of liberal morality. Liberty is not the only goal of men. I can, like the Russian critic Belinsky, say that if others are to be deprived of it—if my brothers are to remain in poverty, squalor and chains—then I do not want it for myself, I reject it with both hands and infinitely prefer to share their fate. (L 172)

In mentioning Belinsky, Berlin was referring to the Russian thinker's moral rebellion against Hegelian historiodicy, to Belinsky's statement (quoted above) that he did not want happiness even as a gift if he were to feel insecure about the fate of his brothers. But in the context of 'Two Concepts of Liberty' the meaning of this quotation acquires a somewhat different connotation. In 'A Remarkable

Decade' it sounded like a defence of individual freedom against the cruelty of Hegelian historical determinism; now its emphasis has shifted, as it were, to the expression of moral solidarity with the victims of institutionalised social injustice. Berlin was right to see this attitude as typical of the moral and intellectual heritage of the nineteenth-century Russian intelligentsia. It is evident (although overlooked by most commentators on 'Two Concepts') that Berlin's moral arguments against the absolutisation of individual liberty were taken from the Russian radicals. The sentiment that practical expertise is more important than cultural refinement was originally enunciated by Turgenev's Bazarov, and later popularised by the radical critic Dmitry Pisarev. The idea that the intelligentsia should not pursue its own freedom at all costs, neglecting social emancipation, was the idea underlying Herzen's 'Russian socialism'. The same idea, albeit somewhat differently accentuated, was also propagated by Chernyshevsky. Similarly, the repayment of the debt owed by the privileged minority to the exploited masses was the central principle advanced by the leading spokesmen of Russian populism, Petr Lavrov and Nikolay Mikhailovsky. They linked the issue to the evolution of capitalism, claiming that it provided conditions of individual freedom for the intelligentsia at the cost of the impoverishment and degradation of the masses. Mikhailovsky reacted to this antinomy in words strongly reminiscent of Belinsky's anti-Hegelian revolt: 'If all the rights arising out of this freedom are merely to allow us to go on playing the role of a colourful and scented blossom, then we reject these rights and this freedom! A curse upon them, if all they do is increase our debt to the people instead of helping us to discharge it!'[24]

I vividly remember discussing this problem at the seminar on Russian populism which I conducted—under Berlin's supervision and with his participation—at All Souls College in 1966–7. I was inclined to agree with Petr Struve that the populist contestation of the struggle for freedom in the name of the people's welfare was not just a political error but also a moral one. Berlin, however, while agreeing with Struve about the utter importance of the struggle for political freedom in Russia, stressed in this context that the particular sensitivity of the Russian intelligentsia to the need to keep political development in line with the norms of elementary justice and equality was a great and unique contribution to the moral evolution of the concept of freedom. On the purely intellectual level, the view of civic and political freedom as merely formal and 'bourgeois' in its class content was, of course, a Marxist commonplace. But the Russian populist intelligentsia, by its refusal to accept constitutional freedom without guarantees of social justice, added to this (in Berlin's view) a powerful moral dimension, which deserved to be taken very seriously by the liberal theorists of liberty.

---

24. Mikhailovsky 1896, 1: 869, trans. Hilda Andrews-Rusiecka in Walicki 1980, 226.

Berlin's long essay 'Russian Populism' (1960)[25] is very instructive for under-standing Berlin's views on the famous dispute concerning the possibility of a non-capitalist path of Russian development. The term 'populism' is used by Berlin in its broadest meaning, embracing all anti-capitalist ideologists of the left—both proponents of a democratic, decentralised socialism, like Petr Lavrov, and repre-sentatives of the 'Jacobin' current, whose chief theorist, Petr Tkachev, believed in the crucial role of the conspiratorial revolutionary vanguard and in post-revolu-tionary dictatorship as a means to achieve egalitarian ends. Predictably, Berlin sympathised with the former as humane believers in freedom, but he also stressed the importance of Tkachev as a predecessor of Lenin.

On the whole, Berlin saw populism as a legitimate protest against 'the capi-talist way' and, by the same token, against the degeneration of individual freedom—that is the negative freedom of non-interference—into freedom 'for the wolves', resulting in the 'bloodstained story of economic individualism and unrestrained capitalist competition' (L 38). He endorsed the basic tenet of the moderate populists: that the welfare of the people is always more important than 'national wealth' (in Adam Smith's sense) and the power of the State. And he extended his sympathy to the Socialist-Revolutionaries, the twentieth-century successors of the populists, whose democratic socialism, respecting individual rights, offered a desirable alternative to Bolshevik tyranny.

The 'largest figure' in the populist movement was, in Berlin's view, Nikolay Chernyshevsky. He was not a man of brilliant, original ideas, like Herzen; nor did he possess the moral genius of Belinsky or the eloquence of Bakunin. He was admirable, however, for his 'unswerving integrity, immense industry, and a capacity rare among Russians for concentration upon concrete detail' (RT 224). Berlin was even ready to acknowledge that Chernyshevsky was not entirely wrong in his conviction that Russian liberals had 'succeeded in betraying both the peasants and themselves' at the time of the land reform of 1861, nor in accusing the Western liberals of political and moral bankruptcy during the Springtime of the Peoples (RT 226–7). This tolerance of, and even sympathy for, Cherny-shevsky's criticism of liberalism was truly remarkable in view of the fact that the Russian thinker was especially critical of Berlin's favourite notion of negative freedom, of which he wrote: 'Liberals will not understand that juridical freedom has value for man only when he possesses the material power to take advantage of it' (1858, 217).[26] No less critical was Chernyshevsky's view of political freedom as a right to participate in political affairs. He stressed that participation in the exer-

---

25. In RT; first published as an introduction to the English translation of Franco Ven-turi's *Il populismo russo*.

26. The translation is taken from Lampert 1965, 199.

cise of political power, or influence on public affairs, depended not on formal rights but on a privileged position in social life.

Especially valuable in Berlin's eyes was Chernyshevsky's capacity to combine his defence of the peasant commune, and of the non-capitalist development of Russia, with faithfulness to the general values of European civilisation, and with a contemptuous rejection of any idealisation of Russia's backwardness, disguised as its alleged 'exceptionalism'. He believed that Russia belonged to Europe and that its 'leaping over the capitalist stage' would be only a minor deviation from the path of European progress. He represented, therefore, a 'Westernising' wing of the populist movement.

Much less acceptable to Berlin was the 'historicist element' in Cherny-shevsky's views (RT 226), which had been presented by Soviet scholars as an alle-giance to scientific determinism. On this question Berlin was on the side of Lavrov and Mikhailovsky (RT 224). Following Herzen, they rejected deter-minism, in both its Hegelian and its positivist forms, setting against it their 'sub-jective sociology', which stressed the role of value judgements and individual choices in history. But Berlin's conviction that Chernyshevsky was really a pre-Marxian historical determinist proved capable of revision, since he later acknowl-edged certain anti-determinist traits in Chernyshevsky's work that moved it closer to the ethical individualism of Belinsky and Herzen.[27] These traits included Chernyshevsky's underscoring of the individual as the only reality of the human world, his Feuerbachian protest against the Hegelian 'despotism of the general', his rejection of historical inevitability as a moral dictate, and his radical scepticism towards theses about objective and universal laws of history.

Among the great critics of liberalism as an outlook of the degenerate upper classes, deeply alien to the idealised peasantry, was Berlin's favourite writer, Lev Tol-stoy. In his article 'Tolstoy and the Enlightenment' (1961), Berlin presented Tolstoy as a thinker close in many respects to the populists (as shown by, among other things, Mikhailovsky's essay on his ideas: cf. RT 238), and very different from the conserva-tive nationalism of Dostoevsky. In contrast to Dostoevsky's anti-rationalism, nour-ished by the culture of the counter-Enlightenment, Tolstoy's ideas—with their common-sense rationalism, consistent and programmatic universalism, idealisation

---

27. Berlin changed his views on this matter under the influence of an article of mine on Chernyshevsky (1959), in which I had focused on the voluntaristic and anti-necessi-tarian strands in Chernyshevsky's philosophy. Berlin, in a long letter to me of 13 March 1962 (Walicki 2005, 53–60), considered this 'a very valuable corrective to the mechanical nonsense written about poor Chernyshevsky'. Under the influence of my argument he dis-tanced himself from his earlier opinions, expressed in his introduction to Venturi's book, and even suggested that Venturi himself had ignored, or tried to smooth out, the compli-cating contradictions in the philosophical views of Russian revolutionary thinkers.

of the simplicity of the 'state of nature', and violent denunciations of irrationality and immorality in social life and in the Church—were deeply rooted in the legacy of the Enlightenment. His religiosity, utterly rationalised, replacing mysticism with angry moralistic fervour, served as a powerful weapon of anarchic negation of all existing institutions—although he did this in accordance with the Evangelical principle of non-violent resistance to evil. Despite its proclaimed allegiance to the Gospel, Tolstoy's doctrine had many affinities with the views of the 'enlighteners' and 'nihilists' of the 1860s. Hence it had many followers among those members of the radical intelligentsia who became disillusioned in revolutionary violence but wanted to remain faithful to their basic ethical commitments.

One of the best known of Berlin's works, 'The Hedgehog and the Fox' (1953), develops an interesting analogy between two very dissimilar writers: Tolstoy, an extreme egalitarian and radical Christian anarchist, and Joseph de Maistre, a theocratic Savoyard traditionalist, supporting extreme forms of social hierarchy and institutionalised violence. What was common to them, in Berlin's view, was a peculiar combination of a single central vision, characteristic of the 'hedgehogs', with a pluralistic pursuit of many ends, characteristic of 'foxes': both of them belonged by nature to the category of foxes, but decided to become hedgehogs out of fear of moral chaos. Discussing the validity of this interpretation does not fall within the scope of this essay. What is important in the present context is Berlin's success in drawing a parallel between two variants of monistic moral fundamentalism, and in setting against both of them the culture of pluralism, which assumes the existence of multiple ends of life.

As is well known, Berlin saw the tradition of moral monism as the ultimate source of modern totalitarianism. In accordance with this diagnosis, he presented Maistre as a precursor of European Fascism.[28] But he never tried to interpret Tolstoy as paving the way for Bolshevism (although such efforts were not lacking in the literature on the subject). This remarkable interpretative restraint reflected his conviction that Tolstoy's combination of moral monism with a rebellious, anarchic spirit could not serve the cause of tyranny.

BERLIN AND THE PERIOD OF 'RELIGIO-PHILOSOPHICAL RENAISSANCE' IN RUSSIA

Berlin's essay on Turgenev was his last work on Russian intellectual history. However, at the beginning of the next decade Berlin returned to the problem of Russian thought in a review article (1981) on two of my own books, *The Slavophile*

---

28. 'Joseph de Maistre and the Origins of Fascism', in CTH.

Controversy (1975), and *A History of Russian Thought: From the Enlightenment to Marxism* (1979). This article, written bit by bit in different countries and cities, provides useful information about Berlin's views on those currents in Russian thought which were not covered in his own essays—in particular, Slavophilism.

Berlin expressed his interest in my book on Slavophilism[29]—which was to be my Habilitation thesis—in his first conversation with me, at All Souls College in Oxford at the beginning of 1960. In a letter to me of 13 March 1962, devoted mostly to my article on Chernyshevsky, he placed the Slavophiles among the most interesting critics of capitalist civilisation, claiming even that they 'said things which are original and fascinating and better than corresponding essays in the West'—more worthy of reading today than, for instance, 'Carlyle or Ruskin who seem [now] absolutely dead'.

In his review article Berlin devoted several pages to my views on Slavophilism, its predecessors and successors. He agreed with my treatment of Slavophilism as the Russian version of European conservative romanticism, and his interest in the subject was closely connected to his works on the Counter-Enlightenment and the romantic upheaval in Europe. But he proved much less interested in the role played by Slavophile religious philosophy in inspiring the Russian metaphysical idealists of the second half of the century to pave the way for Russia's 'religio-philosophical renaissance' of the early twentieth century. He devoted only a few words to Russia's greatest religious philosopher, Vladimir Solov'ev, openly admitting that he had 'no understanding of mystical theology' (1981a, 584). He reluctantly admitted that I may have been right to devote much space to him, but considered as absolutely unnecessary the inclusion in my book of monadological spiritualists like Kozlov, Bobrov, Askoldov or Lopatin. He devoted no more than a sentence to the Hegelian neo-idealism of Boris Chicherin, remarking only that Chicherin opposed everything Herzen stood for. And he did not hide his relief upon passing from 'these somewhat gloomy inland waters' of metaphysical idealism to the chapter on Plekhanov, whom he saw—despite Plekhanov's Hegelian belief in historical necessity—as a clear-minded rational thinker, in the best tradition of Russian Westernism (1981a, 584–5).

My own attitude towards Russian metaphysical and religious thinkers was different from Berlin's. For Berlin, 'religious intelligentsia' was a contradiction in terms, since membership of the intelligentsia necessarily involved commitment to secularisation (CIB 183). By contrast, I sympathised with attempts to rehabilitate Russian religious thinkers in Soviet philosophical literature, and I predicted that the disintegration of the Communist system in the USSR would bring about an

---

29. Berlin persuaded Oxford University Press to assign funds for the translation of the book and publish it in English.

enormous increase of interest in Russia's 'religio-philosophical renaissance' at the beginning of the century.

I proved to be right in this prediction: an enthusiastic reinstatement of religious philosophy took place under Gorbachev's perestroika. But I did not expect that this change would be accompanied by a widespread rejection of the tradition of Belinsky, Herzen and Chernyshevsky. Like Berlin, I wanted and expected a rediscovery of the true message of these thinkers, eliminating from their reception the schemata and outright distortions of the Soviets. In a word, I hoped for a thoughtful reinterpretation of the legacy of the radical Russian intelligentsia, and not its total dismissal. I described my disappointment in a letter to Berlin on 6 November 1991. He shared my bitterness and went further than I did in his criticism of the one-sided fascination with religious philosophy in the new Russia. In a letter of 18 November 1991 he wrote:

> It depresses me, as it does you, that Soviet intellectuals like the Senokosovs, whom you met in Oxford,[30] talk about Berdyaev, Bulgakov and, worse, Frank—Rozanov was at least a remarkable writer—and I keep telling them that they must come out [from] the other end of the tunnel—at the end of their tunnel is darkness. And, of course, our interest in Belinsky, Herzen & Co. annoys them and bores them, because they have been stuffed down their throats as anticipators of Lenin and 'the great thinkers'. But time will pass and there will be a holiday on our side of the street yet, as boring Chernyshevsky once said. (Walicki 2005, 162–3)

The quotation reveals that Berlin, as he himself admitted, was indeed deeply secular and not willing to apply his unusual capacity for empathetic understanding to Russian religious thinkers.[31] We differed in this respect—despite wide common ground in all other matters. Despite his admiration for Anna Akhmatova and Boris Pasternak, the 'Russian strand' in Berlin's complex identity was not rooted in the metaphysical and religious strivings of the Russian cultural renaissance.[32]

Nevertheless, there were at least two important links between this Russian

---

30. Yura Senokosov, a member of the editorial board of *Voprosy filosofii*, was the main organiser of an impressive cultural undertaking of the 'perestroika' period: publishing the works of Russia's idealist philosophers as supplements to the journal (from 1989) under the series title 'Iz istorii otechestvennoi filosofskoi mysli' ('From the History of National Philosophical Thought'). I met him, and his wife, Lena Nemirovskaya, during my visit to Oxford in 1991.

31. Cf. Naiman 2002, 155–64. Naiman's book also contains some interesting observations on Berlin's 'Russianness' (141–3). See also the testimony of Brodsky 1989.

32. Anna Akhmatova was surprised when Berlin told her that Alexander Herzen was a hero for him.

renaissance and Berlin's world of ideas. One was Dostoevsky's Ivan Karamazov, the other was Lev Shestov. Ivan Karamazov's rebellion against historiosophical theodicy, his refusal to accept the prospect of future harmony if purchased by the sufferings of the innocents—so similar to Belinsky's protest against Hegelian justifications of the cruelties of history—exerted a profound influence on the thinkers of the Renaissance period: an influence which caused them to break with the Marxist 'religion of progress' and to seek salvation in metaphysical idealism and modernised forms of Christianity. Sergey Bulgakov described this conversion in his famous article 'Ivan Karamazov as a Philosophical Type' (1901), presenting Karamazov's problems as typical of the moral dilemmas of the Russian intelligentsia, providing decisive arguments for its break with Marxism.[33] In another article, 'The Spiritual Drama of Herzen' (1902), he supplemented this argument by showing a deep similarity between Karamazov's rebellion and Herzen's protest against Hegelianism. Identical references to Ivan Karamazov appeared in Berdyaev's book on Mikhailovsky (which was his first step towards the break with Marxism) and in his systematic deconstruction of Marxism in 'Socialism and Religion' (1906), an article written in the aftermath of the revolutionary events of 1905 in Russia. Among thinkers who had never been Marxists, an enthusiastic admirer of Ivan Karamazov was Lev Shestov—the author of an important book on Dostoevsky and later an outstanding representative of religious existentialism. Shestov referred to Karamazov's rebellion in almost all his books, quoting his words about 'returning the tickets to the future harmony', along with Belinsky's pledge to reject the happy end of progress achieved at the expense of the innocent victims of history.[34]

In *The Brothers Karamazov* the chapter on Ivan's rebellion is followed by the 'Legend of the Grand Inquisitor'—the story of a Catholic prince of the Church who organises his flock under an authoritarian order, offering them bread at the expense of freedom and providing thereby conditions for herdlike, infantile happiness. Dostoevsky intended this tale as a warning against the attempt by revolutionary socialism to create a kingdom of happiness on earth—without suffering, but also without freedom. It is understandable that, after the Revolution, Russian religious thinkers perceived this vision as a prophecy of Communist totalitarianism.

Seen in this context, Berlin's references to Ivan Karamazov and to the Grand Inquisitor acquire great significance. It is true that Berlin did not like Dostoevsky, saw his criticism of the Russian revolutionaries as unjust, and did not write on his

---

33. Reprinted in Bulgakov 1903, 83–112. For a detailed analysis of Bulgakov's and Berdyaev's criticism of the Marxist 'religion of progress' (including their references to Ivan Karamazov) see Walicki 1994.

34. He did so, for instance, in Shestov 1903 and Shestov 1905.

oeuvre.[35] In spite of this, however, at least two of Berlin's references to Dostoevsky are enormously important for the understanding of Berlin's own ideas—of the central intentions of his 'cold war liberalism'.

The first is contained in Berlin's letter to George Kennan of 13 February 1951.[36] Berlin develops in it the idea that no arguments—neither pragmatic (utilitarian) nor historicist (Hegelian)—could justify passive tolerance of totalitarian evil. And—like Berdyaev, Bulgakov or Shestov—he supports this idea by invoking the authority of Dostoevsky. The crucial element of his reasoning reads as follows:

> When, in the famous passage, Ivan Karamazov rejects the worlds upon worlds of happiness which may be bought at the price of the torture to death of one innocent child, what can utilitarians, even the most civilised and humane, say to him? After all, it is in a sense unreasonable to throw away so much human bliss purchased at so small a price as *one*—only one—innocent victim, done to death however horribly—what after all is one soul against the happiness of so many? Nevertheless, when Ivan says he would rather return the ticket, no reader of Dostoevsky thinks this cold-hearted or mad or irresponsible; and although a long course of Bentham or Hegel might turn one into a supporter of the Grand Inquisitor, qualms remain.
>
> Ivan Karamazov cannot be totally exorcised; he speaks for us all.[37]

Strong words: fully concordant with Belinsky's and Herzen's conviction that even the happiest outcome cannot justify the cruelties of progress. Elsewhere—in his article 'Political Ideas in the Twentieth Century' (1950)—Berlin added to this a parallel argument about the inadmissibility of achieving progress by suppressing freedom—also supporting this view by reference to *The Brothers Karamazov*. He wrote:

> This is, of course, the position of the Grand Inquisitor in Dostoevsky's *The Brothers Karamazov*: he said that what men dreaded most was freedom of choice, to be left alone to grope their way in the dark; and the Church, by lifting the responsibility from their shoulders, made them willing, grateful and happy slaves. The Grand Inquisitor stood for the dogmatic organisation of the life of the spirit; Bazarov for its theoretical opposite—free scientific enquiry, the facing of 'hard' facts, the acceptance of the truth however brutal or upsetting. By an irony of history (not unforeseen by Dostoevsky) they have formed a pact, they are allies, and today are often indistinguishable. [...] Whether the refuge is a

---

35. CIB 172–3.
36. Published in L in 2002.
37. L 338.

dogmatic religious faith or a dogmatic faith in social or natural science matters relatively little.[38]

In this manner the liberal from Oxford endorsed the views of the Russian émigré philosophers, most notably Berdyaev, who derived from Dostoevsky a powerful explanation of the origins of totalitarian Communism in Russia: an explanation defining this phenomenon as a result of an unholy alliance between the 'nihilistic' materialism of the Bazarovs and the spiritual, 'ideocratic' authoritarianism of the Grand Inquisitor. Moreover, Berlin wholeheartedly recommended this interpretation (together with Dostoevsky's value judgements) to the main architect of the policy of 'containment' and to the readers of *Foreign Affairs*—that is, to the American political élite.

The Russian religious thinkers of the Renaissance period proclaimed Dostoevsky—together with Solov'ev—the greatest religious genius of Russia. One of the best-known promoters of Dostoevsky's cult was Lev Shestov: a philosopher of consistent individualism and anti-rationalism, constantly protesting against the 'tyranny of reason'. The originality of his interpretation of Dostoevsky consisted in seeing the 'true Dostoevsky' not in the writer's conservative nationalism and orthodox Messianism, but in Ivan Karamazov's rebellious ideas. The most precious tradition of Russian thought was, in his view, the tradition of unceasing protest against human sacrifices on the altar of great, supra-individual and rational ends—a tradition initiated by Belinsky, continued by Herzen, and culminating in Ivan Karamazov. Ivanov-Razumnik presented Herzen, and Shestov as two great representatives of 'immanent subjectivism'—a philosophy systematically contesting all forms of despotic 'objectivism', such as 'objective reason', 'objective laws of history' and an objectively given meaning of life.[39] Herzen represented a secular version of this philosophy; Shestov stood for its religious version, waging a war against theological rationalism in the name of the irrational biblical God, placed above the laws of logic and causality.

It is significant that Berlin, in the last years of his life, became deeply interested in Shestov. In his conservations with Jahanbegloo he mentioned Shestov as one of his favourite Russian writers. He placed Shestov next to Herzen, above Dostoevsky and, of course, above all other religious thinkers of Russia. 'There are two authors', he said, 'whom I make propaganda for: one is Herzen, the other is Shestov. They are both totally decent, open-minded, open-hearted human beings, as Dostoevsky was not.'[40] Despite the uniqueness of his philosophical position, Shestov was one of the representative thinkers of his time, and his interpretation

---

38. L 86.
39. See Ivanov-Razumnik 1908, 273–83.
40. CIB 175.

of Dostoevsky, through the prism of Ivan Karamazov, exerted a profound influence on an entire generation of the Russian intelligentsia.[41] Hence Berlin's great interest in Shestov deserves to be seen—along with his sympathy for Ivan Karamazov's revolt against rational theodicy—as another link between his liberalism and the moral searchings of the Russian intelligentsia of the epoch of 'religio-philosophical renaissance'.

The neo-populist thinker Ivanov-Razumnik considered his own views as a further development of Herzen's and Shestov's 'immanent subjectivism'. His influential *History of Russian Social Thought* (1908) divided Russian thinkers into 'objectivists', bowing down before the allegedly 'objective' laws of development, and 'subjectivists', challenging these laws in the name of the sacred rights of personality.[42] The second group, with which Ivanov-Razumnik identified himself, was presented as the mainstream tradition of the Russian intelligentsia. It is obvious that Berlin agreed with this and that his own views on the intellectual history of the Russian intelligentsia were very close to those of Ivanov-Razumnik.

This was not a result of any direct influence, but a logical outcome of Berlin's position in the great dispute about the Russian intelligentsia, inaugurated by the publication of *Signposts*. He could not side with the Marxists' belief in historical inevitability and teleological progress; neither could he join the authors of *Signposts* in proclaiming a radical break with the traditions of the nineteenth-century intelligentsia in the name of metaphysical idealism, religious revival and accommodation with the authorities. His views placed him in a third camp: among the neo-populists who, like Ivanov-Razumnik, tried to continue the traditions of the classical intelligentsia in a critical way, overcoming populist prejudices against constitutional freedom, and abandoning the anti-individualistic dogmas of the 'religion of progress' without embracing traditional beliefs in a transcendent God. Above all, they extolled the value of free historical choice, setting it against Hegelian historical necessity and the Marxists' objectivist eschatology.

This large area of agreement between the liberal theorist from Oxford and the neo-populist radicals on the eve of the Russian Revolution might seem somewhat odd. But the logic of Berlin's views on the Russian intellectual tradition enables us to see this as natural and fully predictable for a liberal who wanted to remain faithful to the emancipatory tradition of the Russian intelligentsia.

---

41. Lesley Chamberlain is right in seeing anti-Cartesianism (culminating in Shestov's extreme anti-rationalism) as typical of many Russian thinkers. Probably she is also right in attributing the anti-Cartesian bias in Berlin's thought to the 'Russian strand' in his personality (2004, 138–46). In her view 'Isaiah Berlin was himself a Russian-style anti-Cartesian' (145).

42. See 49 above, note 3.

3

A Jew and a Gentleman

SHLOMO AVINERI

In trying to decipher Isaiah Berlin's complex and multi-layered relationship to his Jewish identity, it would seem natural to turn to his own statements about the main sources of his thought. Yet the two instances in which he responded to such queries in print are strangely disappointing.

One of the most detailed accounts Berlin gave of his own thought appeared posthumously as 'My Intellectual Path' (in POI). Though originally written for a Chinese volume, it was first published in English. Its broad sweep includes the dominant philosophical trends which had an impact on his thinking—pluralism, the Enlightenment, romanticism, freedom and determinism. Various philosophers and thinkers are mentioned—those he agreed with as well as those to whose thought he had taken exception—from Rousseau and Marx to Vico, Herder and Herzen.

Yet there is no mention of a Jewish dimension to his thought: true to his basic pluralist approach, Berlin admits his indebtedness to many traditions, though the Jewish angle is totally missing. The only fleeting reference to Jews appears in the context of a paragraph that deals with Plato and Aristotle, when he writes that, in seeking the route to truth, 'Jews and Christians sought the answers in sacred books' (POI 6). A reader without any previous knowledge of Berlin—like the hypothetical member of the Chinese scholarly public for whom the essay was originally intended—would not even know that Berlin was Jewish.

Berlin takes a different approach to his intellectual origins in the address he gave in May 1979 in Israel on receiving the Jerusalem Prize (PI2 255–9). At the outset Berlin recalls how, when the award was announced, an Israeli interviewer telephoned him in Oxford and enquired whether it would be right to state that he was 'formed by three traditions—Russian, British and Jewish'. After his usual tongue-in-cheek disclaimer ('I am not good at improvising answers to unexpected questions'), he admits that the question deserves to be answered, and goes on to relate to these three 'strands' with relish.

Yet once again the reader will be disappointed when arriving at the third—Jewish—strand. The first two strands are described copiously—'to my Russian origins I think that I owe my lifelong interest in ideas', while he credits the British tradition with his commitment to empiricism and individual liberty (PI2 255, 257).

Yet the Jewish strand is somewhat surprising in its vacuousness. Anyone expecting a reference either to the Judaic scholarly tradition or to the existential tensions of a modern Jewish intellectual would look in vain; neither is any Jewish thinker mentioned, not Maimonides nor Spinoza nor Ahad Ha-'am. Berlin does say, though, very movingly, that 'as for my Jewish roots, they are so deep, so native to me, that it is idle for me to try to identify them, let alone analyse them' (PI2 258)—but no clue is given to what they really are. Apparently feeling that this would be disappointing to an Israeli audience, he does declare his basic and deeply felt credo as a Jew and Zionist:

> Two thousand years of Jewish history have been nothing but a single longing to return, to cease being strangers everywhere; morning and evening, the exiles have prayed for a renewal of the days of old, to be one people again, living normal lives on their own soil—the only condition in which individuals can live unbowed and realise their potential fully. (PI2 258)

This statement—an almost uncritical paean to Zionism—does not directly address the question of the Jewish roots of his thought, which remains unanswered even when he is reaching out to an Israeli audience. Yet despite the poverty of Berlin's explicit statements about the Jewish aspects of his thought, this credo may, after all, be a key to understanding the way Berlin dealt with his Jewish identity. While it reiterates a commonly held, slightly romantic version of the continuous Jewish attachment to Zion, it combines this with a statement of universal validity about the need for community and self-reliance inherent in human nature. It is here that one should start.

NATIONALISM

Berlin has frequently maintained that he is not a historian. But as a historian of ideas he always approaches ideas in a historical context—his indebtedness to Vico (and, perhaps, *malgré soi*, to Marx) is obvious. Hence his approach to Jewish themes is an attempt to embed the challenges posed by modernity to the Jewish sense of identity in a general understanding of the modern world. What characterises his various writings on Jewish themes is that his approach starts from the outside—and then moves forcefully to apply his analysis to the place of the Jews in the world.

The best way, then, to understand Berlin's approach to Jewish themes may therefore be to look at his general thoughts on nationalism, as they appeared in a long essay in *Partisan Review* in 1979 (also in AC).

Being well aware that, when it comes to nationalism in the era after the Second World War, one should tread carefully, Berlin tries here to achieve two aims: first, to distinguish between national consciousness and nationalism; secondly, to explain why most nineteenth- and twentieth-century political thinkers—liberals as well as Marxists—underestimated the power of national ideas. It may be argued that both Berlin's distinctions regarding the varieties of national feeling as well as his answer to the latter question are far from totally satisfactory; yet what he says about the phenomenon of nationalism is of general significance—and pertinent to his views about Jewish identity and the emergence of Zionism.

National consciousness, according to Berlin, has to be viewed in the wider context of the understanding of human beings not as disaggregated atoms but as intrinsically connected to one another, so that their mutual links and ties constitute a necessary ingredient of human identity. Over time, a multiplicity of such links has appeared in history, and among them national consciousness is a prime example:

> The need to belong to an easily identifiable group had been regarded, at any rate since Aristotle, as a natural requirement on the part of human beings: families, clans, tribes, estates, social orders, classes, religious organisations, political parties, and finally nations and States, were historical forms of the fulfillment of this basic human need. [...] Common ancestry, common language, customs, traditions, memories, continuous occupancy of the same territory for a long period of time, were held to constitute a society. (AC 338)

It is this Herderian element which is the touchstone of Berlin's idea of national consciousness, and he is insistent that it should not be confused with the excesses of nationalism as expressed in the twentieth century. Herder, he insists in an essay on 'The Counter-Enlightenment', is a cultural, not a political nationalist, who contributed to the spiritual emancipation of downtrodden nations in Central and Eastern Europe.[1] Elsewhere, he maintains that one should acknowledge Herder's insight about the need to belong, '[h]owever greatly we may deplore the appalling consequences of the exaggeration or perversion of what in Herder was a peaceful and humanitarian doctrine' (AC 257).

In his lengthy conversations with the Iranian philosopher Ramin Jahanbegloo, then resident in Europe, Berlin goes even further in distinguishing Herder from his romantic followers: Herder is a democrat who 'rejects passionately the value of conquest. He rejects the idea of superiority of one nation to another. [...] Every nation has a full right to its individual development. [...] There is no political nationalism in Herder' (CIB 99). Herder is also seen by Berlin as an anti-colonialist—even more so, in a way, than the Eurocentric Marx—and had also expressed the hope that the Jews would return to their land (CIB 104–5).

To this Herderian—and Mazzinian—appreciation of the need to belong, Berlin juxtaposes the violent, aggressive political nationalism which he sees especially in Germany and France, and which involves 'the elevation of the interests of the unity and self-determination of the nation to the status of the supreme value before which all other considerations must, if need be, yield at all times' (AC 338).

Liberals, according to Berlin, believed that if each nation had its place under the sun, a harmonious universe would eventually emerge. But what they overlooked was that modernisation created a vacuum that called for a quest for a new focus of identity: and in the case of early nineteenth-century Germany and late nineteenth-century France, a feeling of humiliation, cultural in the first instance, but later political and military, created among the intellectual classes an urge for over-compensation—hence the excesses of German and French chauvinism which led to the major catastrophes of the twentieth century.[2]

Even if one feels that Berlin's explanation of the transformation of a pacific, humanitarian and universalist form of national consciousness into aggressive and xenophobic nationalism needs supplementary historical corroboration, it is clear that the need to belong to a community is basic to his worldview. Such national consciousness is not inimical to liberalism—it is one of the building blocks of his liberal world view. As pointed out by John Gray, Berlin's liberalism is not based

---

1. AC 11–12. See also his distinction between Herder and the Romantics at POI 8–9.
2. AC 349–51. This is repeated at CIB 101: 'acute nationalism is just a reaction to humiliation', hence dominant nations—like the English—have no need for this aggressive compensation.

on a reductivist ontological individualism, as is the case with Popper, Hayek, Rawls and Dworkin—but is a sort of soft communitarianism: 'Berlin sees in nationality the modern expression of a human disposition that appears to be universal and immemorial—the disposition to develop a specific and particularistic identity' (JG 100).

This is the intellectual cornerstone of Berlin's approach to the question of Jewish identity in the modern age, and it informs some of his most spirited essays—on Disraeli, Marx and Hess; it also forms the cornerstone of his radical critique of Jewish assimilation and the foundation for his Zionism and fervent—though far from uncritical—support for the State of Israel.

MODERN JEWISH IDENTITY: DISRAELI AND MARX

Not for nothing is Berlin's bravura 1970 essay on Disraeli and Marx entitled 'Benjamin Disraeli, Karl Marx and the Search for Identity'. This is not only a brilliant analysis of the achievements—and weaknesses—of two of the nineteenth century's most influential persons: it succeeds in relating their two totally disparate careers and modes of thinking to a common quest for identity. Their double marginality, derived from both their Jewish origins *and* their parents' conversion to Christianity, pushed each in a different direction. Yet they had in common a burning need and desire to fill the void in their identity with an idealised alternative construction that existed only in their minds: here that of the British aristocracy, there that of the universal proletariat. Neither real British peers nor real proletarians had a need for such an exalted characterisation of their respective social milieux.

The essay deals not merely with Disraeli and Marx, as is evident from its first sentence: 'All Jews who are at all conscious of their identity as Jews are steeped in history' (AC 253). Berlin's themes are the challenges of Jewish identity once the traditional, pre-Enlightenment exclusion of the Jews from general society gave way to modernity, when a certain class of Jews—first in Germany, but then in other countries as well—ceased to be secure in their own identity and attempted to adopt that of the Other—of the majority society in which they were residing. Mentioning Heine and Börne, to whom he refers as 'the first generation of gifted and ambitious Jews to seek admission to the outside world', he judges their efforts a total and tragic failure: 'The more they insisted that they were Germans, true heirs of German culture, concerned only about German values, or at any rate about bringing the fruits of enlightenment to their compatriots, the less German they seemed to these same Germans.'[3]

---

3. AC 256. This assessment is repeated at POI 166–71 and CIB 21 f.

Both Disraeli and Marx, for Berlin, are emblematic of this conundrum. Admitting that simplistic psychological explanations may be facile, Berlin none the less draws a parallel between these two sons of parents who had chosen conversion not out of deeply felt religious conviction, but from a feeble, submissive accommodationism which led their children into a no man's land in terms of identity, as they could not really identify with the bourgeois world in which their parents' attitude had landed them—and detested it. They reacted to this in different ways—Disraeli by identifying with an idealised aristocracy, Marx by throwing in his lot with an equally idealised proletariat. While their political ideologies went in totally opposing directions, they had their common source in the social and intellectual alienation of both from the bourgeois world of which they were merely nominal members (AC 263).

Yet both Disraeli and Marx went beyond these identifications with a chimerical social class to which they did not belong. Disraeli not only constructed an idealised vision of a British aristocracy, resplendent with knightly images drawn from an equally idealised version of the Crusaders (the choice of name of Tancred is only one example): according to Berlin, he goes one step further, in making aristocracy the moving force of world history. Disraeli then invents for himself a fictitious aristocratic Jewish ancestry connected with the aristocratic republic of Venice—and then proceeds to declare the Jews to be the true aristocracy of humanity. He thus elevates himself from his marginal position in class-conscious England to membership of an élite which 'had given the world its most precious possessions—religion, laws, social institutions, its sacred books, and finally its Divine Saviour' (AC 265). In Disraeli's novels Jews appear as true aristocratic leaders—be it the romanticised false messiah David Alroy, or the imaginary banker Sidonia who actually rules the world from behind the scenes. By turning the commercial realm crafted by the accountants of the East India Company into an Orientalist empire, Disraeli also transcends the ugly capitalism of English society and makes his Jewish marginality into an asset in the process: he, the marginal Jew, offers the Mogul imperial crown to the Queen of England.[4]

Marx's strategy, according to Berlin, in confronting his Jewish ancestry was totally different from that of Disraeli: instead of idealisation, Marx's references to Jews are a combination of occasional denigration with utter distancing and denial, and Berlin tends to agree with the view that Marx's attitude to his Jewish origins can be classified as 'Jewish self-hatred' (AC 280).

Yet at the same time Berlin discerns in the whole structure of Marx's thought a much deeper imprint left by his Jewish origins. He sees in Marx's cosmopoli-

---

4. This idealised Orientalism also gives rise to Disraeli's delightful characterisation of the Arabs in *Tancred* as 'Jews upon horseback' (Diaraeli 1847, 261; cited at AC 270).

tanism and rejection of all forms of nationalism a reaction to the emerging nationalism of his native Germany. Yet this would also lead him to underestimate the role of nationalism in historical development. Moreover, all nationalism has to be eradicated in the future, socialist, society: out of this emerges the construction of the proletariat as a totally alienated, deracinated class, which—according to Marx—has no fatherland, and whose future kingdom will be truly universal.

Berlin is right to point out that Marx had very little contact with real proletarians, and on the few occasions when he met them face to face, he had scant respect or love for them. Marx's proletariat is an abstract category, 'a class to some extent constructed after Marx's own specifications, as a vessel to carry the vials of his justified wrath' (AC 282).

In Marx's condemnation of capitalism and his identification with a notional proletariat, Berlin sees a much deeper echo:

> But when [Marx] speaks of the proletariat, he speaks not of real workers but of humanity in general, or, at times, of his own indignant self. [...] When he [...] prophesies that the last shall be first, that the arrogant enemy who lords it today will bite the dust when the day of the revolution comes, it is the oppression of centuries of a people of pariahs, not of a recently risen class, that seems to be speaking in him. The insults he is avenging and the enemies he is pulverising are, as often as not, his own: the adversary, the bourgeoisie and its executives [...] are the persecutors of the rootless cosmopolitans, the revolutionary Jewish intellectuals [...]. This it is that lends passion and reality to his words, and for that very reason they appeal most deeply to other persons like himself, alienated members of a world-wide intelligentsia [...] it is difficult not to think that the voice is that of a proud and defiant pariah, not so much a friend of the proletariat as of a member of a long humiliated race. (AC 281–3)

There have been many attempts to relate Marx's thought to the Judaic prophetic tradition, to biblical concepts of justice, or to other normative elements of his Jewish heritage. Berlin is right in dismissing these notions, since there is no evidence that Marx was aware—more than any other graduate of a Lutheran German Gymnasium—of this legacy. But he succeeds in salvaging from Marx's social alienation the agonised echo of his quest for identity. This then translates itself into an overall social critique which, in its radical negation of the bourgeois world, is anchored in Marx's own existential conundrums, deriving from his Jewish origins—and their denial by his father's act of conversion. It is in this sense that Berlin re-claims Marx as belonging to a Jewish tradition, albeit alienated and convoluted.[5]

---

5. These themes are less evident, though still present, in Berlin's earlier, magisterial biography of Marx (KM1 11, 33).

THE VINDICATION OF MODERN JEWISH IDENTITY: MOSES HESS

If Disraeli and Marx, despite all the differences between them, are, for Berlin, examples of a loss of identity and authenticity in many people of Jewish descent, Moses Hess epitomises for him the other alternative: a thinker who maintains his identity while constructing it anew and, in the process, offering a radical new message to the Jewish people—independence and self-determination.

Berlin's study of Hess, originally published in 1959, predates his essay on Disraeli and Marx by a decade, but the argument is the same, thus bringing out the continuity and consistency in Berlin's thinking on the subject.

Coming from a similar background to that of Marx—the Rhineland, with its legacy of French revolutionary traditions—Hess is for Berlin the exact opposite of Marx. He did not suffer from Jewish self-hate, and while for many years his socialist thinking would support an assimilationist strategy, he did eventually grasp the significance of the preservation of national traditions, even within a socialist vision.

Berlin admits that Hess was not a system-builder. Consequently his thought does not suffer from the flaws which characterise so many overarching philosophical edifices (AC 242, 247). He sees his contribution in his acknowledgement—in contrast to Marx, where all history is class history—of the historical significance of national identity; and in his realisation that Jew-hatred in modern Europe is aimed precisely at modern, secularised Jews, and thus is not a mere continuation of traditional, Christian anti-Judaism. On both issues, Berlin argues, Hess's predictions 'have proved to be almost uncannily accurate', and are 'a bold and original masterpiece of social analysis' (AC 249, 231), certainly more prescient than Marx's dogmatic views. Thus, while being 'a prophet without much honour in his own generation', he should now be recognised as 'an exceptionally penetrating and independent thinker' (AC 213). Berlin even claims that Hess was vindicated by the events of 1956 in Hungary and Poland (AC 248).

What appeals to Berlin in Hess is his opposition to mono-causal determinism as well as his deep belief in the preservation of historical traditions. He agrees with Hess's acid remark that 'The modern liberal Jew is to be despised with his fine words about humanity and enlightenment, intended only to disguise his disloyalty to his brothers.'[6] He commends Hess's national consciousness and his recognition of national differences while insisting—with Herder and Hegel—that this should in no way lead to ideas of national or racial superiority.

Berlin sees Hess's *Rome and Jerusalem* (1862) as a major intellectual achieve-

---

6. Hess 1862, letter 5, 27–8; cited in this somewhat loose translation at AC 232.

ment. This call for the establishment of a socialist Jewish commonwealth in Palestine is in line with Hess's general support for national liberation. Its very name is inspired by the Risorgimento, then reaching its political apotheosis in the process of Italian unification, and the 'Rome' in the book's title is Mazzini's liberal, humanitarian *Roma terza*, superseding the earlier imperial and papal Romes. At the same time, the book points to the emergence in Germany of modern racism and anti-Semitism, which Hess claims will not be appeased by Jewish assimilation and accommodationism—on the contrary.

Berlin is also impressed by Hess's appreciation of the communitarian nature of much of the Hasidic tradition—in contrast to the bourgeois and quasi-enlightened revulsion of so many German Jews from what they perceived as the unwashed Ost-Juden. Equally, he hails Hess's predictive power in realising that it would be the Eastern European and Middle Eastern Jews who will, eventually, make up the core of the population of the Jewish commonwealth.

And above all he praises Hess's conviction—running so much against the current of nineteenth-century conventional liberal wisdom—that the Jews are a people, not merely a religious group, and that Reform Judaism is nothing other than 'a pathetic and vulgar imitation of Christianity' (AC 239). This was a courageous view when uttered by a socialist Jewish thinker in the 1860s, and Berlin recognises it for what it is: a call for authenticity and pride in one's identity. Hence his acknowledgement of Hess's *Rome and Jerusalem* as 'a masterpiece. It lives because of its shining honesty, its flawlessness, the concreteness of its imagination, and the reality of the problem that it reveals' (AC 241). It is not dated, Berlin asserts, despite its cumbersome language and lack of literary polish.

JEWISHNESS AND ZIONISM

Isaiah Berlin's most outspoken and passionate Jewish and Zionist credo appears in his 'Jewish Slavery and Emancipation', originally published in three instalments in the *Jewish Chronicle* in 1951. Rightly hailed as one of Berlin's strongest statements of his intellectual commitment to his Jewish identity, it also caused—because of its radical criticism of some aspects of Jewish Diaspora life—a storm of criticism, and it must be for this reason that Berlin declined to have it reprinted in his lifetime.

The very title is radical: by juxtaposing 'slavery' and 'emancipation', he consciously uses a very strong term, guaranteed to rub many Diaspora Jews the wrong way. It also echoes—whether consciously or not one cannot say—Ahad Ha-'am's classical essay against Jewish assimilation, 'Slavery in Freedom' ('Avdut be-toch herut', 1891), and Berlin leaves it open whether the 'slavery' in his title refers to the Jewish condition in pre-emancipation days or to the mental state of Jews who viewed emancipation as an opportunity to adopt the mores and cultures of their surrounding societies at the price of denying their own historical identity.

Perhaps surprisingly, Berlin starts with a paean to the pre-modern Jewish community, the *kehilla*, which he calls the Jewish 'establishment' as it developed mainly in Eastern Europe. Not afraid to call it a 'community within a community'—a term consciously playing on the traditional accusation against the Jews that they form 'a State within a State'—Berlin views it as 'one of the most complete and powerful civilisations, albeit persecuted, insulated, and without influence outside the ghetto walls, that can be conceived'. He goes on to suggest that, within this framework, 'The Jews developed a rich and independent inner life of their own, from which sprang those generously endowed, imaginative, free and unbroken Jewish personalities who, even today, compare so favourably with the better educated but, at times, less spontaneous and morally and aesthetically less attractive Jews of the West' (POI 164, 148, 184).

What attracts Berlin to the social and intellectual climate of the pre-modern Jewish *kehilla* is its authenticity—a similar argument to that made by Max Nordau, one of Herzl's main supporters, in his address at the First Zionist Congress in Basle in 1897.[7] Per contra, it is the lack of authenticity which characterises the Jewish attempt at assimilation.

Berlin's attack on nineteenth-century Jewish assimilation, especially in Germany, is rare in its scathing and sometimes extreme language—and undoubtedly imbued with the anger and anguish connected with the Holocaust. How terrible, he comments, that 'The German Jews who believed and practiced [assimilation] with the most sincere conviction have suffered the most tragic fate of all' (POI 163).

The roots of violent German anti-Semitism have to be found, according to Berlin, at least partially in the assimilation project itself: it is not an easy statement to make, especially just six years after the end of the Second World War—but Berlin is adamant. The Jewish Reform Movement in Germany, heralded by Moses Mendelssohn, so much beloved by many liberal and secular Jews, is taken to task by Berlin, when he points out how much people like Mendelssohn—or, for that matter, Heinrich Heine—by over-identifying with Germany and German culture, laid bare their own insecurity and problematic identity:

Such passion surely often derives from a feeling of insufficient kinship and a desire to obliterate the gap [between them and the majority culture]; the more

---

7. Nordau 1897. Similarly, Berlin related how Lewis Namier's main unease with his family's assimilation (and conversion) grew from his inability to abide by their lack of authenticity and pride in their own heritage (PI2 93–4).

obstinate the gap, the more violent the desire to close it, or to act as if it did not exist. And this strikes an unnatural note, audible to all but the stranger himself [...] second nature is different from nature, and the desperate self-identification of the Jew does not ring wholly true.[8]

This is one of Berlin's most eloquent essays, and it is here that he makes famous the oft-repeated phrase that the Jews 'are just like everybody else, only more so' (POI 164). It is here too that he gives currency to the image originated by Lewis Namier that the effect of emancipation on the Jews was like 'that of the sun upon a glacier. The outer crust disappeared by evaporation; the heart of the glacier remained stiff and frozen; but a great portion of the mass melted into a turbulent flood of water which inundated the valleys below' (POI 162), the latter being the first-generation emancipated Jews—the Heines, Marxes and Disraelis—who so much enriched European culture and have been such a fascinating subject for Berlin's studies.

Here also appears the metaphor of the strangers settling in an alien land, who eventually 'grow to be peerless analysts of the social conditions of the tribe' into which they had settled (POI 167), and consequently hated and despised for their superior knowledge by the 'true' natives. Last and not least, here Berlin sets up his powerful parable of the Jews as a tribe of hunchbacks who try, in different ways and with varying degrees of success, to come to terms with their deformity— some maintaining they have no hump, others claiming that it is a special privilege to own a hump, and still others never mentioning a hump, regarding the very use of the term as implying discrimination, and wearing 'voluminous cloaks which concealed their precise contours'. Then, of course, there were those—obviously the Zionists—who admitted that 'a hump was a hump' and should be 'cut off by means of a surgical operation' (POI 174–6).

It was the metaphor of the hump that angered many critics, especially since Berlin uses the term 'deformed' to describe it, thus implying that there was something intrinsically wrong, abnormal or even sick about the Jews as such. It may not

---

8. POI 163. In a sarcastic aside Berlin ridicules Walter Rathenau's contention that the Jews are 'a German tribe, like the Saxons, the Bavarians or the Wends' (1816, 155; cited at POI 170), and scathingly expresses his disgust with the statement attributed to a Jewish German intellectual who, when having to flee the Nazis, declined to seek asylum in France, since he 'could not go to the country of our enemies' (POI 169). This radical criticism of especially German Jewish assimilation is reiterated also in the essay on Disraeli and Marx (AC 258), where Berlin says that the fact that Mendelssohn's children converted to Christianity has to be seen as a testimony to the inherent failure of the German Reform movement, and on this occasion credits also people like Otto Weininger and Simone Weil with Jewish 'self-hatred'.

be a felicitous metaphor, and the pages in which Berlin describes, with obvious relish, the various strategies of the hunchbacks do not make for pleasant reading. When suggesting that the Israeli-born sabra was totally free from any vestige of a hump and was totally 'straight-backed', it is obvious that Berlin is over-simplifying and may have been so much in love with his metaphor that it ran away with him. Yet the very acrimony that the metaphor elicited proved that Berlin had hit on a raw nerve among many Diaspora Jews. Nothing rankles more than an accusation of lack of authenticity, and Berlin's verdict on assimilation was uncompromising: 'As a radical solution [...] it has failed. Nor is there any reason [...] for thinking that it will ever succeed' (POI 163).

It was probably this radical judgement on the chances of assimilation (and the word has obviously more than one meaning) that caused Berlin to be uncomfortable about reprinting the essay. At the time of writing, he was thinking mainly of the European experience, and while his stay in the United States during the war acquainted him with American Jewish life, it is fair to say that it was only later, in the 1960s and after, that he gained a better understanding of the American Jewish experience that would probably have led him to relativise his harsh verdict on Diaspora life.

Be this as it may, this essay is not only Berlin's reckoning with the failure of European Jewish assimilation, but also his own way of justifying Zionism as a return to authenticity, autonomy and self-determination. Yet the essay also has a more subtle agenda, which appears only in its concluding pages. Here he argues on two fronts: on the one hand he disagrees with those 'ultra-nationalist' Zionists who call on all Jews to immigrate to Israel; on the other, he disagrees equally with the point made in *Promise and Fulfilment* (1949) by Arthur Koestler—an erstwhile radical Zionist with sympathies for Jabotinsky—that now that Israel exists, Diaspora Jews have either to immigrate or, if they refuse to do this, give up their Jewish distinctiveness and identity and finally, and peacefully, disappear into the universal stream of humanity. Berlin refuses this 'either–or' alternative, calling it 'an intolerable form of bullying' (POI 181)—and in the process reveals what may have been to him (a Zionist who ultimately chose not to move to Israel) the true meaning of the establishment of the Jewish State.

This is done in a somewhat circuitous way, but the underlying argument is straightforward. The problem of Jewish identity in modern times was communal, not individual. Jews might have thought they could solve their individual problems of identity by various strategies of accommodation, assimilation and even conversion; but, as Nazism has shown, they could not escape—whatever their individual choices—from their communal identity, be they Marranos fleeing the Inquisition or assimilated or even converted Jews in modern-day Germany.

This communal problem has now been solved, Berlin argues. Those Jews who feel, for whatever reason, uncomfortable in the Diaspora now have a homeland to which they can emigrate. Yet there are others—and here Berlin obviously speaks for himself—who will not choose this course, but will continue to live, for a variety of reasons, in 'politically non-Jewish States'. This is a revolutionary novelty, caused by Zionism. Not only did Zionism give a homeland to those Jews who decided to settle in the historical homeland of the Jewish people—but also, *for the first time in the modern age*, every individual Jew is now free to live in a Jewish or non-Jewish environment. This is now 'a purely individual problem which each Jew is free to solve as he chooses' (POI 179). He goes on: 'Every and each individual Jew is in a far better position than he has been since the destruction of the Jewish State by the Romans to choose his own mode of life for himself.'[9]

This is for Berlin the doubly emancipatory message of the emergence of Israel. Its establishment is for him not only the continuation of the narrative of the Risorgimento; it has also freed the Jews of the Diaspora, for their fate is now in their own hands. 'In this sense', Berlin sums up, 'the creation of the State of Israel has liberated *all* Jews, whatever their relation to it.'[10]

From a philosophical point of view, this is an even more radical position than that held by so-called 'radical' Zionists who insist that all Jews should immigrate to Israel. By maintaining that the creation of Israel has emancipated all Jews—not by coercing all of them to emigrate, but by giving *all* of them the freedom of choice, Zionism is a true inheritor of the Enlightenment, and in this way Berlin integrates his Zionism with his liberal credo—and with his own choice not to emigrate to Israel, while remaining an ardent, though occasionally critical, supporter of the Jewish State.

ISRAEL

Berlin's 'The Origins of Israel' (1953), published two years after 'Jewish Slavery and Emancipation', is a natural corollary to it. Like its predecessor, it is still imbued with the heady achievement of the very establishment of a Jewish State, though already at this early stage Berlin is well aware of the fact that the actual Israel does not necessarily live up to the ideals and expectations of its dreamers and founders. Yet—as he would insist until his last days—these blemishes should not be used to deny the very legitimacy—indeed, necessity—of the existence of a Jewish polity.

Despite recent changes in Israeli society and politics, Berlin's analysis of the

---

9. POI 180. This appears also in Berlin 1975, 9–10.
10. POI 184 (italics added). See also MI 178–82.

historical and intellectual origins of Israel has hardly been matched to this day as a profound and sound analysis of its origins. In tune with his own views, developed in 'Historical Inevitability', and in contrast with more conventional and shallow Zionist claims that Israel is the inevitable outcome of the age-old Jewish yearnings for a homeland, Berlin maintains that there is nothing predetermined or necessary in the emergence of the Jewish State. That the contrary is true indicates to him the power of ideas. Israel is almost the paradigmatic case of this power, and of the capacity of human will to overcome the dead weight of circumstance. Herein lies its universal significance:

> [Israel's] career confutes a number of deterministic theories of human behaviour, those offered both by materialism and by the fashionable brands of anti-materialism. And that, I will not deny, is a source of great satisfaction to those who have always believed such theories to be false in principle, but have never before, perhaps, found evidence quite so vivid and quite so convincing of their hollowness. Israel remains a living witness to the triumph of human idealism and will-power over the allegedly inexorable laws of historical evolution. (POI 161)

Berlin is well aware how manifold and sometimes contradictory were the ideas that contributed to the social and political fabric of Israel. He also argued that the vision of how a Jewish commonwealth, once established, would look does *not* come from the Jewish religious heritage—it came from nineteenth-century European ideas, and Berlin has no qualms about referring to it even as a Jewish version of 'the most idealistic liberal conception of the White Man's Burden' (POI 146).

Yet this vision was far from uniform; and, in a somewhat ironic comment, Berlin enumerates the various ingredients that went into the mix that eventually became Israel: English Zionists conceived of it as 'a civilising mission carried on by dedicated personalities who would bring the maturest fruit of the most peace-loving and most humane culture of the West to these [...] rather barbarous Eastern peoples'; French Jews (he had Edmond de Rothschild in mind) hoped for 'a French ideal with pretty French vines and olive trees, elegant, charming and self-contained, an expression of a peaceful, rural, slightly nostalgic nineteenth-century view of the life of tenant farmers and their labourers'; and 'German Jews wanted an orderly, modern, spick and span world [...] well-disciplined, tidy, competent, late nineteenth-century—I will not say Prussian, but at any rate properly regulated and firmly founded—political and economic organisation' (POI 146–7).

But after having his fun at the expense of various Western European Jewish contributions to the emergence of Israel, Berlin recognises that the major contributors to Israel as it eventually emerged were the Eastern European Jews, who were the majority of the immigrants to Palestine in the formative years of the development of the Yishuv and whose imprint has been crucial to its development. The Ost-Juden made their imprint on the course of Israeli society not only because of numbers, but because they came to Palestine with twin political traditions—that of the Jewish *kehilla* and that of the liberal traditions of the Russian intelligentsia:

> The Eastern European Jews, as a result of historical circumstances, possessed a kind of independent establishment of their own. They had, unlike their Western brothers, grown to be a kind of a State within a State, with their own political, social, religious and human ideals. [...] These were the people who to some extent transferred their own institutional basis to the new country. That is what gave Jewish Palestine its profound continuity with the immediate Jewish past. [...] On the other hand [...] they assimilated the humanist-liberal, radical and social-democratic traditions of intellectual revolt [...] [they] were brothers and heirs to the idealistic Russian intellectuals. (POI 148–51)

This combination of a specifically Jewish communal heritage and the liberal traditions of the Russian intelligentsia gave the Jewish project in Palestine both its ideological power and its institutional anchor. For Berlin, this unusual amalgam also meant that his deep commitment to Zionism was not only anchored in his insight into the dilemmas of the Jewish people in the modern world, but also integrated into one of the major spheres of his intellectual endeavour—his fascination with the Russian intelligentsia and his almost uncanny ability, from the perspective of the Oxford of the second half of the twentieth century, to feel deep empathy for the moral heroism—and political failure—of this Russian intellectual liberal endeavour, and to convey this to English and American public opinion. There is a subtext here for Berlin—that what failed in Russia succeeded, after a fashion, in Palestine.

Thus Berlin also points out how the socialist Zionist effort to settle on the land, and the redemptive powers of the 'return' to the soil and to nature, derives from the Russian Socialist-Revolutionaries—the Narodniks—and their wish to 'go among the people'. The Zionist *halutzim* ('pioneers'), who founded the new kibbutzim, were inspired by Russian liberal and socialist ideas, not by Jewish religious sources, much as their quest for a homeland in the land of Israel harks back to Judaic memories and legacies.[11]

---

11. POI 151. In a far less laudatory tone, Berlin also recognises the Eastern European roots of Begin's Irgun, which he calls 'a quasi-Fascist Party', in inter-war Poland: 'It is thence that it derives its terrorism, its heroism, its brutality, and a certain kind of romantic, Byronic [*sic*!] inhumanity' (POI 152).

Two more themes stand out in Berlin's panoramic account in this essay of the origins of Israel. One is his panegyric to Hebrew and its revival in Palestine as a spoken and modern literary and scientific language. His ode to Hebrew is in line with the conventional Zionist preference for it over Yiddish, the common tongue of most—though definitely not all—Jews in Eastern Europe. Here he follows the thinking of the nineteenth-century Hebrew Enlightenment (*Haskala*), which was, after all, the environment in which Berlin had grown up in Riga and Petrograd. Though his historical verdict has been borne out by developments—especially if one imagines how dysfunctional Yiddish would have been in nation-building where Middle Eastern Jewish immigrants were concerned—it is unusually harsh: 'All the warmth, the humour and the raciness, the splendid expressiveness of Yiddish, all the gaiety and tears of the many centuries of exile embodied in it, cannot compensate for the fact that it is an argot; that, like all things created under degraded conditions of life, it is formless, insufficiently disciplined and strict, over-elastic' (POI 154).

Yet his preference for Hebrew is based not solely on its being the historical language of the Jewish people, or on the fact that it was the only common medium that was equally sacred and accessible to all immigrants, but also on its having—dialectically—a cultural dimension relating it to Europe: Hebrew 'was the ancient vehicle of a noble literature, the associations of which have affected the roots of all European thought and imagination. Because of this it has acted as an educational instrument of unique power' (POI 154).

This is a surprising plea for Hebrew, since many (occasionally even Herzl) have linked Yiddish, with its Germanic, and partly Slavonic, roots to European culture, while viewing Hebrew as an antiquated, 'oriental' and hence not really *salonfähig* language. This is obviously in line with Berlin's emphasis on the European sources of Israel's political ideas, and his overall assessment of Zionism as part of the heritage of the European Enlightenment.

This is accompanied, though, by a more ambiguous assessment of the realities of Israel, and, while written in the 1950s, Berlin's thoughts have a contemporary resonance. Berlin admits that many people who visit Israel and expect to find there the efflorescence of Jewish intellectuality may be disappointed by its 'relative coarseness; a kind of stubborn normality and a complacent soundness, wholesomeness, dullness'. On the one hand he is quick to point out that this may be something that 'Jews have surely richly deserved'. On the other, he maintains that it 'may be a cause for regret, or it may not' (POI 156). Berlin is obviously disappointed in what he portrays as a basically true, though somewhat exaggerated, image of the uncomplicated sabra, so dissimilar from the highly cultured European Jew (Koestler at that time made similarly uncomplimentary comments on the Israeli-born youngster, who was grotesquely idealised by such kitsch figures as

Ari Ben-Canaan in Leon Uris's *Exodus*). Yet he tries, in line with conventional Zionist thinking, to see in this a sign of 'normalisation'. But, as the text shows, he is in two minds about this. He is also aware of the enormous challenge posed to Israel by mass immigration from Arab-speaking countries, and although the essay was written in the early 1950s, he asks a question which, while not formulated in these terms today, shows his sensitivity to what for him was the importance of preserving the liberal, European origins of Israel: 'Will the result be Westernisation or "Levantinisation"? It is too early to tell' (POI 159). The ambivalence is obvious.

There is, however, one aspect of his view of Israel on which Berlin has been proven wrong. While expressing his ambivalence about Israel's 'normality', he points out the country's dearth of excellence in fields both material and spiritual—and it is here that Berlin's 1953 perspective is off the mark: 'There are in Israel very few eminent bankers, very few eminent lawyers, not many scientists of genius; there are very few persons principally occupied with the accumulation of wealth. [...] There are no great Israeli novelists [...]. There are on the whole no great thinkers, poets, painters, sculptors, composers' (POI 155–6).

Perhaps even in 1953 Berlin was setting an excessively high standard for Israel: it may equally be that, even then, he did not meet the right people. Be this as it may, few would agree that this dire assessment reflects Israel as it has developed since then, culturally and intellectually—even under conditions of war and siege—and Berlin later came to realise that, after all, Israel, despite its many blemishes—which he was keen to point out—developed much more as an Athens than as a Sparta.

A CLASH OF IDENTITIES?

If I were writing a biographical study, this would probably be the time to ask how, in his private life, Berlin combined his ardent identification with the Jewish people, Zionism and Israel with his emergence as a major British thinker, almost the quintessence of an Oxford don with a powerful public presence. These issues are indeed dealt with in some of the biographies of Berlin—especially in the books by John Gray and Michael Ignatieff—and have sometimes caused controversy and disagreement.

This is not the place to add to this debate, but a number of questions cannot be avoided. There is no doubt that, growing up in 1930s England as the son of immigrants, and as an immigrant himself who never lost his European accent, Berlin had to make a number of tough psychological choices, not least in his academic career. In this respect he was the typical Jewish *maskil* of the nineteenth century, living in two worlds, striving to be 'a Jew in private, and a human being in public' (*Yehudi be-ohalo ve-adam be-tzeto*). This dichotomy obviously exacted its price—perhaps nowhere more apparent than during his service in Washington during the Second World War, when he was responsible for reporting on American moods to the British government. Michael Ignatieff points out in detail how Berlin's loyalty to the British government occasionally put him on a collision course with what some of his Jewish friends in the United States would have liked him to report to London, and some of his reports would not have been pleasant reading to American Jewish leaders at the time, had they had access to them (cf. esp. MI 118–25).

Some of this ambivalence, however, goes deeper. We have seen that Berlin felt uneasy, in his conversations with Jahanbegloo, when asked why he did not immigrate to Israel. He was a frequent visitor to the country, and was involved over decades in supporting it politically and intellectually, but during his visits he moved—as he did in Britain—among a narrow circle of its leaders, political and academic. With all his knowledge and understanding of the country's political and intellectual climate, it cannot be said that he knew the country in the way he knew British society—or, for that matter, the intellectual history of Russia. His accounts of his first visit to Palestine, in 1934, read like the impressions of a white man in the tropics—observed from outside, with much empathy and interest, but without immediate *Einleben* with its Jewish population. Despite his meeting with members of his family living in Palestine, it appears that he felt more comfortable with the high British officials to whom he had generous letters of introduction than with the rough-and-tumble of Jewish life and politics in Eretz Israel (MI 77–80). Some of this aloofness remained even after 1948: while visiting Israel, he was adored by his many friends and acquaintances, he bathed in the love and adoration of his numerous Israeli former students, he hobnobbed with some of the high and mighty—but it may not be unfair to say that the idea of the Jewish State was much nearer to his heart than the (not always pleasant) actual Israel.

Not wearing his emotions on his sleeve might have been a natural outcome of his complex inner life in regard to his own identity, and perhaps he also over-internalised English modes of not showing one's feelings. This does, however, come out in strange ways: one of his first post-1945 published pieces is a music review that appeared in the *Observer* of 19 September 1948 as 'Karajan: A Study', in which he reports on the extraordinary impression made on him by listening to Herbert von Karajan conducting the Vienna Philharmonic Orchestra at the Salzburg Festival.

The musical review as such is beside the point, which is that this was written in the late summer of 1948, when Israel was still fighting for its life, and reported a musical event happening in ravaged post-war Austria, praising a musician who rose to fame under the Nazis. That Israel's agony at the time Berlin was enjoying the festival could not be mentioned is obvious; but the review's reader would not know what happened in Austria—and in Salzburg—during the war, and who Karajan was. Maybe Berlin, then still a young and rather unknown person, had to tread carefully, and in any case his love of music was genuine and deep; maybe the editors of the *Observer* would not tolerate any extra-musical *obiter dictum*. All this is possible, but one still wonders.

This raises the wider issue of Berlin's attitude to the Holocaust. When the first volume of his letters was published, some commentators—notably Clive James (2004)—mentioned how little the Holocaust figures in them. This is also true of his published writings, where the rise and ideology of Nazism is hardly ever discussed. For all that Berlin claims not to be a historian, this is somewhat unusual for a historian of ideas who tried to decipher the riddle and travails of the twentieth century.

Again, some English-bred reticence is understandable. On the other hand, one does not have to agree with those thinkers and leaders who have made the Holocaust the mainstay of Jewish identity to feel a bit uneasy about a strange lacuna and silence. More than on any other occasion, this comes out in his conversations with Jahanbegloo, where his interviewer—young, non-Jewish, coming from faraway Iran, though then resident in Europe—takes liberties which other interlocutors might never have dared to allow themselves.

The section entitled 'Discovery of Auschwitz' in the *Conversations* makes somewhat painful reading (CIB 19–23). When asked 'How did you experience the Second World War as a Jew?', and then what he knew about the Holocaust and when he knew it, Berlin repeatedly takes refuge in what to him is an extremely uncharacteristic turn of phrase: 'I felt exactly like everybody.' He explains, somewhat lamely:

> I never heard about [the extermination of the Jews] until the end of 1944 [...] as I said before, I only discovered the full horror of the Holocaust very late. I do not know why nobody ever told me—perhaps life in an embassy was too protected. Still, I met prominent American Jews from time to time, and nobody ever told me about this. I still feel some guilt about it, even though it was not really any fault of mine.

Berlin goes on to state—as he did on other occasions—that the Holocaust was the ultimate proof of the failure of the emancipation/assimilation project. Then he is brought up short by the interviewer asking him point blank: 'Were any members of your family killed by the Nazis?' Berlin responds: 'Yes. Both my grandfathers, an uncle, an aunt, three cousins, were killed in Riga in 1941'—and leaves it at this, never to come back to it in the interview; never, for that matter, mentioning it on any other occasion in public.

English stiff upper lip? Not wishing to make his family tragedy a key to the understanding of his political thought? Again one wonders, especially as one could imagine numerous occasions on which he could have discussed the ideology that led to the Holocaust—even without mentioning his own family. Yet he chose not to do this.

On the other hand, one should point out—as Ignatieff does—that, like Gershom Scholem, Berlin was scandalised by Hannah Arendt's book on Eichmann and her contention that European Jewry should—or could—have fought against the Nazis while all of Europe failed to show much resistance to German occupation. As he pointed out in numerous letters, he found her comments unfeeling, obtuse and lacking in basic humanity (MI 253).

Yet while Berlin was in Jerusalem during the Eichmann trial in 1961, he never wrote about it or published his own impressions, nor did he take issue with Arendt in public. Was it another example of his not wishing to appear in public as another Jew with a chip on his shoulder? Was it his distaste with the way the Holocaust has been used—and misused—by so many Jewish and Israeli figures? Or was it his pride in his Jewishness, which was reluctant to play the role of victim in what he himself had criticised many times as the lachrymose version of Jewish history? There does not seem to be a clear answer. Again, one wonders.

To this it should be added that a similar blind spot—if one may so call it— appears also in his treatment of the Bolshevik Revolution and Stalinism. During the cold war, Berlin was one of the major contributors to the liberal critique of the Soviet system, and together with Raymond Aron and other Western intellectuals he ensured that criticism of Communism did not come just from professional red-baiters. In his writings on the Soviet Union, one finds a deeply felt critique of the ruthlessness of Bolshevism vis-à-vis the Russian intelligentsia, of which he saw himself as a scion. But there is hardly any reference to the brutality of Stalinism towards the peasantry. The travails of Akhmatova and Pasternak appear frequently in Berlin's writings and speeches—the horrors of collectivisation and the consequent hunger and massive death in Ukraine are barely mentioned. It may be unfair to suggest, though it is probably true, that when one views oneself as a historian of ideas, this may occasionally lead one to overlook the sufferings of those human beings—either in the Holocaust or under Stalin—who have no access to ideas.

Berlin's Jewishness was obvious to all, and he never dissociated himself from it—after all, this was his main criticism of the assimilationists, especially in Germany, and the foundation of his Zionist credo. Nevertheless, it may come as another surprise to his readers to find that, while his writings dealt extensively with thinkers and persons who were Jewish or of Jewish origin—Disraeli and Marx,

Hess and Heine, Weizmann and Einstein—one does not find in his writings references to the historical masters of Jewish and Hebrew philosophy and literature. Not only are medieval thinkers like Maimonides or Yehuda Halevi never mentioned, but the modern Hebrew Enlightenment, the *Haskala*, does not appear in his opus: Bialik and Tschernichowsky, Ahad Ha-'am or Klatzkin—all these stars in the modern Jewish Eastern European firmament—are wholly lacking in his writings. One cannot gainsay Berlin's stature as one of the major Jewish thinkers of the twentieth century—but there are no traces of modern Jewish and Hebrew thought in his writings. Whatever the reason for this, it may also perhaps explain a certain distance from the real Israel formed by these thinkers, writers and poets.[12]

To the end of his life Berlin remained an ardent supporter of Israel. When Prime Minister Ben-Gurion asked him, along with other Jewish luminaries, to address the issue of State and religion in Israel, he responded in a detailed memorandum, which brought out once again his understanding of the complexity of the issues. Israel, he argued, has to be a liberal State, not a theocracy, and 'the question of religious affiliation should make no difference to its laws of citizenship'. Judaism is not merely a religion, but, 'in some sense, a nationality as well'. Hence issues of intermarriage will remain fraught with problems and contradictions, and might be better solved on an interim basis so as to avoid 'a ferocious Kulturkampf'.[13]

This principled yet pragmatic liberalism also informed Berlin's attitude to the vexed problems of the Israeli–Palestinian relationship. In his latter years he was troubled by the more nationalist tone which has characterised Israeli politics since 1967: he opposed Jewish settlements in the occupied territories, and called for a historical compromise with the Palestinians; otherwise, the liberal nature of the country's ethos would be sapped (see Tamir-Rafaeli 1987).

While Berlin insisted that Diaspora Jews should not be drawn into internal Israeli politics, the issue of an eventual compromise between Israel and the Palestinians appeared to him a matter of principle, in line with his general liberalism. Hence a few weeks before his death he wrote a letter to Avishai Margalit in which he supported the Oslo agreements and maintained that only a two-State solution would be in accord with the liberal foundations of Zionism. The letter was published in *Ha'aretz* on 7 November 1997, two days after his death. In it he said: 'Since both sides begin with a claim of total possession of Palestine as their historical right; and since neither claim can be accepted within the realms of realism

---

12. A reflection of this may be seen in the fact that, in the symposium held in Jerusalem to celebrate Berlin's eightieth birthday (Margalit and others 1990), none of the lectures dealt with the specifically Jewish heritage of his thought.

13. This memorandum and a covering letter dated 23 January 1959 were published in Ben-Rafael 2002, 168–76.

or without great injustice: it is plain that compromise, i.e. partition, is the only correct solution.'

Nothing could be a better political expression of his liberal thought when applied to matters Jewish.

4

Berlin's Early Political Thought

Joshua L. Cherniss

This essay explores Isaiah Berlin's political thought from the 1930s to the mid-1950s—the period leading up to the composition of his famous lecture, *Two Concepts of Liberty* (1958; hereafter TCL). In discussing his often neglected early works, I hope to cast new light on the genesis and significance of Berlin's later, better-known, writings—particularly TCL, of which this chapter is to some extent a prehistory.

Examination of these early works suggests that Berlin was less straightforwardly wedded to the 'negative' concept of liberty, and more sympathetic to some elements of the 'positive' conception, than many readings of TCL suggest. While that essay (especially its conclusion) reads as a straightforward argument for viewing political freedom as the absence of external interference (and thus casts Berlin in the role of a champion of Western liberalism against Communism), Berlin's earlier writings on liberty suggest that he was more critical of the West, and more sympathetic to some constituents of 'positive' liberty—particularly the idea of autonomy (defined not as rule by reason or self-given law, but as ability independently to set the direction of one's own life).[1] Berlin's later, reiterated

---

1. Compare the following sentence, in which Berlin speaks from the perspective of a proponent of (one version of) positive liberty, with his heartfelt expressions of his own convictions quoted later in the paper: 'All forms of tampering with human beings, getting at them, shaping them against their will to your own pattern, all thought-control and conditioning, is [...] a denial of that in men which makes them men and their values ultimate' (TCL; L 184).

attacks on paternalism, and his embrace of romanticism as a source of moral and intellectual support for non-conformity and independence, suggest that TCL (and Berlin's other, earlier, criticisms of 'positive' liberty) did not represent an alteration of his position, but rather the adoption of a conceptual scheme which, while it served a purpose in highlighting some of Berlin's insights and convictions, inadvertently obscured others.[2]

Focusing on these earlier works thus alters and enriches our understanding of one of Berlin's best-known ideas, suggesting that in order to understand his position we must go beyond the negative/positive dichotomy, which cannot by itself contain or explain his own conception of liberty. This is the most striking, but not the only, insight into the origins and substance of Berlin's thought yielded by study of his earlier writings.

It was during the decade after the war, too, that Berlin's writings centred most on politics. Later—despite holding a chair in political theory at Oxford, and often being classified as a political theorist—Berlin would write little that was concerned directly with politics or political theory, devoting himself instead (with the exception of a few essays which mainly reiterated or refined elements of his earlier work) to the history of ideas. Therefore, if we are concerned with Berlin as a *political* thinker—as opposed to a historian of ideas, or an exponent of ethical pluralism—it is sensible to concentrate on the period when politics impinged most deeply and decisively on his thought, when his political convictions and concerns were first formed and most directly expounded, and when his work and the political pulse of his times ran closest together.

The story told in this essay—of Berlin's engagement with politics, from its origins in the experience of revolutionary violence and fear of totalitarianism, through its development in his appalled analysis of Soviet Communism and his anxiety about dehumanisation and repression in Western society, to his working-out of his own position in his studies of the history of ideas and the philosophy of history—is not merely one of (justified) horror at political inhumanity. As Berlin wrote, 'men do not live only by fighting evils. They live by positive goals', from 'intense preoccupation' with which 'the best moments come in the lives of individuals and peoples' (L 93). The ideal that most intensely preoccupied Berlin in the years covered by this essay and throughout his life was liberty, in all its forms and complexities; and from his pursuit of this ideal came the best moments in his own life's work.

---

2. Indeed, the 'two concepts' dichotomy—which, far from being original to Berlin, was a commonplace in discussions of liberty in political theory, both in Britain and elsewhere—was always too blunt an instrument for Berlin's purpose. While it has made his essay memorable, and thus durable, it has also masked the subtleties—and exacerbated the confusions—of Berlin's thinking about liberty.

THE PRE-WAR YEARS: AN A-POLITICAL THEORIST?

Few observers encountering Isaiah Berlin before the Second World War would have predicted that the witty, erudite Oxford don would become a renowned political theorist. Berlin described himself at the time as 'not a very political thinker' (1935b); even in the worst depths of the Depression, as Hitler rose, the Spanish Republic fell and Stalin reigned by terror, Berlin lived in a world of personal relationships, philosophical preoccupations and art. Having gone up to Oxford in 1928, he was poised between the frivolous 'Brideshead generation' and the politically earnest generation of the 1930s (CIB 9). This position reflected a more general feature of Berlin's temperament, which was characterised by a tension between aestheticism and moralism, effusiveness and rigour, romanticism and scepticism, amused tolerance and moral sternness. Although he would later recall that, because of his experience of the Russian Revolutions of 1917, he was already ideologically sensitive (CIB 10), this awareness did not translate into political activity. At this point—and arguably later—Berlin was more interested in political *ideas* than actual politics.[3] And for most of the 1930s he did not commit himself, in print, to discussion even of political ideas.[4] Politics feature little in his correspondence from this period; and, oddly for one who lived through the Depression, he was never very interested in, and (beyond a general sympathy towards Keynesianism) lacked strong views on, economic policy.

Yet this picture of the young Berlin as apolitical man should be qualified. Maurice Bowra recalled that, as a young don, Berlin

> saw in many parts of the world ugly forces at work to destroy the civilisation which he valued so highly. [...] Politics were very far from being his only, or even his chief interest, but he could not and would not refuse their challenges [...] he was increasingly troubled by violence abroad and supine indifference at home, and he and his friends helped to create a new seriousness at Oxford. (1966, 185–6)

Berlin himself claimed that the 'dreadful years' of the 1930s had 'conditioned' his political outlook, so that he could not 'think about politics except in terms of a certain amount of black and white'—the 'black' being totalitarianism (Berlin and Hampshire 1972, 6). He packed parcels for the Spanish Republican cause, criticised Britain's failure to oppose Mussolini over Abyssinia, and opposed appeasement. Even his philosophical work had political overtones. Though critical of logical pos-

---

3. Berlin lectured on 'Eighteenth Century Political Theory' at Oxford in Trinity Term of 1940 (*Oxford University Gazette* 70, 553); before that, his lectures centred on logic, epistemology and ethics.

4. For discussion of some possible reasons for this political reticence, see IBLP 15.

itivism's central doctrines, he was sympathetic to its spirit, which he saw as an heir to the Enlightenment, opposed to authority and obscurantism.[5]

Political debate in 1930s Britain was marked by preoccupation with the relationship between ends and means. That it was necessary to judge the means by its end was a common argument among Communists and their apologists. The Communist goal, to 'abolish all the evils of the present and finally establish a free world', was a 'prodigious task', to accomplish which 'one did not have to consider, except from the point of view of their effectiveness, the means which were used nor the fate of individuals. *History did not care about those who were not on its side.*' The intellectual Communist put 'his faith in an *automatism of history* which, even if it is achieved by [...] bad means, will eventually make men good'. In this way, one could 'retain one's faith in the ultimate goals of humanity and at the same time ignore the thousands of people in prison camps, the tens of thousands of slave workers'.[6] These tendencies were intensified by the increasingly desperate fight against Fascism, which convinced many progressives of the justifiability of violence on behalf of righteous causes.

The logic of historical inevitability, the justification of means by ultimate ends, and the political mind-set that these fostered would be central concerns of Berlin's political thought; the combination of utopianism and ruthlessness which was the common property of many Communists and Nazis would be the main target of his mature writings. Yet Berlin's perception of Communist fanaticism predated the 1930s; it was first expressed in 'The Purpose Justifies the Ways', a story he wrote at the age of 12.[7] The story depicts, in the Bolshevik leader Uritsky, a political fanatic who, inured to human sentiment by ideological conviction, 'signed death verdicts without moving his eyebrow'. Uritsky divided human beings into those who stood in his way, and those who obeyed him; the former 'did not deserve to live at all'—his motto was 'The purpose justifies the ways', and 'he did not stop at anything for bringing out his plans' (L 334). Much of Berlin's later work was devoted to uncovering the philosophical roots of the mentality he had portrayed in Uritsky—as well as the historical processes and psychological proclivities that led to the adoption, and in some cases perversion, of these doctrines.

Berlin's first attempt to address politics in print was his essay 'Literature and the Crisis' (1935a), an analysis of the sense of malaise afflicting Britain's intellectuals and artists in the 1930s.[8] Berlin praised young left-wing poets such as Auden

---

5. See e.g. Berlin 1937.

6. Spender 1950, 236, 238, 239 (my emphasis).

7. See L xxviii.

8 The essay, written in 1935, was submitted to, and rejected by, the *London Mercury*; it was finally published in the *Times Literary Supplement* in 2001.

and Spender for using their poetry to convey their personal reactions to the crisis of their time, and criticised those who sought to save 'their doctrine[s] at the expense of their art and the sense of reality with which it is bound up'. 'Literature and the Crisis' anticipated Berlin's later writings in defending personal experience against the demands of dogma, and condemning attempts to achieve security at the cost of freedom. The essay displays an anxiety about freedom—associated with a desire for room, for escape from constriction and 'suffocation'—which, even at this early stage, seems to have been Berlin's primary political priority. In 'Literature and the Crisis' he was concerned with the preservation, not of political freedom, but of inner or mental freedom, which was necessary for individuals to be true to themselves. He therefore emphasised the freedom of the individual *from* externally imposed ideals and demands, as opposed to the freedom of individuals *to* express themselves publicly, and sought to assert limits on what could acceptably be demanded of the individual by society—while also warning against the maiming consequences of self-constriction in the (deceiving) name of inner liberty, and offering a qualified vindication of the value of political engagement.

The seeds of such engagement were thus present in Berlin's mind before the Second World War. Yet the coming of the war did mark 'a genuine change' in Berlin's life and outlook; he became consumed by public events, and was filled with a desire not just to observe and analyse, but to participate.[9] His posting to America immersed him in practical politics, by which he became fascinated; his visit to the Soviet Union after the war inspired in him a sense of moral mission which would drive his work throughout the most intellectually productive period of his life.[10]

ANTI-COMMUNIST MANIFESTOS

Post-war thought was shaped by the horrors of totalitarian dictatorship, the atrocities of modern warfare, and disillusionment with and fear of Communism among Western intellectuals. The political thought of the period was unsurprisingly characterised by pessimism and 'realism', emphasising the centrality of power and conflict, and a general distrust of ideologies and panaceas which derived from the reaction against political messianism and the violence to which it gave rise.[11] Though sympathetic to the veneration of sanity, decency and moderation that

---

9 Letter to Marion Frankfurter, 23 June 1940, L1 304–7.

10. See MI 97–169 for an excellent account of Berlin's wartime experiences. For his visit to the Soviet Union see also SM 28–40, 53–84; IBLP 6, 27–8.

11. On this tendency, see Shklar 1957 and Shklar 1996, 272–3.

this reaction fostered, Berlin thought the atmosphere it created dreary and stifling of individual originality and cultural excellence.[12] He found himself caught between the cultivation of private life that he associated with the older liberalism, and the political commitment demanded by the circumstances of his day.

The dominant political issue for Berlin, as for most of his contemporaries, was the cold war. For all his aversion to zeal and fanaticism, there is no doubt of the depth of his hatred for 'the USSR cesspool'.[13] Indeed, he claimed, 'I have to moderate my acute anti-Communism in order to achieve some degree of objectivity';[14] even having done so, he denounced the Soviet Union as founded on 'an even greater contempt for the freedom and the ideals of mankind than that with which Dostoevsky endowed his Grand Inquisitor'.[15] These remarks were the expression both of liberal principles and of personal loyalty to his friends among the Russian intelligentsia, Stalin's persecution of whom filled Berlin with an anger which he found difficult to contain or express.[16]

In writing about Communist theory and Soviet practice, Berlin emphasised the effects of fanaticism in inspiring cruelty, coarsening thought and feeling, and crushing freedom of the spirit. The ruthlessness of Communist theory—which had given rise to the Soviet regime in the first place—arose from fanatical conviction. Soviet practice, however, had declined into something more cynical and quotidian, as revolutionaries gave way to apparatchiks. Berlin frequently referred to the 'roughnecks' who had come to rule the Soviet Union—'[b]ullying and half-cynical semi-Marxist philistines', 'ruthless and anxious to get on', motivated by opportunism, resentment and blind thirst for domination.[17]

Berlin's analysis of Soviet governance centred on his idea of the 'artificial dialectic', the practice of varying the party line so as to maintain a state of constant uncertainty, alternating campaigns of terror and periods of relaxation. Such 'thaws' saved the regime from being destroyed by its own most devoted servants, and allowed the Kremlin to seem responsive to the cries of the people; they were also prudent, because frightening people too much would leave them numb, paralysed and unproductive. Furthermore, if the people were terrified into total silence, it would be impossible to know what they were thinking; and the government could not allow that. But once symptoms indicated that 'the ties have been loosened too far', 'new calls for conformity, purity, orthodoxy' were issued, the 'guillo-

---

12. See Berlin 1950a, xxii–xxxi; Berlin 1951a, xxii–xxxi.

13. Berlin to Joe Alsop, 1 July 1949, Papers of Joseph and Stewart Alsop, Manuscript Division, Library of Congress, Washington, DC.

14. Berlin to Ruth Lawson, 30 June 1949, MSB 119/186.

15. 'The Artificial Dialectic' (1952), SM 118.

16. Berlin to Philip Graham, 14 November 1946.

17. 'Soviet Russian Culture' (1957), SM 127, 165, 162.

tine begins to work again, the talkers are silenced'. Under this regimen, Soviet society was preserved in a condition of 'permanent wartime mobilisation'.[18] These methods were 'a phenomenon without parallel in the recorded history of human oppression'. Under Stalin, sheer survival depended on 'continuous active support of principles or policies' which were absurd or abhorrent. The effort perpetually to 'chart one's course in fatally dangerous waters' exhausted the mental capacities and constantly tested the moral fibre of those living under the regime. This made it all but impossible to escape 'into an inner citadel in which one can remain secretly heterodox and independent and know what one believes'.[19] Terror was pervasive, and tyranny dominated not only the behaviour of the ruled, but their mental lives. This 'crushed the life' out of Russian society, producing 'a long blank page in the history of Russian culture' (SM 150, 144).

This, according to Berlin, was what Stalin wanted. Stalin realised that the discussion of (even seemingly apolitical) ideas could foster a dangerously critical spirit; he therefore decided to put an end to all controversy. What mattered was not that a doctrine was true, but that it was accepted unquestioningly. This attitude—and the Stalinist values of 'loyalty, energy, obedience, discipline'—resembled Fascism more than classical Marxism. Indeed, life under Communism was marked by the standard vices attributed by Marxists to capitalism: exploitation, the commodification of human beings, the skimming of surplus value by those controlling the means of production. There was 'no society in which one body of men is more firmly, systematically and openly "exploited" by another' than the Soviet Union. Soviet society was organised not for those things valued by liberals—'happiness, comfort, liberty, justice, personal relationships'—but for combat. Bolshevism also differed from Western Marxism in being 'a way of life, all-penetrating and compulsory, controlled absolutely by the Party'. In Russia, Marxism became an eschatological 'metaphysics' which stubbornly ignored awkward facts; it aimed at achieving 'conformity with a set of dogmatic propositions' about 'what men and society must, at whatever cost, be made to be'. Communism had become a 'simple, dogmatic, fanatical faith, relying upon endless repetition of simple formulas and the worship of visible symbols of sanctity and power'.[20]

Berlin suggested that the fanatical revolutionary idealism of the early Bolsheviks and the brutal cynicism of Stalinist apparatchiks emanated from the same

---

18. 'The Artificial Dialectic', SM 107 ff., 112–14; 'Soviet Russian Culture', SM 148.

19. ibid. 144, 149. Hence, in part, Berlin's opposition to the idea of freedom as retreat into an 'inner citadel' where one will be invulnerable to the dangers of the world: for Berlin realised that no such 'inner citadel' was truly secure without being protected by the safeguards of negative liberty.

20. SM 139–40, 143, 151, 155; Berlin 1952, xxiv.

foundations. Russian Communism was founded on monism—the belief that 'there is one truth and one only, which the whole of one's life should be made to serve, one method, and one only, of arriving at it, and one body of experts alone qualified to discover and interpret it'. Monism was, 'even in its most idealistic and unworldly forms [...] in essence, totalitarian'. And, while it was as old as Plato, none had accepted it as naively and fanatically as the Russian revolutionaries. This made Russia fertile ground for Marxism, which (on Berlin's account) held that men and institutions were indissolubly one, that all genuine problems were soluble and 'fundamentally technological', a 'problem of engineering' rather than of politics or morality. Hence Stalin's description of artists as 'engineers of human souls', which so powerfully struck Berlin that he repeated it constantly throughout his writings of the 1950s (SM 134–5).

These totalitarian beliefs were dogmatically held. The essence of dogmatism was the subordination of individual judgement to the demands of theory: the tendency, if the pattern prescribed by ideology fails to fit the facts, to make the facts fit the pattern. Thus, under Communism, Russian society 'was vivisected [...] to fit a theory'. This involved a 'sovereign contempt for history and empirical evidence'—and for the feelings and indeed lives of the individuals affected (SM 154). The lack of respect for reality on the part of those inflamed by revolutionary fanaticism set the stage for Stalinist managerialism's cynical contempt for truth.

Berlin worked out his account of monism and its consequences, which would be at the centre of his later work, as an explanation of the intellectual springs of totalitarianism. This account was developed over the course of the 1950s, in his articles on Soviet Communism and his work on the history of ideas, as well as in more philosophical essays. But its core was first set out in Berlin's lecture 'Democracy, Communism and the Individual', delivered at Mount Holyoke College in 1949, the notes for which (1949a; hereafter DCI) provide a uniquely concise articulation of the core of his liberalism, the kernel from which the whole of his later political thought would grow.

The 'basic proposition' of totalitarianism, according to Berlin, was that 'if one is sure that one has the correct solution to the questions "How should men live?" and "How should society be organised?" one can, in the name of reason, impose it ruthlessly on others, since if they are rational they will agree freely; if they do not agree, they are not rational'. In modern thought, this assumption took the form of scientism—the belief that 'the right answer to questions of behaviour can be discovered by the "scientific" study of society'. Marxism was marked by such scientism, married to a deterministic theory of historical development which 'claimed to be able to demonstrate the proper goals of human existence in terms of a pattern of history of which there was "scientific" proof'. On this view, there was 'only one healthy or efficient condition for the soul, namely when it harmonises with the inexorable movement of society governed by unalterable historical laws'. This 'justifies a despotism of the most absolute kind' in the name of science.[21]

While Marxism was absolutist in its claims to scientific knowledge, its theory of history was relativist, holding as it did that all ideas were 'conditioned by our place in the social and economic structure'. This led to a discounting or devaluing of individuals' values and perceptions, and of moral and intellectual enquiry generally. Furthermore, Marxism regarded history as a struggle with a predetermined and discoverable outcome. Being rational meant being able to cope with reality, which in turn meant being on the winning side of this struggle. Success thus became the sole criterion of truth and the sole basis for respect. This outlook allowed Communists to ignore the beliefs and feelings of their opponents, and justified using any weapon, from censorship to murder, against 'enemies of progress'—that is, those who didn't accept Communist doctrine. Those on the losing side, who placed themselves 'in opposition to the juggernaut of history', could and should be dismissed as 'behaving suicidally, which proves that they are irrational, blind, mad, not worth listening to, and indeed a nuisance'. Such irrational persons did not understand their own condition, and therefore did not deserve to be treated as equals: for the 'pronouncements of the individual soul are valuable only if that soul is in a position to discover the true path'. This attitude undermined the moral foundations of democracy, which 'presupposes that individuals are not made worthless or incapable of rescue by the mere fact that they belong to a class different from your own'.[22]

This view of history as a perpetual struggle fostered ruthlessness: 'to adjust yourself to the movement of history you must carry out the tasks before you without flinching'. Seeing history in terms of class conflict, and themselves as history's ultimate winners, the Soviet leaders regarded individuals as soldiers in an

---

21. DCI 1, 4; SM 135; DCI 5. The historical antecedents of these ideas are treated at PIRA 17–87 and FIB 11–26, 105–30. This account of Communism may have been inspired by Berlin's encounter, in Moscow in 1945, with a member of the old Bolshevik élite, who asked him (he later recalled), 'if there is no room for free thinking in physics— a man who questions the laws of motion is obviously ignorant or mad—why should we Marxists, who have discovered the laws of history and society, permit free thinking in the social sphere? Freedom to be wrong is not freedom [...]. Truth liberates: we are freer than you in the West.' As Berlin remembered remarking at the time (provoking a response of stony silence), this statement came directly out of Comte (PI2 212). It also echoed Lenin's declaration that 'Those who are really convinced that they have advanced science, would demand, not freedom for the new views to continue side by side with the old, but the substitution of the old views by the new views' (1937, 14).

22. DCI 2, 4. Cf. 'Historical Inevitability' (1953), L 126–8, 137–8; FIB 74–104; and Berlin's critiques of E. H. Carr (Berlin 1950b, 1951b, 1962).

army, and other, non-Communist nations as antagonists in a death-struggle.[23] This justified the unlimited and unhesitating use of the coercive apparatus of the State, which was like a 'pistol wrested from the grasp of the enemy but not to be thrown away until it has been used to shoot the enemy. So long as enemies occur anywhere no holds are barred.'[24]

The denial of human moral equality by totalitarianism was connected to the belief that 'the proper way to live is discovered by experts wise enough to detect the direction of history'. Those who 'know which way things are moving [...] have a right to coerce the dissentient minority in the name of the verdict of history'. Their task was 'to adjust the individual soul' to society, without regard for 'its own conscious desires, ideals, aspirations'; this justified the assumption by 'experts' of 'unlimited power' (DCI 4–5). Communism sought to 'attune' the minds of its subjects to the scientific truths of Marxism, so that the subjects came to respond as 'the harmonious constituents of a properly regulated and efficiently functioning mechanism'. The task of education for Communists was 'not to supply knowledge and develop the faculty of assessing critically', but so to adjust the individual 'that he should only ask those questions the answers to which are readily accessible, that he shall grow up in such a way that he would naturally fit into his society with minimum friction'. The values of Bolshevism, and of totalitarianism generally, were 'tidiness, security', and freedom to do only 'that which alone will make for true, everlasting universal happiness'. This outlook condemned the personal and intellectual virtues of a liberal culture—'Curiosity for its own sake, the spirit of independent individual enquiry', the wish 'to pursue ends because they are what they are and satisfy some deep desire of our nature'—as failing to conduce to the 'harmonious development of a monolithic society' (SM 136; DCI 5–6).

AGAINST 'ENGINEERS OF HUMAN SOULS'

This provides ample support for the picture of Berlin as a Cold Warrior whose work amounted to an 'anti-Communist manifesto' (Strauss 1961, 138). Yet for Berlin Communism was merely 'the most consistent and extreme expression' of a mentality that was 'widespread beyond the confines of Russia today'. The charac-

---

23. Berlin late 1940s, 3.

24. DCI 3. This image echoes Benjamin Constant's argument—later endorsed by Berlin—that it was more important that coercive power be limited, and individuals protected against it, than that the power be vested in the 'right' hands: 'It is not against the arm that one must rail, but against the weapon. Some weights are too heavy for the human hand.' Constant 1815, chapter 1, 'De la souveraineté du peuple', 312, quoted at L 209.

teristic evil of Soviet Communism, and even of Nazism, was 'an extreme and distorted [...] form of some general attitude of mind from which our own countries are not exempt'. This attitude sought 'to mould human beings in ways likely to make them fit [...] into preconceived patterns of social life'. It marked all parts of the world and all portions of the political spectrum, from Communists to anti-Communist crusaders such as Senator Joseph McCarthy, and even many avowedly liberal administrators and philanthropists (DCI 6; L 343; 1950, xxvii).

As a liberal Cold Warrior, Berlin consistently warned against the danger of adopting the very dogmatism that liberals sought, or should seek, to combat. The answer to Communism was not 'a counter-faith, equally fervent, militant' and doctrinaire. Nothing was gained by seeking the same sort of scientific authority or social conformity as that sought by Communism: 'I see no purpose in defeating the other side if our beliefs at the end of the war are simply the inverse of theirs, just as irrational, despotic etc.' Berlin's opposition to calls for conformity and attempts to develop rigid, unquestionable political and moral doctrines were thus not directed against Communist ideologues alone. His correspondence suggests other (albeit lesser) targets, from McCarthy to the neo-Thomist intellectual crusader Mortimer Adler, and other proponents of various orthodoxies in the West.[25] It was not Communism alone, but orthodoxy and ideological tyranny as such, that Berlin opposed.

Berlin's first substantial essay in political thought, 'Political Ideas in the Twentieth Century', like most of his writings from this period, centred on the repressive, technocratic, conformist spirit which he saw sweeping the world. The essay contends that the twentieth century was distinguished from preceding periods by seeking to suppress, rather than to answer, troubling questions about human life, and thereby secure agreement by 'removing the psychological possibility of alternatives'. The elimination of friction (both social and internal), and therefore of the disruptive influence of disagreement and doubt, was necessary to enable individuals to 'pursue socially useful tasks, unhampered by disturbing and distracting reflections'. Such goals were not compatible with the existence of a wide array of choices, which made it impossible to maintain a 'well-adjusted' or 'integrated' social whole. As a result— and in the name of humanitarian goals—many were prepared to suppress 'any tendencies likely to lead to criticism, dissatisfaction, disorderly forms of life'.[26]

This 'new Zeitgeist' sought 'the organisation of society as a smoothly working machine', in which human behaviour could be 'manipulated with relative ease by technically qualified specialists'. There was a tendency 'to reduce all issues to technical problems', particularly the problem of how to achieve 'a condition in

---

25. Berlin, letter to Herbert Elliston, 30 December 1952, MSB 131/301–2.
26. 'Political Ideas in the Twentieth Century' (1950, hereafter PITC), L 77, 81, 79.

which the individual's psychological or economic capacities are harnessed to producing the maximum of unclouded social contentment', which in turn depended
on suppressing 'whatever in the individual might raise doubt or assert itself
against the single all-embracing, all-clarifying, all-satisfying plan'. Berlin particularly stressed the tendency to see human problems and conflicts as psychological
'maladjustments', 'dangerous deviations from that line to which individuals and
societies must adhere if they are to march towards a state of well-ordered, pain-
less, contented, self-perpetuating equilibrium'. All anxiety and doubt were dismissed as 'dislocations which the expert can set right', 'purely destructive dis-
eases' best cured 'by so treating the patient that the problem no longer troubles
him', that is, 'by removing it—like an aching tooth. Instead of unravelling you cut.
Instead of answering the question you remove it from the questioner's consciousness.' This view rejected the individualism of earlier liberal thought—according
to which society existed for, and policy was only justifiable in terms of the goods
of, individuals—in favour of a collectivist conception according to which individuals were 'parts—interchangeable, almost prefabricated—of a total pattern'
which existed for the sake of society.[27]

The reference to 'a total pattern' is telling. Berlin opposed these trends
because they violated liberty and devalued individuality, and because he was convinced that those who hankered after a 'final solution' would 'always end by
repressing and destroying human beings in their march towards the Promised
Land'.[28] But he was also moved by an aversion to tidiness itself. He was haunted
by the vision of a 'fanatically tidy world of human beings joyfully engaged in fulfilling their functions, each within his own rigorously defined province, in the
rationally ordered, totally unalterable hierarchy of the perfect society'.[29] Indeed,
for Berlin liberty was associated, even equated, with untidiness and the rejection
of harmony.

Related to this was Berlin's opposition to orthodoxy. He believed that there
was in 1950 'all too little disbelief'; ideologies were adhered to with 'unreasoning
faith' and a 'blind intolerance' which ultimately stemmed from an 'inner bankruptcy or terror' and the desperate desire for 'a safe haven'.[30] In a time of uncertainty, men had taken refuge in new or old faiths, religious or scientific, which
offered certainty and security in exchange for obedience. Against this, he called
for 'a greater degree of self-examination, less organised, precipitate, uncritical

---

27. 1949b, 1187; L 78, 82, 87; 1949b, 1188; L 83; cf. 'Philosophy and Government
Repression' (1953, hereafter PGR; SR 66, 69, 73.

28. PGR, SR 75. Berlin had used the phrase 'final solution' before Hitler made the
words infamous, in a translation of a passage from Blok in Berlin 1935a, 11.

29. 'Historical Inevitability', L 112.

30. PITC, L 83.

mass pursuit of things however intrinsically noble, in which too much is trampled under foot, too little is allowed for the gap between theories and the infinite complexity of individuals'.[31] And he insisted on the need for 'the inestimably precious gifts of scepticism and irony' (1949b, 1133). The age called for

> not (as we are so often told) more faith, or stronger leadership, or more scientific organisation. Rather it is the opposite—less Messianic ardour, more enlightened scepticism, more toleration of idiosyncrasies. [...] Since no solution can be guaranteed against error, no disposition is final. And therefore a loose texture and toleration of a minimum of inefficiency,[32] even a degree of indulgence in idle talk, idle curiosity, aimless pursuit of this or that without authorisation [...] will always be worth more than the neatest and most delicately fashioned imposed pattern. (PITC, L 92–3)

Another marked feature of both Soviet Communism and Western technocracy was instrumentalism—the tendency to treat human concerns and activities as valuable only as means to some ultimate goal. Against this, Berlin endorsed Herzen's belief that (in Berlin's words) 'Everything in nature, in history, is [...] its own end. The present is its own fulfilment, it does not exist for the sake of some unknown future.'[33] This would become a central part of value pluralism, which holds that genuine human values are not derived from other values, but are independent, intrinsic ends-in-themselves;[34] but it was clearly enunciated, independently of pluralism, in Berlin's writings on cultural and intellectual trends in the post-war period.[35]

This position echoed Berlin's opposition to the view that the end justifies the means, and to the consequent tendencies both to commit atrocities in the name of ideals or distant goals, and complacently to discount the tragedy of the compromises inherent in politics. Berlin's preoccupation with the ethics of political action thus cut two ways, against fanatical idealists and cynical 'realists'.[36] His resistance to the justification of vile means in the name of ultimate ends—which involved a rejection both of what Weber termed the 'ethic of conviction' on the one hand, and of an instrumental conception of politics (and of rationality) on

---

31. Letter to Henry Luce, 4 May 1950.

32. Berlin's early political writings are studded with attacks on efficiency as a social ideal; it was this belief that liberty and efficiency were not associated, were indeed in conflict, and that liberty should (within limits) generally take priority, that decisively distinguished Berlin from, for instance, F. A. von Hayek.

33. 'Herzen and Bakunin on Individual Liberty' (1955), RT 93–4.

34. See e.g. 'Equality' (1956), CC 102.

35. See, e.g., RT 94–5, 197; PGR; SR 54.

36. See RT 89, 193, 197–8, 200.

the other—was clearly shaped by his response to Soviet politics. But it also emerged from his reading of polemics between revolutionaries and reformists, voluntarists and determinists, in late nineteenth-century Russia; and from his reaction against 'realists' (such as the pro-Soviet historian E. H. Carr), managerial administrators and social scientists who advocated an instrumentalist, 'value-neutral' approach to the study of humanity and society.[37] It was central to his intellectual stance and ethical outlook, shaping his liberalism and value pluralism, as well as his responses to the political controversies of his times.

His recoil from the brutalisation of individuals in the name of abstractions, combined with the empiricism instilled in him at Oxford, led Berlin to a general rejection of general principles, 'because they bear down too cruelly upon actual human beings in actual situations too often'. Understanding could be achieved only by 'looking at the actual situation & then indicating the truth without fear of disloyalty to principles. Once principles are applied rigorously absurdities follow.' Therefore 'one must [...] not commit oneself to campaigns for general principles: only for liberation from specific wrongs & then for liberation from the defects of the remedy, & so on'. There could be 'no general solution' to human problems, but only a constant struggle to steer a course between dangers and towards improvement.[38]

BERLIN'S HUMANIST LIBERALISM: MORAL INDIVIDUALISM AND EGALITARIANISM

The publication of 'Political Ideas in the Twentieth Century' occasioned an appreciative letter from Berlin's friend, the American diplomat George Kennan. In his reply,[39] Berlin sought to express 'what I myself [...] deeply believe' about 'the fundamental moral issue on which everything turns': that 'every human being [...] possess[es] the capacity to choose what to do, and what to be'. Therefore, 'the deliberate act of tampering with human beings' was 'heinous' because it created 'unequal moral terms', in which the victim was treated 'as a mere object and not as a subject whose motives, views, intentions have [...] intrinsic weight'. In opposition to this, Berlin declared himself 'more concerned with making people free than making them happy', and preferred 'that they [choose] badly than not at all'. Without the ability to judge and choose freely, human beings could be neither happy nor unhappy in any way 'worth having', since the very notion of worth depended on having 'a choice of ends, a system of free preferences' (LGK, L 336–7, 339, 342).

---

37. These themes are developed further in section 5.2 of Cherniss and Hardy 2005.
38. Letter to Elliston, 301; letter to Myron Gilmore, 26 December 1949.
39. Published in L as 'Letter to George Kennan' (hereafter LGK).

His letter to Kennan highlights the influence on Berlin of Kantian ethics, which his later emphasis on pluralism has tended to obscure. Berlin was never an adherent of Kant's rationalistic moral theory; but his conception of human dignity was deeply influenced by Kant, to whom he traced his belief in the evil of using human beings 'as means to ends that are not their own, but those of the manipulator, the treatment of free beings as if they were things, tools'.[40] Kant's notion of human beings as ends in themselves was central to Berlin's rejection of utilitarian and historicist instrumentalism: 'the one thing which no utilitarian paradise, no promise of eternal harmony in the future within some vast organic whole will make us accept is the use of human beings as mere means' (LGK, L 339).

Berlin generally used Herzen as his mouthpiece for expressing his conviction that to 'trample' individuals in the name of allegedly higher goals was 'always a crime because there is, and can be, no principle or value higher than the ends of the individual, and therefore no principle in the name of which one could be permitted to do violence to or degrade or destroy individuals' (RT 112). But he also acknowledged his indebtedness to Kant; and it was from Kant that he derived important aspects of his own theory of values. Kant, Berlin explained, argued that individuals were ends in themselves 'because they were the sole authors of moral values'. Values existed, not in nature, but only in the wills of individuals. Human beings, as the authors of all genuine values, could not be sacrificed to anything other than their own purposes, without 'stultifying the absoluteness, the end-in-itselfness' of values. From this it also followed that all individuals were morally equal, because all were equally creators, carriers and fulfillers of values. This was the basis of the liberal belief in the 'right to develop one's individual capacity' and protest against 'any form of despotism, however benevolent and rational, not because it diminishes human happiness but because it is intrinsically degrading, a falsification of what human relationships between equal and independent (and ideal-pursuing) beings ought to be' (PIRA 151, 154).

The influence of this Kantian moral sensibility is reflected in Berlin's opposition to paternalism. Paternalism was premised on the belief that 'Human beings are children. We must first herd them together, create certain institutions, make them obey orders.' Such an attitude could be honourable and benevolent; but 'it always leads to bad consequences in the end'. Berlin objected to such moral infantilisation—to 'being treated like a child'—as a denial at once of equality, freedom and dignity.[41] Painfully sensitive himself, he was firmly committed to upholding

---

40. 'The Apotheosis of the Romantic Will' (1975), CTH 222; cf. 'Kant as an Unfamiliar Source of Nationalism' (1972), SR 238–9. That these passages come from the 1970s suggests that Kant remained an important figure for Berlin.

41. Quotations from Berlin 1964, 14, 10. Berlin admitted that individuals do not, at birth, have the power of choice and the means of understanding the world. Education was

human dignity; and his writings burn with a special indignation when discussing paternalism. This remained true throughout his life, but is particularly prominent in his early political thought.

Central to both Berlin's liberalism and his pluralism were his moral individualism and egalitarianism. These latter positions are not logically entailed by or necessary to pluralism; but his adherence to them shaped the sort of pluralist (and the sort of liberal) that Berlin was.

In DCI Berlin characterised liberalism as holding that 'the ultimate and only source of authority for the rightness or wrongness of legislation and wider social action is the moral sense of the individual' (DCI 3); he later wrote that 'all that is ultimately valuable are the particular purposes of particular persons' (RT 112). From this position, he defended the 'value of individual experience over the impersonal needs of society', and insisted that 'problems, social and personal, must be decided ideally by each person asking himself, in accordance with his own lights, what he should do and how he should live and how he should behave to his fellows' (DCI 4–5).

Berlin's moral individualism, with its valuation of the uniqueness of—and therefore differences between—individuals, as well as his recognition of the inevitability of divergence and conflict, admiration for individual excellence, and 'negative' conception of liberty, made him resistant to policies of levelling, which, he feared, invariably led to uniformity. Yet despite this 'aristocratic' element in his liberalism, Berlin was committed to egalitarianism as a moral principle. His moral individualism was essentially egalitarian, based as it was on the presupposition that 'every man is in principle capable of giving answers to personal and social questions which are as worthy of respect as any other man's' (DCI 2). Berlin tended to emphasise the importance of liberty more than that of equality; but he also recognised the importance of equality, and believed that it should sometimes take precedence over liberty. Furthermore, he recognised that liberty itself should be egalitarian—liberty for all, and not merely for those in possession of the 'right' ideas or attributes.

This egalitarian impulse extended to Berlin's pluralism, which holds that there is no stable, permanent, objective hierarchy of values, and that each genuine value is valuable in itself rather than in relation to some higher value. Thus in

---

thus necessary: but it was important that it be designed to foster independence and make the exercise of freedom possible. Its purpose was 'not an inculcation of obedience but its contrary, the development of power of free judgement and choice' (L 342; see also DCI 3–4 and, for Berlin's fullest treatment of the relationship between education and liberty, PIRA 125–6). In setting out this (now unexceptionable) vision of the goals of education, Berlin was responding to contemporary thinkers who asserted that the aim of education was indoctrination. See e.g. Carr 1946, 103.

DCI Berlin declared that the 'necessarily precarious balance between incompatible ideals' at which liberal society aims must be 'based on the recognition of the equal or nearly equal validity of human aspirations as such, none of which must be subordinated to any single uncriticisable [...] principle'; and that 'different ideals of life, not necessarily altogether reconcilable with each other, are equally valid and equally worthy' (DCI 3, 1). Therefore, while it asserted the conflict between liberty and equality,[42] Berlin's pluralism was itself premised on a belief in the basic moral liberty and equality of individuals.

This belief informed not only his ethical theory, but his political stance, which was anti-paternalist, anti-authoritarian, and anti-élitist. Despite his comfortable position at the heart of the Establishment, Berlin distrusted the authority of 'all the great managers of society [...] who confidently and tidily arrange the destinies of others'.[43] He accordingly devoted much of his work to criticising 'belief in the privileged status of the elect appointed by history to guide and govern the rest'.[44] Berlin sympathised with underdogs, misfits and eccentrics, and hated bullies. This inspired his attacks on the 'realist' view that 'Only the victors deserve to be heard', while 'the rest—[...] all the critics and casualties of Deutschtum or White Man's Burdens, or the American Century, or the Common Man on the March'—could, being merely 'historical dust, [...] poor little rats', be ignored or silenced. Seeing the worship of toughness and success in the ascendant in the post-war world, he exclaimed, 'Surely there never was a time when more homage was paid to bullies as such: and the weaker the victim the louder (and sincerer) his paeans.'[45]

Although this moral egalitarianism, and consequent opposition to authoritarianism and élitism, seem eminently democratic (if democracy is defined in terms of a belief in political equality, or respect for the equality, and equal empowerment, of all individual citizens), in TCL Berlin insisted on the difference, and potential conflict, between liberalism and democracy; and he has been associated with other post-war liberals whose work was marked by a suspicion of plebiscitary democracy and an 'aristocratic' desire to protect individual liberties against the 'tyranny of the majority'.[46] While DCI can be seen as part of the larger liberal

---

42. Indeed, one of his first expressions of pluralism focused on this conflict: 'we now know that liberty, if not restrained, leads to inequality, and equality, if rigidly carried through, must lead to loss of liberty. This is the lesson of the nineteenth century, of which Communism denies the truth' (DCI 1). Cf. 'Equality' in CC.

43. 'Montesquieu' (1955), AC 149.

44. DCI 2–3; cf. 'European Unity and its Vicissitudes' (1959), CTH 179–80.

45. L 343. The figures Berlin had in mind here were the pro-Soviet E. H. Carr and Harold Laski, and the anti-Communists James Burnham and Arthur Koestler.

46. e.g. Hacohen 2000, 506–8.

battle to wrest the term 'democracy' away from Communist opponents—who insisted on distinguishing between 'Western' and 'Eastern' democracy, and claimed that the latter was as valid as, or superior to, the former[47]—Berlin's later work claimed liberty rather than democracy as its guiding political ideal. One possible reason for this was the influence of Jacob Talmon's *The Origins of Totalitarian Democracy* (1952). Berlin and Talmon were friends, and discussed their shared interests and ideas before the publication of Talmon's book. Berlin later maintained that he had come to his account of liberty and its betrayal independently of Talmon;[48] in any event, after Talmon's book was published, Berlin laid more emphasis on the tension between liberty and democracy, and ceased to label his own position as democratic. Yet there remained a 'democratic' element in his thought, which can be seen in his sympathy for the Russian populists, in his passionate opposition to paternalism and managerialism, and in his egalitarian and anti-hierarchical pluralism.

THE IDEA OF LIBERTY

The various elements in Berlin's early political thought were brought together in his analysis of liberty. The best statement of this is, of course, TCL; but the crystallisation of Berlin's political thought around the concept of liberty began earlier, and the process was carried out most extensively in a manuscript first composed in 1952, 'Political Ideas in the Romantic Age' (PIRA, published in 2006).

In PIRA Berlin defines the 'nuclear, central, minimal' meaning of 'liberty' or 'freedom', common to all valid uses of those words (which he here, as elsewhere, used interchangeably), as the '*absence of restraint*' or interference which prevents individuals or groups from realising their 'wishes, inclinations, impulses'; all other interpretations of freedom tend to be 'artificial or metaphorical'. 'Freedom is in the first sense freedom against; liberty is liberty from.' More specifically, *social* or *political* freedom meant freedom from interference or oppression *by other human beings*. Freedom was thus 'in its primary sense a negative concept'; while other senses of freedom may be valid, the negative sense was for Berlin 'more basic'. The recognition of this was the basis of the liberal conception of political freedom as a 'frontier beyond which [...] interference must not go'. On this classical liberal view, liberty was not a positive goal, but the condition necessary for positive goals to be pursued (PIRA 155, 88, 90, 160).

PIRA makes clear the connection between Berlin's early works directed

---

47. See e.g. Carr 1945.
48. Berlin 1992, 98; Berlin 1980, 1.

against the pursuit of social harmony and the elimination of maladjustment and discontent, and his later writings on liberty. Berlin attacked as 'specious' the definition of freedom as the absence of frustration, the fulfilment of one's desires through 'self-adjustment to the unalterable pattern of reality in order to avoid being destroyed by it'. Freedom on this false view was 'obedience to laws, understanding of necessity', recognition and adoption of 'that true, unique order in which every human soul is fully realised', the elimination of gaps between striving and fulfilment. Berlin charged that this view substituted the notion of 'adjustment, or happiness, or frictionless contentment' for that of freedom proper (PIRA 169, 166, 186, 99, 167).

This view of freedom as the elimination of frustration and irrationality through the acceptance of necessity was 'founded on a confusion' which had 'cost a great many human lives': that freedom is necessarily equivalent to rationality and fulfilment. This, in turn, was an aspect of the 'vast metaphysical fantasy' of monism —the belief that the universe was 'a harmonious system', a 'logical schema', that, because the truth is one, 'no true values can come into collision with each other if they are properly understood', since 'the good cannot conflict with the good, nor right with right'. This view trivialised human tragedies by ascribing them to error and holding them to be illusory, and thus took 'all dignity from human experience and human ideals'. Berlin's pluralism was thus, from the start, inspired by an opposition to what he saw as the callousness and emptiness of theodicy; once again, human dignity was his central concern (PIRA 205, 192, 95, 98, 137).

Monism fostered the pursuit of conformism. If freedom consisted in being rational and virtuous, it meant wanting that which it is right to want. And if there is only one right thing to want, and what is right for one individual cannot conflict with what is right for any other individual in the same situation, then freedom must involve all individuals pursuing the same goal. This meant that self-realisation consisted in being and doing the same things as others; freedom thus consisted in conformity. Furthermore, if what it is proper to be or do is knowable, then any person or body that possesses such knowledge may exercise 'unlimited power' in order to bring others into line (PIRA 140).

In PIRA Berlin thus joined together the evils and errors that he had spent the previous several years exposing: monism, determinism, the elimination (rather than solution, or acknowledgement) of problems and conflicts, the pursuit of adjustment, contentment, orthodoxy and conformity, and the absolutist rule of an elite of 'experts'; and sought to make sense of these dangers in relation to his own ideal of liberty.

Berlin also confronted an (arguably) even darker perversion of liberty, whereby liberty came to mean 'self-obliteration' through the submergence of oneself in some collectivity, 'self-immolation on the altar of State or race or religion or history or the "dynamic" pursuit of power for its own sake', or the 'violent destruction of others or oneself'. This was 'the precise opposite' of the liberal notion of freedom, centred on 'civil liberties [...] limitation of interference, and [...] the sanctity of certain areas dedicated to private life' (PIRA 203–4). What tied this irrationalist perversion to the 'rationalist' one was that both involved the subordination of individuals to abstractions; in the process, liberty, far from protecting individuality, became the denial of it, the imposition of a pattern or the absorption of the individual into something larger—so that the individual's own unique character and personal inclinations were lost.

Both of these perversions rested on the notion of the 'true' or 'real' self. What this self willed could be discovered by determining what it was proper to will. From this, Berlin insisted, the natural step was for the wise to impose what was good or rational on everyone. By being made to do what was rational—what their true selves willed—individuals were in fact being ruled by themselves. Thus was coercion identified with 'complete self-government', and freedom with obedience to authority. This was 'one of the most powerful and dangerous arguments in the entire history of human thought'. To deprive an individual of liberty with the explanation that in so doing he or she was 'given a higher, nobler liberty' was a 'grotesque and hair-raising paradox', a 'particularly repulsive form of mockery' which 'enabled some men to torture and kill others [...] because [...] their natures demanded it'. It was at the heart of all totalitarian theory; for it justified both coercion, and disregarding the expressed wishes or opinions of individuals (PIRA 123–4, 143, 141–2).

Berlin sometimes seemed to apply this criticism to 'positive' liberty as a whole. But, as PIRA reveals, while he believed that the positive notion of liberty tends to give rise to or be associated with the notion of the 'real' will as that which individuals should will (or would will if only they were rational), that conception of the self is not necessary to it. It emerges from Berlin's discussion in PIRA, and from his other early works, that there is a valid element in 'positive' liberty. This is the recognition that liberty involves the right of individuals to choose goals, determine courses of action, and make decisions for themselves. To deprive an individual of freedom was

> to refuse him the right to say *his* word: to be human at all; it was to depersonalise him, to degrade or destroy his humanity [...] a diminution of that in man which made him man—a moral agent, the source of all morality, the being whose rights were worth fighting and, if need be, dying for, the only goal to which total sacrifice could be justified. (PIRA 114–15)

This was precisely the point that Berlin had passionately espoused in his letter to Kennan. And in *Freedom and Its Betrayal*—which substantially repeated the account offered in PIRA—he even put his own words from that letter in the mouth of Rousseau (of all people), when he wrote that, for Rousseau, to use others for one's own purposes, to rob them of their freedom of choice, was 'the sin against the Holy Ghost' (FIB 33; L 340). Elsewhere he asserted that

> the essence of liberty has always lain in the ability to choose as you wish to choose, because you wish so to choose, uncoerced, unbullied, not swallowed up in some vast system; and in the right to resist, to be unpopular, to stand up for your convictions merely because they are your convictions. That is true freedom, and without it there is neither freedom of any kind, nor even the illusion of it. (FIB 103–4)

This position was the essence of the defence of individuality and free choice against conformity, coercion, conditioning and all the other forms of control that Berlin condemned in his earlier writings. It has often been equated with 'negative liberty'; but it contained an element of 'positive' liberty as well, for it included not only freedom from coercion, but also the exercise of the ability to choose and to will, to act in accordance with one's own beliefs, to select and pursue ideals for oneself—that is, a form of self-rule or autonomy.

Or perhaps it would be more appropriate to say that both the 'negative' and 'positive' (before its perversion) concepts of liberty contained elements of, and were important to, this 'essential' or 'basic' concept of liberty as the ability to make choices for oneself. In Berlin's early writings 'negative' liberty is depicted as closer to this basic liberty; but it is not identical to it. Basic liberty—'Freedom reduced to its narrowest terms'—consisted of 'freedom to choose between alternatives: it cannot be *less* than that' (PIRA 187). 'Negative' liberty was important in protecting this basic freedom—in providing the space necessary for its existence. But 'positive' liberty could also be an expression or realisation of basic freedom; it was only when it came to be interpreted in a way contrary to the essence of freedom that it became invalid.

Nor did Berlin simply reaffirm the classical liberal view of freedom. In PIRA he presents classical liberalism as conceiving of freedom's value in purely instrumental terms, as a condition for other goods, and the theorists of 'positive' liberty as regarding liberty as an end in itself. Berlin's own position involved a combination of the 'negative' conception of freedom characteristic of earlier liberal thought with the vision of freedom as 'an absolute end, needing no justification in terms of any other purpose, and worth fighting for [...] for its own sake, independent of its value in making people happy or wise or strong' which came from such proponents of 'positive' freedom as Rousseau, Kant and the romantics (SR 54).[49] Berlin also departed from classical liberalism in his reiterated emphasis on choice as an existential condition, which lent his liberalism a dramatic—and at times tragic—quality more reminiscent of Camus than of Mill.

The account of liberty in PIRA ultimately centres on the opposition, not between positive and negative freedom, or between classical liberalism and its critics, but between what Berlin termed 'humanistic' and 'non-humanistic' notions of freedom. The difference between these hinged on conceptions of the self and of the 'ultimate ideal of life' (PIRA 207). The non- (or anti-) humanistic conception viewed individuals as components of larger forces; individuals were defined, not by their own characters or (empirical) wills, but by the 'unalterable function which history or some other abstract despot has laid upon them'. Liberty in the non-humanistic view consisted of 'collective self-sacrifice, some Messianic mission' (PIRA 204). This view was anti-empirical and anti-individualist. It commanded individuals to bow to the demands of larger forces or collectives—history, or class, or race, or some aesthetic ideal.

Against this stood the 'humanistic' view, which defined the individual as 'an empirical being in time and space, pursuing such ends as he pursues, for whatever reasons, and requiring, in order to be what he wishes to be, a certain area protected from invasion by others'. Berlin's 'humanist' position was based on a combination of an empiricist conception of human agents with the Kantian contention that the wishes and ideals of individuals should be respected because individuals are 'the sole source of all morality, the beings for whose sakes alone whatever is worth doing is worth doing', and that therefore there is nothing outside individuals 'to which they can in principle be deemed worthy of sacrifice' (PIRA 206). It held that freedom, and particularly freedom of thought, was a 'natural right', a 'basic interest and need and craving of human beings' *qua* human beings, and that the best society was one 'in which the largest number of persons are allowed to pursue the largest number of ends as freely as possible'.[50] It thus united what was valid in the 'positive' with what was best in the 'negative' concept of freedom, and grounded both in a view of 'basic' freedom as an essential characteristic of or condition for humanity.

It was commitment to this 'humanistic' moral position, born of the experience of violent political fanaticism, and forged in the shadow of totalitarianism

---

49. Conceptually, neither the positive nor the negative conceptions necessarily assign either instrumental or intrinsic value to liberty; Berlin's point was rather that, historically, proponents of the negative conception had tended to an instrumental valuation, and proponents of positive liberty had more frequently insisted on liberty's intrinsic value; but these were historical rather than logical linkages.

50. SR 73–4; letter to Elliston, 302.

and amidst the fog of fear and repression, more than to any particular definition of freedom, or alliance with romanticism or the Enlightenment, with socialism or capitalism, the East or the West, that defined Berlin's early political thought, and that inspired and guided his work throughout his life.

Acknowledgements

I have benefited from the generosity of many people while working on this essay. My greatest debt is to George Crowder and Henry Hardy for their invitation to contribute to this volume and their subsequent patience and guidance; I am further indebted to Henry Hardy for saving me from numerous errors. I am also most grateful to Stanley Hoffmann for his support and encouragement while I was working on this piece; to Richard Tuck, Sean Ingham, Matthew Landauer, Patti Lennard, Lucas Stanczyk, Don Tontiplaphol and other friends at Harvard for incisive and clarifying discussion of individual points discussed here; and to Ryan Hanley, José Harris, Steven Smith and the late Robert Wokler (whose death is a great sadness to me) for advice and encouragement over the years.

5

Berlin on Liberty

MARIO RICCIARDI

W hat makes a contemporary classic? The answer is seldom uncontroversial. Popularity, originality, depth—each of these is proffered in turn as the defining property of this elusive class of artefacts. Disagreement is just as great among the experts: each connoisseur has his own favourite classic. So it might come as a surprise that in the field of political philosophy few would deny classic status to 'Two Concepts of Liberty' (TCL). Isaiah Berlin's essay, originally a lecture given in Oxford in 1958, is widely recognised in the field as one of the outstanding achievements of twentieth-century political thought, almost everybody's choice at or near the top of the list for an ideal anthology of contemporary political philosophy.

Part of the explanation for this amazing popularity, which spreads far beyond those sympathetic to Berlin's political outlook, may be found in its distinctive 'voice'.[1] In sharp contrast to the dominant tendency of the age, which conceives the academic author as an impersonal agency whose style, tastes and idiosyn-

---

1. Arthur C. Danto has aptly characterised this feature of those he calls 'star-philosophers'. They 'have pretty distinct voices, possibly in consequence of the fact that so much of what they have written has been composed to be read before audiences, and hence is filled with devices of a kind calculated to hold an audience: turns of phrase, ingenuity of examples, sparks of wit, and an aura of presumed intimacy between speaker and hearer' (1999, 228).

crasies are better excluded from the written page, Berlin features prominently in his essay. Quite literally, he 'speaks his mind'. The result is somewhat less transparent than the best contemporary philosophical prose, as exemplified by authors such as John Rawls or Thomas Nagel, but has an unmatched capacity to capture the reader's attention. We find ourselves thrown into the middle of an intellectual battlefield which Berlin brings to life with the same realism that one finds in Paolo Uccello's fresco *The Battle of San Romano*. We can almost hear the clash of different understandings of liberty, feel 'the power of ideas' as they take hold of our imagination and feeling (L 167).

To those familiar with the golden period of Oxford philosophy, Berlin's personal approach is not a surprise. One finds the same quality in the writings of all the major authors who belong to the generation and intellectual environment notoriously dubbed 'our age' by Maurice Bowra (Annan 1990). The same highly personal tone is present in the writings of philosophers otherwise as diverse as J. L. Austin, Stuart Hampshire and Iris Murdoch. To the contemporary reader, trained in the strictures imposed on academic writing by the practice of blind refereeing, the carefree attitude these authors had to footnotes, bibliographic references and allusions to the ideas of other people (often identified just by surname) is sometimes maddening, but preserves the taste of a conversation.[2] This is a style of philosophical writing that bears the marks of philosophy's oral, face-to-face origins.

Reading TCL, one should always remember that the essay was conceived as a lecture, that it is based on earlier lectures, and that even in its final, revised, form, it should be thought of as addressed to a lay audience.[3] These features account for the complexity of the text, which covers more ground than the title announces, and for the apparent inconclusiveness of some of the arguments. On issues such as coercion or freedom of the will Berlin confines himself to general remarks, sailing at a safe distance from the shallow waters in which more analytically minded authors frequently find themselves stranded. It is clear that his aim is not analysis as such, but rather to give his public a broad view of the intellectual landscape.

In the lecture Berlin draws an intellectual map, charting the terrain with its slopes and asperities, tracing the paths followed by different authors and political movements. The starting point is the distinction between negative and positive liberty—a distinction that, as Berlin points out, is not meant to be exhaustive of the different senses in which 'this protean word' has been used in the history of mankind (L 168). Next, he assesses different interpretations of 'positive liberty',

2. According to Danto, this contrasts sharply with the 'bottom-line view' of philosophy that underlies blind reviewing (1999, 241).

3. Berlin's lecture is a distillation of material from two previous sets of lectures, now published as FIB and PIRA.

the implications of which can gradually lead to results that turn out to be inimical to the enjoyment of freedom in the negative sense. This is the peculiar 'inversion' in the meaning of 'liberty' which Berlin denounces in the lecture because it leads to an understanding of the political community that is the very opposite of a liberal society (IBLP 68–71). The remainder of the lecture deals with other aspects of freedom that, though grounded in its ordinary use, are extensions of its core meaning to different areas of experience. In the final part Berlin puts forward an early version of his idea of pluralism, and shows its critical connection to liberalism and to the idea of a political regime that recognises an area of non-interference with the activities of its subjects. As this highly compressed summary suggests, it is only an examination of the map as a whole that can make sense of Berlin's agenda.

Although it is ostensibly about a conceptual distinction, Berlin's essay is relatively sketchy when it comes to analytical fine tuning. Nevertheless, even a superficial glance at the current literature on freedom reveals the remarkable fertility of the essay. He touches on several points that are still at the forefront of the debate. These aspects of Berlin's approach are worth mentioning because they help the newcomer to understand an otherwise puzzling feature of Berlin's attitude to the debate that took its lead from TCL. With few exceptions, to be found in his 'Introduction' to 'Five Essays on Liberty' (in L), Berlin did not reply to the criticisms of his own formulation and defence of the distinction between negative and positive liberty. As time passed, a huge number of articles dealt with his treatment of freedom, but the author himself took a rather Olympian attitude towards the debate, emerging from his self-imposed discretion only once, to issue a short reply to an article by David West.[4] Such self-restraint is unusual, even in a writer who notoriously entertained serious doubts about the value of his own philosophical work.

There is, of course, an easy explanation, supported by Berlin's own statement that he 'left philosophy for the field of the history of ideas' (CC vii–viii). One might argue that Berlin was not interested in the niceties of the analytical debate because he conceived of them as belonging to philosophy, an intellectual activity in which he no longer regarded himself as engaged by the time the debate reached its height. The fine-grained analyses of the likes of Felix E. Oppenheim, J. P. Day or Hillel Steiner[5] are as far from the history of ideas as one can imagine. Hence the lack of interest, and the silence.

Despite the authority that Berlin himself has lent to such an explanation, there is a better account of his attitude towards the analytic treatment of freedom,

---

4. West 1993. Berlin's reply (1993b) is in the same issue of the journal.
5. Oppenheim 1961; Day 1970; Steiner 1975.

which sheds light on TCL as a whole. This is suggested by the difference between the first reactions to TCL and the subsequent debate. Earlier commentators such as Richard Wollheim and Gerald MacCallum raised specific points about Berlin's presentation and defence of the distinction between negative and positive liberty that he (quite reasonably) felt under an obligation to address, irrespective of their importance for his own intellectual agenda, but most later contributions mention the essay without engaging in any sustained discussion or criticism of the overall argument. With the sole exception of a footnote in which Berlin deals with the problem of the measurement of freedom, the essay is treated as a classic, if somewhat superseded, statement of a conceptual distinction still relevant to the contemporary debate. Very little attention is devoted to the overall structure of the text and to its different strands of argument. It is almost as if what follows the introduction and discussion of the distinction—more than half of the essay—was just a very long footnote, an afterthought. If, as I suggest, Berlin had an overall aim, he might be excused for not having felt the need to engage in this new phase of the debate. It is not the philosophical character and style of the subsequent discussion that explains Berlin's silence, but rather its irrelevance to his own intellectual agenda. His broader purpose, I believe, is to restate the importance and methods of political philosophy.

OVERTURE: THE RESILIENCE OF POLITICAL PHILOSOPHY

A brief survey of the structure of the essay illustrates my claim. As is customary with inaugural lectures, the original version of TCL included an 'overture' whose aim was to show the general relevance of the topic and to pay the author's respects to the previous holder of the chair. Berlin discharged his duties towards his predecessor as Chichele Professor with grace, acknowledging G. D. H. Cole's multiple talents as teacher, thinker, writer and political activist. This latter, occasional, part of the text was omitted when the essay was published in its final form in 1998 and in 2002 (PSM, L). The remainder of the 'overture' reads like a short manifesto for Berlin's understanding of his mission as Professor of Social and Political Theory. It contains, in compressed form, a defence of the relevance of political philosophy and a statement of method for the discipline, which together provide a preface to the essay. Berlin warns the reader against the tendency to underestimate 'the power of ideas'. It is likely that he had two different targets in mind in issuing such a warning: on the one hand, historical materialism, with its devaluation of ideas and culture—the superstructure—as contrasted with the material conditions of society—the structure;

on the other, logical positivism, with its dismissive attitude towards moral and political concepts. Today the reader might find such a coupling odd, but Berlin persuasively pointed out a remarkable similarity in their practical consequences in the field of political philosophy:

> To neglect the field of political thought, because its unstable subject-matter, with its blurred edges, is not to be caught by the fixed concepts, abstract models and fine instruments suitable to logic or linguistic analysis—to demand a unity of method in philosophy and reject whatever the method cannot successfully manage—is merely to allow oneself to remain at the mercy of primitive and uncriticised political beliefs. It is only a very vulgar historical materialism that denies the power of ideas, and says that ideals are mere material interests in disguise. (L 167–8)

Seeing through differences in style and form of argument, Berlin recognised a common trend in two of the most powerful intellectual movements of the age. The connection becomes clearer if one considers the attitude prevalent at the time among logical positivists. A. J. Ayer comes most naturally to mind, but perhaps the writings of Margaret Macdonald illustrate this attitude better. She was a student and teacher at Bedford College, London, and attended Wittgenstein's lectures in the 1930s. A pioneer in a world that was still male-dominated, she wrote several papers on political and legal philosophy which were widely read in the 1950s, as is shown by the fact that two of them were included in a famous anthology edited by Antony Flew (1951). Almost completely forgotten now—she died in 1956—Macdonald was a bold writer and thinker whose approach to political language was marked by complete scepticism towards its cognitive content. She subscribed to a version of the subjectivist theory of value, popular among logical positivists, which held that human choice is the only source of value.[6] Dealing with the problem of the foundation of political obligation, she wrote that there is 'an indefinite set of vaguely shifting criteria, differing for different times and circumstances' (1951, 185–6). Linked to a determinist explanation of preferences, this theory of political obligation was remarkably close to the thoroughgoing historicism of some of the Marxist thinkers of the time. Political judgement is reduced to the selection of the most efficient means to achieve ends chosen on ideological grounds. The consequences for political philosophy were momentous. According to Macdonald, 'The value of the political theorists [...] is not in the general information they give about the basis of political obligation but in their skill in emphasising at a critical moment a criterion which is tending to be over-

---

6. According to Macdonald, 'value utterances are more like records of *decisions* than propositions' (1956, 49).

looked or denied' (1951, 186)—an ancillary, almost technical role, whose aim seems to be persuasion rather than knowledge.[7]

Given such premises, it is not surprising that, two years before the publication of Berlin's essay, Peter Laslett announced the violent death of political philosophy, naming logical positivism as the culprit (1956, vii–ix). Laslett's denunciation is still quoted today as evidence of attitudes in the 1950s, but it was always far-fetched. A survey of what was published and taught in Britain at the time shows that in the late 1950s political philosophy was still alive and well. Although it was more marginal in the philosophical community than it was up to the early 1940s (see O'Sullivan 2004, 20–40), its value was not negligible—not at least if thinkers such as Michael Oakeshott, John Plamenatz or J. D. Mabbott qualify (as seems reasonable) as political philosophers of outstanding ability. Nevertheless, Laslett's announcement is evidence of a widespread prejudice, with which Berlin meant to take issue in his lecture. Berlin's bellicose attitude is not simply the natural reaction of somebody who has just been elected to a chair in political theory and is eager to show that his own calling is not devoid of interest for the academic community and the general public. The methodological remarks at the beginning of the essay should be read as the outcome of his evolution as a thinker, and were put forward as serious arguments against the devaluation of political philosophy. In order to understand, and not merely explain away, political disagreement, one should put words, concepts and deeds in their proper context. This context, as the content and structure of the essay show, has to be historical. Otherwise, as Berlin says, 'our own attitudes and activities are likely to remain obscure to us'. To make sense of political problems, we should 'understand the dominant issues of our own world' (L 168). The phrasing is not accidental. The shallow image of political theorists as caretakers of ideologies is swept aside to be replaced with the traditional idea of philosophy as self-understanding, conjugated in the historical mood.[8]

Berlin recognises the importance of words and their meanings for the understanding of politics, but disagrees with the selective attitude of most of his contemporaries towards the proper starting point for conceptual investigations. He suggests that 'the best among them look with disdain upon a field in which radical discoveries are less likely to be made, and talent for minute analysis is less likely to be rewarded' (L 167). The adjective 'minute' is interestingly ambivalent. For people such as Austin and his followers it had a positive resonance, pointing towards the careful and patient fieldwork that they regarded as an essential part of a philosophical analysis of language; but for Berlin it clearly had a more critical

---

7. Berlin elaborates his criticisms of this way of conceiving political philosophy in 'Does Political Theory Still Exist?' in CC, 152–3, 156.

8. This feature of Berlin's treatment of freedom went unnoticed, surprisingly, in Skinner 1984.

connotation. There may be an allusion to R. G. Collingwood's sharp criticism of those he called 'minute philosophers' (1939, 15–21). These were people such as H. A. Prichard and H. W. B. Joseph, who, under the influence of their teacher and mentor John Cook Wilson, pioneered the kind of painstaking analysis of ordinary language commonly associated with Austin and his school.

Berlin was a close friend and associate of Austin, and had a leading role in shaping the activity and intellectual agenda of what he himself later called 'Oxford Philosophy' (PI 130–45). Nevertheless, by the time he delivered his inaugural lecture as Chichele Professor he was completely out of tune with the direction in which Oxford Philosophy was heading. His published letters show that even in the early 1930s he was critical of 'the futility of the wrangles indulged in by [his] colleagues, young especially'. Hence the determination to read 'a lot of Hegel, Marx, Engels & the Russians in order to climb out into a different even if not wider universe' (L1 43). A careful examination of Berlin's early philosophical writings bears witness to such an attitude. His critique of verificationism, and his defence of the autonomy and significance of areas of ordinary language, such as metaphor, that were looked on with suspicion by most of his Oxford contemporaries, are evidence of a growing dissatisfaction with their way of doing philosophy.

There is a continuity between Berlin's defence of a pluralistic approach in the philosophy of language and his account of the different uses of the word 'liberty' (CC 56–80). The meaning of this word is 'so porous that there is little interpretation that it seems able to resist' (L 168). Here, again, the choice of words is not accidental. The use of 'porous' is likely to be an allusion to Friedrich Waismann's thesis on the 'porosity' of ordinary language (1945, 41–5; 1946, 95–7). According to Waismann, 'porosity' should be distinguished from 'vagueness'. Vagueness can be reduced by sharpening definition, but porosity is an inherent feature of concepts, not just a matter of how they are used in ordinary parlance. Our efforts to discipline language, to reduce it to a precise instrument, are bound to be frustrated by this characteristic of the words we use. As the epithet 'porous' suggests, Waismann alludes to a disposition to absorb and retain matter that should properly be regarded as external to the nature of the item in question. Like sponges, our words carry with them contents that exceed their core meaning. Hence 'every definition stretches into an open horizon' (1944, 44). Waismann's highly personal approach encouraged the kind of large-scale account of areas of experience and thought that people such as Austin were likely to consider wild, almost charlatanesque, flights of the imagination.

CONCEPTS AND CATEGORIES

Berlin's lecture is ostensibly about 'two concepts' of liberty, but very little atten-tion has been devoted to what exactly he meant by 'concept'. A survey of the text shows that the answer to this question cannot be taken for granted. Berlin employs, somewhat promiscuously, different words and expressions that are not obviously synonymous. He talks about 'political words and notions', 'meaning', and the 'sense of the word'. What is clear is that he thinks that the same word can be used in different ways and that, among these different uses, some have suffi-cient stability to be regarded as expressing concepts (or 'conceptions' or 'notions': Berlin seems to use such terms interchangeably). In the case of 'liberty' (or 'freedom'—Berlin treats the two as synonymous) the very same word expresses at least two different concepts, 'negative' and 'positive'. In our post-Fregean era such liberality in the use of terminology might appear a sign of sloppy thinking, but it was not necessarily so at the time Berlin wrote his lecture. Philosophers of out-standing distinction such as Gilbert Ryle and H. L. A. Hart employed the word 'concept' with the same liberality to investigate very large areas of experience. Readers of Ryle's *The Concept of Mind* (1949) or Hart's *The Concept of Law* (1961) who open these books in search of something like a clear-cut definition, a set of necessary and jointly sufficient conditions for the use of a word, will be severely disappointed. They will find instead a careful analysis of the uses of the words 'mind' or 'law', and of several other words connected with them in different ways. In addition, both books contain an impressive array of interrelated philosophical arguments and explanations concerning the different things and events about which all these words are used in ordinary language. For Berlin's contemporaries, to write a book or a paper on 'the concept of X' was to put forward a philosoph-ical account of X.

Nevertheless, in Berlin's writings there are traces of a general account of concepts that is worth examining, given its importance for the proper under-standing of TCL. Berlin himself gave a hint of what he meant by 'concept' in a conversation with Bryan Magee, where he described concepts as 'the structural units of our thinking'. The two concepts of liberty examined in the lecture are indeed something like structural units in so far as they are the items around which different debates and political disagreements seem to cluster. Berlin's conversa-tion with Magee is interesting also for the qualification that immediately follows this characterisation of concepts. According to Berlin, 'we make use in our thinking not only of structural units but also of structures'. These structures

> are often called 'models'. For example, when talking about society some people
> will think of it as a sort of machine, put together by man to accomplish certain

tasks, in which all the various moving parts connect up with each other in certain ways. But others will think of it as a sort of organism, something that grows like a living thing, in the way an oak tree develops out of an acorn. Now whether you think of society as a sort of machine or as a sort of organism will have enormous practical consequences, because—depending on which of these models is dominating your thinking—you will derive significantly different conclusions and attitudes regarding government, politics and social questions, not least regarding the relationships of the individual to society. You will also have a different attitude towards the past, and to the various ways in which change can come about. (Magee 1978, 38)

Berlin's conversation with Magee was recorded for the BBC in the mid-1970s. He had already given a more detailed account of 'models' or 'paradigms' in two essays published in the early 1960s, 'Does Political Theory Still Exist?' and 'The Purpose of Philosophy' (both in CC). Here the 'large-scale' items of our intellectual endowment are distinguished from 'categories'—'central features of our experience that are invariant and omnipresent, or at least much less variable than the vast variety of its empirical characteristics' (CC 165). According to Berlin, freedom is one of the basic categories in terms of which we conceive and study man and society. He does not use the word 'concept' very much in these earlier methodological reflections, but it does not seem unreasonable to think that concepts are the historical building-blocks out of which models or paradigms are composed. One might say that the two concepts examined in the lecture are among the interpretations of the basic category of freedom that emerge from what Oakeshott calls 'the conversation of mankind'.[9] In the light of such evidence, and if my account of its significance is correct, the thesis that in 1958 Berlin was doing 'harmless' history of ideas instead of philosophy should be rejected. Many years after his supposed 'retirement' from the philosophical profession, Berlin articulated and defended, in his conversation with Magee, the same approach he had adopted in TCL.

In the study of the external world, what counts as a category seems to be determined by invariable, though metaphysically contingent, properties of human beings, but when we come to the study of society and politics, categories appear more liable to change. This might happen as the result of a slow, almost imperceptible, shift in the way people talk and think, or as the outcome of radical, revolutionary, subversions of perspective. The publication of the two texts[10] from which TCL was distilled has sharpened our understanding of the lecture,

---

9. Oakeshott 1962.

10. FIB, for all its many differences from PIRA, is essentially a re-presentation of parts of the same body of material.

showing the crucial background role that the 'romantic revolution' and its consequences play in the confrontation between negative and positive accounts of
freedom. Berlin's decision to introduce the two concepts as developed out of the
possible answers to two different questions is designed to bring to light this 'dramatic' dimension of the philosophical and ideological approach to freedom. The
passage is worth quoting in full:

> The first of these political senses of freedom or liberty [...], which (following
> much precedent) I shall call the 'negative' sense, is involved in the answer to the
> question 'What is the area within which the subject—a person or group of per-
> sons—is or should be left to do or be what he is able to do or be, without interfer-
> ence by other persons?' The second, which I shall call the 'positive' sense, is
> involved in the answer to the question 'What, or who, is the source of control or
> interference that can determine someone to do, or be, this rather than that?' (L 169)

Some commentators have pointed out that Berlin's deployment of interrogatives
to elucidate what is involved in, or presupposed by, the use of a concept bears a
striking resemblance to the role that 'the logic of question and answer' plays in
Collingwood's search for 'absolute presuppositions'.[11] The comparison is indeed
suggestive, and finds further backing in Berlin's Prologue to PIRA, where the
intellectual debt to Collingwood is explicitly acknowledged (13). In any event,
this interpretation of Berlin's method reinforces the sense in which TCL sets out
a role for contemporary political theory within the broader field of philosophy.

According to Berlin, models and paradigms shape the way people think and
talk in a way that can be, and at the ordinary level is very likely to be, unconscious
(CC 154). They exercise a hold on the imagination mainly through metaphor (CC
158). The task of philosophy is to attend to such modes of expression so as to
sharpen our awareness of their presuppositions. Since this kind of investigation
deals with assumptions that have slowly taken their current form with the passing
of generations, its method should be alert to the peculiarities of historical
analysis. Of paramount importance among these is a sensitivity to the relative
instability of models and paradigms, to the constant strain to which they are subject under the pressure of experience, and to their consequent susceptibility to
change (CC 9–11).[12] Philosophical understanding is something that should not be
taken for granted, once and for all.

These features of Berlin's method explain an otherwise puzzling peculiarity
of TCL that has frequently been misunderstood. Many commentators have com-

---

11. The first to point out such a similarity was Bernard Williams (CC xv–xvii).
Recently, the matter has been investigated further in Skagestad 2005.

12. CC 9–11. See Collingwood 1940, 48 note, 350–5.

plained about the supposed lack of rigour in the analysis of negative and positive liberty. But such a criticism ought to be seen as misplaced once one has understood that Berlin is not merely analysing the logical connections between different uses of a word. When, for example, he warns that some interpretations of positive liberty can lead to conclusions incompatible with freedom understood in the more basic, negative, sense, his thesis should not be read as if it were the discovery of a logical possibility. A statement about positive liberty does not 'entail' any such consequences (L 198). It is the play of political imagination, the 'power of ideas', that can lead to such conclusions.[13] This also explains why some of the analytical criticisms of the lecture are fundamentally wrongheaded. They fail to take seriously Berlin's overall undertaking on its own terms, which are basically those of Collingwood.

This objection certainly applies to Gerald MacCallum, possibly the most influential of the early critics of TCL. According to MacCallum there is just one concept of freedom, since every statement about liberty can be reduced, by means of analysis, to the following formula: an agent, x, is free from 'preventing conditions', y, to do something (or to become something), z. By 'preventing conditions' MacCallum means 'constraints', 'restrictions', 'interferences' and 'barriers'. In this way, controversies concerning the definition of 'freedom' can be restated as disagreements over the interpretation of the three variables (agents, restrictions and actions or modes of being)—for example, over whether restrictions are natural or social, whether agents are individual or collective (MacCallum 1967). The success of MacCallum's definition is due in great part to John Rawls, who uses it in the formulation of his principles of justice (1971, 202). But despite its clarity and usefulness, MacCallum's formula fails to capture all the shades of meaning of 'liberty'. Most notably, it obliterates the opposition between the two concepts of freedom that Berlin meant to clarify.[14] This, of course, is not an objection to the adoption of a 'triadic' definition of 'freedom' when it suits one's needs. But it is a crucial consideration in assessing the merit of MacCallum's criticisms of Berlin's essay. MacCallum's formula may still be valid for the category of freedom, despite failing to convey the contrasts between the different shades of meaning of the historical concepts of liberty. If Berlin's aim was to bring

---

13. Berlin himself clarified his position by saying that, when he wrote the lecture, he saw the idea of 'inner' or 'real' freedom characteristic of the positive account of liberty as a metaphor, although he did not emphasise the point. Political freedom is 'an altogether different matter, and directly concerned with coercion, whatever its relation to the impregnable life of reason' (1993b, 297).

14. It is surprising that Berlin's rather half-hearted reply to MacCallum does not point this out. Berlin instead confines himself to minor observations on what is or is not the case when persons or peoples struggle against their chains or enslavement (L 36).

to light these shades of meaning he was right to reject MacCallum's criticism: he and MacCallum were working at different levels of abstraction.

NEGATIVE LIBERTY: DESIRES AND MEASUREMENT

Berlin introduces the notion of negative liberty by pointing out that, in ordinary discourse, people are said to be free 'to the degree to which no man or body of men interferes' with their activity. Hence political liberty, is 'simply the area within which a man can act unobstructed by others'. What counts as obstruction is explained as follows: 'If I am prevented by others from doing what I could otherwise do, I am to that degree unfree; and if this area is contracted by other men beyond a certain minimum, I can be described as being coerced, or, it may be, enslaved' (L 169). This, however, is a revision of the original text of the lecture. In the first version, political liberty was characterised as not being prevented from doing what one wants to do (1958, 7). As was pointed out by Richard Wollheim, liberty or the absence of it are in this way dependent on desire. This would lead to the counterintuitive result that if somebody has no desire to do what he is prevented from doing, he is nevertheless not unfree (Wollheim 1959, 90). So a perfectly contented slave would turn out to enjoy perfect freedom.

In *Four Essays on Liberty* (1969), Berlin recognises the error and the text of TCL is modified accordingly. In the introduction he elaborates on the relation between liberty and desire, referring to the 'Stoic' view of freedom, according to which freedom consists in consciously adjusting one's desires to what it is possible to achieve. The 'discipline of desire' of the desert fathers, the 'contented slave', and what in contemporary economics are called 'adaptive preferences' are all instances of this psychological device. Berlin recognises that allowing freedom to be dependent on desire would rule out a non-subjective criterion of political liberty. Being free or unfree would become a matter of feeling oneself to be so. This would render meaningless any criticism of a political regime for suppressing liberty, so long as its subjects were psychologically adapted to their condition. The relevance of this point to understanding Berlin's liberalism has seldom been underlined, but is nevertheless of the utmost importance. It is clear from his reaction to Wollheim's criticisms, and also to those of Macfarlane (1966), that Berlin is determined to preserve freedom, or the lack of it, as a viable standard for the evaluation of a political regime. If the presence or absence of liberty in a given situation were a matter of perception, such a goal would be unattainable.

Being negatively free or unfree, then, is for Berlin a matter of fact. This fits with a plausible interpretation of a large class of quantitative statements and judgements, in political theory as well as in ordinary discourse. The most important of these are comparative. One might say, for example, that John has more freedom than Paul, or that the average Afghan citizen has less freedom than the average British subject. Of course, such comparisons, if taken literally, need a unit or a standard of measurement.[15] Berlin was aware of the relevance of this issue for a theory of negative liberty, and proposed his own account of the measure of freedom in a long footnote to the text of TCL. He enumerates five aspects of freedom that are relevant for its measurement:

> The extent of my freedom seems to depend on (*a*) how may possibilities are open to me (although the method of counting these can never be more than impressionistic; possibilities of action are not discrete entities like apples, which can be exhaustively enumerated); (*b*) how easy or difficult each of these possibilities is to actualise; (*c*) how important in my plan of life, given my character and circumstances, these possibilities are when compared with each other; (*d*) how far they are closed and opened by deliberate human acts; (*e*) what value not merely the agent, but the general sentiment of the society in which he lives, puts on these various possibilities. (L 177, note 1)

This statement has raised a heated controversy in the literature.[16] One thing strikes the reader immediately: Berlin's account brings together dimensions of freedom of different sorts. The number of possible actions open to one (*a*) and their relative difficulty (*b*) may be conceived as quantitative standards that, at least in principle, could be expressed mathematically; the importance (*c*) or value (*e*) of such actions are more aptly classified as qualities. Dimension (*d*), on the other hand, concerns a prerequisite for the application of the concept of freedom rather than a standard of measurement. The heterogeneity of the items in this list has given rise to the criticism that Berlin is aggregating incommensurables. The remainder of the footnote shows that he was aware of this objection, but his response to it is tentative, and far from clear. He says that all these magnitudes must be integrated, 'and a conclusion, necessarily never precise, or indisputable, drawn from this process', and then qualifies this by saying that 'It may well be that there are many incommensurable kinds and degrees of freedom, and that they cannot be drawn up on any single scale of magnitude.' He seems thereby to deny the possibility of aggregative comparative judgements, while granting that of simple comparative ones. The footnote ends with what sounds like a compromise: 'the vagueness of the concepts, and the multiplicity of the criteria involved, are

---

15. This view is not shared by all liberals. However, those who reject it admit that its rejection implies the rejection of the idea of liberty as a fundamental value. See Dworkin 1977, 270.

16. For a survey of the debate, see Carter 1999.

attributes of the subject-matter itself, not of our imperfect methods of measure-ment, or of incapacity for precise thought'. As it stands, this compromise is far from persuasive, because it fails to address the objection that it was meant to over-come, and, therefore, to fulfil the requirement that negative freedom should pro-vide an independent standard of evaluation.

NEGATIVE LIBERTY VERSUS ABILITY AND SELF-GOVERNMENT

The success of Berlin's essay depends in good part on the success of the distinc-tion between 'negative' and 'positive' freedom. As we have seen, for Berlin, nega-tive freedom has to do with the space within which a person can be or do certain things without interference, whereas positive freedom concerns who governs—that is, who or what determines that a person does something or pursues a certain project. In the debate following the publication of Berlin's essay one encounters three different, not necessarily related, versions of 'positive freedom': (1) freedom as individual self-mastery (rule by the 'real' self); (2) 'ability' (the power to do something); (3) collective 'self-determination' (not being governed by another State or society).[17] For Berlin, positive liberty is to be understood only in sense (1). He does not identify positive liberty with (2), although he has been frequently misquoted in this respect.[18] He also tries to separate (3) from liberty, including positive liberty, although on this point he is more ambivalent (IBLP 71–2). All three of these versions of positive freedom display what Berlin called its 'porous' character to the highest degree, absorbing certain natural or social characteristics alongside the true features of liberty. Negative freedom, on the other hand, depends strictly on external conditions, and in particular on actions by other per-sons that may interfere with one's opportunity to act.

Berlin is clear that the idea of freedom, whether negative or positive, should not be confused with the idea of ability, which is sometimes referred to as 'effec-tive freedom' (Swift 2001, 55). Berlin's insistence on this point was liable to pro-voke criticism from the Left, and it did. Socialists complained that to describe a person deprived of physical or financial means as free is profoundly misleading. One might as well say that a tramp is 'free' to dine at the Ritz—a statement that, though not meaningless, raises obvious problems. It was easy for these critics, in particular the Marxists, to relate Berlin's own social situation to his understanding

---

17. These three senses of freedom are clearly distinguished by Adam Swift, who wrongly supposes that Berlin confuses them (2001, 55–68; cf. IBLP 67–8).

18. Especially by economists, who in fact take their lead from Amartya Sen (1988).

of liberty: they were reassured in their belief that 'Freedom for an Oxford don' is indeed 'a very different thing from freedom for an Egyptian peasant' (L 171). Nevertheless, Berlin held his ground. In so far as the criticisms bore on conceptual analysis, he rebutted some of them, while also conceding that political consequences did not follow automatically from the conceptual autonomy of negative liberty (L 171–4). Returning to this point in 1969, he added a helpful clarification, distinguishing liberty from the conditions in which it can be exercised (L 38). To be negatively free is one thing; to have the financial means to use this freedom is something else. Confusing liberty with its conditions does not foster the cause of emancipation or equality, and is very likely to give rise to dangerous illusions. A careful reading of the lecture shows that exposing this kind of conceptual confusion was one of Berlin's aims. 'Everything is what it is', and 'nothing is gained by a confusion of terms' (L 172).

Berlin's responses to the standard socialist objections to negative freedom might appear to today's reader the most outdated part of the lecture. Berlin himself explicitly recognised that the historical situation in which the essay was conceived and written influenced the internal organisation of the text, and the relative emphasis given to different parts of his analysis. Had he written the lecture today, the 'search for status' would no doubt have been allotted a much larger role. The increased attention that nationality and the 'struggle for recognition' receive in Berlin's later writings can be traced back to his inaugural lecture. But it would be misleading to say that Berlin's defence of the conceptual autonomy and meaningfulness of negative liberty rests only on contingent motivations. If, as I have argued, the lecture should be read as a contribution to philosophy, Berlin's theoretical preoccupations should be taken at face value. Among these, the determination to dispel confusion and promote understanding is clearly paramount (IBLP 71–2). The same considerations apply when Berlin underlines the importance of agency for the identification of those instances of prevention that create unfreedom. If the impossibility of doing something depends on natural accidents (as when one is prevented from crossing the road by a tree that has been felled by lightning), clearly such prevention lies beyond the pale of freedom.[19]

Another notion that Berlin is eager to keep distinct from liberty is collective self-government. From the point of view of the history of ideas it is easy to see

---

19. Miller 1983. Bernard Williams has pointed out another aspect of the importance of agency that is compatible with Berlin's approach. According to Williams, 'the restriction of our activities by the intentional activities of others, as contrasted with the ubiquitous limitations we face in nature, can give rise to a quite specific reaction, resentment; and if resentment is not to express itself in more conflict, non-co-operation, and dissolution of social relations, an authoritative determination is needed of whose activities should have priority' (2001, 82).

why these notions are confused in ordinary parlance. The struggle for collective self-rule has often found its expression in the language of liberty. This issue was raised by Charles Taylor in a seminal contribution (1979), and has been revived recently by Quentin Skinner. According to Skinner, Berlin's understanding of negative freedom as non-interference does not rule out the possibility that freedom is compatible with non-democratic government. Starting from Berlin's premises, one has to deny that there is a logical connection between freedom and democracy, a conclusion Skinner regards as untenable. As evidence for the prosecution, Skinner quotes TCL, mentioning the passage where Berlin distinguishes liberty from other values, such as equality or self-government (Skinner 1998, 113–15). According to Berlin, negative freedom is indeed compatible with autocracy or with the absence of self-government (L 176). This conclusion might sound shocking to some, but it is only a consequence of the idea that being free or unfree is a matter of fact, contingent on the degree of other people's interference. The outcome of such interference, in so far as it amounts to prevention, is clearly logically independent of the kind of political regime one happens to live under.

Skinner regards Berlin's solution as flawed. Accordingly he has put forward what he sees as a third concept of liberty. This 'neo-Roman' theory of freedom (the name is a tribute to the republican *libertas* of the Romans) can be summed up by saying that (i) there is a connection between the freedom of an individual and the freedom of the community to which he or she belongs; and that (ii) there is a further connection between the freedom of an individual and the fact that he or she is not subordinated to an arbitrary power. If these two conditions are not fulfilled, a person cannot be said to be politically free (Skinner 1998, 23–57). Skinner's objection assumes that TCL is meant as a complete list of the legitimate uses of the word 'freedom'. In any event, there are passages where Berlin comes close to the acknowledgement of non-domination as a reasonable extension of liberty.[20]

Recently Skinner has returned to the third concept of liberty in a lecture that is more sympathetic towards the complexity of Berlin's arguments (2002b).[21] But he has not altered the substance of his position or the fundamental character of his criticisms. In particular, he assumes too straightforward a connection between Berlin's analysis and defence of negative liberty and his liberalism. These are cer-

20. L 32, 201. See IBLP 88, where George Crowder argues that Berlin could accept non-domination as a form of liberty 'either by extending negative liberty to include the absence of dependence, or by interpreting the positive idea to embrace non-domination as an aspect of authentic self-direction, or by conceiving of non-domination as a different kind of freedom altogether'. Berlin's approach leaves all these options open, but the structure of the lecture suggests that he would have regarded them as analogical extensions, not as expressions of the core meaning of liberty.

21. See the discussion of the 'republican' critique of Berlin in IBLP 87–90.

tainly related in so far as Berlin is convinced that the recognition of an area of protection from interference is a necessary feature of a liberal regime. However, according to Berlin, this is not a sufficient condition of liberalism. A social and cultural environment that is friendly towards a variety of life-plans, lifestyles and modes of thought is a further condition whose satisfaction is not guaranteed simply by non-interference.

Contrary to widespread opinion, Berlin's defence of the conceptual autonomy of negative liberty should not be interpreted as if it were a straightforward political statement. The distinction between the two concepts of liberty is, in the first instance, a contribution to the understanding of the category of freedom. Only after we have freed ourselves from confused notions of freedom can we examine the rival merits of different social arrangements. According to Berlin, a liberal regime, which includes a measure of negative freedom, is better than the alternatives, including those based on positive liberty. This, however, is not sufficient to show that Berlin is a 'negative libertarian', as Skinner seems to suggest (2002b, 264–5), if that means that negative liberty is overriding.

NEGATIVE VERSUS POSITIVE LIBERTY

The distinction between negative and positive freedom is paradigmatic in contemporary political theory, and it bears witness to the impact of TCL that Berlin is often credited with its introduction. This widespread impression, as Berlin himself says, is historically inaccurate.[22] The remote origin of the distinction is in Kant, who uses 'negative' and 'positive' to describe two different ways of defining practical freedom. In the first sense, freedom is said to be negative because it is characterised negatively as independence of determination by sensible impulses. In the second sense, freedom is said to be positive because it is characterised positively as determinability by the moral law.[23] This is not the place to pursue the complex issues of interpretation that the Kantian doctrine of practical freedom has provoked (see Engstrom 2002, 294–8). Nevertheless, there is one aspect of

---

22. For educated readers raised in the first half of the twentieth century the distinction was familiar because it was used by the British Idealists, and through their influence had entered the wider social and political debate. See Green 1895, 2–27; Bosanquet 1899, 124–40. Among Berlin's contemporaries in Oxford, the distinction had already been employed by John Plamenatz (1938, 68). The distinction is also used by de Ruggiero (1925, 338–9; 350 in the English translation). Although Berlin does not mention de Ruggiero's book, it is very likely that he knew it through Collingwood, its English translator.

23. Immanuel Kant, *Critique of Practical Reason* (1788), part 1, book 1, chapter 1, section 8, theorem 4.

Kant's treatment of freedom that is worthy of attention because it sheds further light on Berlin's essay. Kant says that it is not possible to grasp the essence (*Wesen*) of freedom through the negative definition. The positive definition, on the other hand, flows from the negative and is richer and more fruitful. This way of characterising the difference between the two kinds of freedom is very likely to be the origin of Green's and Bosanquet's assumption that positive liberty should be seen as the 'real', hence superior, version of freedom. As his discussion of positive liberty shows, Berlin was aware of the intuitive appeal of such a thesis.

Nevertheless, Berlin saw a fundamental problem in the positive definition. If liberty consists in not being a slave to someone, such a definition also applies reflexively. One can be at the mercy of one's own desires, even if also aware of good reasons to resist them. A smoker knows he must quit because smoking is bad for him, but cannot resist a cigarette. Such a situation, as Berlin pointed out, gives credibility to the idea of a divided self, one part claiming control over its actions and one part shunning such control (L 180). In the case of the hypothetical smoker in conflict with himself, control is not exercised, as it should be, by the rational part that orders him to quit, but by the irrational part that prefers the pleasure of a cigarette and ignores the damage caused by smoking. But what is it that the rational part of the self does? Given common presuppositions about rationality, it is natural to say that the rational self applies universal criteria for the selection of goals. This capacity, however, is not uniformly spread among the population, because we know that some people do not act rationally. Given this premiss, if one is absolutely convinced that one knows the real goals at which a person's actions should aim, one can feel authorised to compel others to realise their proper goals. Can one say that a person who compels someone else to do something is a liberator? Does that not involve a paradox according to which 'real' freedom consists in being compelled to act in one's best interest? For Berlin, historical experience suggests, as a natural development of such an idea, that a person who is compelled in this way is no longer treated as autonomous, but instead as part of a collective being whose rational soul must impose its own free will on its recalcitrant limbs. With this last conceptual slide, we reach the bottom of a slippery slope. The idea of freedom seems to justify totalitarianism, with its complement of torture, censorship and violence.

The leading character in this intellectual drama is Kant. His ideas on liberty, as authors such as Green and Bosanquet show, can lead to conclusions that are inimical to the very possibility of leading an autonomous life. Under a regime in which a 'rationalist' interpretation of positive liberty is paramount, a person might end up being treated as a means, not as an end in itself (L 183–4). Having realised, on the basis of the historical evidence, that the concept of positive liberty is particularly liable to distortion, Berlin turned to negative liberty in search of an antidote to positive liberty's paternalist disease. As his treatment of the measurement of freedom shows, he is convinced that negative liberty, whatever its defects from other points of view, is less vulnerable to such distortions.[24] The peculiar 'objectivity' of negative liberty lies in its being a fact, something whose existence depends ultimately on causal interactions among bodies.

Berlin inverts Kant's order of priority between the two concepts:

> The fundamental sense of freedom is freedom from chains, from imprisonment, from enslavement by others. The rest is extension of this sense or else metaphor. To strive to be free is to seek to remove obstacles; to struggle for personal freedom is to seek to curb interference, exploitation, enslavement by men whose ends are theirs, not one's own. (L 48)

A moment's reflection on the paradigmatic case of unfreedom—being prevented from doing something by the interference of others—brings out the reason for this inversion. Negative liberty is 'fundamental' because it is closer to the basic experience of bodily interaction, which Berlin rightly regards as belonging to the solid background of the objective material world.[25] With positive liberty we enter a different realm, whose intentional dimension opens up the possibility of a much wider range of interpretations.

As the subsequent debate has shown, Berlin's reliance on the objectivity of negative liberty loses its strength progressively as one moves further from the paradigmatic case. As he recognises, in effect, in TCL, the extent to which the stockbroker's action prevents the shopkeeper from doing something is highly disputable, and depends on larger issues such as the susceptibility of different kinds of event to different kinds of explanation.[26]

Berlin's equivocation on the topic of measurement opened up a gap in his defence of negative freedom as a political standard—a gap that Charles Taylor exploited to put forward a new version of the idea of positive liberty (1979). A crucial step in Taylor's argument relies on comparative judgements between different people or societies. In an underdeveloped country with a dictatorial regime that imposes atheism there is no freedom of religion, but neither are there traffic-

---

24. According to Berlin, negative liberty is not immune to distortions. However, his reconstruction of the thought of positive libertarians such as Rousseau, Hegel and Fichte shows that he regarded their understanding of freedom as more likely to be incompatible with the defence of an area of non-interference in a person's activities.

25. Bernard Williams calls this basic sense of freedom 'primitive'. He writes: 'this is the place to start because [primitive freedom] involves a quite basic human phenomenon, and that phenomenon already points in the direction of politics' (2001, 79, 82).

26. L 169–70; Gray 1980, 521–3.

lights that restrict the freedom of motorists. A democracy in an industrialised country, on the other hand, will probably have a system that recognises the freedom of all forms of religion, but also roads full of traffic-lights. A quantitative understanding of negative freedom might lead to the conclusion that there is more freedom under the dictatorship than under the democratic regime. For Taylor, the intuitive implausibility of such a conclusion suggests that purely quantitative criteria are inadequate for the assessment of freedom. This means that we should look elsewhere. Restrictions on the circulation of traffic are not particularly significant from an evaluative point of view, and are therefore of little relevance to our freedom.

Taylor's solution to the problem of assessing degrees of liberty relies on the idea that the notion of freedom has a built-in reference to purposes. He claims that our judgements about freedom are a function of purposes and their relative evaluations. But this amounts to a rejection of the whole notion of negative freedom, which involves a claim of fact, independent of purposes. The alternative, teleological, account of freedom developed in Taylor's essay is close to the traditional understanding of positive liberty. Taylor claims that once this link between freedom and purpose is accepted, we are compelled to slide a fair way down the slippery slope that so preoccupied Berlin. In particular, we need to recognise that internal restrictions are 'real' (there is such a thing as acting against one's own best judgement), and also that there are goals that have objective value. However, Taylor thinks it is still an open question whether the truth of these contentions amounts to a slide towards totalitarianism.

Taylor's argument has been criticised by pointing out that he conflates the measurement and evaluation of freedom (Carter 1999, 148–65). Such a conflation, for those who do not subscribe to his objective theory of values, is clearly a mistake. Whether this would also have been Berlin's reply is not clear, at least if one takes seriously his unclarity about the qualitative dimensions of freedom. Nevertheless, his scepticism towards the idea of objective reason, which has a crucial role in his criticism of positive liberty, is incompatible with Taylor's views on purpose. Berlin was certainly not a perfectionist. He believed in the objectivity of at least some fundamental human values, but his pluralism allows that such values can be legitimately combined in many ways, thus ruling out 'thicker' theories of the human good such as Taylor's.

Even if the analysis of freedom as a political value leaves room for views such as Taylor's (Williams 2001, 81), a recognition of the plurality of values and the creative role of human choice in interpreting them seems bound to require areas of individual liberty where people can pursue their projects without interference (Gray 1995, 31).

TCL is not the last statement of pluralism in Berlin's thought. However, it is here that its connection with liberalism is made explicit for the first time. The ultimate motivating force of Berlin's classical statement of liberalism is the possibility that a distortion of the concept of liberty may lead to a society that systematically obstructs the plurality of value. Berlin could have adopted Montaigne's description of life as 'un mouvement inégal, irrégulier et multiforme'[27] as the epigraph for his inaugural lecture. Its contribution to our understanding of this feature of humanity, and of the conditions for its preservation, guarantees its lasting value.

Acknowledgement

I should like to thank Ian Carter, George Crowder, Henry Hardy and an anonymous referee for helpful comments on a previous draft.

---

27. 1588, paragraph 2 ('a rough, irregular progress with a multitude of forms': Montaigne ed. Screech 1991, 922).

6

Strange Reversals
BERLIN ON THE ENLIGHTENMENT
AND THE COUNTER-ENLIGHTENMENT

GRAEME GARRARD

THE BATTLE FOR BERLIN

According to Isaiah Berlin, the Enlightenment was one of 'the best and most hopeful episodes in the life of mankind' (POI 52). That is why its values are, he claims, 'deeply sympathetic to me'. The *philosophes*, he tells us, 'liberated people from horrors, obscurantism, fanaticism, monstrous views. They were against cruelty, they were against oppression, they fought the good fight against superstition and ignorance and against a great many things which ruined people's lives. So I am on their side' (CIB 70). Certainly there are few individuals one can more easily imagine blending into the eighteenth century 'republic of letters' than Isaiah Berlin—'the Diderot of our age'.[1]

Yet Berlin devoted much of his remarkable scholarly career to exploring the ideas of a rogues' gallery of Counter-Enlightenment figures such as Maistre, Hamann, Sorel and Fichte.[2] His essays are also liberally spiced with references to even more obscure reactionary writers, such as Knut Hamsun, Friedrich Jahn and Ernst Arndt. Berlin's interest in these half-forgotten (in some cases entirely forgotten) figures of the Counter-Enlightenment is not merely the morbid curiosity

---

1. Siedentop 1994, 8. Wokler 1995 makes the same comparison.
2. See Berlin's essay 'The Counter-Enlightenment' (1973), in AC.

of a liberal wishing to provide his enlightened readers with a *frisson* of excitement in the face of reactionary madness. He genuinely believed that we have something to learn from these losers in the struggle of ideas.

Berlin's fascination with these dark figures has led to accusations that he has 'gone native'. Mark Lilla writes that, in reading Berlin's essays, 'one has the uncomfortable impression of watching someone welcome harmless stray puppies into his home, only to discover years later that they are all grown up, straining at their leashes, teeth bared'.[3] John Gray has attempted to enlist (some say hijack) Berlin in his own crusade against the Enlightenment. 'The idea that animates all of Berlin's work, both in intellectual history and in political theory,' Gray writes with enthusiastic approval, 'is one which, if true, as I take it to be, strikes a death-blow to the central classical Western tradition—and, it must be added, to the project of the Enlightenment.'[4] This view is shared by Richard Rorty who, in *Contingency, Irony, and Solidarity*, includes Berlin among other philosophical anti-foundationalists such as John Dewey, Michael Oakeshott and John Rawls who were sceptical about the possibility of grounding liberalism on trans-historical philosophical foundations (1989, 57).

In response to this attempt to drive a wedge between Berlin and the Enlightenment, Robert Wokler has answered that 'if Berlin's occasional writings lend some support to Gray's hostility to an Enlightenment Project, by far his most substantial essays on eighteenth- and nineteenth-century thought display his deep affinities to Enlightenment thinkers and his emulation of their style' (1995). Steven Lukes endorses this view, writing of Gray's anti-foundationalism as follows: 'What Berlin says, speaking in his own voice, and in his central texts, is the very opposite of this. [...] something far more robust than reluctance would prevent Berlin from following Gray down his Rortian path' (1995). Claude Galipeau, while less categorical on this point than Lukes, none the less concludes that '[e]ven though he is aware of the dogmatism and narrowness of some Enlightenment thinkers, Berlin still remains with this tradition' (1994, 82). Michael Rosen concurs, albeit with significant qualifications, referring to Berlin's 'deeply Weberian [...] "yes-but" to the Enlightenment' (1993, 4). Roger Hausheer agrees, describing Berlin's 'project' as 'continuous in spirit with that of the Enlightenment, whatever radical breaks he may make with some of its more rigidly unempirical assumptions' (PSM xxxiii).

In the first part of what follows I argue that these latter interpreters of Berlin have seriously underestimated the depth of his reservations about the Enlightenment (as he understands it) and the extent of his sympathy for its enemies. For

---

3. Lilla 1994, 13. See also Lilla, IBCE 1–12.
4. Gray 1993, 64–5. This argument is developed more fully in JG.

Berlin, the Enlightenment was a form of monism with a dangerous tendency—like positive liberty—to lead to intolerance and even despotism (Schmidt 2000, 741–51). He believed that many of the political disasters of the last two centuries, beginning with the French Revolutionary 'Reign of Terror', originate in the Enlightenment project to unbend 'the crooked timber of humanity' in order to make it conform to a single, universal ideal. The Enlightenment's monistic conception of truth and its utopian belief in the rational compatibility of values is prone to perversion into forms of despotism that undermine its liberal commitments. However, by preferring the more modest claim that political despotism is the *likely*, but not logically necessary, outcome of Enlightenment monism, Berlin has adopted a position that is much more plausible while still setting himself decisively (if not totally) against the Enlightenment. I conclude that the question of whether Enlightenment monism is likely to have the undesirable political consequences that Berlin believes is more an empirical than a philosophical question, and is probably impossible to answer definitively.

In the second part of the essay I argue that, just as the *philosophes* unintentionally brought about tragic consequences that subverted their own professed goals, according to Berlin, so many of the thinkers of the pluralistic Counter-Enlightenment inadvertently promoted liberal ends, in spite of their reactionary intentions. Examples of such 'strange reversals' (as Berlin calls them) abound in his work, and constitute one of the major themes of his thought. However, as I show in the case of *philosophes* such as Rousseau and Montesquieu, his Enlightenment/Counter-Enlightenment schema leads Berlin into an intellectual Procrusteanism that results in some odd and inconsistent conclusions. Yet, as with his refusal to accept a logical connection between Enlightenment monism and political despotism, Berlin wisely rejects any such connection between Counter-Enlightenment pluralism and political liberalism, thereby saving him from a conceptual trap into which other liberal pluralists have fallen.

BERLIN'S ENLIGHTENMENT

According to Berlin, the *philosophes* shared a belief that the world possesses a permanent, unalterable structure governed by universal laws. These laws are discoverable by a combination of reason—when unclouded by myth, prejudice, religious dogma and emotion—and disinterested empirical observation, following the model and method of the natural sciences as established in the seventeenth and eighteenth centuries, above all by Isaac Newton. The empiricism of the Enlightenment held that experience is open to all, which means that, in the absence of internal and external obstacles to direct sensory perception, everyone is capable of knowing the world as it really is. The Enlightenment sought to eradicate error by removing impediments to knowledge. Hence its emancipatory drive to free the minds of human beings by attacking all forms of authority and superstition that impede progress towards this goal. 'According to this doctrine,' Berlin writes, 'all genuine questions were in principle answerable: truth was one, error multiple; the true answers must of necessity be universal and immutable, that is, true everywhere, at all times, for all men, and discoverable by the appropriate use of reason, by relevant experience, observation and the methods of experiment, logic, calculation' (AC 163). Societies will tend to converge to the extent that they are based on the universal truths of science, thereby reducing, if not eliminating, a major source of human conflict and suffering. Hence the common belief of the 'party of humanity', as the *philosophes* were sometimes called, that there is one universal human nature, one universal civilisation, and, in an ideal world, one universal language. A typical example of this account of the Enlightenment appears in Berlin's essay 'The Decline of Utopian Ideas in the West':

> The Enlightement programme seemed clear: one must find out scientifically what man consists of, and what he needs for his growth and for his satisfaction. When one had discovered what he is and what he requires, one will then ask where this last can be found; and then, by means of the appropriate inventions and discoveries, supply men's wants, and in this way achieve, if not total perfection, at any rate a far happier and more rational state of affairs than at present prevails. Why does it not exist? Because stupidity, prejudice, superstition, ignorance, the passions which darken reason, greed and fear and lust for domination, and the barbarism, cruelty, intolerance, fanaticism which go with them, have led to the deplorable condition in which for too long men have been forced to live. Failure, unavoidable or deliberate, to observe what there is in the world has robbed man of the knowledge needed to improve his life. Scientific knowledge alone can save us. This is the fundamental doctrine of the French Enlightenment, a great liberating movement which in its day eliminated a great deal of cruelty, superstition, injustice and obscurantism.[5]

For Berlin the Enlightenment was basically—but not exclusively—a French affair, just as the Counter-Enlightenment was fundamentally German.

Berlin believes that the monism he associates with the Enlightenment (although not *just* the Enlightenment) is prone to authoritarianism, just as positive liberty is susceptible to perversion into tyranny. In his famous lecture on 'Two Concepts of Liberty', he concedes that negative liberty has occasionally been perverted into tyranny as well, but this is much less common than the 'strange [...]

5. CTH 34. Other statements of this view can be found at AC 3–4, 163; RT 83–4, 137; TCE 276–7; and in 'The Philosophers of the Enlightenment', in POI.

reversal' of positive liberty into heteronomy (L 198). 'The perversion of each', he claims in an interview, 'has led to bad consequences, but one of them has, it seems to me, historically been more cruelly perverted than the other. I think that positive liberty has been distorted more disastrously than negative liberty, but I do not deny that negative liberty has been perverted into a species of laissez-faire which has led to terrible injustices and sufferings' (CIB 147). However, as a matter of fact this has happened far less often than the perversion of positive liberty into despotism. The reason for this tendency is that positive liberty rests on assumptions that have, historically, proved to be extremely tempting to well-meaning despots who have sought to 'liberate' humans through force. One assumption is that we have two 'selves', a higher, rational and autonomous 'true self', and a lower, irrational and heteronomous 'empirical self'. Another is the monist belief that 'some single formula can in principle be found whereby all the diverse ends of men can be harmoniously realised' (L 179–81, 214). Berlin finds evidence of these beliefs throughout Western history, where they have been repeatedly twisted and abused to justify countless forms of despotism across the political spectrum.

Berlin makes a similar argument about the Enlightenment, which he claims is monistic in its basic assumptions about truth, reason and nature. He argues that these beliefs have tended to undermine the Enlightenment's emancipatory goals, which he shares. Although he denies that such beliefs *necessarily* entail despotism, they are sloped towards such forms of oppression,[6] since the *philosophes* believed in a 'final solution' to knowledge and values valid at all times and in all places. According to Berlin, many of the political disasters of the last two centuries, beginning with the 'Reign of Terror', originate in this Enlightenment project 'to bring the many into a coherent, systematic unity' (TCE 200), by education and socialisation if possible, by force if necessary. As such, it is a secular form of fundamentalism ironically exhibiting many of the same zealous and intolerant tendencies as the religious fundamentalism it opposed. Hence his belief that 'the great eighteenth-century *philosophes* were ultimately responsible for a lot of intellectual tyranny, for the rule of the intellectuals, ending in the Soviet Union [...] with the Gulag [...] these good men, who were against superstition, against tradition, against every kind of falsification, against authority, great liberators [...] nevertheless preached a doctrine which, in a somewhat perverted form, maybe, led to some rather tragic consequences'.[7]

---

6. Charles Taylor applies the term 'value-slope' to some factual descriptions that claim to be neutral (1985, 73).

7. Berlin speaking to Humphrey Carpenter in an interview for Carpenter 1996, and quoted somewhat inaccurately in that work at 127. The discrepancies between the taped interview with Berlin and the version printed by Carpenter were brought to my attention by Henry Hardy, who corrected it for me.

Berlin's depiction of the Enlightenment as monistic in its basic assumptions about truth and value is both correct and not particularly controversial. Virtually all of the *philosophes* and *Aufklärer* agreed that 'the truth is one', a basic belief which is the common property of virtually *all* Western thought since Plato, according to Berlin. More contentious is his claim that Enlightenment monism, like all monisms, contains an authoritarian temptation to those who subscribe to it, since Berlin thought that few of those who really believe that they possess the truth will see much, if any, reason to tolerate error. He regarded this temptation as very powerful, but not wholly irresistible. It is just much easier to justify intolerance, coercion and despotism if one assumes that 'the truth is one' and that you possess it. Berlin never claimed that this basic belief *necessarily* leads to dire political consequences, but he thought that it strongly disposes those who hold it that way. Hence the repeated tendency of monists to favour illiberal and intolerant political systems designed to unbend the crooked timber of humanity. There is no *logical* connection between the belief that one possesses the truth and the belief that it should be imposed on those who do not. Logically, toleration of error is just as compatible with monism about basic beliefs as intolerance of it. Berlin granted that there are some monists who successfully resisted this temptation and denied that it is the role of the State to enforce the truth; 'the business of laws', John Locke wrote in *A Letter concerning Toleration*, 'is not to provide for the truth of opinions, but for the safety and security of the commonwealth, and of every particular man's goods and person' (1689, 88). This is also true of John Stuart Mill's 'harm principle', according to which 'the only purpose for which power can be rightfully exercised over any member of a civilised community, against his will, is to prevent harm to others', which Berlin called 'the ultimate basis of political liberalism'.[8] Yet, for Berlin, the Enlightenment produced relatively few such political liberals because the desire to drag the ignorant and deluded out of their caves into the light of truth is so powerful and poses a constant temptation, and this desire is much stronger for monists than for pluralists, making the former much more politically dangerous than the latter. Only monists believe that a 'final solution' is possible in the realm of values, and it is this mistaken belief that makes it so difficult to resist the temptation to impose it.[9]

Berlin's argument about the disposition of monism towards political despotism is less a philosophical argument than a psychological observation, since it pertains not to any logical connection between monism and despotism but merely to an unfortunate propensity that tends to breed fanatics. This explains why

---

8. L 236. The quotation is from Mill 1859, chapter 1, 223. Berlin refers to Mill as 'the man who [...] founded modern liberalism' (L 218).

9. Berlin uses the term 'final solution' to describe this belief at L 212 and CIB 143.

Berlin believes that the Enlightenment is so prone to a 'strange reversal' into well-meaning authoritarianism, which was already evident before the French Revolution in the popularity of enlightened despotism among many *philosophes* and their authoritarian patrons, such as Joseph II of Austria, Catherine II of Russia and Frederick II of Prussia. However, it is no *more* prone to this than other forms of monism, which has been the norm in the West since Plato.

For Berlin, pluralism was a minority tendency in Western thought until the advent of late-eighteenth century romanticism, which emerged in reaction to Enlightenment monism. His claim contrasts with, on the one hand, the much bolder claim that Enlightenment monism *necessarily* entails political despotism, which is clearly untrue, and, on the other hand, the much more modest claim that it *can* promote political despotism, which is a truism that says very little indeed. Berlin's position seems to be that Enlightenment monism is very *likely* to subvert its own liberal values, which is a serious charge indeed. He is no less critical of the Enlightenment than he is of positive liberty and monism generally: he regarded them all as politically very dangerous beliefs. While he admired the Enlightenment for destroying one form of despotism, he condemned it for erecting another form in its place. So, at best, the Enlightenment leaves us no better off. At worst, we are worse off (perhaps *much* worse off) since these new forms of despotism are often more extreme and destructive than those they have replaced:

> For the tyranny of ignorance, of fear, of superstitious priests, of arbitrary kings, of all the bogies fought by eighteenth-century enlightenment it substitutes another tyranny, a technological tyranny, a tyranny of reason, which, however, is just as inimical to liberty, just as inimical to the notion that one of the most valuable things in human life is choice for the sake of choice, not merely choice of what is good, but choice as such. It is inimical to this and in this way has been used as the justification both for Communism and for Fascism, for almost every enactment which has sought to obstruct human liberty and to vivisect human society into a single, continuous, harmonious whole, in which men are intended to be devoid of any degree of individual initiative. (FIB 26–7)

Unfortunately, the question of whether Enlightenment monism is *likely* to give rise to political despotism is probably impossible to answer definitively because of the difficulty of establishing the role that such basic beliefs play in the minds of real political actors, and how significant the intentions of these actors are in the events that actually shape history. The most that can be said with any certainty about Berlin's claim is that it is neither as simplistic nor as obviously wrong as many of his detractors assume. He prudently stressed the contingency of the relationship between monism and political despotism. Yet he still held that the tendency that contingently links them is very strong indeed, thereby raising very serious questions about the Enlightenment, which he viewed as extremely dangerous, *malgré lui.*

A good example of Enlightenment intolerance is the attitude of most of the *philosophes* in France towards Christianity. While there were relatively few atheists among them, there were also few Christians; most were deists who believed in a remote, non-interventionist God stripped of Christian attributes. They viewed Christianity as not only wrong, but as extremely harmful, the most serious of all impediments to human understanding and progress. Tolerating such false beliefs was tantamount to tolerating the principal obstacle on the road to knowledge, without which civilisation could not advance and happiness would not increase. The enlightened despotism that many *philosophes* such as Voltaire advocated was intended to purge false beliefs such as this from the minds of men as a necessary (if not sufficient) condition for progress and happiness. The Jacobins—who put their hero Voltaire in the Panthéon in Paris in 1791—inherited this Enlightenment belief and used the coercive power of the State to impose a policy of intolerance towards false and (as they saw it) harmful beliefs such as Christianity. According to Berlin, much of the well-meaning despotism that has blighted Western political and intellectual history since springs from this basic outlook, which has taken many forms.

For Berlin, the authoritarian political tendencies in Enlightenment monism were nowhere more apparent (and baleful) than in the writings of Jean-Jacques Rousseau, a *philosophe* who had an enormous influence on the leading Jacobins of the French Revolution. Hence Berlin's strong antipathy to, if not actual hatred of, Rousseau, whose belief that individuals must sometimes be 'forced to be free' (1762, 141) proved highly serviceable to tyrants like Robespierre. Berlin, who was heavily influenced by Benjamin Constant's dim view of Rousseau, believed that the latter's doctrine was 'not very different from that of the Encyclopaedists. [...] The actual substance of what Rousseau said was not so very different from the official enlightened doctrine of the eighteenth century' (RR 53). Although Rousseau regarded liberty as an 'absolute value' and a 'religious concept', it underwent a 'great perversion' in his thought to become a doctrine leading to slavery (FIB 31, 48). Thus, the greatest eighteenth-century advocate of liberty was also 'one of the most sinister and most formidable enemies of liberty in the whole history of modern thought' (FIB 49). Berlin subscribed to what might be called 'the continuity thesis' of the Enlightenment and the Revolution, the belief that they were connected in some intrinsic way, as cause and effect, for example—and Rousseau personified this link.

Yet if, as Berlin claims, Machiavelli is a pluralist, then so too is Rousseau. In his essay on 'The Originality of Machiavelli', Berlin credits the Florentine with being one of the earliest 'makers of pluralism' in modernity because he recognised the existence of two irreconcilable and incommensurable value systems: the Christian and the pagan/republican. For Machiavelli Christianity is politically disastrous because it has 'rendered the world weak and given it in prey to criminal men'. So he offered his readers a choice between Christianity and political success (1531, 131–2). For Berlin this was a historic moment in Western thought because it created a 'serious rift in the idea of *philosophia perennis* in ethics and politics. The idea that there can be only one true answer to any question, whether of fact or of value'. By posing this choice Machiavelli became 'the first thinker who in the same sense allowed that there were at least two ways of life, either of which men could lead, seeking salvation either in this world or the next, which are not compatible' (CIB 54).

Rousseau makes the very same argument as 'the illustrious Machiavelli' in his *Social Contract*, where he rules out Christianity as a candidate for the civil religion that he advocates. Although Rousseau professed his belief in Christianity as the 'holy, sublime and true' faith that deserves the utmost respect and admiration, and regarded the life of a true Christian as a good life, perhaps the best that a person can live in this world, he thought that it contains a teaching fundamentally at odds with the republican ideals of civic identity and active public engagement that are central to the principles of political right spelled out in his famous political treatise. The Christianity of the Gospels is socially and politically ruinous because it is 'uniquely concerned with Heavenly matters' and utterly indifferent to 'whether things go well or badly here on earth' (1762, 220–1). The severe 'republic of virtue' that Rousseau hoped might survive in a few remote corners of an otherwise corrupt and decadent Europe would need a patriotic civil religion with a message wholly contrary to the spirit of the Gospels. This very same argument qualified Machiavelli as a pluralist in Berlin's eyes, yet Berlin presents Rousseau as an Enlightenment monist, indeed, as the quintessential Enlightenment monist. If Rousseau was actually a pluralist (as he must be if Machiavelli was), then Berlin must either revise his account of the Enlightenment to include pluralists like Rousseau or revise his account of Rousseau as an Enlightenment thinker. My own view is that Berlin is correct about the Enlightenment being monist in its basic beliefs but wrong about Rousseau being an Enlightenment thinker.[10]

Berlin had a similar problem fitting Montesquieu into his Enlightenment/Counter-Enlightenment schema. The author of *The Spirit of the Laws* affirmed the variety of human forms of life and emphasised the decisive role of external factors in shaping diverse *moeurs* and beliefs. For Berlin this qualifies him as a pluralist, and should therefore exclude him from the Enlightenment, just as he includes Rousseau by denying that he is a pluralist.[11] Montesquieu *should* fall out-

---

10. I make this case in Garrard 2003.

11. Berlin describes Montesquieu as a pluralist in 'Montesquieu' (AC 157) and (by implication) at CIB 107.

side of the circle of the *philosophes*, which is where Berlin appears to situate him in the following passage:

> In fact the whole system of values upon which the Enlightenment rested began to crumble if the very possibility of a single universal method for obtaining true answers to moral and metaphysical questions, true for all men, at all times, everywhere, *quod ubique, quod semper, quod ab omnibus*, was doubted or denied. Indeed, the very tone of Montesquieu, the whole tenor of his work, was somehow felt to be subversive of the principles of the new age. (AC 148)

Given this, it is not surprising that Berlin professed his puzzlement at Montesquieu's affirmation of universal laws of nature, since his 'whole aim is to show that laws are not born in the void' (AC 153). His only significant criticism of Montesquieu is that he contradicted himself by adhering to a belief in transcendent and immutable natural laws which are inconsistent with the idea of laws as organic, adaptable and amenable to change, which is the key to his thinking for Berlin. Elsewhere, he appears to retreat from the idea that Montesquieu's views were really subversive of the Enlightenment, since 'even he did not deny that all men wanted peace rather than war, warmth rather than cold, food rather than starvation, sexual procreation rather than total celibacy, and the like. [...] The goals of men are not all that different' (1971, 9).

BERLIN'S COUNTER-ENLIGHTENMENT

Having defined the Enlightenment as monistic—according to which 'all true solutions to all genuine problems must be compatible: more than this, they must fit into a single whole: for this is what is meant by calling them all rational and the universe harmonious' (L 193)—Berlin characterises the Counter-Enlightenment as a movement that arose in opposition to this. He sees it as a form of pluralism, based on an affirmation of cultural diversity and a rejection of the belief in the singularity of truth or human nature. 'Its most important influence on European thought', for Berlin, 'is the belief that science and reason do not have all the answers, that to some central questions of value—ethical, aesthetic, social, political—there can be more than one valid answer' (CIB 68).

As a pluralist himself, Berlin is committed to the belief that 'some values are not compatible, historically compatible, with others, so that the notion of an order in which all true values are simultaneously present and harmonious with each other is ruled out' (AC 124). Hence the tragic necessity to choose some goods over others. He believes that this truth was not widely recognised until the late eighteenth century and the early nineteenth, when romantic writers (particularly in Germany) revolted against the dominance of the French Enlightenment and Revolution. For Berlin this was a decisive turning point in Western intellectual history, since it represented the first *major* rebellion against the monistic mainstream of Western thought for 2500 years. According to Berlin, in the late eighteenth century the Germans 'rebelled against the dead hand of France in the realms of culture, art and philosophy, and avenged themselves by launching the great counter-attack against the Enlightenment' (CTH 196). This German reaction to the imperialistic universalism of the French Enlightenment and Revolution, which had been forced on them first by the Francophile Frederick II, then by the armies of Revolutionary France, and finally by Napoleon, was crucial to the epochal shift of consciousness that occurred in Europe at the time, leading eventually to romanticism.

Berlin believed that this unlikely ground proved to be fertile soil for liberal pluralism, which owes more to the Enlightenment's enemies than it does to its proponents, many of whom were monists whose tragic political legacy has often been terror and despotism. Just as the liberal Enlightenment tends to undergo a strange reversal into despotism because of its underlying monist assumptions, so the reactionary Counter-Enlightenment tends to undergo a no less strange reversal into liberalism because of its underlying pluralist assumptions. 'The result of romanticism', Berlin concludes, 'is liberalism, toleration, decency, and the appreciation of the imperfections of life', the opposite of the Enlightenment's legacy (RR 147). His sympathy for romanticism is clear, if qualified:

> One is not committed to applauding or even condoning the extravagances of romantic irrationalism if one concedes that, by revealing that the ends of men are many, often unpredictable, and some among them incompatible with one another, the romantics have dealt a fatal blow to the proposition that, all appearances to the contrary, a definite solution of the jigsaw puzzle is, at least in principle, possible, that power in the service of reason can achieve it, that rational organisation can bring about the perfect union of such values and counter-values as individual liberty and social equality, spontaneous self-expression and organised, socially dictated efficiency, perfect knowledge and perfect happiness, the claims of personal life and the claims of parties, classes, nations, the public interest. If some ends recognised as fully human are at the same time ultimate and mutually incompatible, then the idea of a golden age, a perfect society compounded of a synthesis of all the correct solutions to all the central problems of human life, is shown to be incoherent in principle. (CTH 236–7)

Berlin's essay on 'The Counter-Enlightenment' ends abruptly in the early nineteenth century, thereby suggesting that it was a single movement centred in

Germany that arose in reaction to the French Enlightenment. But the war between the Enlightenment and its enemies continues to this day with no less intensity than 200 years ago. So it makes little sense to refer, as Berlin does, to *the* Counter-Enlightenment as though it is a single movement, which it most definitely is not.[12] Although a good case can be made for viewing the Enlightenment as a single movement (as Berlin does), the same is not true of 'the' Counter-Enlightenment. The range of Counter-Enlightenment thought extends far and wide, much further and wider than the Enlightenment itself, from the mid-eighteenth century to the present; it appears in a variety of national contexts, and comes from all points of the ideological compass, from conservative Catholics and German romantics to liberals, neo-Marxists, feminists, environmentalists and postmodernists. Each opponent of the Enlightenment has his own particular conception of what it was, and his own specific reasons for opposing it, although there is much overlap and many strange bedfellows among them. That is why it is best to speak of Counter-Enlightenments rather than *the* Counter-Enlightenment (see Garrard 2006).

For Berlin, the monism of the Enlightenment is both wrong (as a matter of fact) and politically dangerous in its consequences. The former is apparent in its view of human nature. He believes that simplistic Enlightenment assumptions about human nature have been rightly replaced in the nineteenth and twentieth centuries by 'an increasingly complicated and unstable picture as new and disturbing hypotheses about the springs of action were advanced by psychologists and anthropologists' (AC 323). On the one hand, Berlin writes of the *philosophes* as follows:

> The central doctrines of the progressive French thinkers, whatever their disagreements among themselves, rested on the belief, rooted in the ancient doctrine of natural law, that human nature was fundamentally the same in all times and places; that local and historical variations were unimportant compared with the constant central core in terms of which human beings could be defined as a species, like animals, or plants, or minerals. (AC 1)

Berlin clearly rejects this view, which he contrasts unfavourably with that of Edmund Burke, who emphasised the diversity, rather than the uniformity, of human nature:

---

12. The term 'Counter-Enlightenment' first made its appearance in English in a 1949 essay in *Partisan Review* by William Barrett, where it is mentioned only in passing (1949, 663–4). He also employs it in his popular 1958 book on existentialism (1958, 244). The German expression *Gegen-Aufklärung* is older, probably coined by Friedrich Nietzsche in the late nineteenth century (1877, 478, fragment 22[17]). This latter reference is due to Robert Wokler: IBCE 26 note 4.

Burke said some very wise things. He said that the idea that there can be discovered such an entity as pure human nature if one strips away all the layers of civilisation and art, that you can penetrate to 'the natural man', i.e. a creature who embodies what is common and true of all men everywhere, at all times, and nothing beside this, that this idea is false. To make a revolution in the name of true human nature […] is absurd and wicked. There is for Burke no such thing as a universal human nature. (CIB 74)

This view is shared by the Catholic reactionary Joseph de Maistre, for whom 'there is no such thing as *man* in the world'.[13] Berlin commended Maistre (another admirer of Burke's) for his 'genius', consisting 'in the depth and accuracy of his insight into the darker, less regarded, but decisive factors in social and political behaviour'.[14] His comments on Maistre are liberally spiced with words such as 'bold', 'uncannily penetrating', 'original', 'brilliant', 'sharp-eyed', 'effective', 'lucid', 'exceedingly pungent', 'sharp[ly] realistic' and 'acute'. He believed that Maistre's dark depiction of man and nature, while grotesquely exaggerated, was not without an important kernel of truth often denied by thinkers of the Enlightenment. His grim portrait of the natural world, according to which '[t]he whole earth, perpetually steeped in blood, is nothing but a vast altar upon which all that is living must be sacrificed without end',[15] won Berlin's grudging approval when considered next to the Panglossian optimism of Condorcet. '[W]hen, against [Condorcet], Maistre says we are told to follow Nature, but that this leads to curious consequences, what he says is not absurd,' Berlin concludes (CIB 76). He did not merely *describe* Maistre's psychological 'realism'; to a surprising extent he *subscribed* to it as well.[16] This can best be seen in the following, revealing passage, which deserves to be quoted in full:

13. Maistre 1797, 53 (emphasis added), cited at CTH 100.

14. CTH 166. Berlin's surprisingly positive response to Maistre was probably influenced by his reading of Tolstoy. The great Russian novelist was much impressed by Maistre, whose work he read while writing *War and Peace*, in which Maistre is mentioned by name. Berlin's *The Hedgehog and the Fox* (1953) devotes considerable attention to a comparison of the ideas of Tolstoy and Maistre, and is his first significant published engagement with the latter's thought. In it he describes both as 'acute observers of the varieties of experience' and 'sharp-eyed foxes' (RT 77, 80). The essay that eventually became 'Joseph de Maistre and the Origins of Fascism' was broadcast as part of a radio series around the same time that Berlin wrote his essay on Tolstoy. It is hard to imagine that Tolstoy's interest in and generally favourable view of Maistre did not significantly influence Berlin's reception of him, particularly given that Berlin speaks appreciatively of those very aspects of Maistre's outlook that seem to have made the greatest impression on Tolstoy, such as his account of war.

15. Maistre 1821, 25; CTH 111.

16. For a detailed analysis of Berlin's attitude towards Joseph de Maistre, see Graeme Garrard, 'Isaiah Berlin's Joseph de Maistre', in IBCE.

While all around him there was talk of the human pursuit of happiness, [Maistre] underlined, again with much exaggeration and perverse delight, but with some truth, that the desire to immolate oneself, to suffer, to prostrate oneself before authority, indeed before superior power, no matter whence it comes, and the desire to dominate, to exert authority, to pursue power for its own sake— that these were forces historically at least as strong as the desire for peace, prosperity, liberty, justice, happiness, equality.

His realism takes violent, rabid, obsessed, savagely limited forms, but it is realism nevertheless. [...] Blindly dogmatic in matters of theology (and theory generally), in practice he was a clear-eyed pragmatist [...].

No one who has lived through the first half of the twentieth century, and, indeed, after that, can doubt that Maistre's political psychology, for all its paradoxes and the occasional descents into sheer counter-revolutionary absurdity, has proved, if only by revealing, and stressing, destructive tendencies—what the German romantics called the dark, nocturnal side of things—which humane and optimistic persons tend not to want to see, at times a better guide to human conduct than the faith of believers in reason; or at any rate can provide a sharp, by no means useless, antidote to their often over-simple, superficial and, more than once, disastrous remedies. (CTH 167–8)

As this passage reveals, Berlin believed that Maistre had a dangerous tendency to exaggerate, to push things too far. Yet, while it is true that Maistre was playing with very dangerous ideas that took him beyond orthodox Catholicism and traditional conservatism in the direction of a sinister 'ultra-modernism' with Fascist affinities, Berlin also perceived what he believed were some important, if unpalatable, truths in Maistre's thought, mixed in with a great deal that is hyperbolic, polemical and frequently repulsive (CTH 96). For Berlin, Maistre was what might be called an 'exaggerated realist'. This ambivalent attitude is encapsulated in Berlin's claim that Maistre 'revealed (and violently exaggerated) central truths, unpalatable to his contemporaries, indignantly denied by his successors, and recognised only in our own day' (CTH 174).

Given all of this, it is not so surprising after all to find that Berlin, the 'patron sage of English liberalism' (Bull 1993), was not only interested in, but actually had some appreciation for, Joseph de Maistre, the 'lion of illiberalism' (Holmes 1989). In some of his basic assumptions he is remarkably close to the 'realist' enemies of the Enlightenment such as Maistre, whose pessimistic views history has tragically vindicated in his eyes, particularly in the twentieth century. Unlike these reactionary Counter-Enlightenment figures, however, Berlin believed that it is precisely *because* of these grim realities that we must cultivate the liberal virtues of self-restraint, tolerance and mutual respect. Whereas these pessimistic assumptions led Maistre to reactionary conclusions, for Berlin they pointed in the opposite direction, towards a liberal politics of pluralism designed to secure as tolerable a life as possible in the tragic circumstances in which human beings commonly find themselves. It is a dark, Hobbesian liberalism that has strong affinities with Judith Shklar's 'liberalism of fear' (1989). Both political conclusions—liberal and illiberal—are logically compatible with pluralist assumptions and with the pessimistic conception of human nature Maistre and Berlin appear to have shared.

Like Burke and Maistre, Berlin also attacked eighteenth-century cosmopolitanism and its 'ideal of a single, scientifically organised world system governed by reason' which, he claims, lies at 'the heart of the programme of the Enlightenment' (AC 353). Echoing Herder, one of his intellectual heroes, Berlin states that 'I regard cosmopolitanism as empty. People can't develop unless they belong to a culture. [...] if the streams are dried up, as, for instance, where men and women are not products of a culture [...] that would lead to a tremendous desiccation of everything that is human' (Gardels 1991, 22). Berlin's sensitivity to cultural diversity and his Herderian belief in the importance of language to the formation of identity have led him to sympathise with some of the 'communitarian' and nationalist critics of both Enlightenment cosmopolitanism and liberalism (in some forms), the former of which he charges with a 'curious failure of vision' for consistently underestimating the importance and persistence of national identity. However, as a liberal, Berlin was supportive of a commitment to national community only to the extent that it is compatible with negative liberty. The freedom of the individual thus constitutes the acceptable outer limit of his communitarianism. Only essentially benign forms of community can be reconciled with this view, which falls far short of the full-blooded nationalism characteristic of many of the Enlightenment's reactionary opponents.

Another 'central dogma of the Enlightenment' that Berlin scorns is the belief in progress, the idea, as he puts it, that each successive civilisation in history is 'either a stepping-stone to a higher one, or a sad relapse to an earlier and lower one, that gives force, sense of reality, and persuasive power to this vast panoramic survey' (TCE 234). Berlin regards this facile belief as not only wrong—as 'history follows no libretto'—but dangerous, since it has so often been used as a pretext for political crimes and atrocities (RT 86). For Berlin, the *philosophes* were 'true forerunners' of Marx, who inherited their faith in progress, a faith that the tragic experience of the twentieth century has made impossible for us to share, as far as Berlin is concerned (CIB 72). 'It is by now a melancholy commonplace', he wrote of his century, 'that no century has seen so much remorseless and continued slaughter of human beings by one another as our own', a fact that belies the belief in history as progressive (CTH 175).

While Berlin did not rule out the possibility of pluralism issuing in illiberal and oppressive political consequences (Machiavelli, for example), he saw it as much less likely to do so than monism.[17] Conceptually, the relationship between liberalism and pluralism is just as contingent for Berlin as that between monism and political despotism. 'Pluralism and liberalism are not the same or even overlapping concepts,' he claims. 'There are liberal theories which are not pluralistic. I believe in both liberalism and pluralism, but they are not logically connected.'[18] Pluralists are not relativists. Like monists, they acknowledge the existence of objective goods although, unlike monists, they deny that all goods are reconcilable or can be arranged in an objective hierarchy of value. However, pluralism for Berlin *tends* to be more resistant to illiberal practices than monism. The Enlightenment, as a form of monism, is therefore more *likely* to lead to despotism in practice (despite its intentions) than the pluralistic Counter-Enlightenment (despite its intentions).

But there is nothing *illogical* for Berlin about a pluralist promoting one good over others, provided it is not done on the grounds that the chosen good is *intrinsically* preferable to the goods not chosen. This conclusion is rejected by some liberal pluralists such as George Crowder, who argues that to accept value pluralism 'is to have good reason to take seriously and promote a diversity of goods and ways of life', which in turn commits us to liberalism, since that is the political system he believes is best suited to the promotion of value diversity.[19] Berlin wisely resists this bolder version of liberal pluralism. Even if Crowder is right that a life with a wide variety of goods is itself a good worth promoting, it cannot claim rational priority over other goods, if we take the incommensurability of goods seriously, since there is no common currency for judging between the good of diversity and other goods. In such cases, a pluralist must acknowledge that these two goods are simply incommensurable.

---

17. For a detailed discussion and assessment of the relationship between liberalism and pluralism, see chapters 6 and 7 of IBLP.

18. CIB 44. The claim that there is a link between pluralism and liberalism is criticised in Crowder 1994. Berlin wrote a reply to Crowder with Bernard Williams, printed immediately after Crowder's article. Crowder argues that 'the plurality of values in itself gives us no reason to support liberalism, indeed no reason to prefer any particular political arrangement to any other' (1994, 293), a position that he later rejected in LVP.

19. IBLP 157. See also LVP 136–45. Crowder's case for the connection between pluralism and liberalism in LVP rests on three main pillars, only one of which is diversity. I do not have space here to address the other two. I have discussed this subject with Gunnar Beck in depth and I am grateful to him for helping me formulate this argument.

CONCLUSION

Berlin once described the German philosopher J. G. Herder as 'not an enemy but a critic of the French Enlightenment' (1981b, 8). It is very tempting to include Berlin among the Enlightenment's 'friendly critics' alongside his hero Herder. The fact that Berlin was a liberal makes it seem highly counter-intuitive to cast him as an enemy of the Enlightenment, since most liberals see themselves as its natural heirs. Yet his belief that Enlightenment monism is likely to lead to political despotism precludes this possibility; if the Enlightenment is prone to a 'strange reversal' into despotism, then it is extremely politically dangerous, notwithstanding its own liberal values. Yet Berlin's deep sympathy with those values precludes him from being classed as an outright enemy of the Enlightenment such as J. G. Hamann. On balance, I believe that Berlin was more hostile than sympathetic to the Enlightenment. He sided with its liberal values, rejected its basic monist beliefs, and condemned the political despotism that, he argued, it had a tendency to foster.

While most liberals regard themselves as descendents of the *philosophes*, there is 'another liberalism' that derives more from the pluralist enemies of the Enlightenment than it does from the Enlightenment itself.[20] Berlin's liberalism has its roots in this pluralist soil. While liberalism and the Enlightenment share a common concern for individual freedom, he believes that only the former is able consistently to uphold this value in practice, since it is based on pluralism. By contrast, the Enlightenment aspiration to organise society rationally in accordance with a universal conception of truth is incompatible with its belief in individual freedom, which is a core value of liberalism for Berlin. He thought that the likely political consequences of this belief were usually disastrous for liberalism.

---

20. See Rosenblum 1987 for an account of the neglected 'romantic experience of liberalism' (1).

7

Berlin and History

RYAN PATRICK HANLEY

'I am no historian.' Such was Isaiah Berlin's warning to a Princeton audience in 1973, and it was not the first time he had issued such a disclaimer.[1] Yet to the ears of that Princeton audience the warning must have sounded odd. The occasion of his visit was to deliver that year's Gauss Seminars under the title 'The Origins of Cultural History', and the lecture in which the disclaimer occurs, the first of three, bears the title 'Two Notions of the History of Culture: The German versus the French Tradition' (Berlin 1973).[2] The lecture itself examined the history of eighteenth-century political ideas, with the goal of discerning the origins of the contemporary approach to cultural history. As both the means and the ends of the lecture were historical, the audience might not unreasonably have wondered, in the light of his disclaimer, whether these were topics best suited to this speaker. Yet, at the same time, the reader of this lecture and of Berlin's other writings on the study of history may well find here an attraction that owes much to the fact that Berlin was a historian neither by instinct nor by training. His main concerns were political and philosophical rather than historical, and these governed his excursions into history. Yet it is precisely his political and philosophical orientation that makes his approach to the philosophy of history and the history of phi-

---

1. See SR xiv.
2. References for quotations from these lectures will be given by lecture and page number in the form 'OCH 1.15' (the reference for the opening quotation).

losophy relevant not only to historians of ideas, but also, and perhaps more importantly, to students of contemporary politics and philosophy.

The story of Berlin's attempt to marry his political, philosophical and historical interests begins with his biography.[3] In the 1930s, Berlin was a leading participant in the philosophical discussions then reaching their height in Oxford. But by the end of the Second World War, in which Berlin had been posted to the British Embassy in Washington, a shift in his academic interests had occurred. Berlin himself credited the shift to his talk with the Harvard mathematician H. M. Sheffer, who convinced him that 'there were only two philosophical disciplines'—logic and psychology—'in which one could hope for an increase of permanent knowledge'. But the real impact of their exchange lay in Sheffer's hint that progress might still be possible in the study of the history of philosophy as well, even if such study 'was not part of philosophy itself'. Thus Berlin's account of the 'profound impression' the conversation left on him:

> In the months that followed, I asked myself whether I wished to devote the rest of my life to a study, however fascinating and important in itself, which, transforming as its achievements undoubtedly were, would not, any more than criticism or poetry, add to the store of positive human knowledge. I gradually came to the conclusion that I should prefer a field in which one could hope to know more at the end of one's life than when one had begun; and so I left philosophy for the field of the history of ideas, which had for many years been of absorbing interest to me. (CC vii–viii)

But what exactly does this mean? It is surely right that during the later 1940s and the 1950s Berlin's principal academic interests moved from philosophy to areas today more directly associated with the history of political thought. But many of his readers have felt that his enterprise cannot be wholly subsumed by this or by any other single label. David Pears in particular has suggested that what Berlin meant in the account above was not that he left philosophy *per se*, but rather 'that he left *analytic* philosophy, because his interest in the philosophy of history, which started with his book on Marx in the middle 1930s, was something that he never abandoned'.[4] This seems correct; to read Berlin's later historical work is indeed to realise that he cannot be said ever to have 'left' philosophy, and this essay aims to uncover the relationship of Berlin's understanding of history to his training in philosophy, and particularly to locate the centrality of anti-positivism in his historical thought. Yet, at the same time, philosophy was not the only influence on

---

3. For accounts of the intellectual and professional significance of the following biographical episode, see MI 130–1; White 1999, 221; and Cracraft 2002, 279–80.

4. IBAC 36.

Berlin; his conception of history was shaped by his engagement as much with his political as with his philosophical world. The study of his views on history thus requires an examination not only of the relationship of his philosophical commitments to his historical thought, but also of the relationship of his political theory—and especially his idea of liberty and his value pluralism—to his philosophy of history. To see this is ultimately to see the central place occupied by history in Berlin's political philosophy as a whole.

Berlin's understanding of history has, however, been largely underemphasised by some recent readers.[5] This neglect can be partly explained by Berlin's failure to address the study of history in a sustained or systematic way. His best-known contribution, the 1953 lecture 'Historical Inevitability', would in time prove to receive some of the most critical treatment of any of his writings, largely on the grounds of its disorganisation—a charge that might be applied to his thoughts on history as a whole, which are scattered over a wide range of writings on a broad array of subjects. For this reason, perhaps the best place to begin a review of his understanding of history is the Gauss Seminars. These admittedly have a broader intention than to present Berlin's historical thought; indeed, at their heart they might be considered a crucial step in the evolution of his thoughts on value pluralism. But for the student of Berlin and history the lectures have two considerable advantages: first, they touch within a comparatively small compass on a number of the principal historical themes that Berlin would develop at greater length in other places; secondly, they present these themes in a way that makes clear their relationship to the political and philosophical ideas for which Berlin is today best known.

SCIENTIFIC HISTORY

Berlin's aim in the lectures is to trace 'the origins of the idea of the history of culture'—or to identify the birth of 'the very notion of culture as a possible subject for history' (OCH 1.2). In tracing these origins he sets up a characteristic

---

5. Important exceptions to this rule include the critique of Berlin's philosophy of history offered in Mazurek 1979; John Gray's more sympathetic examination of the same in chapter 3 of JG; and James Cracraft's recent presentation (2002) of Berlin's writings on history as a 'philosophical guide' for 'ordinary working historians' (277; cf. 299). On the role of history in Berlin's political philosophy, see Galipeau 1994, 165–79; and IBLP, esp. 18–21. My study of Berlin's understanding of the relationship between political science and statesmanship also takes his understanding of historical methodology as a point of departure, and in so doing briefly treats several of the themes addressed below at greater length: see Hanley 2004, esp. 328–30.

dichotomy.[6] Here the dichotomy separates 'two approaches' to or 'two notions' of cultural history. The first, he says, he has 'rather crudely called the French approach' because of its association with Voltaire (OCH 1.3–4). This approach he rejects, and in developing his case against it he relies on and further develops some of his most characteristic political ideas. Indeed the starting point for his critique of Voltaire's philosophy of history is its indebtedness to what Berlin famously called 'monism': the conviction, fundamental to the political thought of the Enlightenment, that 'to all serious questions there is only one true answer, all the other answers being false, because it must be so: if the question is a serious question then presumably there can be only one true answer to it' (OCH 1.4). Berlin further develops this point in his second lecture, in which he identifies 'the fundamental and central ideal of the Enlightenment' as the conviction that

> even if we cannot reach it, it must at any rate in principle be possible to formulate a kind of existence in which all human virtues reach perfection, and all these virtues harmonise with each other, on the simple principle that, since to all questions there must be one true answer and one true answer only, and since no true proposition can be incompatible with—or certainly cannot contradict—any other true proposition, the accumulation of situations described by all these true propositions must in fact constitute human perfection. (OCH 2.5)

Herein of course lies the master idea of Berlin's philosophical defence of value pluralism, and in turn his political argument against all forms of idealism and utopianism from Plato to Lenin.[7] But the Gauss Seminars reveal that this same anti-monism served as the basis for Berlin's understanding of how individuals should orient themselves to the past. The monistic historian who believes that the past can best be understood by uncovering a single category—in Voltaire's case, the exploitation of the weak and naive by the wicked and powerful—is doomed to historical reductionism and misunderstanding, Berlin insists.

Yet monism was hardly Voltaire's only failing, according to Berlin. Voltaire, he continues, also participated in the second failing of enlightened thought: for not only did Voltaire embrace the monistic assumption that one true answer exists for every problem, he also embraced the Enlightenment's insistence that the methods

---

6. Berlin himself acknowledges this propensity in the lectures, asking for the indulgence of his audience as he presents 'a dichotomy which, like all dichotomies, is over-general, over-dogmatic, and if taken too seriously will certainly distort the facts, but which nevertheless is perhaps in a limited way useful' (OCH 1.13).

7. As a characterisation of Enlightenment political thought, however, this broad-brush treatment has been seen as wanting, and also mitigated by Berlin's more nuanced treatments elsewhere: see e.g. Robert Wokler, IBCE 18 ff.

of natural science are the most effective means of discovering this answer. Voltaire, that is, was among the most strident partisans of the Enlightenment's characteristic faith that 'nature, if it is properly tortured, properly probed, properly looked at, if the proper technique is adopted, will supply the answer' to any question human beings might ask. What troubles Berlin about this claim is its scope. Berlin himself of course was no friend of irrationality, and applauded many of the Enlightenment's efforts to reground intellectual enquiry in empiricism.[8] Where the Enlightenment erred, on Berlin's account, was in its ambition to apply the methods of natural science to human phenomena, and particularly to the study of the history of human cultures. Having seen the advantages of using 'the technique of the natural sciences' as a means of uncovering the errors of 'metaphysics and theology', Voltaire and his contemporaries, Berlin claims, then took the fatal misstep of concluding that 'there was no reason for supposing that, if the same technique was applied to moral, or aesthetic, or political, or religious questions as well, equally lucid, interconnected answers could not be found' (OCH 1.4–5).

Berlin considers this a misstep because it confuses two types of knowledge. In particular, the misstep lies in the confusion of the sort of knowledge capable of precision and quantification with the sort of enquiry whose subject matter by nature precludes such quantification. Berlin's interest in this distinction is not new to the Gauss Seminars. In making this claim he drew on a line of enquiry that he had been developing since at least the 1950s regarding 'the great issue of *Naturwissenschaft* versus *Geisteswissenschaft*, of the natural sciences versus the humanities' (OCH 3.3). In the Gauss Seminars he speaks of 'the division, which then becomes more and more patent in the nineteenth and twentieth centuries, between the fields in which we demand truth and the fields in which we appear not to demand truth, if I may put it in this very bold fashion'. The former sort of enquiry is dedicated to the discovery of truths capable of being legitimised via replication. Employing a term from analytic philosophy, Berlin explains that in fields like 'mathematics, or physics, or even common sense to a large extent, or history for that matter, we really demand verification of some sort' (OCH 1.22).

It is striking that Berlin included history in his list; as we shall see, his mature work largely separated history from other fields—especially mathematics and experimental science—in which truth is capable of verification. But on some level Berlin thought it natural to include history in this list of the fields of 'descriptive knowledge'. He certainly considered the data of history empirically verifiable, and in this sense he never denied that its data can be organised scientifically; in

---

8. Peter Skagestad nicely demonstrates Berlin's sympathy for the Enlightenment's aims even as he criticised the way in which its monism engendered 'irrationalism' (2005, 111). For further discussion of Berlin's status as an heir of the legacy of the *philosophes*, see Wokler, IBCE, esp. 20–1.

fact, he claims, it is impossible for historians to 'dispense with empirical investigation' (AC 105). But historical research, Berlin would also insist, involves more than merely identifying facts; genuine historical consciousness requires in addition a capacity to synthesise such facts and then elicit conjectures and conclusions from them. It is in this sense that he suggests the methods of the natural sciences are insufficient for a working historian. Where the natural sciences seek to demonstrate the truth of facts, in history we 'demand tolerance, and we demand it to a large extent because, whatever the quality is that we are looking for, it is not quite truth in the sense in which we demand it in these other more positive fields. What it is to be called I do not know—acceptability, plausibility' (OCH 1.23). Here too we discover a positive link between Berlin's historical and political thought. The 'tolerance' that Berlin deems fundamental to historical understanding is the same virtue that his theory of value pluralism would posit as a prerequisite for cultural understanding.

   Given the necessity of tolerance for historical understanding, it is somewhat ironic that the Enlightenment's most visible champion of political and religious tolerance was the chief target of Berlin's critique in the Gauss Seminars. But, as Berlin would insist in an essay published in the following year, Voltaire's philosophy of history was better suited to monism—and hence fanaticism—than pluralism. Voltaire, he there explains, 'looks on history, in a loose fashion, as an accumulation of facts, casually connected, the purpose of which is to show men under what conditions those central purposes which nature has implanted in the heart of every man can best be realised: who are the enemies of progress, and how they are to be routed' (AC 92). With Gibbon and Hume, Voltaire is here identified as representative of the Enlightenment's characteristic efforts to employ the techniques of natural science to uncover the fundamental uniformity of the cosmological and ethical mechanisms that animate and thus direct the movements of both nature and human nature.[9] But Berlin rejects the proposition that history either can or should uncover nature; this belief, he claims,

> is one which eliminates the whole dimension of what might be called historical-mindedness, the whole genetic aspect of why human beings were as they were when they were, what their particular values were, what sort of attitudes they had, and why they had these attitudes, and how these attitudes affected their lives, or placed them in the frame of mind in which certain things appeared to them right or wrong, in which they lived the kind of lives they did or produced

9. Berlin's account of this aspect of the Enlightenment's understanding of history has not gone unchallenged. John Pocock, for example, in the context of a discussion of Berlin's account of the aftermath of the Enlightenment, points to Adam Smith's understanding of historical conditioning of humanity and its role in the evolution of cultural stages (1999, 131).

the kind of works of art they did. [...] To explore these questions is, I should have thought, one of the proper functions of historians, whether cultural historians, or other kinds. (OCH 1.10)

'Historical-mindedness' on Berlin's account requires an appreciation of the concerns of its subjects—an appreciation that cannot be achieved via a search for uniformity.

In making this claim in the Gauss Seminars, Berlin drew on and further expanded views he had first expressed in his two most comprehensive previous studies of history: 'Historical Inevitability' (1954) and 'The Concept of Scientific History' (1960). The latter of these directly treated the theme of the Gauss Seminars. There Berlin argues that 'scientific' history is founded on a false hope. Scientific historians, he claims, believe it possible to achieve an objective or neutral perspective on human events akin to that of the experimental researcher studying natural phenomena in the laboratory. Berlin, however, is sceptical that human beings can achieve such a perspective on human affairs. He claims that in the study of human affairs the 'total texture is what we begin and end with', and its 'web is too complex' to be studied objectively, for there is in fact 'no Archimedean point' where an observer might stand the better to survey our own doings; such detachment is impossible given the nature of both ourselves and our culture (CC 114; cf. 119, 123).[10] Berlin's claim, then, is that it is not detachment from but rather immersion in culture that historians need. Indeed the principal and frequently reiterated theme of the piece is that we must continually seek an internal perspective on the human objects of study, and reject the search for inexorable laws that remain outside culture.[11]

This distinction between the historical enquiry that focuses on the sensibili-

10. It would be a mistake to label Berlin a 'postmodernist' *tout court*; as Cracraft has noted, Berlin's emphasis on the place of judgement and responsibility in historical study render his conception a constructive resource in countering the ethical relativism characteristic of postmodernism (2002, 291). But, at the same time, Berlin's prominent emphasis here on the inescapable web of human knowledge, in conjunction with his critiques of scientific rationality and Enlightenment instrumentalism, clearly parallel the scepticism towards metanarratives characteristic of postmodernism (297, 300). To this one might also add Berlin's striking account of Vico's understanding of mathematics in the Gauss Seminars (see OCH 2.18). On Berlin's possible debts to postmodernism—especially on issues related to those touched on by commentators cited below (175 note 34)—see McKinney 1992; and Berlin's response (1992b).

11. This aspect of Berlin's historical practice has been described as 'strikingly similar' to that developed by Collingwood: namely the understanding of 'the historian's central task as the grasping of the historical agent's relatively alien concepts and categories through the historian's own concepts and categories'; see Skagestad 2005, 101–2.

ties of peoples and the historical enquiry dedicated to uncovering the 'laws' of historical change lies at the heart of 'Historical Inevitability'. Scientific history, we are told, focuses not on people, but on 'impersonal forces', in an effort to uncover the larger patterns that control historical change and thus the direction in which history inexorably moves (L 103; cf. CC 105–8). Here the legacy of Berlin's early engagement with Marx's political philosophy and philosophy of history is evident.[12] In the face of this challenge, Berlin advocates what has been called his 'deeply "personal" approach to the history of ideas' and to political and cultural history more generally.[13] In 'Historical Inevitability', this conflict between the 'personal' and the 'impersonal' can be seen in Berlin's efforts to counter the debilitating effects of historical determinism.[14] Determinism, Berlin insists, requires a direct response for two reasons. First, determinism precludes free will and a sense of moral responsibility on the part of the agent. Second, determinism denies a capacity for evaluation or judgement of the agent on the part of the historian.

This is perhaps the central idea that Berlin is concerned to develop: that determinism commits its holder to the belief that 'the notion of individual freedom is a delusion', and thus to seeking 'the elimination of the notion of individual responsibility' (L 131, 115; cf. 107, 110, 122, 136, 138). Again and again Berlin returns to the claim that historical determinism rests on such a trade of liberty for absolution; to believe in it is to 'transfer responsibility for what happens from the backs of individuals to the causal or teleological operation of institutions or cultures or psychical or physical factors' (L 118; cf. 128, 131, 160, 164; RT 43). Ultimately Berlin would insist that this flight from the responsibility necessary for liberty, encouraged by both the hubris of scientific history and the humility of a theological or teleological history, was not merely a failing of historical method, but also threatened to lead to more significant ethical and political failings (L 132).[15] And with this in mind we can see another important connection between Berlin's historical thought and the central themes of his political thought. The defence of individual liberty that Berlin famously developed in contemporary essays such as 'Two Concepts' lies at the heart of his critique of scientific history;

---

12. For the influence of his study of Marx on his historical thought, see especially JG 87-95; and Cracraft 2002, 287.

13. Cherniss 2006, xxxvi–xxxviii.

14. In his abstract of 'Historical Inevitability', Berlin himself would insist that the conflict between determinism and the responsibility that comes with free choice was at the heart of the piece: see POI 18–21. For helpful sympathetic treatments of Berlin's account of this conflict, see Geyl 1955, 240–1; Cracraft 2002, 289–90; JG 78–81; Galipeau 1994, 71–80; IBLP 51–6; and section 2.4 of Cherniss and Hardy 2005.

15. I treat these failings and their moral and political consequences at greater length in Hanley 2004: see esp. 329, 332–3.

the rejection of the unwillingness to embrace liberty and the responsibility its exercise entails is indeed the central theme uniting his otherwise separately developed accounts of positive liberty and historical determinism.

Contemporary readers of 'Historical Inevitability' tended to be sceptical of its account of the conflict between determinism and free will. In the piece Berlin himself asked whether 'any ordinary human being' or 'any practising historian' could 'begin to believe one word' of 'this strange tale' of determinism that he had just told, and the same question was asked by Berlin's critics, who actively wondered whether his critique, for all its polemical force, captured either the essence or the subtleties of its target (L 154).[16] Perhaps the most visible and scathing critique came from the historian E. H. Carr. Carr insisted that the entire debate between free will and determinism that Berlin constructed was itself a 'red herring'. In addition, Berlin 'pokes fun at people who believe in "vast impersonal forces" rather than individuals as the decisive factor in history', which Carr labelled 'the Bad King John theory of history', also insisting that 'The desire to postulate individual genius as the creative force in history is characteristic of the primitive stages of historical consciousness', and warning us that 'we should probably recognise that there is something childish, or at any rate childlike, about it'. But what Carr thought especially immature in Berlin's view was its moralising tendency. Carr recognised that Berlin thought determinism not only implies the rejection of the free will of historical actors, but also 'encourages historians to evade their supposed obligation [...] to pronounce moral condemnation on the Charlemagnes, Napoleons and Stalins of history'.[17]

But readers of Berlin will wonder whether this is a fair criticism. Berlin himself was hardly a moralist; in several places, including the Gauss Seminars, he took care to distance himself from the facile moralism Carr described. In 'Historical Inevitability', Berlin's own position is clear: historians, he claims, 'need not—

---

16. Erich Kahler charged Berlin with having treated the question of freedom and determinism 'a little bit too lightly' (1964, 204). Christopher Dawson's review emphasised that Berlin's 'arguments are overpowering and bewildering rather than convincing' (1957, 585; cf. 587). Ernest Nagel questioned the very incompatibility on which Berlin insisted, arguing that 'Belief in determinism is therefore not incompatible, either psychologically or logically, with the normal use of moral discourse or with the significant imputation of moral responsibility' (1960, 316). John Passmore insisted that Berlin 'makes our blood run cold by associating naturalism with a particularly primitive species of Laplacean determinism, in order to entice us into an anti-naturalistic doctrine of "free acts"' (1959, 100; cf. 102). Nathan Rotenstreich noted that Berlin's castigation of determinism as 'deflationary', even if true, hardly constitutes a disproof of it (1963, 385–7).

17. Carr 1961, 92, 39, 86; see also the useful account of Berlin's response to Carr, which I follow below, in Cherniss and Hardy 2005, section 2.4.

they are certainly not obliged to—moralise; but neither can they avoid the use of normal language with all its associations and "built in" moral categories' (L 163–4). To the degree that Berlin's approach to history can be said to have a 'moral' aspect it is certainly not prescriptive or normative; his claim is more modest. It is rather that the very practice of being a historian inevitably requires one to judge, and consequently any system that privileges value neutrality violates a deep and natural human propensity. To use a Humean distinction much admired by Berlin (see, e.g., PIRA 260–5), Carr's error lies in his confusion of 'ought' and 'is': in this case Berlin's ostensible prescription for what historians ought to do with his actual—and far more modest—description of what historians in fact do, and indeed cannot help but do. Historians, being human, simply cannot abstract themselves from the natural process of judging that is implicit in the human approach to the world. A positive approach to history must therefore seek to recover this natural form of human judgement, and in so doing resist both the abdication of judgement characteristic of scientific history, and the monistic judgement characteristic of Voltaire's history.

EMPATHETIC HISTORY

In the Gauss Seminars Berlin presents this positive approach as an alternative to Voltaire's. He locates its origins in the nineteenth rather than the eighteenth century, seeing it as a product of the romantic rather than the enlightened age. In terms of the cast of characters he assembles, it is a 'German' rather than a 'French' phenomenon, the progeny of Herder rather than Voltaire (OCH 1.15). It is also the approach to the study of history and culture to which Berlin himself subscribed; in describing its origins, Berlin clearly manifests his oft-noted propensity to identify himself with the objects of his study.[18] But what did both Herder and Berlin find so attractive in this approach? The answer lies in its thoroughgoing rejection of the scientific ambition to understand historical phenomena by forcing them into larger patterns of explanation. This construction of unitary wholes is precisely what Berlin means to avoid. Eric Auerbach described its opposite, and Berlin quotes a long passage from his *Mimesis* to illustrate the approach that he embraces:

> When people realise that epochs and societies are not to be judged in terms of a
> pattern concept of what is desirable absolutely, but rather in every case in terms
> of their own premises [...] when in other words they come to develop a sense of
> historical dynamics, of the incomparability of historical phenomena, so that each

---

18. See e.g. Cherniss 2006, xxxvi and note 2.

epoch appears as a whole, whose character is reflected in each of its manifestations; when finally they accept the conviction that the meaning of events cannot be grasped in abstract and general forms of cognition, and that the material needed to understand it must not be sought in the upper strata of society, and in major political events, but also in art, economy, material and intellectual culture, in the depths of the workaday world and its men and women, because it is only there that one can grasp what is unique, what is animated by inner forces, and what in a more concrete and more profound sense is universally valid [...][19]

Berlin's description of this as 'a perfectly good statement of what cultural history is about' illuminates several aspects of his own approach to the study of history. First it dramatically reveals his rejection of the search for patterns, characteristic of the Enlightenment's pursuit of a 'universal civilisation', which, it has been said, must necessarily culminate in 'the evanescence of particularism'.[20] In resisting this tendency, Berlin instead embraces what has been called his 'relentless pursuit of the particular'[21]—that is, his concerted emphasis in his philosophy of history and his own writings in the history of ideas on uncovering the discrete and the specific in their multiplicity instead of seeking to force discrete and specific data into intellectually satisfying, but reductionist, theoretical wholes. This propensity, which has been called 'anti-Procrusteanism', again shows his historical thought emerging directly from his political concerns.[22]

Berlin's move is then a shift of emphasis from patterns to particulars. But this shift itself raises two further questions. First, how are these discrete data themselves to be studied? And second, what are we to do with these data once they have been uncovered? The first of the two questions gave rise to Berlin's emphasis on the necessity of 'empathy' for genuine historical understanding, while the second question led him to emphasise the necessity of historical judgement. In the case of the first of these categories, 'empathy' enters into Berlin's story as an alternative to the objective approach of scientific historians. Where they sought to understand historical phenomena from a neutral vantage-point, Berlin emphasised that genuine understanding requires not distance from but rather closeness to a subject. Not neutrality's lack of feeling but rather the genuine fellow-feeling of empathy is what is required for true understanding. Berlin locates the origin of this position in the reaction of Hamann and his contemporaries to the character-

---

19. Auerbach 1968, 443–4, cited at OCH 1.12.

20. JG 87.

21. Cracraft 2002, 292–4. Berlin's understanding of the conflict of a sensitivity towards particulars with the scientific search for absolute laws is also nicely treated in Mazurek 1979, 394–5; and section 2.3 of Cherniss and Hardy 2005.

22. The term 'anti-Procrusteanism' is Jonathan Allen's (1998).

istic French Enlightenment claim 'that science replies to all our questions, and that the life of man can be illuminated by large scientific generalisations and not by some kind of direct inspection of the human character and human activities on the part of people who truly understand other human beings'. Their rejection of this proposition in favour of a focus on language as a means of understanding led them to suggest that

> the proper way of understanding life is to understand other human beings, and to understand other human beings you need the gift of some kind of artistic empathy, some kind of sympathetic insight into the emotional, intellectual and other movements of the human spirit, rather than the capacity for calm, rational analysis characteristic of the way in which physicists, mathematicians and chemists are wont to use their talents. (OCH 1.20)

Here Berlin drives his strongest wedge between the methods of enquiry appropriate to the natural sciences and those appropriate to the humane sciences. Neutrality is fatal to the ends of the latter enterprise, even though necessary for the former. Berlin expands on the nature of the unique gifts needed for each sort of enquirer in his glosses on Herder. To understand human phenomena—especially art and language—Herder claimed, 'what you needed were not the gifts which were needed by a genuine scientist, namely the capacity to generalise, the capacity to create abstract models for the purpose of comparing the jagged, uneven surface of life against these idealised models; not the capacity for generalising or for formulating hypotheses which could be verified or falsified in experience'. Instead one needed something very different:

> What you needed was not knowledge, above all, which is what the Enlightenment had praised—not knowledge of facts, but a quality called understanding. If you are reading a book, and wish to understand what it is the author is telling you, if you are looking at a picture, and wish to know what the painter is trying to convey to you, you do not need factual information. It may help, but that is not what you need above all. What you need is some capacity for entering into the purposes, the motives, the outlook which the painter, the writer, the architect, whoever it might be, is in some way, either consciously or unconsciously, attempting to convey; the picture of the world which he is trying to embalm in his work, immortalise, give some kind of concrete embodiment to; and the capacity for understanding which he is the first to elaborate. This famous *Einfühlung*, which he invented as a word[23]—the idea of empathy, the idea of insight, which is not an intellectual faculty at all, of course—is the faculty which we

---

23. Henry Hardy tells me that he has not found this word in Herder's works. The nearest equivalents he has encountered are *hineinfühlen* and *mitfühlen*. see Herder 1774, 503.

need for the purpose, at any rate, of understanding what might be called the emotional or the spiritual life of mankind. (OCH 1.21–2)[24]

Here Berlin makes clear precisely what he means by frequently referring to history as a humanistic discipline. History is not merely non-scientific; rather, history is a humane study in so far as it draws upon all of the resources of the human person, rational and emotional, to bring one closer to the totality of another human being. Berlin's source for this idea is Herder, who taught that 'man was one and not compartmentalised', and that to treat men as if they were divisible, as 'specialisation' or 'division of labour' are wont to do, is an act of 'self-falsification' or 'self-mutilation' or 'de-humanisation' (OCH 1.24). It was also Herder who taught Berlin that the limits of ratiocination as a means to genuine human understanding compel us to have recourse to empathy.[25] Yet it was another figurehead of the Enlightenment, Adam Smith, who perhaps best articulated the process that Berlin here describes. In his account of the operations of the imagination, Smith explains that when we, by sympathy, attempt to conceive the thoughts or feelings of another, 'by the imagination we place ourselves in his situation, we conceive ourselves enduring all the same torments, we enter as it were into his body, and become in some measure the same person with him, and thence form some idea of his sensations'.[26]

So too Berlin, who insists that the art of empathy consists in attempting to conceive of 'what we should have done if someone very unlike us had been there, into whose skin, in some mysterious way, we are able to enter' (OCH 3.14). Precisely this same capacity is required by historians who wish fully to understand the individuals and ideas they seek to describe. Hence his advice to the would-be historian of philosophy: 'To write a good illuminating history of philosophy you must try to see these problems from the "inside", so far as you can. You must try and enter imaginatively into the mental world of the philosophers you are discussing.'[27] But this advice applies not only to intellectual historians, for here too we find a crucial link

---

24. This passage parallels and synthesises several other passages in Berlin's published corpus: see for example AC 105-06; CC 133; CTH 58–60. I develop this account further in terms of its implications for political science and statesmanship in Hanley 2004, 335–6.

25. Skagestad notes that Berlin's emphasis on empathy goes beyond what Collingwood proposes, even as Berlin is identified as 'perhaps the most important successor' to his former teacher (2005, 105, 112).

26. Smith 1759, I. i. 1. 2, 9.

27. CIB 24; cf. 28: 'The history of ideas is the history of what we believe that people thought and felt, and these people were real people, not just statues or collections of attributes. Some effort to enter imaginatively into the minds and outlooks of the thinkers of the thoughts is indispensable, an effort at *Einfühlung* is unavoidable, however precarious and difficult and uncertain'; cf. CTH 69.

to Berlin's political thought. Berlin's cosmopolitanism, the very qualities of humane toleration across cultures that he strove to inculcate through value pluralism, was itself founded upon an 'empathy' that 'allows us to recognise unfamiliar values as genuine avenues for human flourishing'.[28] His own historical methods thus reaffirmed the central conclusions of his value pluralism, in that each emphasised the need to suspend one's own standards to appreciate those of the individual or culture under study.

Berlin has specific reasons for insisting that cultures and individuals should be judged internally. In the Gauss Seminars he presents these in his discussion of Vico. Vico, on Berlin's account, served as Europe's hope for countering Cartesianism. Cartesianism, as Berlin describes it, postulates that all true knowledge is subject to verification; seen from this perspective, the humanities seem like 'nothing but amusements, they are just a collection of old wives' tales' (OCH 2.15; cf. AC 85–6; CC 103). But herein lies what Berlin calls Vico's 'big move', namely his realisation of the essential difference between the subjects of scientific study and the subjects of human study, and it is this difference that makes a historian's imaginative empathy both possible and necessary. 'History', Vico is said to have claimed, 'is something which human beings make':

> I cannot attribute motives or purposes to things, largely because I do not think they have any. But even if they did have them I would not know what they were. But in the case of human beings I can do this, because I know what it is to have a motive, I know what it is to have a purpose, I know what it is to plan, I know what it is to strive for something, I know what it is to wish to create something. Therefore when I speak to other human beings or write about other human beings, I have what might be called an inside view. (OCH 2.20)

Herein lies the uniqueness of the humanities, as well as what Berlin calls 'the heart of Vico's doctrine': the belief that our understanding of human beings 'cannot be fitted into the normal categories of physical or biological interpretation and speculation', and the recognition that 'there is an inner knowledge which is to be differentiated, discriminated, from outer knowledge. There is something called human studies, or humane studies, which are to be discriminated from the natural sciences' (OCH 3.2–3; cf. 3.12).

---

28. See Zakaras 2004, 507. On the importance of the inside view in historical writing, see also Cracraft 2002, 295–6.

THE SENSE OF REALITY

Berlin's positive historical method as both a historian of philosophy and a cultural historian, then, is founded on the claim that the nature of the human subject requires an empathetic approach distinct from the 'data gathering' characteristic of the sciences. But a second question still awaits resolution: What is a historian to do with such information once assembled? Berlin has an explicit answer: The historian must synthesise his information into a larger framework. But here we should take care not to misstate Berlin's aim. We know already that Berlin is deeply suspicious of the search for wholes; how then is his move towards synthesis to be distinguished from the aspirations to pattern-creation that, in his estimation, vitiated determinism? Berlin's distinction lies in his claim that construction of narratives, or historical system-building, is a legitimate, and even necessary, enterprise, provided that it is founded on an empirical base—that is, provided that it is founded on the study of particular experience, and ascends only from there.

This ascent from discrete particulars to synthetic conclusions lies at the heart of Berlin's many invocations of the importance of 'judgement' for the historian. He gives an indication of what this judgement entails in his essay on scientific history. There he explains that what historians require is

> a capacity for integration, for perceiving qualitative similarities and differences, a sense of the unique fashion in which various factors combine in the particular concrete situation, which must at once be neither so unlike any other situation as to constitute a total break with the continuous flow of human experience, nor yet so stylised and uniform as to be the obvious creature of theory and not of flesh and blood. The capacities needed are rather those of association than of dissociation, of perceiving the relation of parts to wholes, of particular sounds or colours to the many possible tunes or pictures into which they might enter, of the links that connect individuals viewed and savoured as individuals, and not primarily as instances of types or laws. (CC 140)

Good historians, that is to say, are possessed of a certain skill at perceiving 'fittingness'; in this sense they are the direct opposite of the Procrustean who would fit the data to the pattern rather than the other way around. Vico and Herder, on Berlin's account, each cultivated this sense of 'a general feel for what belongs where, of the notion of belonging in general' (OCH 3.8; cf. 3.12). This 'general feel' is what Berlin would elsewhere describe at length as the 'sense of reality' (see e.g. RT 69; CC 128, 134).[29]

---

29. For a detailed account of the passage quoted above and the place of the sense of reality in both historical and political understanding, see Hanley 2004, 330–3.

Berlin's claim, then, is that the historian requires a certain sensibility. But can this sensibility be defined more rigorously? There is an elusive feel to what he calls 'this mysterious capacity of being able to enter into the imaginations of those early peoples' (OCH 3.13). Some of his commentators have taken this imprecision, characteristic of his claims about historical gifts, as one of the 'obscurities'[30] he admits to in his approach to history. In particular, his reference to the 'gift' of 'genius'[31] at the heart of this mysterious capacity has been criticised on two grounds. First, it violates, on some level, Berlin's otherwise faithful adherence to his claim that common sense is the necessary departure-point for historical enquiry: how, one wonders, is Berlin to reconcile his attachment to common sense with his invocations of elusive genius? Secondly, it has struck some as élitist—and hence inconsistent with his commitment to value pluralism—for him to call for historical judgement: is Berlin, it has been wondered, arguing for 'a world of historians playing the role of philosopher-kings'?[32]

Given Berlin's manifest antipathy to Plato's philosopher-king as the arch-monist, this latter criticism may seem incongruous. But it does point to an important question about Berlin's consistency. As we have seen, he is committed to the claim that it is possible for human beings of one culture or age to empathise with those of another age or culture. Empathy, he suggests, depends on the possibility of those of one culture or age 'entering into' the values of another: there must exist some sort of commonality that makes empathy feasible. At the same time, he repeatedly insists on 'the incommensurability of the values of different cultures'. This, indeed, may have been the principal lesson that Berlin took from his study of Herder: namely that, in the comparative study of cultures, 'to ask for any kind of general standards of value between them, for any kind of criterion in terms of which their excellences can be compared, becomes intrinsically and logically absurd. [...] [Herder] flatly lays down the proposition that the happiness of one people cannot be compared with the happiness of another; that there is no way of comparing the excellence of one culture with the excellence of the other' (OCH 2.4–5). A culture can thus be judged only 'in its own internal terms', not by criteria developed from cultures foreign to it (OCH 2.6).[33] But if indeed, as Berlin

---

30. L 3, 4 note 1, 54.

31. CC 109; L 144 note 1.

32. These are the two central objections developed in Mazurek 1979, 398–400, 403 (for élitism see 399, 403; for the quotation, 400); for his references to Berlin's 'obscurities' see 393, 396.

33. And here it should be noted that both Berlin's Zionism and his 'anti-Procrusteanism'—two explicitly political positions—are themselves directly presented in the course of his review of Herder on cultural history; see especially his comments on 'natural kinship or affinity' and 'assimilation' (OCH 2.8–11).

himself says elsewhere, 'the possibility of human understanding' rests on some commensurability (POI 12), one is led to wonder how he can support empathy and incommensurability simultaneously.

This tension might be put somewhat differently. As several commentators have noted, Berlin is a consistent critic of the teleological understanding of human nature, and rejects faith in a discoverable, universal human nature and the role of natural law therein, a faith characteristic, on Berlin's account, of both the Enlightenment and the classical and medieval understandings of human nature that the Enlightenment sought to repudiate. Yet in his pleas for a cosmopolitan, humane politics, Berlin depends on the positive existence of what has been called a 'common human nature' or 'universal moral minimum' that leads us to assert definite boundaries to human action.[34] This tension is perhaps clearest in his essay 'My Intellectual Path', in which Berlin seeks to reconcile his attachments to pluralism and a shared human nature by making the claim that, despite the existence of a plurality of human values, there is yet not 'an infinity of them: the number of human values, of values which I can pursue while maintaining my human semblance, my human character, is finite—let us say 74, or perhaps 122, or 26, but finite, whatever it may be' (POI 12). But whether this position—which one is tempted to call his 'natural law postmodernism'—is sustainable requires further consideration.[35]

BERLIN NOW

Berlin, we can conclude, advocated a warmer, deeper and more empathetic approach to the study of history than that adopted by those of his contemporaries with a more deterministic or scientific bent. But what implications, if any, does Berlin's critique have for contemporary historians, and particularly for contemporary historians of ideas?

---

34. These terms are taken from Franco 2003, 496–8. Similar charges are made in Mazurek's accusation that Berlin depends on an ' "unchanging pattern" of human universals' (1979, 402); and in Cherniss's identification of a 'major tension' in Berlin's thought as 'the idea that there are indeed inherent and unalterable truths about human nature as well as individual selves' (2006, xliv); cf. Zakaras 2004, 497, 500, 514; Galipeau 1994, 64; and Frisch 1998, esp. 423–4.

35. Though such a synthesis may be less radical than it might at first appear. Berlin's own account of the political thought of Montesquieu emphasises his simultaneous embrace of the ideals of a universal human nature and a plurality of cultural ends: see AC 142. A helpful recent examination of this problem in Berlin's thought and an attempt to solve it in a manner faithful to his original understanding of liberalism is offered in George Crowder's IBLP, esp. 132–6 and 148–70.

On one level, Berlin's influence has been limited. He has on occasion been identified as working within a distinctive British school, namely the Oxford 'political theory' school, along with John Plamenatz.[36] Yet in the Anglo-American world this has hardly been the dominant school of interpretation over the past several decades. The study of the history of ideas—and in particular the study of the history of political thought and the study of the history of political philosophy—has rather been largely driven by scholars working in methodological traditions broadly defined by Leo Strauss and by Quentin Skinner; few contemporary historians of political ideas would point to Berlin as a primary influence before these two figures. Unlike Berlin, Strauss and Skinner defined specific ways of reading historical texts and developed sophisticated methodologies to further such studies.[37] Where then does Berlin fit into this contemporary landscape?

My suggestion is that Berlin cannot serve as the figurehead of an alternative school, but that he nevertheless has much to contribute to those already working within the broad traditions mentioned above. For the chief value of Berlin's approach to the history of political philosophy lies in his consistent claim that such study ought to be governed by a concern for what is both philosophically and also politically most important.[38] The latter point was particularly emphasised by Berlin. Hence his critique of certain approaches:

> Some histories of philosophy throw little light on it because, unless the writer is or has been a student of philosophy himself, unless he has thought about philosophical problems as such, he cannot have any idea of what it is that made someone else think these thoughts or be tormented by these problems. He cannot truly grasp what questions philosophers have attempted to answer or analyse or discuss. He will simply transcribe—he will write that Descartes said this, Spinoza said that, but that Hume did not think that either was right. That is all quite dead. Unless you have yourself spent sleepless nights about philosophical problems, you cannot possibly tell that there exists such a subject.

Berlin continues by making clear the place of empathy in the study of the history of ideas. Historians of philosophy, no less than other types of historians, need to see subjects 'from the "inside"': 'You must try to enter into what the ideas meant to those who entertained them, what were the kinds of things that were central to

---

36. See Kelly 1999, 48, 51–2.

37. The general approaches of these two authors are well known; readers seeking further illumination are referred to their own accounts. Skinner's influential methodological essays have been republished as Skinner 2002b; for Strauss, see especially Strauss 1952.

38. The following section further develops claims introduced in the conclusion to Hanley 2004, 336–8.

them. Without that there can be no true history of ideas.' So far from insisting that historians should be objective, Berlin considers it an asset—even a prerequisite—that the historian of philosophy be actively engaged in the problems posed by the thinkers under study. Indeed, 'unless you are yourself involved in such topics and are puzzled by such problems, you cannot write a significant history of the similar preoccupations of others'.[39]

Now, to say this is to take a specific view of the study of the relationship of ideas to contexts, perhaps the principal source of the methodological disagreement between the two schools above mentioned. In particular, to say this is to counter the historicist claim that the past is to be understood only on its own terms. Berlin is of course partly sympathetic to this view, as his critique of Voltaire's universal standards reveals. But at the same time he repeatedly notes his aversion to a thoroughgoing historicism or contextualism:

> Philosophy is not a cumulative discipline. The major ideas, outlooks, theories, insights, have remained the central ideas of philosophy. They have a certain life of their own which is trans-historical. Some people disagree. They say you can only understand questions and ideas in terms of the historical environment in which they occur. How can you understand Machiavelli without accurate knowledge of events in Florence, life in Italy, in the fifteenth century? How can you understand Spinoza if you know nothing about Holland or France in the seventeenth?[40]

Berlin is quick to grant that 'there is some truth in that'—'but only some'. The fact remains that, while contextual knowledge can help illuminate the project or problems of a given thinker, it cannot by itself explain why his ideas remain relevant or why they might be worthy of our study or attention; only the substance of those ideas can tell us that. Berlin observes that, while we know comparatively little today about the conditions of life in ancient Athens, it yet remains the case that

> Plato's ideas mean something, indeed, a great deal to us today, even without the environmental knowledge that ideally is needed to understand what Greek words mean. Central ideas, the great ideas which have occupied minds in the Western world, have a certain life of their own—we may not understand precisely what they meant to Athenians, we may not know how Greek or Latin were pronounced, we may not understand inflexions, nuances, references, allusions—

---

39. CIB 23–4; cf. 28; and the letter from Berlin to Morton White quoted in White 1999, 252. This would seem to require Berlin to accept that empathetic position-changing is possible; but cf. Skagestad's identification of Berlin's occasional hesitation on this front (2005, 104).

40. CIB 25–6. See also IBLP 191–5.

but major ideas survive in some sense despite the ignorance of the material aspects or historical details of the world in which they were born and exercised influence.[41]

Language alone is not a sufficient barrier to prevent us genuinely entering into the conditions and contexts of intellectual worlds dissimilar to our own (see L 148–9). More important than sensitivity to historical context is sensitivity to or appreciation of the great, perennial ideas, the ideas that transcend an individual culture.

In this respect, Berlin's dichotomy between Voltaire and Vico in the Gauss Seminars and elsewhere (see AC 88–9) breaks down when applied to Berlin himself. For while it may be tempting to identify Berlin as 'pro-Vichian' and 'anti-Voltairian', his reservations about historicism led him to distance himself from Vico and to embrace or incorporate certain aspects of Voltaire's approach to history. First and foremost, Berlin admires Voltaire's biographical portraits, which reveal him to have been 'one of the gayest, most delightful and most fascinating storytellers, I think, whom humanity has ever known' (OCH 1.7). Berlin might well have been describing himself, as his own most successful writings were often biographical studies of individual characters, many of which were collected in *Personal Impressions*. But Berlin also adopts another aspect of Voltaire's historical practice. As we have seen, he criticises Voltaire for bringing all of history before the bar of utility; but he also wished to emulate Voltaire's sense of historical judgement as a means of sorting historical data. Hence the complexity of his critique of Voltaire's single-minded concern for utility: 'All the rest is of not the slightest importance, and he says: Why should we spend pages and pages on telling the stories of how one barbarian despot followed another barbarian despot? Why should we want to know whether Quancum succeeded Kincum, or whether Kicum succeeded Quancum?' (OCH 1.6; cf. AC 90; CTH 51–3).

But this is one of Berlin's own most hallowed positions. Repeatedly in his work, in his own name, Berlin insists on a rejection of the value-neutrality which might otherwise compel one to examine everything indiscriminately. Some form of choice and value judgement is inescapable, even in the very selection of which materials we will focus on. Hence that 'minimum residue of value judgement which no amount of conscious self-discipline and self-effacement can wholly eliminate, which colours and is part of our very choice of historical material, of our emphasis, however tentative, upon some events and persons as being more important or interesting or unusual than others' (L 119). What is needed, Berlin here and elsewhere insists, is a talent for separating the wheat from the chaff, the talent of the artful eye capable of determining what is politically relevant and

---

41. CIB 26.

hence worth our time, and what is not. Like Voltaire's, Berlin's history of ideas is always governed by a concern for what is most useful to us today.[42]

This brings us to Berlin's ultimate claim about the choice of subject matter: not only should the history of philosophy emphasise what is philosophically important, but it should also be governed by a concern for what is most politically relevant. In this respect Berlin might be thought to have been outmanoeuvred by the other schools of interpretation; it is unlikely that we can discover for Berlin an analogue of the Cambridge school's application of their distinctive study of early modern republicanism to the study of modern Europe, or of the well-received though largely unfounded claim that 'Straussianism' explains American foreign policy in the Middle East.[43] Berlin's political engagement is somewhat different from this more direct sort of involvement. To explain what it is, it might be helpful to turn again to what Berlin shares with Voltaire, even as he criticises him in the Gauss Seminars:

> Voltaire's notion of culture is this: there is a perfectly clear criterion for what is good and what is bad. That is what I mean by saying that to all true questions there is one correct answer, if you have the criterion for obtaining it. If you ask what is worthy of existing and what is not, what kind of life is worth living and what kind of life is not, what is beautiful and what is ugly, what is good and what is bad, what is noble and what is ignoble, any intelligent person living at the beginning of the eighteenth century is armed with weapons which can establish this with complete dogmatic certainty. (OCH 1.8)

It is important to define the target of Berlin's objection with precision. What he finds objectionable are not the questions themselves. Indeed, among the most distinctive features of Berlin's career was his engagement with what is beautiful and what kind of life is worth living. What he rejects is Voltaire's characteristic 'dogmatic certainty' that any one answer to such questions could be 'perfectly clear'. Historians of philosophy must be philosophers in a genuine sense: open to persuasion, characteristically diffident and sceptical, even in their pursuit of answers to the questions that matter most.

It is often noted that historical accuracy was not the chief virtue of Berlin's own writings.[44] Yet his keen sensitivity to what matters most perhaps redeems

---

42. Thus Cherniss notes that Berlin 'sought to make past ideas speak to present problems' (2006, xxiii), which parallels Pears's observation that Berlin's 'concentration on a finely formulated problem would always be informed by his awareness of its place in some larger system of ideas and ultimately of its place, if it had one, in human life': IBAC 32.

43. See the essays collected in Gelderen and Skinner 2002; and the reliable explanations of Strauss's intentions and influence contained in Zuckert and Zuckert 2006 and Smith 2006.

44. See, e.g., Cherniss 2006, xxxiv.

them, at least in part. Indeed perhaps even the loudest detractor might properly say of Berlin's work in the history of ideas what he himself said of Vico's historical writings: 'The historical details may be wrong, even absurd, the knowledge may be defective, the critical methods insufficient—but the approach is bold, original and fruitful' (CTH 61–2).

8

Crooked Timber or Bent Twig?

BERLIN'S NATIONALISM

DAVID MILLER

There is a puzzle in understanding Isaiah Berlin's attitude to nationalism that no one (to my knowledge) has yet been able to resolve. The nature of the puzzle can be indicated in various ways. Berlin, as is widely known, was a stout defender of negative liberty—the idea that 'there ought to exist a certain minimum area of personal freedom which must on no account be violated' (L 171)—and in that capacity he criticised those, including many nationalists, who interpreted liberty to mean the collective self-determination of the group as opposed to the absence of constraints on its individual members. Yet throughout his life he was a Zionist,[1] and this commitment to the national liberation of the Jews was not an idiosyncrasy, but extended to other nations struggling to free themselves from colonial or imperial rule. So how, if at all, did Berlin's liberalism and his apparent nationalism cohere?[2]

Another way into the puzzle is through spelling out the two arboreal metaphors of Berlin's that I have used in the title of this essay. 'The Crooked

---

1. MI 79–80, 106–8, 179, 181–4, 292–3; CIB 85.

2. Both JG and Galipeau 1994 have chapters on Berlin's nationalism, but in neither case is this aspect of his thought critically probed in the way that I shall attempt here. A much less sympathetic treatment of Berlin, and of liberal nationalism generally, can be found in Cocks 2002, chapters 3–4. Cocks's critique, however, misrepresents Berlin's position in several respects: see Miller 2004.

Timber of Humanity' is the phrase used by Berlin to signal both the imperfection and the cultural diversity of the human species, and the resulting moral impossibility of laying down any single set of rules, any common framework of government, to encompass the very different ways human beings have chosen to live their lives together.[3] As he says when expounding his favourite philosopher, Herder:

> [...] there is a plurality of incommensurable cultures. To belong to a given community, to be connected with its members by indissoluble and impalpable ties of common language, historical memory, habit, tradition and feeling, is a basic human need no less natural than that for food or drink or security or procreation. One nation can understand and sympathise with the institutions of another only because it knows how much its own mean to itself. Cosmopolitanism is the shedding of all that makes one most human, most oneself. (AC 12)

This, then, seems to indicate strong endorsement of the idea that not only individuals but also nations must be allowed to live in their own way and under their own institutions. But when he speaks of nationalism, Berlin often switches to the metaphor of the Bent Twig, attributed by him to Schiller:[4] nationalist movements, he suggests, must be understood as responses to wounds that are inflicted on peoples, which lead them to lash out blindly against their oppressors, like a twig that springs back and whips the face of the person who has touched it (CTH 251; Gardels 1991, 19; Magee 1992, 4). Notice how the metaphor works: the twig is deformed by an unnatural outside force, then when released it strikes uncontrollably against the source of the deformity. In this image nationalism is not only identified with its destructive consequences—insurrection, bloodshed and the like—but would not exist at all in a world where no people inflicted psychic wounds on another. If the Crooked Timber metaphor presents nationalism as a natural expression of human diversity, the Bent Twig metaphor presents it as a blind, irrational response to collective humiliation.

Matters are not made any easier if we look at Berlin's various accounts of what nationalism *is*. Here are some examples:

---

3. The phrase comes from Kant 1784, 23, line 22—and Berlin's preferred rendering of the relevant quotation is 'Out of the crooked timber of humanity no straight thing was ever made.' It is used in many of his essays: see L 92, 216, 238; AC 148, 353; CTH 19, 48; SR 192; POI 181. Cf. L1 72.

4. The attribution is unconfirmed: see Henry Hardy's note at RR 161. Joshua Cherniss has suggested that Berlin's source was actually Plekhanov 1896, vii: see <http://berlin.wolf.ox.ac.uk/ information/a-z.html#twig> (accessed 9 May 2006).

Nationalism is an inflamed condition of national consciousness which can be, and on occasion has been, tolerant and peaceful. (CTH 245)

Nationalism is not consciousness of the reality of national character, nor pride in it. It is a belief in the unique mission of a nation, as being intrinsically superior to the goals or attributes of whatever is outside it [...]. (CTH 176–7)

Nationalism, even in its mildest version, the consciousness of national unity, is surely rooted in a sharp sense of the differences between one human society and another, the uniqueness of particular traditions, languages, customs—of occupation, over a long period, of a particular piece of soil on which intense collective feeling is concentrated. (SR 232)

Nationalism simply means that we say to ourselves that nobody is as good as we are, that we have a right to do certain things solely because we are Germans or Frenchmen. (CIB 102)

Nationalism—the elevation of the interests of the unity and self-determination of the nation to the status of the supreme value before which all other considerations must, if need be, yield [...]. (AC 338)

Each of these accounts of nationalism is significantly different from the others. One might be tempted to conclude that Berlin was simply a loose and sloppy thinker capable of defining 'nationalism' in whatever way suited the polemical purpose of the argument he was making at the time. But this, I think, underestimates him. This after all was a man who had spent hours in the company of precise philosophers like Ayer and Austin, presumably wrestling over the details of what exactly it is that we mean when we say ... and who was perfectly capable of drawing careful distinctions between ideas that others had confused. That he failed, repeatedly, to give a clear and consistent definition of nationalism indicates more than mere sloppiness—it indicates, I believe, that there were deep internal tensions in Berlin's thought in this area that he never satisfactorily resolved. I shall try to unearth these tensions as I proceed. But first let me consider two 'quick-fix' solutions to the inconsistencies between the accounts of nationalism listed above.

The first is to say that two quite different things are going on in the accounts I have presented. On the one hand, Berlin is indicating what it means to be a nationalist—looking at nationalisms from the inside, and showing us what is distinctive about what nationalists believe. On the other hand, he is explaining the source of nationalism—indicating the conditions under which nationalist ideologies arise. Clearly these two enterprises are complementary rather than competing, and when Berlin says, for instance, that nationalism is a condition of wounded consciousness, he is engaged in the second, explanatory, task, whereas when he says that nationalism is a belief in the uniqueness and superiority of the national mission, he is engaged in the first.

This solution won't do, however, because on both fronts Berlin turns out to be inconsistent: he tells us different stories about what it means to be a nationalist, as I shall illustrate later, and he also gives different accounts of how nationalism arises; as the set of quotations above illustrates, he is capable of seeing it as an 'inflamed' condition of consciousness that arises only in certain quite specific circumstances, but he is also capable of seeing it as a natural response to human diversity that can be expected to prevail so long as human societies retain their distinctive languages, customs, cultures and so forth.

A second quick-fix solution is to say that (although he does not make this very explicit) Berlin is always in practice working with a distinction between 'benign' and 'malign' forms of nationalism, a distinction that runs roughly parallel to the more familiar distinctions between 'Western' and 'Eastern' or 'civic' and 'ethnic' nationalism.[5] This is sometimes indicated by a contrast he draws between nationalism proper and 'the consciousness of national unity', the latter being the benign version, as in the third quotation above. Now it's clear that Berlin does discriminate quite sharply between different versions of nationalism—indeed one of his later interviews was entitled 'Two Concepts of Nationalism' in recognition of this fact. But what is much less clear is how the line is to be drawn—by virtue of what features a particular form of nationalism falls on one or other side of it. Are malign forms of nationalism essentially *political* and benign forms essentially *cultural*, for instance, as some of Berlin's remarks about Herder might suggest? We shall see that in place of a simple two-way distinction Berlin draws different contrasts between nationalisms on different occasions.

Finally, why does it matter to try to dispel the clouds of confusion surrounding Berlin's writings on nationalism? It matters, I believe, because Berlin has some claim to be considered the founding father of contemporary liberal nationalism, that strand of liberal thought that tries to reconcile liberal freedoms with the value of national belonging and national self-determination.[6] Many have thought that 'liberal nationalism' is an oxymoron, an attempt to combine incompatible

---

5. The first distinction was drawn in Kohn 1944, chapter 8, and in Plamenatz 1973, 22–36. For a more elaborate geographical classification of nationalisms, see Gellner 1997, chapter 7. The second distinction has been drawn in Smith 1991, 8–14, and in Ignatieff 1993, 3–6.

6. The term 'liberal nationalism' was first self-applied in Tamir 1993, but it has been extended to include a number of other theorists, including Neil MacCormick (1982), Avishai Margalit and Joseph Raz (1995), Will Kymlicka (2001) and David Miller (1995).

political values (Vincent 1997; Benner 1997; Brighouse 1998; Cocks 2002, chapter 4). If Berlin's views turn out to be internally inconsistent at the deepest level, this may cast more general doubt on the idea of liberal nationalism. So there is more at stake here than just the analysis of one man's writings on nationalism. Having conducted that analysis, I shall come back in the last section of the paper to compare Berlin's ideas with those of later exponents of liberal nationalism.

WHAT DO NATIONALISTS BELIEVE?

The best place to begin an analysis is perhaps with Berlin's most systematic account of nationalist doctrine, found in his essay 'Nationalism: Past Neglect and Present Power', in which he identifies four features of that doctrine (AC 341–5). The first of these is 'the belief in the overriding need to belong to a nation'. This is the view that human beings are profoundly influenced by the particular cultural group they are born into, which gives them not only their language, but also their beliefs, customs, social practices and so forth, with the implication (presumably) that if the nation is destroyed, or an individual member is torn away from it, this is a very significant loss. The second feature is a belief 'in the organic relationships of all the elements that constitute a nation'. This organic conception of the nation entails that membership is not to be conceived on the model of a voluntary association, and also that relationships of other kinds must be subordinated to the demands of nationhood. The nation, in other words, has an overriding claim on its members' loyalty. The third feature is a belief 'in the value of our own simply because it is ours'. Nationalists, Berlin claims, subscribe to a form of moral relativism which refuses to recognise universal values, holding instead that we have no reasons for action beyond the principles and values of the particular national culture to which we belong. Finally, the fourth feature is the belief in the supremacy of national claims: nothing must be allowed to stand in the way of a nation fulfilling its mission, even if this brings it into conflict with other nations.

Notice first that this four-part definition identifies nationalism as a set of beliefs, a doctrine, indeed a doctrine of a fairly abstract and philosophical kind. In giving it, Berlin has in mind, as the text reveals, nationalist ideas as expounded by late eighteenth- and early nineteenth-century European philosophers—Herder, Burke, Fichte, Michelet, Hamann, Hegel, Maistre and Bonald are among the thinkers mentioned. Would Berlin, if challenged, have maintained that holding these four beliefs is a necessary condition for being a nationalist? Almost certainly not: we have seen already that he recognises a sense of nationalism in which it is equivalent to 'the consciousness of national unity'—the consciousness of belonging to a distinct people with whom one has special ties of culture and history—and he freely admits that nationalism in this sense is a far more pervasive phenomenon. And even if we add to this a political claim about the need to maintain and protect such special ties, this does not appear to commit us to any of the four beliefs that Berlin presents as constituting nationalism. So 'nationalism' as presented in this essay seems really to mean 'romantic nationalism in post-Enlightenment European philosophy', not nationalism in a broader sociological sense.

Notice second that even if we take Berlin's account on its own terms as an account of nationalist philosophical *doctrine*, the four elements do not stand or fall together in the way that he implicitly suggests. Not only that, but in the case of each element we can distinguish two alternative positions that someone might take, without in any obvious sense ceasing to be a nationalist. So we have sixteen possible 'varieties of nationalism', none of which can so far be ruled out as theoretically incoherent. Let me illustrate.

If we take the first element, the belief in the overriding need to belong to a nation, then while nationalists certainly agree about the significance to individual people of their membership in national communities, they disagree about whether this has direct political implications—especially about whether it entails a right of national self-determination in the political sense. So we might distinguish *cultural* forms of nationalism from *political* forms on this basis, as indeed Berlin himself does when he says of Herder that:

> [his] nationalism was never political. If he denounces individualism, he equally detests the State, which coerces and mutilates the free human personality. [...] Even though he seems to have coined the word *Nationalismus*, his conception of a good society is closer to the anarchism of Thoreau or Proudhon or Kropotkin, and to the conception of a culture (*Bildung*) of which such liberals as Goethe and Humboldt were proponents, than to the ideals of Fichte or Hegel or political socialists. For him *die Nation* is not a political entity. (TCE 205–6)

In other words, the idea that human beings are deeply shaped by the particular culture of their nation can be interpreted in such a way that it implies that each nation should have a State of its own—the political version of nationalism—or alternatively as implying simply the right of each culture to develop autonomously—the cultural version.

Consider next the organic metaphor—the idea that nations are not merely aggregates of individuals but organic wholes in which each part is dependent upon the rest. Berlin takes it to follow from this that national values must be supreme—that the claims of lesser groupings, families, provinces, Churches, and so forth, must always give way to the demands of the nation itself, which means that in one important sense nationalism must be illiberal: it must limit the freedom of individuals to form groups that might compete for supremacy with the nation as a whole. But does it follow? Nationalists must reject atomic individualism, let us agree, but they do not need to attribute to the nation itself the kind of supremacy over smaller groupings that Berlin supposes. Instead they can regard national communities as constituted, in part, by smaller communities of various kinds, so that preserving the 'social organism' (if that metaphor is used) involves sustaining a balance between the whole and the parts. Burke, for example, did precisely this when he attacked the centralising tendencies of the French Revolution as entailing that:

> [...] the people should no longer be Gascons, Picards, Bretons, Normans, but Frenchmen, with one country, one heart, and one assembly. But instead of being all Frenchmen, the greater likelihood is, that the inhabitants of that region will shortly have no country. [...] Such divisions of our country as have been formed by habit, and not by a sudden jerk of authority, were so many little images of the great country in which the heart found something which it could fill. The love to the whole is not extinguished by this subordinate partiality. (1790, 244)

The organic metaphor, then, is ambiguous between what we might call *unitary* and *pluralist* versions of nationalism, the former being for obvious reasons more illiberal in its implications than the latter.

The third element in Berlin's account of nationalist doctrine is the claim that national values are supreme—that there is no higher source of moral authority from which universal principles might be derived, setting limits to what might be done in the name of the nation. Once again, it is important to distinguish what is common ground among nationalists from what is held by only certain among them. All nationalists recognise that nations are ethical communities, in the sense that membership brings with it special obligations, the content of which varies somewhat from one nation to the next. But they disagree about whether these special obligations exhaust the ethical universe, so to speak, or whether there are not also universal obligations that a person has simply by virtue of being human. Thus many nationalists have subscribed to some version of natural law or natural rights, interpreted perhaps more narrowly than anti-nationalists would like, but nevertheless setting limits to the values that nations can legitimately pursue. This is true of both Rousseau and Burke, for example, and more recently of thinkers such as Michael Walzer, whose 'thick' local (effectively national) account of morality is complemented by a 'thin' moral minimalism that is universal in scope—'a set of standards to which all societies can be held—negative injunctions, most likely, rules against murder, deceit, torture, oppression, and tyranny' (1994, 10). So we can draw a contrast between *morally unrestricted* and *morally restricted* forms of nationalism.

Finally we come to Berlin's fourth element, the belief in national *supremacy*, which, as he points out, may or may not be accompanied by a belief in national *superiority*—though sometimes he combines the two ideas, as a glance at the five accounts of nationalism above (183) will reveal. National supremacy is the idea that the nation has a mission or a destiny which nothing must be allowed to impede, justifying not only the suppression of internal divisions, but also the sweeping aside of groups and people outside, through territorial conquest, for example. When national superiority is invoked, supremacy is justified by the claim that those who are suppressed or pushed aside are culturally inferior. So are nationalists by definition committed to such an idea? Here again we need to draw a distinction, this time between nationalists whose sole object of concern is the flourishing of their own nation, and nationalists who, while inevitably giving greater *weight* from a practical point of view to the interests of their own people, are also concerned to promote the well-being and autonomy of nations every-where. Mazzini embodied this second position, defending the rights of Italians first, but also the rights of all the other European peoples who lacked self-determination.[7] More recently Walzer (1990) has introduced the concept of 'reiterative universalism' to capture the idea that in claiming a right to political autonomy for our own nation, we must recognise a parallel right in others: whatever justifies our claim must also justify theirs. The relevant distinction in this case is between nationalisms that are *singular* and nationalisms that are *reiterative*, in that they attach ethical weight to the claims of all peoples who are recognised as forming potentially self-determining nations.

We have, then, four possible dimensions along which nationalist philosophies or ideologies might vary. Berlin, in presenting his account of romantic nationalism, takes it for granted that nationalism must be political, unitary, morally unrestricted and singular, whereas it is not difficult to see how other combinations are possible. For instance, someone might hold a political and unitary view of nationalism, and yet concede that national self-determination was subject to moral limits, and that other nations had rights to political autonomy equivalent to those of one's own. Again, one might be a cultural nationalist and either believe or not believe that one had duties to protect cultures other than one's own, and so on. I don't suggest that every box in the matrix can plausibly be filled—for instance it would be hard to hold a reiterative view on the issue of national supremacy without also placing moral restrictions on the exercise of national autonomy—but many of them can, and Berlin's account in this essay conceals that fact. The effect is to make nationalism appear irredeemably hostile to liberal values, which is not, as we shall see, Berlin's considered view.

---

7. 'I am an Italian, but at the same time I am a European. I love my country because I love the concept of country. I believe in freedom for Italians because I believe in the concept of freedom. I want rights for Italians, because I believe in rights for all', he wrote. Mazzini 1861, 178, trans. 99.

I mentioned earlier that Berlin often seems to work implicitly with a contrast between benign and malign forms of nationalism, and in the light of 'Nationalism: Past Neglect and Present Power' we might be tempted to think that he sees 'good' nationalism as cultural, plural, morally restricted and reiterative, and 'bad' nationalism as political, unitary, morally unrestricted and singular. But this is not so; instead he draws different contrasts on different occasions, highlighting sometimes one and sometimes another of the elements we have separated. In his later interviews, for instance, he counterposes 'aggressive' nationalism to 'non-aggressive' or what he sometimes calls 'sated' nationalism—the latter referring to the form of nationalism prevailing in long-established territorial States like Britain that no longer have expansionist aims (Magee 1972, 2–4, 13–14, 22; 1992, 3–5; Gardels 1991, 19–20). This contrast evidently picks up the fourth element in our analysis above: the issue is whether nationalism licenses acts of aggression against other States or peoples. Elsewhere, the line is drawn between cultural and political nationalism—when praising Herder, for instance (POI 8–9), but also on other occasions, as when asked 'What political structure can possibly accommodate this new age of cultural self-determination?', he replies 'Cultural self-determination without a political framework is precisely the issue now' (Gardels 1991, 21). This is not Berlin's final word on the subject, as I shall show later, but it does indicate an inclination on his part to depoliticise nationality—to hope for a world in which rich cultural variety is not accompanied by deep political divisions. From this perspective, 'bad' nationalism arises when culture and politics become intertwined.

Given his general philosophical outlook, one might have expected that Berlin would have preferred pluralist to unitary forms of nationalism, but interestingly enough, in those few places in which he touches upon the issue, he displays little sympathy for what we would now call multiculturalism. Nations matter to Berlin as inclusive forms of community. 'I believe', he says, 'that the common culture that all societies deeply need can only be disrupted by more than a moderate degree of self-assertion on the part of ethnic or other minorities conscious of a common identity' (Gardels 1991, 21).[8] And when discussing the possibilities open to Jews living in societies in which they form a small minority—a question, as we shall see shortly, that preoccupied Berlin—he forcefully rejected 'galut' (that is to say, Diaspora) nationalism, 'based on the notion of modern nations as a motley amalgam of highly diverse and quasi-autonomous communities, in which Yiddish-speaking Jewish groups, living lives full of picturesque native colour, with folk-song and ancient crafts, and quaint traditional customs, would form a rich, if exotic, ingredient'. Such notions he calls 'sorry absurdities' (POI 180). What this reveals is that Berlin's celebrated pluralism is a pluralism about moral ideals,

---

8. See also his comments on multiculturalism in Berlin 1992a, 116.

values, personal ways of life, or what Rawlsians would call 'conceptions of the good'; it is not social pluralism of the kind that would welcome 'a motley amalgam of highly diverse and quasi-autonomous communities' as a richer kind of society than one based on a shared common culture. Or, as he puts it elsewhere, 'we like variety, but we need sufficient assimilation not to create injustice, cruelty and misery' (1992a, 121).

Berlin's pluralism is also constrained by his recognition that there are universal values, that it is integral to our understanding of what human beings are that they share a minimum set of values in common, despite great moral diversity in other respects (L 21–6; Lukes 1994; Galipeau 1994, chapter 3). He thinks, in particular, that every culture has recognised a minimum set of human rights: 'The idea of human rights rests on the true belief that there are certain goods— freedom, justice, pursuit of happiness, honesty, love—that are in the interest of all human beings, as such, not as members of this or that nationality, religion, profession, character; and that it is right to meet these claims and to protect people against those who ignore or deny them' (CIB 39). It follows immediately from this that for Berlin any acceptable form of nationalism must be morally restricted, in the sense that it must regard human rights (or universal human values more generally) as setting limits to what can be done in the name of national self-determination.[9] The problem here is not to understand the general shape of Berlin's nationalism, but to decide exactly how much moral diversity he would be prepared to tolerate before the bedrock is reached: he leaves few practical clues. But this raises a more general problem about Berlin's pluralism and its relation to his liberalism that I shall not attempt to address here.[10]

Let us take stock of what we have discovered so far about Berlin's attitude to nationalism. We know that it is equivocal—as he says at one point, 'I do not wish to praise or attack nationalism. Nationalism is responsible for magnificent achievements and appalling crimes' (SR 251). We know that he wishes to distinguish between *varieties* of nationalism, a distinction that is sometimes, but by no means always, signalled by a contrast between nationalism proper and something else, for instance 'national consciousness'. We know that, in his most detailed account of the kind of nationalism that he fears, he combines four separate elements, but that on other occasions he focuses on just one of these, for instance the 'aggressive' character of certain nationalisms. But we do not yet have a clear picture of the kind of nationalism he is prepared to defend; in particular we do not yet know how far he thinks that 'benign' nationalism entails national self-

---

9. 'I don't believe in total self-determination. I believe that self-determination has its limits if it inflicts too much trampling on human rights, and it can' (Berlin 1992a, 122).

10. On this issue, see JG 141–68; Lukes 1994; Crowder 1994 and LVP; Berlin and Williams 1994; Gutmann 1999.

determination in the political sense—having a State or some other form of political authority to protect and shape national culture. To throw further light on this question, I want next to examine Berlin's account of the sources of nationalism: if nationalism arises as a response to human needs, what more precisely are the needs to which it responds?

THE SOURCES OF NATIONALISM

At the most general level, Berlin's answer to this question is that nationalism stems from the human need to achieve dignity and avoid humiliation. But if we survey his writings on nationalism, we find these ideas being interpreted differently on different occasions, as he gives sometimes a more positive and sometimes a more negative gloss on nationalist aspirations. We are still caught between Crooked Timber and Bent Twig.

The most strongly positive gloss on nationalism occurs when Berlin is writing about Zionism, against the background of a remarkable analysis of the Jewish condition in European societies before the foundation of the State of Israel.[11] His diagnosis is that Jews in these societies have been faced with a choice between three unpalatable options. The first is to attempt to assimilate completely to the national culture of whichever society they find themselves in, altogether denying the significance of their Jewish descent. But this attempt, Berlin argues, can never succeed. Assimilationist Jews try too hard to master and copy the social and cultural norms of their adopted nation, distorting their own lives in various ways, but without convincing the natives that they genuinely belong. Berlin likens them to people who are thrown among a tribe whose language and customs are unfamiliar. In order to survive they become expert students of the tribe's culture, but never cease to be strangers, since, as Berlin puts it:

> [...] their whole existence and all their values depend upon the assumption that they can by conscious effort live the life of the natives, and acquire complete security through pursuing, if need be by means of artificial techniques, those activities which the natives perform by nature and spontaneously. This must not be questioned, since, unless it is true, the presence of the strangers among the natives can never be wholly free from danger, and their enormous sustained effort, culminating in the acquisition of a special kind of intellectual and moral

---

11. I use Berlin's Zionism to throw light on his general understanding of, and attitude towards, nationalism, though some commentators suggest that it stands somewhat at odds with the rest of his thought—see for instance Avishai Margalit, LIB 147–59, and Richard Wollheim, LIB 161–8.

vision with which they have seen into the heart of the native system, might turn
out to derive from a gigantic delusion: a delusion which has taken them in, perhaps, but has not taken in the natives whose instincts continue to tell them that
the strangers, who by this time look like natives, speak like them, even react like
them, nevertheless lack something, want of which prevents them from being
natives. (POI 168)

Berlin uses this analogy to explain, on the one hand, the considerable success
achieved by assimilationist Jews in certain cultural fields, often involving a
romanticising of the national achievements of their adopted country, but, on the
other, the sense of perpetual unease, of trying too hard to be like the natives while
living in constant anxiety that they will be found out. Unlike other cultural
minorities who have, over time, simply been absorbed into the larger societies
they inhabited, and for reasons that Berlin does not make wholly explicit—
whether the latent or overt anti-Semitism of the majority, or some special feature
of Jewish identity—Jews can never feel fully at home in Gentile societies despite
all their efforts to convince themselves that they have discarded their Jewishness
and 'gone native'.

If this form of assimilation cannot succeed, the second strategy open to Jews
is to proclaim their Jewish identity and try to turn it into a badge of honour rather
than a cause for shame. Berlin's most detailed discussion of this strategy can be
found in his psychological portrait of Benjamin Disraeli (in AC). Disraeli, in love
with the English aristocracy and desperate to find a way of including himself in
their company, did so by way of inventing an 'aristocratic' Jewish identity. He saw
himself as the descendant of an ancient great race of Jews whose triumphs he cat-
alogues in his novels, and this self-image was in one way successful, both for Disraeli's own self-confidence and for his ability to impress others. But, according to
Berlin, Disraeli lived in a world of fantasy, his political successes notwithstanding.
'Unable to function in his own proper person, as a man of dubious pedigree in a
highly class-conscious society, Disraeli invented a splendid fairy tale, bound its
spell upon the mind of England, and thereby influenced men and events to a considerable degree. [...] His entire life was a sustained attempt to live a fiction, and
to cast its spell over the minds of others' (AC 273, 5).

Why then, more generally, must the second strategy fail? In order to proclaim
one's Jewish identity in a way that will gain one recognition from the surrounding
society, one has, Berlin implies, to romanticise it, to exaggerate certain Jewish traits
and become exotic. But this in turn must involve fantasy, and therefore an inability
to live in a way that is true to one's own personality. We can connect this, I believe,
to Berlin's dismissal of 'galut' nationalism, which he rejects in part because he
thinks that a modern society cannot function as 'a motley amalgam of highly

diverse and quasi-autonomous communities', as we saw earlier, but also because it prescribes a certain way of being Jewish, involving speaking Yiddish and so forth, which many Jews, left to their own devices, would choose not to embrace.

If neither outright assimilation nor exaggerated Jewishness are successful ways for Jews to live with freedom and dignity in Gentile societies, the third strategy sketched by Berlin is a kind of compromise whereby a person's Jewishness is not denied, but is suppressed—something to be treated as relatively unimportant, to be discussed only on occasion and in selected company. Using an analogy that some critics have found distasteful, Berlin suggests that Jews might be thought of as hunchbacks who had found different ways of coping with their deformity. The first group, the assimilationists, simply denied that their humps existed—they had long since vanished; the second group maintained that to have a hump was a privilege, that those with humps were superior beings; the third group tried not to talk about humps, and hoped in that way that they would become less noticeable. 'They tended to wear voluminous cloaks which concealed their precise contours' (POI 175–6). One senses that for Berlin this was the least bad of the three strategies. But evidently it involves a certain kind of self-deception and self-alienation, and in that sense is not compatible with a fully dignified human existence.

Behind Berlin's analysis lies his assumption that the Jewish identity is indeed a form of national identity, such that Jews can only live free and dignified lives under circumstances in which they have somewhere to be 'at home'; they have available to them a cultural milieu in which being Jewish becomes the normal state of affairs, so that each person can choose his own path in life without having to negotiate the issue of identity in one or other of the above three ways. What deeply impressed Berlin about Israel was precisely the 'normality' of everyday life there. Noting the relative absence of 'extreme' personalities, whether in the arts, the sciences or business—especially 'sophisticated, chess-playing café intellectuals'—he remarked that tourists 'are much disappointed by the relative placidity, relative coarseness; a kind of stubborn normality and a complacent soundness, wholesomeness, dullness which the Jews have surely richly deserved' (POI 156). And this also profoundly affected the position of those Jews who continued to live in the Diaspora, for it was now a matter for each individual to decide how to conduct his or her life. The strategic dilemma did not disappear, but it was no longer '[a] matter of tragic and desperate concern to the Jews as a whole'. For 'If the Jews are to continue to suffer for failing to please their neighbours by behaving like apes and parrots, they will at least do so individually' (POI 184).

This last argument of Berlin's is in certain respects puzzling. He says that 'The creation of the State of Israel has rendered the greatest service that any human institution can perform for individuals—has restored to Jews not merely their personal dignity and status as human beings, but what is vastly more important, their right to choose as individuals how they shall live' (POI 182). One thing that Berlin is claiming here is that the existence of Israel as an independent State grants a kind of recognition to Jews everywhere, and he is surely right to say that this has greatly enhanced the self-confidence of Jews who have remained in the Diaspora as well as those who have emigrated to Israel. But Berlin also adds a claim about Jews having the right to choose *as individuals* how to live, and this is more mysterious. In general (though with notable exceptions) they have had the opportunity either to remain in their present country of citizenship or to migrate to Israel, but for those who elected to stay in the Diaspora—and Berlin vigorously defends their right to make such a choice—the social pressures they face do not seem to have changed as a result of Israel having come into existence. If Berlin's diagnosis of the Jewish condition in Gentile societies is correct—if none of the three strategies of assimilation he identifies as having been adopted by Jews in such circumstances is successful, and as a result Jews continue to suffer from what he calls 'social uneasiness', if not outright persecution—it is not clear why the existence of Israel as a sovereign State with a Jewish majority should change this.[12]

This problem aside, we can extract a general account of the roots of nationalism from Berlin's reflections on Zionism.[13] He assumes, first, that Jewish identity and culture are distinct and deep-rooted, which, when taken together with the latent or overt hostility displayed by members of the dominant culture, shows that outright assimilation into existing European cultures could never be a successful path for Jews to follow. By extension this applies to many other national cultures, for instance those subject to outside colonial rule, where Berlin argues that abandoning one's own culture and trying to assimilate to that of the colonising power is always a mistake (SR 249–66). For the culture to flourish, it needs a secure space in which it is the dominant form of life—it needs a cultural 'home', in other words. But does this also require political self-determination? Berlin sometimes implies that it does, but if we think about the question more closely, we can see that, from this perspective, the value of political self-determination can only be instrumental. Cultures are more likely to be secure in their 'homes' when they have States to protect them. If, on the other hand, we postulate an external power committed to protecting the culture in question, there is nothing in this account of the sources of nationalism to rule out such an arrangement (suppose, for instance, that the

---

12. It might be said—and Berlin himself appears to suggest this in places—that the very fact that Jews now have a choice whether to stay or to move to Israel guarantees their freedom: such disabilities as they suffer in Gentile societies are self-imposed. But this is surely implausible, neglecting as it does the very great costs that may be involved in uprooting oneself from one's country of origin and moving to a new society.

13. It is not my aim to assess Berlin's Zionism itself. For a critical appraisal, see Cocks 2002, chapters 3–4.

British had been willing to extend their mandate in Palestine forward in time to provide a secure national home for the Jews). The idea that in order to live a dignified life one must live among people who share one's cultural identity is not linked to the idea of political self-determination. What I earlier called Berlin's 'strongly positive' gloss on nationalism does not give us much more than cultural nationalism plus the claim that, as things now are, cultures that do not enjoy political protection are liable to be crushed.

What now of the Bent Twig, Berlin's much less favourable account of the psychological roots of nationalism? Here the main exhibit is German nationalism of the late eighteenth and early nineteenth century, and although the account can once again be spelt out using the language of human dignity, what is doing the work is not the idea of being at home with people who respect you, but the idea of resentment at being treated as inferior by outsiders. Nationalism, Berlin says in this vein, 'is in the first place a response to a patronising or disparaging attitude towards the traditional values of a society, the result of wounded pride and a sense of humiliation in its most socially conscious members, which in due course produce anger and self-assertion' (AC 346). Germans were liable to respond in this way because they were regarded as culturally and politically backward by comparison with the nations of Western Europe—Spain, Italy, Britain and, especially, France. Resentful at being made to feel provincial, German intellectuals began to announce the superiority of their own cultural values, contrasting themselves with 'the rich, worldly, successful, superficial, smooth, heartless, morally empty French' (CTH 246). What began as a movement for spiritual and cultural revival, however, turned in time into a political movement whose aim was to demonstrate German superiority by force. Other factors were also necessary for this transformation to occur, Berlin admits. But the basic idea here is that nationalism is driven, not just by the desire for recognition as such, but by the desire that one's own culture should be recognised as at least equal, if not superior, to rival cultures. In other words, recognition here intrinsically involves comparison between forms of cultural belonging. It is not enough to be securely at home in a culture whose other members treat you as an equal. If you feel that people from other cultures look down on yours, then you will find this humiliating, and take steps to force them to recognise the value of your traditions.

Two points are worth emphasising about this explanation of nationalism. First, it links cultural and political nationalism much more closely together. It is hard to see how cultural recognition can be achieved without political self-determination and the range of resources, which typically will include military resources, that go with it. Second, even if we think in terms of a world of culturally homogeneous units each of which possesses its own State, there is no guarantee that aggressive forms of nationalism will not arise. For it is still possible for some nations to resent the perceived cultural superiority of others, and to engage in aggressive actions accordingly.

When Berlin talks in general terms about the origins of nationalism, he often uses language that is ambiguous as between the two explanations I have distinguished. He speaks, for instance, about the need for recognition, or the 'search for status', describing this as among the most powerful of human motives (POI 195–9; L 200–8). He seems here to have particularly in mind the nationalisms of colonised peoples, who prefer to be ruled autocratically by leaders drawn from among themselves than by 'some cautious, just, gentle, well-meaning administrator from outside' (L 204). But in describing the motive involved, he conflates three separate elements: first, the need to belong, meaning the need to live among people who, because of their cultural and other characteristics, can recognise me for what I am; second the need not to be patronised or looked down upon by outsiders who inevitably *misrecognise* me; third, the need to be politically independent, to have a sense that I am in control of my life along with others who share my aims and values.[14] These three elements are obviously connected, and perhaps in the case of colonised peoples they naturally combine to produce movements for national liberation, but in other cases they may come apart. In Berlin's analysis of the Jewish predicament, for instance, it is the first element that predominates. What Jews are said to need is not primarily recognition by others, nor indeed political independence, but simply an environment in which they can live together without 'social uneasiness' and achieve individual self-fulfilment. In the case of post-Enlightenment Germany, by contrast, the second element comes to the fore. The Germans already lived surrounded by other Germans; their problem was not a failure of recognition by 'the members of the society to which, historically, morally, economically, and perhaps ethnically, I feel that I belong' (L 202). Nor was it lack of political independence: although of course there was at this point no unified German State, the Germans were not a colonised or occupied people, and Berlin does not explain their nationalism in terms of the experience of political division. The problem, rather (according to Berlin), was a shared perception that German culture was regarded as inferior to the cultures of other European States, and that Germans, as a people, were therefore not being given adequate recognition by outsiders. Finally, although Berlin does not take this step, we might well envisage forms of nationalism in which the third element predominates: the nationalisms, that is, of established and confident peoples who simply wish to be politically independent—who already have a sense of collective belonging, and who do not regard themselves as being treated as inferiors by

---

14. Compare Avishai Margalit's analysis of the diverse emotional roots of nationalism, according to Berlin, at LIB 151–4.

outsiders, except in so far as they have up to now been denied rights of self-government. For such peoples, the 'search for status' is a search specifically for *political* status, not for cultural recognition.[15]

Perhaps because he does not distinguish clearly between the different forms that the demand for recognition can take, Berlin tends to treat what he calls 'this profound and universal craving for status and understanding' as a deep-rooted aspect of human nature, and therefore as not susceptible to ethical assessment. His concern is only to distinguish it from a desire for liberty in the proper sense. Normatively, however, it matters a great deal which form the need for recognition assumes. Indeed, as we have seen, Berlin himself wishes to applaud (moderate) Zionism and condemn (romantic) German nationalism. Unfortunately, just as he fails to draw a clear line between 'good' and 'bad' versions of nationalist doctrine, so here he fails to separate different motives for nationalism in a way that would allow relevant ethical distinctions to be drawn. In order to see how far a normative account of nationalism can be found in Berlin, I shall attempt in the final section of this paper to compare his thinking with later theories of liberal nationalism.

BERLIN AND LIBERAL NATIONALISM

Liberal nationalism, as I shall understand it, is more than just the claim that there is no outright opposition between the principles of liberty and nationality—that there can be versions of nationalism that do not require sacrificing the freedoms and other rights that liberals cherish. If that were all that was meant by liberal nationalism, then it is clear, on the basis of what has been said already, that Berlin was a liberal nationalist: he was a liberal who recognised that at least some forms of nationalism could be reconciled with personal liberty, even if (as we have seen) he was less than clear about precisely *which* forms this was true of. I take the idea of liberal nationalism to involve more than this—to imply that the relationship between liberal and nationalist values is symbiotic. In particular, liberal nationalists hold that liberal goals cannot reliably be achieved except in societies whose members share a common national identity; they may also think that national self-determination cannot be achieved except in societies that enjoy liberal rights and freedoms. But do these claims conceal an inner tension between the two sets of values, manifested in practical divergences over questions of policy? Berlin, his value pluralism notwithstanding, remained firmly committed to the protection of negative liberty as the first priority of liberals. How far did this commitment con-

---

15. This analysis might apply to minority nationalist movements in liberal States, the nationalisms of the Scots, the Catalans or the Québécois, for instance.

strain his nationalism, and what can we learn as a result about the prospects for a coherent form of liberal nationalism?

The oldest and perhaps best-known of liberal nationalist claims is the one made by John Stuart Mill in the sixteenth chapter of *Considerations on Representative Government*, namely that 'free institutions are next to impossible in a country made up of different nationalities' (1861, 547). Briefly stated, Mill's argument is that, in multinational societies, inter-group hostilities will mean that there is no united public opinion capable of forming an effective check on government; instead each group will attempt to use the powers of the State to exploit and suppress the others. Berlin never argues explicitly to this effect. Nevertheless, his comments, noted above, about the need for a common culture, and his hostility towards certain kinds of multiculturalism, seem to have been inspired by a similar thought. Liberty requires social peace, and confidence among different groups that each will abide by a commonly agreed set of rules; and these conditions are threatened by deep cultural divisions. As Berlin put it in the course of an interview, 'I think liberalism is essentially the belief of people who have lived on the same soil for a long time in comparative peace with each other' (1992a, 121).

The converse of this argument is that there is a liberal case for nation-building in societies whose populations are culturally divided, an argument endorsed by Mill in his notorious remarks about the benefits to the Bretons and the Basques of being absorbed into French nationality, and to the Welsh and the highland Scots of being converted into Britons (1861, 549). Perhaps because of changed circumstances, no such remarks are made by Berlin. This does not mean that he excluded all nation-building policies as a matter of principle. When he writes about Israel, for instance, he lavishes praise on the creation of (modern) Hebrew as a national language, arguing that this has served to bind together Jewish immigrants from different backgrounds, while at the same time connecting them to a noble past. 'Of all the factors at work in creating a democratic and liberal nation in Israel today, not even excluding the army, it is the most penetrating, the most influential, and the most successful' (POI 154). And in his tribute to the Indian nationalist Rabindranath Tagore, he praises the latter for wanting to reclaim distinctive aspects of Indian culture, including reviving the Bengali language, in the face of a 'shallow internationalism' whereby 'Races, communities, nations were constantly urged to abolish their frontiers, destroy their distinctive attributes, cease from mutual strife, and combine into one great universal society' (SR 264). But it is important to observe that these policies are non-coercive, and therefore do not involve any hard choices between liberty and the goal of nation-building. To put liberal nationalism to the test, we need to consider cases where nation-building policies involve limiting individual freedom in certain respects. Consider, for example, the laws governing the language of commercial signs in

Quebec, or the enforcement of a national curriculum in education, limiting the autonomy of schools to tailor the content of what they teach to the religious or ethnic background of their pupils. Although we have no direct evidence of Berlin's views on these matters, in the light of what we know about his political philosophy in general and his attitude to nationalism in particular, it seems likely that he would have come down on the side of individual liberty. So although Berlin sees and accepts the argument connecting national unity to liberal democracy, he would have been reluctant to draw from it the practical conclusion that many liberal nationalists have wished to derive—namely, that nation-building goals, justified in part by their contribution to liberty in the long run, may none the less in the short term justify restricting the freedom of some individuals and some groups to live as they wish.

A second claim made by liberal nationalists concerns the cultural preconditions for individual autonomy. The argument here is that, in order for individuals to choose autonomously how to live, they must have access to an adequate range of social practices and other options, and these are provided by what Kymlicka calls a 'cultural structure' (1989, chapter 8). In the absence of such a structure, individuals might still have choices to make, but they would not be able to make intelligent decisions about the comparative value of the different possibilities open to them, and so genuine autonomy, which involves choosing for good reasons, would be impossible. The most important cultural structures are those that Kymlicka later refers to as 'distinct and institutionally complete societal cultures', and these in practice must be national in scope (1995, chapter 5). Because of global pressures in the contemporary world that tend to erode these societal cultures, they are only secure when they are protected by institutions of political self-determination. In this way, national self-determination can be justified by appeal to the indisputably liberal value of autonomy.

What would Berlin have made of this argument? We know that he regarded the idea of autonomy as one that must be treated with considerable care. In itself autonomy—choosing one's values and plan of life for oneself—is a valid ideal of freedom; but it is liable to be transformed, by what Berlin calls 'sleight of hand' (L 181), into versions of positive liberty that have sinister consequences. In any case, autonomy, in this sense of choosing for oneself, should not be conflated with having many options to choose between, an external condition distinct from the internal state of the chooser. And he seems more concerned that individuals should have as many options as possible when deciding how to live their lives than that these options should be coherently structured as a result of forming part of a single 'societal culture'. From this perspective, Berlin's position seems closer to that of Jeremy Waldron (1995), who defends what he calls cultural *'mélange'*—being able to combine options drawn from many different cultures in a single life—than to Kymlicka's defence of cultural integrity. So again it seems unlikely that Berlin would have approved of policies designed to protect cultures from invasion by foreign elements—for instance, attempts to safeguard minority languages in danger of being swamped by international languages by requiring children to learn them in schools, or measures designed to block the import of foreign films or television programmes—even though in general he celebrates cultural diversity and condemns cosmopolitanism as shallow. His liberalism is in this respect more classical than that of recent liberal nationalists: it is about protecting individuals from outside interference, especially State interference, rather than about using the State to protect the cultural conditions under which people can lead autonomous lives.[16]

As I suggested above, liberal nationalists typically connect cultural integrity to political self-determination.[17] But it is important to distinguish a weaker and a stronger version of this argument. The weaker version sees political self-determination as a kind of protective shell within which a culture can remain secure and develop through its own internal processes. The evil to be avoided here is cultural suppression or distortion by outside agents—imperial emissaries, say, who either from animosity or misguided benevolence try to shape a culture in their own image, passing laws to prohibit traditional practices, for instance. By having institutions of self-rule, a space is created in which those whose culture it is can either preserve or develop it as they see fit. The stronger version sees political self-determination as integral to cultural development itself. Politics is the vehicle through which existing cultural values can be debated, priorities established, and

---

16. It is not of course classical in the socio-economic sense: Berlin was always a firm supporter of the New Deal and the Welfare State.

17. One exception is Yael Tamir, who explicitly defends a cultural interpretation of the right of national self-determination, which she contrasts with the political idea of self-rule. As we shall see, this may align her most closely with Berlin's position. Yet Tamir's distinction remains obscure to me. She says: 'In its communal aspect, national self-determination entails a process whereby individuals seek to give public expression to their national identity. Hence, it is often described as the right of individuals to a public sphere, thus implying that individuals are entitled to establish institutions and manage their communal life in ways that reflect their communal values, traditions, and history—in short, their culture' (1993, 70). But if institutions in the public sphere are not political institutions, what are they? Tamir also makes the point that national self-determination need not imply democratic political participation. This is true: nations can be self-determining so long as those who make political decisions on their behalf are recognised by the remainder of society as legitimate representatives of the national culture. But this shows that the right of national self-determination need not be implemented in a democratic form, not that it is a cultural rather than a political right.

policies enacted to implement the decisions reached—for instance, language policies in schools and the media, State funding for cultural events, and so forth.

In so far as Berlin subscribes to either of these arguments, it is clearly to the weaker version. This conclusion can be deduced from the way he expresses his support for Zionism. Nowhere does Berlin suggest that Jewish culture cannot flourish except through having a national State whose aim is to promote it. Instead, as we have seen, he argues that what Jews need is first and foremost a *society* of their own—a place where being Jewish is the normal, taken-for-granted state of affairs, and in which, therefore, Jews can feel at home, at ease with themselves. That this requires the creation of an independent Israeli State is contingent on the fact that such a society could exist, securely, only under its protection. Moreover, he would probably have regarded the politicisation of cultural questions implied in the second argument with suspicion. He was drawn, evidently, to Herder's view of culture as a spontaneous growth in which the unique spirit of a particular people is expressed. From this perspective, setting cultural priorities by political decision, no matter how democratic the procedure, would appear too mechanical a process.

The upshot is that, for Berlin, national self-determination was only of instrumental value. Unlike later liberal nationalists, he did not see collective autonomy—the experience of determining, along with others, the direction in which your society will develop—as intrinsically good. Self-determination mattered because, other things being equal, it was most likely to create the conditions under which individuals could develop freely, and avoid the discomfort of being governed by those who did not share or even perhaps understand their values. Again we see how Berlin's liberalism conditions and limits his nationalism.

A final argument that I want to consider links national self-determination with justice. To deny self-determination to nations capable of exercising it, some would argue, is an injustice in the same way as, say, denying voting rights to a competent adult citizen. This argument is usually put forward on behalf of minority nations such as the Catalans, the Québécois and the Scots, and the claim is not primarily about material injustice. These peoples might be doing perfectly well in material terms, but it is simply unfair that they should not be allowed to control their collective life—language policy, cultural matters, national symbols etc.—in the way that people in established nation-States are able to. This can be interpreted as a demand for equal status, and, as we have seen, Berlin recognises the force, and to some extent the legitimacy, of such demands as a general matter. But apparently he does not see the failure to grant national self-determination in cases such as this as an instance of injustice, nor does he appear particularly sympathetic to the demand itself, on those few occasions when he refers to contemporary nationalist conflicts (AC 350; Gardels 1991, 21). Perhaps these cases

remind him too much of the original Bent Twig: these are not the nationalisms of
oppressed peoples, but of peoples who resent the fact that their nationhood is not
being given equal recognition by their more powerful neighbours.

THE COHERENCE OF LIBERAL NATIONALISM

What, then, can an examination of Berlin tell us about the possibility of developing a coherent version of liberal nationalism? As noted earlier, several critics
have argued that this is at best an unstable compound: faced with real political
choices, would-be liberal nationalists have to decide between their liberalism and
their nationalism. Consider issues such as these: restrictions on immigration, the
rights of cultural minorities, the claims of (potentially illiberal) secessionist
movements, and responsibilities to the global poor. In each case there appears to
be a liberal position on the issue, and an opposing nationalist position (on the first
issue, for instance, liberals will privilege individuals' rights to free movement,
whereas nationalists will privilege the right of political communities to determine
their own membership). Depending on which choices are made, liberal nationalism collapses either into unqualified liberalism or unqualified nationalism: there
is no third way. And our analysis of Berlin's thought appears to confirm this diagnosis: the positions he adopts are wholly grounded in liberal principles. His partly
sympathetic response to nationalism is to be explained, first, by the value he
attaches to cultural diversity, to a world in which many different patterns of life
are realised in different places, as opposed to cosmopolitan uniformity which he
saw as 'a tremendous desiccation of everything that is human' (Gardels 1991, 22);
second, by his recognition of human beings' need for cultural belonging, of being
at home in familiar surroundings, which in Berlin's case sprang from reflection on
his own deep-rooted Judaism (PI2 258–9). But these values have no direct political entailments for Berlin. Indeed, as we have seen, he is strongly inclined to
depoliticise cultural nationalism entirely, following his reading of the much
praised Herder. In the end this apolitical stance cannot be sustained: Berlin recognises, above all in the case of Israel, that a cultural 'home' requires the protection
of an independent State if it is to be secure. But the value of political self-
determination is always instrumental. As Stuart Hampshire has suggested, Berlin's
nationalism, such as it is, has a broadly utilitarian character: people are happy
only when living according to familiar customs and habits, and they need political independence to sustain that accepted way of life (IBAC 129).

But although Berlin's own political thought exemplifies the final triumph of
liberalism over nationalism, we can still learn much from him about the kind of liberalism and the kind of nationalism that can be successfully combined. For these are

both loose and flexible ideologies, capable of being interpreted in very different ways. Take nationalism first. As our analysis of Berlin has revealed, nationalist *doctrines* can vary along at least four different dimensions, and there are also sharply contrasting stories to be told about the psychological motivations that underlie nationalism—the human needs to which nationalism responds. Is nationalism to be understood in terms of a universal human need to live in a cultural community in which one feels at home, or it is to be understood much more narrowly as a response to feelings of inferiority or humiliation provoked by comparisons with other communities? If the first story is true, we may expect nationalism, or some equivalent of it, to be a perennial feature of human society, and one that any plausible version of liberalism must comes to term with. If the second story is true, by contrast, then liberal cosmopolitanism, which aims to create a just world order in which all individuals, and all cultures, are equally respected, can plausibly claim that nationalism is no more than a passing phase of human history—as Einstein once said, it is an infantile disease, 'the measles of the human race'.

So how should a liberal nationalist understand nationalism? I suggest that the following six theses delineate a form of nationalism that can cohere with liberalism.

1. Although nationalism may make its appearance only in the transition from pre-modern to modern society, it nevertheless is a form of human community appropriate to large, anonymous and highly mobile societies. It creates a sense of shared identity, and allows people to see themselves as part of a transgenerational community with a distinctive character and culture.

2. National identities are not, however, primordial. A people's self-understanding develops over time, and adapts to new circumstances. In particular, criteria of membership can change, and need not, for example, be understood in racial or ethnic terms.

3. Nationality is an important source of personal identity, but it need not and should not be exclusive. Belonging to a nation does not exclude, and may often be supported by, membership in sub-national groups of many kinds: local communities, religious and cultural groups, political associations and so forth.

4. By belonging to a nation, a person incurs special obligations to his or her compatriots, but this is consistent with having duties to outsiders that are universal in character (for example, the duty to respect human rights). In other words, what nationality requires is a *reasonable* partiality towards compatriots, not out-and-out moral parochialism (Miller 2005).

5. All nations have valid claims to self-determination, so no nation is entitled to pursue policies in the name of self-determination that prevent others from doing the same. The political institutions that cater for self-determination must respond even-handedly to such claims, for instance through federal arrangements or forms of devolution for national minorities.

6. Political self-determination is important because, in general, cultures cannot flourish and develop without political support. But at least as much weight should be attached to the instrumental reasons for making political and national boundaries coincide—for instance that this may prove to be an essential precondition for democracy and social justice.

Embracing these six theses means adopting a form of nationalism that is pluralist, morally restricted, and reiterative, but still political—to use the terminology developed in the second section to analyse Berlin's nationalism. Nationalism of this kind seems at least potentially consistent with liberal principles, but before reaching this conclusion we need to turn the spotlight on to liberalism itself, and again draw some distinctions.

One relevant distinction is that between classical and modern liberalism—between a liberalism that centres on individual rights to life, liberty and property, the free market and the minimal State, and a liberalism that incorporates democratic citizenship, social justice and the Welfare State. Liberals of the first type have often argued, with justification, that nationalism of whatever stripe poses a threat to classical liberal principles by virtue of its implicit collectivism. Nations are communities whose members can make claims on each other that go beyond non-interference, and that pursue collective projects of various kinds, all of which requires the State to play a more active role than classical liberalism permits. By the same token, however, nationalism and modern liberalism are natural allies—a shared nationality provides the motivational basis for democratic citizenship and the pursuit of social justice, as I have argued elsewhere (1995, chapter 4).

Perhaps less familiar is a distinction that can be drawn between deontological and sociological versions of liberalism. Deontological liberals see liberal principles as mandatory guides to action that can be derived from abstract reflection on the circumstances of human life—for instance, by considering basic human interests, we can derive a set of rights that must be respected under all circumstances, such as rights to freedom of speech and movement. A liberal State is one that adheres to liberal principles so derived. Sociological liberals, by contrast, ask about the social and political circumstances in which liberal aims and values are most likely to be achieved, without assuming that it is possible to adhere to liberal principles in all cases. In particular, one such principle may have to be compromised now in order to improve the chances of creating or sustaining a liberal society in the future. An issue such as allowing free speech to racists illustrates this distinction. A deontological liberal will ask whether racist speech violates some condition such as Mill's harm principle, and if it does not, will defend the racist's right to air his views. A sociological liberal will ask about the consequences of permitting racist speech: will it create a climate of violence in which other liberal values are put at risk, or even threaten the stability of liberal democracy itself? If so, this may be sufficient reason to clamp down on it. The distinction I am drawing here is no doubt too crude, since many flesh-and-blood liberals will be sensitive to considerations of both kinds. Nevertheless, by seeing liberals as standing at different points on a line between these two poles, we can throw further light on the coherence of liberal nationalism.

In a number of areas, nationalists are likely to support policies that deontological liberals will find unacceptable. They may, for example, impose national curricula on schools, with the aim of encouraging national integration, thereby lessening educational freedom of choice. They may impose language requirements on business or the public services. They may pursue immigration policies that discriminate between applicants on cultural grounds, thereby infringing the equal rights of the unsuccessful applicants. But whereas deontological liberals are likely to dismiss such policies out of hand, the question for sociological liberals is whether over the longer term they will help to build a society in which liberal rights and values are more securely enjoyed. The liberal nationalist argument is that liberalism depends upon the solidarity and sense of common identity that nationhood provides; so policies such as those outlined above may be justified if indeed they are necessary to consolidate national identities in the face of the social fragmentation endemic in contemporary societies.

Where should we place Berlin on the liberal dimensions we have just been considering? As already noted, his liberalism is clearly modern rather than classical—so far, so good. But was his liberalism deontological or sociological? There is evidence in both directions. There are places in which he seems to treat the defence of an area of negative liberty as something close to a fundamental principle, not to be overridden in the name of other values. But, as we saw earlier, there are also places in which he recognises that liberalism itself has social preconditions, and he makes the connection between cultural community, trust and willingness to abide by liberal principles. Let us say that he stands somewhere towards the middle of this spectrum. His liberalism is such that a coherent liberal nationalism remains an open possibility for him. Why, then, was he reluctant to take that final step?

The reason, I believe, is that Berlin was convinced (along with many later critics of liberal nationalism) that nationalism, as a real political phenomenon, is always unstable. Theoretically we can delineate a benign form of nationalism, as I have done above, and as Berlin also, though with limited success, attempted to do. But there is no way to ensure that any actually existing form of nationalism remains within the limits we have set, and every chance that circumstances will arise in which it becomes aggressive, intolerant, authoritarian etc. National consciousness, in other words, is always liable to become 'inflamed'; the Bent Twig is an ever-present danger. And this, I think, is the deepest challenge that liberal nationalism faces. So long as we remain at the level of theory, we can interpret both liberalism and nationalism so as to make their relationship not only consistent but mutually supportive. But when we move from theory to practice, it becomes much harder to identify conditions under which our favoured form of nationalism will remain stable, or to find political mechanisms that will ensure this. This challenge represents Berlin's final legacy to the liberal nationalists who have succeeded him.

Acknowledgements

I am very grateful to Henry Hardy for his help in finding some of the sources on which this paper is based, and in particular for supplying transcripts of two broadcasts in which Berlin discusses nationalist ideas. I should also like to thank Erica Benner, Jerry Cohen, George Crowder, Henry Hardy and the referees for *Political Studies* for illuminating commentary on earlier drafts, and Zofia Stemplowska and Sarah Fine for their help in preparing the final manuscript.

9

Value Pluralism and Liberalism

BERLIN AND BEYOND

GEORGE CROWDER

At the heart of Isaiah Berlin's political thought there is a tension between its two key elements. On the one hand, Berlin is proud to call himself a liberal, standing up for individual liberty against tyrannical regimes such as the Soviet Union. On the other hand, he is just as strongly committed to the concept of value pluralism, the idea that fundamental values are irreducibly plural, potentially conflicting, and sometimes incommensurable with one another. Value pluralism points to the centrality in human life of hard choices. If values are 'incommensurable', there is no common standard by which they can be weighed against one another when they conflict; each possesses its own unique force. Applied to the claims of liberalism, this creates a major problem of justification: Why should we choose the values characteristic of liberalism—personal liberty, respect for the dignity of the individual, toleration, and so forth—in preference to rival packages of values, such as those of conservatism, or socialism, or even Soviet Communism?

I believe that Berlin never resolved this problem, indeed that he never gave it the sustained and systematic attention it deserves. His most explicit attempts to answer it are either flawed or limited. Nevertheless, those same attempts provide valuable hints that can be improved on and developed into a distinctive and persuasive value-pluralist theory of liberalism. In the following I have space only to sketch the outlines of a case I have developed in greater detail elsewhere (LVP; IBLP chapters 7–8). I hope to add a clearer view of where my argument departs from Berlin's, and I shall pay more attention than I have previously to the question of whether the kind of universal values assumed by Berlin can be a basis for liberal pluralism.

I begin by setting out Berlin's position: his concept of value pluralism, his various accounts of choice under pluralism, and the corresponding explanations that he provides, or that have been attributed to him, of the relation between pluralism and liberalism. In the second part I argue for my own view of the pluralism–liberalism link, a view that to some extent revives certain of Berlin's arguments, but also transforms and adds to them. Finally, I briefly compare the kind of liberalism indicated by my arguments with that supported by Berlin, highlighting the main points of continuity and contrast, and assessing the extent to which my view goes beyond Berlin's. I argue that, despite significant differences, my position remains within the general spirit of Berlin's liberal-pluralist outlook.

BERLIN ON VALUE PLURALISM AND LIBERALISM

Berlin's idea of value pluralism emerges in opposition to the 'moral monism' he sees as the 'perennial philosophy' of Western thought (CTH 7–19; POI 11–14; L 212–17). According to moral monism, all ethical questions have a single correct answer, deducible from a single formula. Monist formulas are dominated by a single value, or by a small set of values, which either overrides or serves as a common currency for all others. Plato's Form of the Good, Aristotle's ideal life of contemplation, and Marx's liberation of the proletariat are all instances of overriding super-values. Bentham's concept of utility exemplifies the notion of a single value as common currency.

Berlin sees two major problems with moral monism. First, the notion of a single right answer to all moral conflicts is an encouragement to utopianism, and consequently to authoritarian or even totalitarian visions in which utopia is realised by force, which in turn is justified by utopian goals. Second, moral monism is false, because no single formula can resolve all ethical conflicts. Rather, 'the world that we encounter in ordinary experience is one in which we are faced with choices between ends equally ultimate, and claims equally absolute, the realisation of some of which must inevitably involve the sacrifice of others' (L 213–14).

In this passage Berlin sketches the heart of value pluralism. Basic human goods cannot be easily ranked or commensurated, but are irreducibly multiple, frequently incompatible and sometimes incommensurable with one another. The world of value pluralism is a world of moral conflict, disagreement and dilemma. Irreducibly plural values may clash. Incommensurable values, when they clash, cannot be ranked or traded off according to a single formula that is correct in all cases. Each value is its own measure and, depending on the circumstances, there may be many reasonable ways of responding to conflicts among them. Consequently there is no possibility in a pluralist world of a 'final solution' to all moral and political problems, and therefore no justification of authoritarian politics in the name of utopia (L 212).

Here, however, a problem arises. If pluralism means that there are many legitimate ways of ranking values, does it mean that anything goes? Does pluralism amount to a form of relativism, in which all ethical perspectives are equally authoritative? What then could be said for Berlin's liberalism—his general defence of minimal 'frontiers' of negative liberty against tyrannies like the Soviet Union (L 52–3, 171–4, 211)? If pluralism is really a species of relativism, then Berlin's liberal commitments could be dismissed as no more than his personal preferences or the values of certain cultures among others. So much, then, for his opposition to Soviet Communism, or to scientism, or to the historical abuse of positive liberty.

It has to be said that Berlin does sometimes come close to equating pluralism with relativism. In his studies of Vico and Herder in particular, he appears to endorse what he sees as their shared picture of cultures as distinct and incommensurable, each with its own 'centre of gravity' (e.g. TCE 61, 75, 211, 233–5). In his later work, however, he rejects that conclusion and tries to show how pluralism and relativism are distinct—indeed that pluralism is the superior view. The key point in this respect is that we are capable of understanding other cultures. What makes this possible is our ability to project ourselves into alien points of view by using our imaginations. This 'inside view' is in turn made possible by the 'human horizon' we all share: the basic common experience and responses that identify us as human beings (CTH 10–11; 79–80). What makes those shared attributes distinctively human is that they include conduct oriented to ends or purposes or values, even if these are not consciously or explicitly formulated. It follows that some (highly generic) values are, and must be, universal. Berlin gives no systematic account of the precise content of these universal values, although he occasionally refers in this connection to liberty, equality, justice, and courage (L 172; CIB 37). At any rate he is convinced that, compared with relativism, pluralism is truer to our experience of universal values that cross cultural boundaries.

Choice under pluralism: the subjectivist and contextualist interpretations

The existence of moral universals does not, however, solve the problem of justifying liberalism in the face of value pluralism. There is still the pluralist emphasis on hard choices. Liberalism involves the privileging of certain values over others. If such basic values are incommensurable, why should we choose the liberal package of values rather than some alternative, such as conservative, socialist or Communist packages?

Berlin never answers this question systematically, and never really gives it his concerted attention. From what he does say, however, we can extract three different responses. First, he sometimes seems to believe that incommensurable values are wholly incomparable with one another, and that consequently choices among them must be ultimately non-rational, or not guided by any reason that is decisive over others (AC 74–5). If this is his view then his commitment to liberal solutions in preference to the alternatives looks arbitrary. Indeed, on this strong reading of incommensurability, no political position is rationally justifiable since any such position rests ultimately on a non-rational plumping for one set of values rather than another.

However, Berlin repudiates this subjectivist interpretation of choice under incommensurability in a later article (Berlin and Williams 1994). There, he insists that reasoned choice among incommensurable goods is possible, if not in the abstract then at least in (some) particular cases. He gives no examples, but one can imagine a conflict between liberty and equality. There is no good reason to rank equality above liberty in every case, or in the abstract, but there may be good reason to do so for the specific purpose of welfare redistribution (L 172–3). Consequently, Berlin's second view of choice under pluralism allows at least some room for rational choice. Incommensurability rules out simple formulas that apply in all cases, but not the possibility of reasoned choice within a particular context. I shall call this his 'contextual' approach.

This contextual view is an improvement on the crude subjectivism of Berlin's first position, but its upshot remains hard to separate from the cultural relativism he is supposed to reject. What sort of context should we look to for guidance? One obvious candidate is cultural context, and Berlin does sometimes speaks in just those terms, referring to the possibility of resolving hard choices by appeal to 'the general pattern of life in which we believe' (L 47), or 'the forms of life of the society to which one belongs' (CTH 18). In these passages cultural convention seems to be authoritative.

Choice under pluralism: the conceptual interpretation

In 'Two Concepts of Liberty', however, Berlin also hints at a third response to the problem of pluralist choice, and in particular of the status of liberal values under pluralism. In certain passages Berlin seems to find liberal principles implicit in the concept of pluralism itself. I shall call this his 'conceptual' interpretation of pluralist choice. The text contains two arguments along these lines, corresponding roughly to two elements of pluralism: value conflict and incommensurability.

First, Berlin believes that the pluralist emphasis on value conflict yields an argument for freedom of choice. If pluralism is true, 'the necessity of choosing between absolute claims is then an inescapable characteristic of the human condition. This gives its value to freedom [...]' (L 214). The value-pluralist outlook emphasises moral plurality and conflict, therefore the unavoidability of choice. If we must choose, Berlin argues, we must value freedom of choice, hence by implication a liberal order based on negative liberty. Pluralism implies liberalism.

This argument suffers from an obvious logical flaw: it violates 'Hume's law', according to which values cannot be derived logically from facts. To say simply that pluralist choices are unavoidable is not to say that they are desirable, or that our freedom to make them should be maximised (Crowder 1994, 297; JG 160–1). To the necessity of difficult moral choices an equally valid response might be to keep such choices to a minimum, and that would be a recipe for authoritarian rather than liberal politics.

A reply to this objection might be that Berlin does not really intend to claim a *logical* connection between pluralism and liberalism, but some other kind of link. On this matter of Berlin's intentions, the evidence is highly equivocal. On the one hand, the possibility that Berlin is claiming a logical link between pluralism and liberalism is supported by the last section of 'Two Concepts', with its references to the way the experience of pluralism 'gives its value to freedom', and to 'pluralism, with the measure of "negative" liberty that it entails' (L 214, 216).[1] On the other hand, there is Berlin's declaration in an interview that pluralism and liberalism 'are not logically connected'—although this is immediately followed by the claim that 'pluralism entails that [...] a minimum degree of toleration, however reluctant, becomes indispensable' (CIB 44). Most recently it has been argued that 'the connection between pluralism and liberalism is not *logical* in character, but *psychological*' (UD 226, 290–2, 296–7). If that were so, then Berlin's apparent leap from is to ought might not be so easily criticised as a logical error.

There are two problems with the 'psychological' defence of Berlin, however. The first is that its precise terms are unclear. Berlin himself mentions the idea of a psychological link between pluralism and liberalism on a couple of occasions in very late correspondence and interviews, but he does little more than name it as an alternative to the possibility of a logical link. He does not explain what he means by a 'psychological' connection, and his comment that 'everything is ultimately psychological' is not helpful (UD 99). A similar idea is given more substance by Michael Walzer and William Galston, who both see pluralism and liberalism as linked by overlapping temperaments or general dispositions (Walzer

---

1. Henry Hardy points out that the second phrase may refer to contingent rather than logical entailment, but it seems to me that the latter meaning is more natural for a professional philosopher such as Berlin.

1995, 31; Galston 2002, 61–2). As Walzer puts it, 'I don't know anyone who believes in value pluralism who isn't a liberal'. 'Receptivity, generosity and scepticism' are 'qualities of mind' that tend to be present in both liberals and pluralists. Pluralists, in short, tend to be liberals, and vice versa. However, not all pluralists are psychologically disposed to be liberals. Two notable exceptions (if they are exceptions rather than the rule) are John Gray and John Kekes, who both accept value pluralism but argue against liberalism. Gray rejects liberal values as universally applicable; Kekes opposes liberalism root and branch.[2] On the 'psychological' view of the pluralism–liberalism relation, what can liberals say to Gray and Kekes: that they are psychologically abnormal?

Even if we accept that most pluralists tend to be liberals and vice versa, what is the force of this observation? Gray and Kekes claim that pluralists who are inclined to be liberals are making a mistake. The reason they give is that pluralism leads logically away from liberalism. For both Gray and Kekes, if value pluralism is true then many different rankings of goods are equally reasonable: no single ranking can be universally authoritative. Therefore the universalist claims of the traditional liberal project are invalid. At best (in Gray's account), liberalism represents only one locally valid ranking of values in competition with other locally valid rankings. To respond to this kind of argument, liberals need to do more than simply point to a supposed temperamental convergence, since that merely begs the question. They need logical arguments of their own.[3]

So far, Berlin has not given us such an argument, but he hints at another possibility when he discusses the implications of value incommensurability. 'If [men] had assurance that in some perfect state, realisable by men on earth, no ends pursued by them would ever be in conflict, the necessity and agony of choice would disappear, and with it the central importance of the freedom to choose' (L 214). Here he suggests that the incommensurability of values implies the imperfectibility of human lives in general and of political life in particular. His critical targets are views like classical Marxism and anarchism, which anticipate the pos-

---

2. Gray 1993, 1995; JG; Gray 2000, 2006; Kekes 1993, 1997, 1998. For more detailed responses to Gray and Kekes, see LVP chapter 5; IBLP chapter 7; Crowder 2006; Galston 2002, chapter 5.

3. This suggests a response to Graeme Garrard's claim in this volume (156 above) that the relation between value pluralism and liberalism is 'contingent' rather than logical. It is unclear what Garrard means by 'contingent' here, other than that the truth of value pluralism makes it 'more likely' that liberalism is justified (universally or locally, objectively or only for value pluralists?). Perhaps he has the 'psychological' connection in mind, but that provides no answer to Gray and Kekes. On the other hand, if there is something about the concept of pluralism itself that makes adherence to liberalism more likely, then what is that something, and how is this argument different from my 'conceptual' case?

sibility of human societies in which all genuine goods are realised simultaneously and harmoniously, and in which significant disagreement and conflict concerning the nature of the good life is a thing of the past. If pluralism is true, Berlin argues, such positions must be dismissed as dangerous utopian fantasies. Value incommensurability implies the permanence of conflict among goods and ways of ranking goods, and it therefore rules out as conceptually incoherent some of the main ideological rivals of liberalism. Moreover—although Berlin does not spell this out—it provides liberalism with positive support, since it implies that a realistic and humane form of politics must be one that accepts and accommodates serious moral conflict and disagreement. Liberalism, with its values of toleration and personal liberty, arguably falls within this latter class of realistic positions.

This argument is persuasive as far as it goes, but limited. It fails to single liberalism out as the *best* political response to pluralism. Liberalism is not the only political form that is consistent with pluralist anti-utopianism. Conservatism is another obvious candidate—a superior candidate, Kekes would argue. And if conservatism is acceptable, then liberal pluralists are forced back to the problem of relativism, since conservatism counsels reverence for local tradition. Liberals need a stronger principle than imperfectibility if liberalism is to be picked out as uniquely or best fitted to the pluralist outlook.

I conclude, then, that Berlin's actual attempts to argue from the concept of value pluralism to liberalism fall short. The argument from choice is either logically flawed or psychologically indeterminate, and the argument from anti-utopianism fails to specify liberalism as the best response to social imperfectibility.

Berlin's universal values

Before moving on to consider ways of reviving and adding to these arguments, I want to look at a claim that has been attributed to Berlin, but that he does not make—indeed, it is undermined by much that he actually says.

The claim is that Berlin's commitment to the universality of at least some values suggests a principle of respect for a minimal universal morality that is best satisfied by liberalism. Jonathan Riley, for example, refers in this connection to starvation, arbitrary killing and slavery as experiences that are universally disvalued, and argues that such judgements imply an embryonic notion of human rights, hence the beginnings of a case for liberalism (2000, 2001).

Berlin does not himself argue along these lines, and what he does say about moral universals does not get us very far in this direction. He presents two different accounts of universal values, but neither of them identifies values that are substantial or thick enough to amount to, or even approach, distinctively liberal values.

First, there is the idea of the 'human horizon' introduced earlier: I take this to imply that universal values are presupposed by our ability to understand other cultures. This is possible because the specific values of alien cultures, even values that we reject, are expressions of very general human purposes that we do share. Clearly, such purposes must be very general indeed, since they are limited, according to Berlin, only by what is recognisably human, and so fall within the human horizon (CC 166; CTH 11, 80). For example, he declares explicitly that the values of the Nazis are, regrettably, recognisably human, and so fall within the human horizon (POI 12–13; CIB 38). We reject these values, but we can nevertheless understand them because they express, albeit in a grossly distorted way, generic human purposes that we all share. Berlin does not spell out what these purposes are that we share with the Nazis, but one can imagine that they may include the desire for cultural belonging that has led historically in various directions, including both liberal and aggressively illiberal forms of nationalism (AC 333–55). At any rate, it is clear that the values implied by the human horizon must be too thin or generic to recommend liberalism, or indeed to have any critical force. They are by definition values that are expressed in all recognisably human cultures. Berlin appeals to them not in order to make any substantial ethical or political case, but to explain how we can empathise with alien ways of life, which in turn helps to separate the pluralist outlook from relativism.

Sometimes, however, Berlin speaks in apparently different terms of universal values as 'an empirical fact about mankind [...]. There are values that a great many human beings in the vast majority of places and situations, at almost all times, do in fact hold in common, whether consciously and explicitly or as expressed in their behaviour, gestures, actions' (CIB 37).[4] I shall call this Berlin's notion of 'core' universals.[5] Again, he says very little about the content of these values, apart from occasionally mentioning liberty, equality, justice and courage. Riley's proposals would also be plausible candidates as core universals, since most people in most human societies have regarded starvation, 'arbitrary' killing and slavery as misfortunes to be avoided, at least for themselves.

Does Berlin's notion of core universals get us any further towards a more substantial set of common values that point towards liberal institutions? Not as he presents it, I believe. Part of the problem is that the core universals are still too thin or generic to have any real critical teeth. On one interpretation, they might be seen as coextensive with the horizon, a set of ultra-generic values that are

---

4. See, similarly, L 45; CTH 18.

5. Here I follow Henry Hardy's use of the term 'core', which is used rather differently by Berlin (AC 1; TCE 277). See the Appendix to this volume, which contains a diagram of the relation between the core and the horizon suggested by Hardy and approved by Berlin. I have reservations about this diagram, noted in the accompanying discussion.

expressed in various ways in all human societies. This fits with Berlin's definition of the core as consisting of values that have actually been held by most societies. Alternatively, it may be argued that the core universals should be thought of as thicker than the values of the horizon—that is, as more substantial or demanding values that are not so easily satisfied, and so capable of providing critical leverage against some societies or social practices. But if the relevant values are said to be 'held' by 'the vast majority' of human societies, then that might seem to leave little scope for pointing critically to cases where such values have been dishonoured. In fact the matter is not quite so simple. Later I shall look at a non-Berlinian account of moral universals that does explain how values can be both 'held' by a society and dishonoured at the same time. For the moment I simply note that no such account appears in Berlin. Once again, he shows no sign of wanting to use his notion of moral universals as a critical standard.

Indeed, it is hard to see how he could do so, given the strength of his empirical emphasis when he discusses values.[6] In referring to 'values'—whether those of the horizon or the core—Berlin usually makes the purely factual claim that these are ends that people value or have valued historically; he is not usually making any normative judgment about whether such ends are really valuable. So, when he says there are universal values, he is merely reporting that certain ends have in fact been valued by most human societies, without making any judgement of his own about whether these ends ought to have been valued. This approach has the advantage that it enables Berlin to stay out of controversies about the true nature of the human good. But the price of this abstention is that his notion of universals is normatively sterile. Hume's law comes in again. From the mere fact that most human societies have valued warfare, for example, it does not follow that human societies ought to value warfare, or that a society that rejected war is worthy of criticism. Even if Berlin's notion of the core universals had more substance than it has, no normative commitment would follow.[7]

Finally, even if Berlin's universals did have critical force, he gives us no reason to believe that this will be sufficient to support distinctively liberal commitements. He does assert that all societies are committed to 'a minimum of what I have called "negative" liberty', but this turns out to mean only that 'no society literally suppresses all the liberties of its members' (L 207). This liberty is minimal indeed, and Berlin himself acknowledges that it falls well short of defining

---

6. On Berlin's 'empiricism' in general, see POI 1–2; IBLP 15–21; and 20 above.

7. He does, in one place, refer to 'rules so long and widely accepted that their observance has entered into the very conception of what it is to be a normal human being' (L 211). But his subsequent unpacking of 'normal' is very unclear, oscillating between generic, 'horizon'-type notions of 'humanity' and 'sanity' on the one hand, and specifically liberal standards of due process of law on the other.

liberal demands, such as those of J. S. Mill and Benjamin Constant, for a 'maximum' degree of individual liberty. Similarly, the universals listed by Riley—avoidance of starvation, arbitrary killing and slavery—are too thin to single out liberalism as their best political expression. The most one could say is that liberalism is compatible with the moral implications of pluralism on this score, since liberals do accept these universals. But liberals are clearly not alone in accepting these values: conservatives, socialists and Communists, indeed virtually all human societies, could say the same.

I shall argue later that there may yet be potential to develop a pluralist notion of moral universals in a critical, indeed a liberal, direction. For the present, though, I conclude that there is little to support such an argument in what is actually said by Berlin. The values implied by the horizon are ultra-generic, compatible with anything that is humanly recognisable. The core universals may be thicker, but we are given little reason to believe that they are thick enough to possess any significant critical teeth. What bite they do have does not amount to a specific case for liberalism. Indeed, Berlin's usual notion of moral universals lacks any direct normative force because it is strictly empirical.[8]

BEYOND BERLIN

Can the pluralist case for liberalism be restated in more persuasive terms than those provided by Berlin? I believe it can. In part such a restatement will consist of a resuscitation and amendment of Berlin's arguments, in part it will appeal to additional arguments not found in Berlin. I begin by briefly reconsidering the contextual strategy before focusing on the conceptual approach.

The contextual strategy

Recall that Berlin sometimes suggests that we can rank competing incommensurable values for good reason in context. This implies the possibility of a contextual case for liberalism: liberal values should be prioritised in certain contexts. The problem with this was that by 'context' Berlin usually seems to assume the context of a particular cultural tradition—'the general pattern of life in which we believe' —which makes his position hard to distinguish from cultural relativism. On such a view, liberal politics will be justified only where there is already a liberal culture—a view that does not seem robust enough to support Berlin's liberalism.

---

8. This is not to say that such empirical universals are wholly irrelevant to normative commitments. I return to this point below.

Might it be possible to broaden the contextual case for liberalism by broadening the understanding of 'context' on which it is based? A broader view would understand context as including not only pre-existing culture but also wider social, economic or civilisational circumstances. If liberal values could be identified with such a wider context, that might suggest their validity across cultural boundaries. For example, Joseph Raz argues that the central liberal ideal of personal autonomy is appropriate, even unavoidable, not only for currently liberal societies but for all societies under 'the conditions of the industrial age and its aftermath with their fast changing technologies and free movement of labour' (1986, 369).

Without wishing to reject this line entirely, I think it suffers from a major difficulty. The wider the context, the more likely it is to be consistent with a whole range of ethical and political responses among which liberalism occupies no privileged position. For example, 'the industrial age' or 'modernity' is too wide a context to single out liberal ways of life as uniquely appropriate or successful. Raz's argument on this score is countered by John Gray, who points to the apparent success under modern economic conditions of Asian cultural groups that do not value individual autonomy highly (1993, 308; 1995, 83). On the other hand, if liberals narrow the context to focus only on those circumstances that favour liberal commitments, they will be accused of cooking the books. In short, the contextual approach to liberalism is troubled by an awkward tension between excessively wide and excessively narrow versions that either fail to point distinctively to liberalism or do so only in a question-begging way. I do not say categorically that it would be impossible to strike a perfect balance between these extremes, but such a course would obviously be tricky.

The conceptual strategy

Liberal pluralists would therefore do well to consider the alternative, 'conceptual' strategy, where links with liberalism are sought from within the concept of value pluralism itself. I shall now consider four arguments along these lines, each corresponding to one of the elements of the pluralist idea. Three of these will be attempts to reformulate and strengthen the conceptual arguments I have already introduced: the argument from moral universals, and Berlin's arguments from choice and imperfectibility. To these I add a further argument that is not found in Berlin but that has, I believe, crucial implications—not least for the prospects of reviving the arguments from choice and imperfectibility. This further argument focuses on the 'plurality' component of value pluralism. It generates a principle I shall call 'respect for plurality', which in turn implies a commitment to the promotion of value diversity. It also transforms Berlin's arguments from imperfectibility and choice into more effective arguments from 'reasonable disagreement' and 'personal autonomy' respectively. Although I see the commitment to universal values as playing only a limited role in constructing a distinctive and convincing pluralist case for liberalism, I argue that such a case does emerge from the principles of value diversity, reasonable disagreement about the good life, and personal autonomy, all underwritten by the principle of respect for plurality. I begin with the argument from moral universals.

1. *Universal values*

Recall that while some people might be tempted to seek a direct route to liberalism from the universal values presupposed by pluralism, Berlin himself gives us little reason to believe that such a strategy will succeed. Whether conceived as horizon or core, Berlin's notion of moral universals possesses no significant critical force, for two main reasons: first, his universal values are too thin or generic; second, they are merely empirical descriptions rather than normative commitments.

Might it be possible to solve these problems by reformulating the pluralist account of moral universals in terms that are both normatively committed and also thick enough to have real critical bite? A model for such a view may be provided by Martha Nussbaum's theory of human capabilities.[9] For Nussbaum, people need certain fundamental 'capabilities' in order to live lives worthy of human dignity, and the extent to which these capabilities are promoted is a universal criterion for evaluating the performance of ethical, social and political systems around the world.

Unlike Berlin, Nussbaum spells out her universal values explicitly and systematically, listing them under ten main headings: life; bodily health; bodily integrity; senses, imagination and thought; emotions; practical reason; affiliation; relations with other species; play; control over one's environment. And unlike Berlin's, Nussbaum's universals are normative commitments: the capabilities are not merely valued by people de facto, but objectively valuable for human well-being.

A standard objection to this approach is that Nussbaum's universals are selected in an arbitrary or biased way. Indeed, someone might argue that this is where Berlin's strictly empirical view is superior: Berlin simply reports what people have valued, while Nussbaum lays herself open to objection by committing herself to a view of what is really valuable.

Nussbaum is alive to this objection, and replies that her capabilities possess both critical force and empirical grounding. On the one hand, the list includes some items that could serve as bases for cross-cultural criticism. 'Practical reason', for

---

9. Nussbaum has advanced this theory in many places. The most recent account at the time of writing is Nussbaum 2006. Nussbaum 2000 chapter 1 also contains a clear statement and defence.

example, involves 'being able to [. . .] engage in critical reflection about the planning of one's life' (2000, 79). This seems to point to a respect for personal autonomy that often appears to be denied in practice by many traditional forms of life, especially for certain categories of people, notably women. On the other hand, the list is said to reflect the actual commitments of human cultures the world over. It is based on evidence from the literatures of many cultures, especially the 'tragic' literature that reveals what different societies have regarded as harms and misfortunes. Nussbaum's conclusion from these enquiries is that certain losses—of physical capacities, loved ones, basic freedom, and so forth—have been regarded as disastrous in all cultures at all times. This account of universal misfortunes suggests a theory of the human good. It is not that Nussbaum's theory of the good is derived logically from her empirical account of cultural norms, since that would breach Hume's law. The link is the looser idea that the de facto norms constitute *evidence* of what a theory of the good ought to contain. Regularities of human experience and evaluation tend to suggest what really contributes to a good human life, but the final commitment in this respect is a matter of judgement rather than deduction.

Note also how this account enables Nussbaum to explain how certain goods can be both 'held' by most societies and, at the same time, grounds for criticising those same societies. This was a question raised earlier in connection with Berlin's notion of a set of 'core' universals, but it did not receive an answer from Berlin. For Nussbaum, practical reason, for example, is valued by most human societies in the sense that most cultures contain streams of thought and practice that emphasise the contribution made by practical reason to human well-being. On the other hand, cultures are complex constructions containing many streams, not all of them in harmony. In some societies the value of critical reflection comes into conflict with other powerful concerns, with the result that practical reason is not as fully or consistently institutionalised as it might be. The value of independent thought is acknowledged in aspects of these societies (as in all others), but such societies may still be criticised for failing to promote that value more fully—for example, as a capability appropriate to women as well as men. In this way, the empirical universality and the normative universalism in Nussbaum's theory are linked.

This step from empirical to normative universals is one that Berlin might have taken but does not. His universals are usually stolidly empirical. By and large, he is suspicious of theories of the human good, which he tends to associate with speculative approaches to philosophy, and more pointedly with ethical monism. I think this hostility is unnecessarily monolithic, preventing him from drawing on philosophical and moral resources, especially in the natural law tradition, that might have given more substance to his ethical and political theory.[10]

---

10. There is a parallel here with Berlin's hostility to positive liberty in 'Two Concepts of Liberty', although the nature of that hostility needs careful qualification: see IBLP 83–6.

Nussbaum is an interesting case in point, since she is a value pluralist—the capabilities represent incommensurable goods—yet combines this with an explicitly normative starting point and a much fuller account of the content of moral universals than anything in Berlin. In these respects I believe Nussbaum's work makes a valuable contribution to a liberal reading of value pluralism.

It may be, then, that Berlin's account of moral universals could be fortified, and thus turned to real critical account, by Nussbaum's theory or something like it. However, it seems to me that liberal pluralists should still be wary of pinning their hopes on a case based on moral universals alone. Nussbaum's view is far from uncontroversial. It has frequently been accused of containing—especially in its emphasis on critical reflection—a liberal or individualist bias that prevents it from being truly universal in the empirical sense (Miller and Fabre 2003, 13). Indeed, Nussbaum herself has recently sought to allay this objection by (among other things) distinguishing critically reflective 'practical reason', which she insists is genuinely universal, from a distinctively liberal notion of 'personal autonomy' (2003, 39–43). This suggests that the tension between the empirical and critical elements of such a theory never goes away; at best it might be managed or negotiated. How far Nussbaum succeeds in this, and whether some other view might do better, are complex questions I cannot answer here. In view of the difficulties associated with any strategy of this kind, I believe that liberal pluralists should at least be prepared to consider further alternatives.

2. Diversity of goods

One such alternative can be found by focusing on another aspect of the concept of pluralism: the irreducible plurality of human goods. The basic argument goes as follows. Value pluralism is the idea that there are many intrinsic goods—that is, goods valuable for their own sake. Each of these goods makes its own unique claims on us, requiring our respect. Prima facie, we should respect all such goods equally—that is, we should respect all such goods across their full range. This is what I mean by 'respect for plurality'. To respect plural goods involves promoting them where possible. In principle, then, pluralism commits us to the promotion of as many goods as possible in a given situation—that is, pluralism generates a principle of 'value diversity'. This idea is captured by Bernard Williams, who writes, 'If there are many and competing genuine values, then the greater the extent to which a society tends to be single-valued, the more genuine values it neglects or suppresses. More, to this extent, must mean better' (1978, xvii). Roughly speaking, it is generally better that a society embrace a greater rather than narrower range of values. When it comes to determining the best political vehicle for advancing this diversity of goods, liberalism surely has a strong claim. Its traditional emphasis on individual liberty, toleration and personal autonomy clears social spaces within which individuals and groups can pursue a wide range of different purposes.

A number of qualifications and observations are in order. First, the argument favours certain forms of liberalism over others. In particular, value diversity is a criterion that is more convincingly satisfied by 'social' or 'egalitarian' types of liberalism, which balance individual liberty with equality and social justice, than by 'classical' or 'laissez-faire' or 'neo-liberal' forms, which elevate negative liberty (i.e. liberty as non-interference) and the free market above all other considerations.[11] This view is supported by Berlin's attack on laissez-faire capitalism. The problem with laissez-faire, according to Berlin, is that it maximises the amount of negative liberty in a society, but at the cost of ignoring other important values, such as social justice, equality and compassion (L 37–9).[12]

Second, my argument from pluralism to liberalism by way of diversity has been accused of breaching Hume's law (UD 295–6). The objection is that value pluralism makes a claim of fact (about the nature of values) from which I then illicitly try to deduce a value judgement (that we ought to promote a diversity of values). This would be true if I followed Berlin's strongly empirical understanding of values, but in this respect I depart from him, for reasons explained in the last section. I understand the universal values presupposed by pluralism as contributing objectively to human well-being—as argued by Aristotle, the natural law tradition and Nussbaum. Consequently, my argument does not violate Hume's law because it does not move from fact to value but from value to value. The starting point is not a claim of fact about what people happen to value, but a value judgement to the effect that certain generic goods (and more specific local expressions of these) contribute to human well-being.

Third, I say that a society ought 'prima facie' to promote 'more' rather than fewer goods, because for pluralists the goal of diversity cannot be a simple matter of maximising a quantity of goods whatever the circumstances. For one thing, pluralists cannot accept that there is any common measure according to which different goods can be quantified. Further, to 'respect' a good is not *always* to promote it, because sometimes there will not be enough 'social space' in which to pursue in practice all the goods we may wish to honour in principle (Rawls 1993, 57). This may be because of lack of time or resources, or it may be that certain goods conflict with one another as a matter of necessity—as when someone cannot simultaneously

---

11. Representative 'social' liberals include T. H. Green, L. T. Hobhouse, John Rawls and Ronald Dworkin. 'Classical' liberals in this sense include Adam Smith, Friedrich Hayek and Robert Nozick.

12. For a similar argument, directed against Robert Nozick's theory of the minimal State, see Hart 1979.

enjoy the distinctive benefits of single life and married life. The goal of value diversity, then, should be understood in terms of a tolerably coherent package of values that can be judged to express a greater range of human goods, overall, than the alternatives. The comparison will not be precisely measurable, but rather a matter of judgement. Judgement need not invoke measurement, and moral and political judgements are, by and large, cases in point. Quantification is not required, for example, for the judgement that a more diverse package of goods was promoted by the liberal Western societies of the twentieth century than by the Soviet Union.

Fourth, my linking of pluralism with diversity might be thought to be unpluralist because it makes a single value overriding, namely diversity, when the central claim of value pluralism is precisely that no single value, or narrow range of values, is overriding.[13] However, the idea of value diversity, as I conceive it here, is not really 'a single value' on a level with, say, negative liberty. Rather, 'diversity' is a meta-value expressing the notion of 'respect for plurality'—that is, to respect diversity is to respect *all* genuine human goods.

A final set of qualifications responds to John Gray's objection that although pluralism implies an ethic of diversity, diversity is not best served by liberalism. The reason is that Gray understands the diversity in question as a diversity of cultures or forms of life. Because different forms of life generate different political systems, pluralist diversity therefore endorses a diversity of political regimes. Liberalism will be one of these, but only one among others—it will possess no privileged status. The optimal pluralist world will contain both liberal and non-liberal regimes (JG 152). The problem with this view is that it blurs the boundary between pluralism and cultural relativism. On a distinctively pluralist view it is particular goods, such as liberty and equality, that are incommensurable, not whole cultures. (Whole cultures cannot be incommensurable because pluralists accept that at least some values are shared universally.) Consequently, the ideal of diversity implicit in pluralism refers, primarily, not to political regimes or forms of life, as assumed by Gray, but to goods or values. Rather than valuing and promoting a diversity of regimes or cultures without regard to their content, value pluralists should value and promote a diversity of regimes and cultures that are themselves internally diverse—that is, that exhibit internally a diversity of goods and (secondarily) ways of life. Once more, liberalism has a strong claim to being acknowledged as the political form most accommodating of this kind of diversity. This is not to say that liberalism is limitlessly accommodating or wholly neutral among conceptions of the good life, merely that a liberal order leaves more room for a variety of goods and conceptions of the good to be pursued than does any known alternative.[14]

---

13. See Graeme Garrard, 156 above.

14. Even if whole cultures *were* incommensurable, that would not necessarily rule out the possibility of ranking them, on the model of the reasoned ranking of incommensu-

3. Reasonable disagreement

Berlin's argument from imperfectibility, it is recalled, got us a certain distance from pluralism to liberalism, but then stalled. It ruled out utopian rivals, but then failed to privilege the claims of liberalism over those of conservatism. I believe that this next step, a pluralist argument for liberalism against conservatism, can be taken by turning the argument from imperfectibility into an argument from 'reasonable disagreement'.

This move links value pluralism with an idea made familiar by the leading defenders of 'political' liberalism, John Rawls (1993) and Charles Larmore (1996).[15] For these thinkers a salient feature of the modern world is 'the fact of pluralism': there is widespread disagreement about how people ought to live their lives. Further, much of that disagreement is 'reasonable': even if some views of the good life are mistaken, there is no way this kind of mistake can be rationally demonstrated, and those who adhere to these views must be regarded as doing so on reasonable grounds. Where disagreements are reasonable in this sense they are likely to be permanent. A realistic and prudent form of politics will therefore accept and accommodate reasonable disagreement rather than trying to over-come it. Liberalism, with its characteristic acceptance of plural conceptions of the good, is such a realistic and prudent political form.

Much the same case can be made in distinctively value-pluralist terms. Conceptions of the good life can be thought of as essentially schemes for ranking basic human goods in most cases. Christians, for example, emphasise humility and love for one's neighbour as especially important values for all human beings in all or most circumstances; imperial Rome celebrated manly strength and self-assertion in the same general terms (CTH 8). If at least some basic values are incommensurable, then many such general rankings will be prima facie reasonable. This is not to say that pluralism endorses all conceptions of the good without exception, since some do better than others when judged by pluralist standards such as value diversity and perhaps respect for universals. But within those limits there will be much legitimate variation. Consequently, many disagreements concerning the merits of rival conceptions of the good will also be reasonable. Reasonable disagreement ought to be accommodated, and liberalism provides the appropriate political vehicle for such accommodation.

---

rable *values*, either in context or according to the principles implicit in pluralism itself. Consequently, even if Gray were right about the incommensurability of cultures, that would not be enough to eliminate arguments for the superiority of liberal cultures.

15. But note that the relation between Berlinian liberal pluralism and Rawlsian 'political liberalism' is not without friction: see the criticism of liberal pluralism in Larmore 1996 chapter 7. Liberal-pluralist responses to this critique include LVP chapter 7 and Galston 2002 chapter 4.

It might be objected that there is a hidden assumption here. Even if disagreements about the good life are 'reasonable' in the sense that many substantial claims in this area are not demonstrable, how does it follow that such claims should be accommodated rather than overruled by an orthodoxy asserted by force? To put this another way, the reasonableness of this kind of disagreement makes it permanent *unless* it is ended by force—for example, the enforcement of a particular religion. From a pluralist point of view, why should enforcement of orthodoxy be trumped by liberal accommodation? Does liberal accommodation award an un-pluralist priority to toleration or respect over unity or righteousness?

One response to this challenge would be to appeal to the traditional Lockean point that, since beliefs in such matters are private to the believer, attempts to use the blunt instrument of the state to enforce belief are likely to be futile (Locke 1689). Second, Berlin makes the point that 'drastic action' tends to lead to consequences that are predictable only in that they always involve 'the avoidable suffering of the innocent' (CTH 17). This second reply can be supplemented by a more distinctively pluralist consideration, based on the principle of 'respect for plurality'. Coercion always has costs, and the massive degree of coercion that would be required (at least under modern conditions) to enforce allegiance to a single 'thick' conception of the good would have massive costs. From the pluralist point of view, which requires respect for the full range of human goods, such costs are highly unlikely to be acceptable. History, it is true, is full of instances where people have believed that no cost was too great in order to realise some supreme end. But that kind of view has tended to rest on the monism that pluralists oppose.

How does 'reasonable disagreement' give liberalism an edge over conservatism? Conservatives agree with liberals about the general imperfectibility of human societies, but they are not as well placed to cope with reasonable disagreement. The problem is the conservative reliance on tradition. The typical conservative response to social imperfectibility is to seek a stable order through uncritical adherence to an inherited conception of the good. But that possibility is ruled out by the reasonable disagreement characteristic of modernity.

Again, the same point can be approached in a distinctively value-pluralist way. The disjunction between pluralism and traditionalism was touched on earlier, when I argued that even so far as pluralism implies the importance of context in decision-making, context need not be narrowly identified with tradition. The idea of reasonable disagreement drives a further wedge between pluralism and tradition. On the pluralist view, traditions themselves embody rankings of incommensurables that are subject to reasonable disagreement. Moreover, for the pluralist this is not just a fact about the modern world but a feature of the human condition: traditions have always embodied particular value-rankings that may be disputed. Of course, one could say the same thing about liberal traditions or conceptions of the good. But liberals are typically prepared to see their own deepest convictions questioned, and even regard this as essential—as in Mill's arguments for freedom of expression (Mill 1859, chapter 2). More importantly, the peculiarity of liberal conceptions of the human good is that they tend to be more 'open-textured' than conservative conceptions. That is, they leave room for people to pursue different ends and projects, including many of those valued by conservatives. Conservatives, on the other hand, tend not to repay the liberal compliment.

4. Individual autonomy

A final link between pluralism and liberalism is suggested by Berlin's argument from choice. Earlier I concluded that that argument was either logically flawed or psychologically indeterminate. It can be made to work, however, when it is converted into an argument from a particular kind of choice: namely, autonomous choice.

The argument from reasonable disagreement showed that we cannot resolve conflicts among incommensurables simply by appealing to tradition. Similarly, we cannot rely on monist rules like utilitarianism to resolve our difficulties—since these, too, represent rankings of incommensurables that reasonable people may contest. How, then, can we decide such questions? Pluralists, I believe, are obliged in such cases to think for themselves in a strong sense. Ideally, they should be prepared to deal with each choice on its own terms, weighing all relevant competing considerations, including those that conflict with rules and customs. They should be able to stand back from received rules and customs, recognise the value rankings these embody, and critically assess their application in the circumstances. This may involve appeal to background values such as personal and collective conceptions of the good, but these too should be subject to revision. Pluralists ought, that is, to be capable of autonomy when they are faced with such fundamental conflicts. And since individual autonomy is one of the most distinctive ideals of liberalism, it is in a liberal political order that the capacity for individual autonomy is most likely to be nurtured.

In short, to cope well with the hard choices that pluralism imposes on us is to be able to choose autonomously, or critically. This argument is essentially a reworking of Berlin's argument from choice, but it avoids Berlin's leap from is to ought. What grounds the case for autonomy here is not merely the necessity of choosing among incommensurables, but the goal of choosing *well*—by which I mean choosing for good reason. It is the need to choose rationally among incommensurables, not simply the need to choose, that requires us to choose autonomously.

This move raises a question of its own: Why is good choice under pluralism the same as rational choice? Why not say that from a pluralist point of view rational choice is itself merely one value among others, no more inherently worthy than arbitrary plumping? The answer appeals once again to the principle of respect for plurality. This does not mean that every human good must be pursued in every situation, since obviously goods often conflict and we have to be selective. It does mean that we should, in making such choices, 'honour' all genuine goods so far as circumstances allow. To determine how far circumstances allow the pursuit of a particular good or combination of goods is the province of practical reasoning. In the absence of practical reasoning our choices would be arbitrary and incoherent, resulting in lives in which goods are pursued or neglected at random, without attention to their real value (Kekes 1993, 97–8). Pluralism does not imply indifference; on the contrary, it stresses the intrinsic value of many goods. Practical reasoning is essential to the honouring of these goods. Since practical reasoning under pluralism requires personal autonomy, respect for plurality requires autonomous thinking.[16]

This pluralist case for individual autonomy has significant ethical and political implications. The political implications I shall come to in a moment, but the immediate ethical message is that the capacity for autonomy is a characteristic of the best lives from a pluralist point of view. People who are not equipped to think critically will be to that extent ill-equipped to cope well with the hard choices that, on the pluralist view, will inevitably confront them. This does not mean that heteronomous lives are valueless. Such lives may exhibit many genuine goods. But heteronomous lives cannot be among the best possible overall, judged from a pluralist perspective, since they lack a capacity for good decision-making in the face of inevitable and profound value conflict.[17]

Someone might object that my conclusion here is un-pluralist, because I have in effect accorded a universal privilege to a single good, namely individual autonomy. But my argument does not require that autonomy be privileged in every case. I do not deny the possibility of situations where personal autonomy appropriately yields to rival considerations such as urgency or security or the demands of personal relationships. The point is that these and other moral decisions are unavoidably made within a political framework that is shaped by *some* general ranking of values. The question is whether, and to what extent, this ranking answers to fundamental pluralist concerns. Among these are concerns for

---

16. Martha Nussbaum presents a similar picture of practical reason as necessary (along with 'affinity') to 'organise' other goods (2000, 82). She does now distinguish practical reason from liberal autonomy (see 220 above), but I believe that distinction is questionable.

17. My argument is that under pluralism lives can count as good to the extent that they exhibit a *capacity* for personal autonomy rather than its actual, or continual, exercise. This leaves open the possibility that people may choose autonomously to live in traditional, non-autonomous ways. For versions of the distinction between capacity and exercise in relation to personal autonomy, see Brighouse 2000, chapters 4–5; Reich 2002, 92–6.

moral universals—although I left open the question of how far these are likely to possess much critical force. More telling are the criteria of value diversity and reasonable disagreement, which suggest a politics capable of accommodating many goods and (secondarily) ways of life. Finally, the exigency of choosing well among incommensurables points to an emphasis on personal autonomy. Together, these values amount to a case for an identifiably liberal political order, and for a liberal order that upholds individual autonomy as a public ideal. But the principles that ground and regulate such an order need not be conceived as absolutes. William Galston captures the appropriate liberal-pluralist view here when he refers to the possibility under pluralism of strong but rebuttable presumptions—in favour, for example, of human rights (2002, 69-78). The same point may be made in favour of the main principles for which I have argued: diversity, reasonable disagreement and individual autonomy.

TWO CONCEPTIONS OF LIBERAL PLURALISM

If these arguments are correct, they add up to a distinctive and compelling pluralist case for liberalism. Moreover—especially if the argument from autonomy is accepted—they add up to a case for a particular kind of liberalism. In this final section I briefly compare the vision of liberalism found in Berlin with the kind of liberalism that emerges from the refurbished and extended case I have presented. The question of whether my view develops or departs from Berlin's is raised by Beata Polanowska-Sygulska, who concludes that my contribution 'does not in the end amount to finishing the old cathedral, but to putting up a new, semi-detached edifice' (UD 299). I think there is some truth in this, but how much is a matter of judgement. I shall point to both continuities and departures.

The general picture of liberalism advanced by Berlin has the following features. First, as we saw earlier, Berlin is deeply ambivalent about liberalism's ethical foundations. Sometimes he seems to regard liberalism as valid only locally or relatively, as in the 'contextual' reading of choice under pluralism; at other times he appears to see the claims of liberalism in more universal terms, as in the hints he offers of a 'conceptual' case, and in his strictures, both explicit and implicit, against tyrannical regimes such as the Soviet Union. It may be that his deepest inclination is to seek a position somewhere between the poles of relativism and abstract universality, a position akin to Raz's broader, 'civilisational' contextualism. If so, Berlin never really makes this clear, and I leave this possibility open.

A second feature of Berlin's liberalism is more definite: his 'realism'. For Berlin, the task of liberalism is not the ambitious, optimistic mission of social perfectibility that he associates with the scientistic *philosophes* of the Enlightenment, but a more modest holding action in which excesses are contained and conflicts managed. This view is generated by his stress on social and political imperfectibility, which in turn derives from his emphasis on the incommensurability of basic human goods.

Third, there is Berlin's emphasis on negative liberty—perhaps the best known aspect of his thought because of the fame of 'Two Concepts of Liberty'. That essay is often misunderstood. Berlin does not claim that the negative liberty of noninterference is the only coherent conception of liberty, or that the positive liberty of self-mastery has no value. However, the general tenor of the essay is that, especially when it comes to political matters, we should prefer the negative to the positive ideal more often than not. Negative liberty is not as vulnerable to the kind of conceptual distortion and misapplication that has historically been the fate of positive liberty. In Berlin's liberalism, negative liberty has a special place.

That does not mean, however, that Berlin is a proponent of minimal-State or laissez-faire liberalism in the mould of Friedrich Hayek or Robert Nozick. On the contrary, he is an explicit defender of economic redistribution—this is a fourth feature of his liberalism, although it is true that he does not develop this defence in any detail. As a value pluralist, he denies that even negative liberty always overrides other values, and indeed argues expressly that concerns for equality and social justice sometimes require restrictions on liberty (L 172–3). Further, Berlin argues, negative liberty is one thing, the 'conditions' for its enjoyment something else (L 38). When people are left wholly at the mercy of the market, they are often left without the resources necessary to take advantage of the 'opportunities' they are said to have in formal, negative-liberty terms.

Fifth, however, Berlin's emphasis on negative liberty does lead to a somewhat conservative attitude to cultural minorities. For Berlin, cultural belonging is a primary human good. This commitment is deeply rooted in his own experience in the Jewish Diaspora, and accounts for his support for Zionism and his sympathy with nationalism more generally. Nevertheless, he does not approve of the politicisation of minority cultural claims that is characteristic of contemporary multiculturalism.[18] In this area he seems definitely to prefer toleration to group rights or minority self-determination.

How does this picture compare with the kind of liberalism indicated by the case I have presented? First, my case is, for better or worse, more forthrightly universalist in its claims. On my view, liberalism is the best political expression of principles that are implied by the concept of value pluralism. These principles are universally valid because value pluralism is itself a universal feature of human morality. Conflicts among incommensurable goods have always been part of

---

18. See Gardels 1991, 21.

human ethical experience, even if not recognised in quite those terms, as shown by the tragedies of Shakespeare and Sophocles. So the foundational case I have constructed looks bolder than that presented by Berlin, who is more apt to appeal to local and historical context. On the other hand, I do not mean to reject contextualism as a possibility either, although I regard it as a second best. Further, my conceptual case is inspired by hints given by Berlin himself, especially in 'Two Concepts'. Arguably, my case is less a departure from Berlin than a resolute following through of one of his own lines of thought.

Second, I see no significant difference between Berlin's view and my own on the score of realism. Again, my development of Berlin's pluralist-based notion of social and political imperfectibility into a version of Rawlsian reasonable disagreement can be seen as a more thorough working out of Berlin's own logic— more vigorous because reasonable disagreement rules out not only liberalism's utopian rivals but also conservativism's reliance on tradition.

Third, however, where Berlin's emphasis falls on negative liberty as the quintessential liberal conception of liberty, my argument stresses the centrality of positive liberty in the form of personal autonomy. If the conditions for personal autonomy are among the primary components of human well-being, as pluralism (on my view) implies, then the securing of those conditions must be a central concern of the liberal State.

How should the conditions for autonomy be secured? The fourth element of Berlin's liberalism was a commitment to economic redistribution rather than laissez-faire. I believe my argument leads in the same direction. While Berlin saw redistribution as required to secure the conditions for enjoyment of negative liberty, I would make the same point about personal autonomy.

Finally, however, my stress on personal autonomy suggests an attitude to culture that is closer to contemporary (liberal) multiculturalism than to Berlin's reliance on toleration alone. Will Kymlicka (1989, 1995) has argued convincingly that the exercise of personal autonomy depends on conditions that are as much cultural as material or economic; further, that the maintenance of cultures cannot be achieved through 'benign neglect', but must be a policy goal of the liberal state. Yet, once again, this conclusion can also be reached through a consistent application of Berlin's own principles. If cultural belonging is such an important part of human well-being, as Berlin believes, then this is true not only for politically dominant cultures but also for minorities, including 'national' minorities.[19]

---

19. Note, however, that my argument, like Kymlicka's, makes multiculturalism subject to the universal value of personal autonomy. It differs from the version of liberal-pluralist multiculturalism advanced by William Galston, where groups may legitimately determine the lives of their members subject only to a 'right of exit' conceived in largely negative-liberty terms: see Galston 2002, especially chapters 8–9. A genuine right of exit

In short, my reformulated and extended case for liberal pluralism, although leading in certain respects to different emphases from those in Berlin, and even to different conclusions, remains broadly in keeping with most of his basic commitments: to individual liberty, 'realism', redistribution, and diversity of both cultures and values. Indeed, in some respects it could be argued that my conclusions—on multiculturalism, for example—are more faithful to the fundamentals of value pluralism than Berlin's own.

This is not to deny that my case departs from Berlin's in significant respects: first, in the claims I make for the universality of liberal pluralism by way of the conceptual argument, compared with the generally contextualist or historicist tenor of Berlin's approach; second, in my stress on personal autonomy compared with Berlin's negative liberty. Yet even these arguments represent, to some extent, the following through of intuitions tentatively expressed by Berlin.[20] On the whole, I am inclined to see my case as going 'beyond' Berlin's mainly in the sense that it develops rather than abandons what he started.

---

requires more than non-interference, I would argue; it requires a capacity on the part of the individual for independent thought (see Crowder 2007). Galston seems to accept this now, but continues to see a distinction between independent thought in the required sense and liberal autonomy (2005, 182–3). I see no such distinction.

20. See, for example, Joshua L. Cherniss's observation (95, 114–16 above) that concern for personal autonomy is prominent in some of Berlin's early work.

10

A Liberal-Pluralist Case for Truth Commissions

LESSONS FROM ISAIAH BERLIN

JONATHAN ALLEN

O ver the past three decades, we have been presented with a remarkable spectacle—a series of regime transitions, occurring first in Southern Europe and Latin America, then in Eastern Europe and South Africa. Totalitarian and authoritarian regimes have been succeeded by more open, representative political systems—and in all these cases, the new societies have had to confront the challenge of deciding what to do in response to abuses of human rights committed by agents of the predecessor regimes. Various responses have been adopted, ranging through inaction, the granting of official pardons, the publication of official records, decisions to offer full or conditional amnesties, criminal prosecution and other penalties (see Kritz 1995, Teitel 2000, Elster 2004). Perhaps the most striking response has been the creation of a new kind of institution, which has come to be called a 'truth commission'. This has attracted a great deal of attention, especially in the form manifested in the South African case, where victims of politically motivated violence were invited to present their stories and confront the self-confessed perpetrators in public hearings. Many observers have concluded that the South African Truth and Reconciliation Commission (TRC) offers a model of 'transitional justice' to be emulated in other societies undergoing political transformation, and perhaps even in more settled societies with a past marked by violence and injustice.[1] Differing accounts of the nature of the truth commission model compete for our attention.

---

1. For these claims, see Rotberg 2000, 4–5, and Valls 2003.

The aim of this chapter is to show that the liberal pluralism articulated by Isaiah Berlin provides a promising framework for interpreting the purposes—and limitations—of truth commissions such as the TRC. But this immediately raises a question: Why Berlin? There are at least two possible objections underlying this question. First, even the most partial admirer of Berlin's work would have to admit that it displays little or no concern with political institutions or questions of policy.[2] Second, some critics have argued that Berlin's thought was moulded—and permanently limited—by the context of the cold war, and that the extent of this influence has not been fully acknowledged in recent appropriations of his work (see Kenny 2000, 1037–8).

It is indeed clear that Berlin's work is above all an attempt to trace the intellectual roots of modern totalitarianism, and to identify views and habits of thought that contributed to its rise and persistence.[3] It is also true that his most important intellectual contributions lie in the areas of meta-ethics, the history of ideas, the analysis of political belief-systems, the elaboration of normative concepts central to political life such as liberty or equality, and the articulation of a liberal disposition. Either for personal reasons, or because of the lingering influence of his early association with logical positivism, Berlin chose not to address the institutional and policy dimension of politics. But this does not signify that his thinking simply has no institutional implications, or that it cannot be applied beyond its original context. Many contemporary public policy controversies are readily comprehensible as conflicts of values—conflicts over the value of the environment and the livelihood of workers, or over liberty and life in the case of abortion, to take just two prominent examples.[4]

Even more important, it is doubtful that the general attitudes Berlin saw at work in Leninist and Stalinist Communism have died along with that ideology. In what follows, I want to show, among other things, that one particularly influential account of the purposes of truth commissions is marked by a troubling tendency towards what Berlin referred to as monism—the view that moral goods are ultimately unitary, and that conflicts of value are more apparent than real, simply the

---

2. For example, in his essay on Montesquieu, Berlin makes only scant reference to the idea of 'countervailing powers', focusing instead on Montesquieu's 'pluralist' appreciation for the diversity of ends pursued by different people, classes and cultures. See 'Montesquieu' in AC. In a similar vein, Berlin's pluralism makes no mention of the institutional pluralism of figures such as Maitland, Cole, Figgis and Laski.

3. This has been ably argued by George Crowder in his excellent book on Berlin: IBLP 2–5.

4. See the cases collected in Gutmann and Thompson 2006. For arguments about ethics and public policy that draw explicitly on value pluralism, see Ignatieff 2001, 2004; Galston 2002, 110–23; Raz 1995; LVP 226–55; IBLP 176–87.

result of faulty understandings of the goods in question. This defence of truth commissions—I shall refer to it as the 'restorative justice' view—is certainly not, in any sense, totalitarian. But it conflates distinct moral values and, in so doing, threatens to deplete the critical vocabulary available to individuals in their political life.

In order to demonstrate the value of Berlin's thought for reflection on truth commissions, I begin by briefly stating my understanding of the nature of the idea of value pluralism espoused by Berlin. I then offer a more extended discussion of the phenomenon of truth commissions and of the TRC in particular, singling out two accounts of the purposes of truth commissions for critical consideration—a 'simple sacrifice' defence, characterised by a crude or casual understanding of the implications of value pluralism, and the 'restorative justice' argument to which I have already made reference. In both cases, I argue that a judicious understanding of value pluralism is able to counter the weaknesses of these two views. I then conclude by discussing Berlin's distinctive form of liberalism, and sketch an account of the function of truth commissions suggested by his liberal pluralism, though this is by no means its only source of inspiration. While my primary aim is to show how Berlin's thought contributes to the formation of a distinctive understanding of truth commissions, I hope that this application will in turn allow us to see the significance of key aspects of Berlin's views in a new light.

UNDERSTANDING VALUE PLURALISM

As George Crowder has recently noted, the two major themes of Berlin's intellectual career are his 'liberal commitment to freedom' and his value pluralism.[5] There is an important sense in which both of these themes have a remedial function for Berlin—both offer a diagnosis of the intellectual sources of modern totalitarianism, as well as an alternative to totalitarian ideologies. It is thus at least plausible that Berlin's liberal pluralism has a role to play in other political settings in which serious harms have been facilitated by ideological commitments—as was certainly the case in South Africa. In later sections of the chapter, I want to show that the idea of value pluralism, rightly understood, offers a vital counter to two problematic defences of the idea of truth commissions. I begin here by outlining a general understanding of value pluralism.

---

5. IBLP 124. The relation between Berlin's pluralism and his commitment to liberalism has become a matter of intense controversy recently, largely as a result of John Gray's argument (JG; Gray 1995, 2000) that a consistent value pluralist disallows a commitment to universal principles, including the principles of universalist liberalism. I shall make no direct contribution to this debate here, although my approach is based on the view that Berlin's value pluralism and his liberalism are best understood as related, but distinct commitments.

Value pluralism, for Berlin, is to be understood as a set of evaluative and descriptive claims, anchored in ordinary experience, about the values or goods rightly recognised by human beings as genuine. Such values are objectively valid, and some of them are universal, that is, valuable for all people everywhere and at all times. However, there are many goods (including some universal goods) that are not reducible to others, though this irreducible plurality is bounded by features of humanity rather than infinite. The plurality of values means that there is the potential for conflict—conflict among goods (such as justice and mercy), within goods (between negative and positive liberty, for example), or between bundles of goods (ways of life or cultural practices). When such conflicts do occur, they force us to make choices that cannot be arrived at simply by appealing to a single decision procedure or rank-ordering such as Bentham's 'felicific calculus', because the goods in question are 'incommensurable'. While it is sometimes possible, in a particular context, to resolve such conflicts more or less satisfactorily and more or less rationally, they confront us with the loss of something that is genuinely valuable in its own right, so that it would amount to a form of blindness simply to see our choice as a net gain, without recognising an ineliminable residue of loss.[6] Some of these losses may not trouble us a great deal, but others, involving basic or ultimate values, are more dramatic, and are rightly perceived as tragic or even in some cases as involving the commission of some wrong.[7]

Of course, this rather terse summary of Berlin's views on value pluralism does not address, let alone answer, a number of critical questions. However, it should serve to indicate one general feature of the idea of value pluralism, as well as a puzzle arising from it. Value pluralism is best understood as a response to, and is in competition with, an alternative (and dominant) model of how we should understand the world of values, which Berlin calls monism. At its broadest and most dramatic, monism is the view that ethical questions have a single correct answer, derivable from a universally valid moral law, itself based on a single, universally valid conception of human good. This belief is a deep characteristic of Western thought, evident as far back as Plato, but in Berlin's view, it is also a crucial source of twentieth-century totalitarian ideologies, operating in conjunction with ideas of authentic selfhood and the belief that science enables us to formulate coherent systems of rules for regulating human conduct rationally. Yet not all

---

6. Although it is not an account of individual choice, Adam Ferguson's depiction of the displacement of traditional or 'rude' ways of life by more complex commercial societies recognises the value of commercial society and the attitudes associated with it, but insists that the loss of civic virtue resulting from this process should continue to trouble us. See Ferguson 1767.

7. This summary draws chiefly on the careful analyses of Crowder, IBLP 126–41, and Plaw 2004.

monist views directly support the drive to impose ideological coherence that is characteristic of totalitarian political systems.

Although Berlin's famous essay 'Two Concepts of Liberty' is directed against Marxist totalitarianism, a less dramatic conception of monism may be derived from it. This monist temptation or tendency exists wherever there is a drive to integrate diverse and conflicting values into a harmonious system of ideas—that is, into a system in which the conflicts disappear as a result of a reconstruction of the values in question. Thus, the appearance of a conflict between liberty and equality may be met by an attempt to demonstrate that the conflict is simply the result of inadequate understandings of liberty and equality.[8] In the case of the TRC, one attempt to defend it against the charge that it involved a reprehensible sacrifice of justice to the goal of social unity or reconciliation simply denied that any such sacrifice had occurred. The appearance of sacrifice was instead attributed to a defective conception of justice, a conception that supposedly mistook punishment for the 'restorative' core of justice.

Yet it is by no means a simple matter to identify what, if anything, is especially troubling about the (non-totalitarian) monist tendency. In a recent challenge to Berlin's account of value pluralism, Ronald Dworkin warns that while monism has provided some tyrants with a justification for great crimes, a facile acceptance of the inevitability of conflict among values may also serve those who seek to justify their decision to withhold a good legitimately demanded by some set of people (LIB 75). Dworkin insists that when confronted by apparent conflicts between values, we *should* in fact proceed in the manner designated here as monistic. In his view, 'integrity among our concepts is itself a value', and therefore we have a 'standing reason for preferring conceptions of our values that do not conflict' (LIB 127). A value pluralist may respond that the monist drive to coherence typically conflates distinct values. While I take this to be correct, it may easily be misconstrued to commit one to a belief in the existence of a number of readily intelligible, clear, simple and discrete objective values, values in principle in conflict with one another—a view perhaps suggested by Berlin's endorsement of Bishop Butler's comment: 'Things and Actions are what they are, and the Consequences of them will be what they will be: Why then should we desire to be deceived?'[9] Such a picture seems over-simple. Values such as equality may be complex and multifaceted, or may not be especially clearly understood. If so, should we not heed Dworkin's insistence that 'we cannot declare [...] for conflict right away' (LIB 139)?

In what follows, I concede the point that it is possible to arrive too quickly at

---

8. This example is suggested and defended by Ronald Dworkin in LIB.

9. Butler 1726, sermon 7, 136 [§16]. Berlin quotes Butler's comment on at least three occasions in his published writings: KM 1 (inaccurately); L 101–2; L1 692. See also MI 103.

the judgement that one is confronted with an all-or-nothing conflict among values, and that such a judgement may be as morally problematic as the monist tendency itself. One of the early defences of the TRC—what I am calling the 'simple sacrifice' argument—is vulnerable to this kind of objection.

However, value pluralists need not be committed to the oversimplified picture of value-conflict presupposed by the 'simple sacrifice' view. Moreover, the monist tendency remains troubling—but not because it is uniquely and directly supportive of ideological imposition. Rather, it remains problematic when its drive for system or 'integrity' among values threatens to collapse their distinct character completely. In such a case, we are confronted not with a systematisation of the critical vocabulary available for political argument, but with its depletion. This is the heart of Berlin's criticisms of the idea of positive liberty. While he recognises the validity of the concept of positive liberty, his concern is that conceptions of positive liberty display a monistic tendency to equate liberty with some other value (justice, equality or reason) and then in consequence deny us the right to use the word 'liberty' in any sense that might conflict with this value. This deprives individuals of conceptual resources that may prove indispensable in their struggle against an official ideology claiming to represent true freedom (see L 216–17). Thus, even if it stops well short of endorsing the total system of an ideology, to the extent that the monist tendency deprives us of critical resources, it should be resisted.

Berlin's opposition to the monist tendency not only derives from value pluralism, but is further reinforced by his commitment to a distinctive form of liberalism, based on a recognition of individual complexity, which will be considered at a later stage of the argument. My focus now is on the relevance of value pluralism for assessing competing accounts of the purposes of truth commissions. Before considering these accounts, however, it is necessary to review the history of truth commissions and the forms they have assumed.

A NEW TYPE OF INSTITUTION

Truth commissions have emerged in the context of recent political struggles, as practical responses to the political challenge of finding ways to confront a violent past and move beyond it, rather than as the result of philosophical fiat. As a result, these institutions display an array of diverse features. While all (at least twenty-two, at the latest count), have aimed to uncover facts about past abuses, some have been sponsored by presidents, others by parliamentary bodies, and still others have been conducted by private institutions. Some have made recommendations concerning compensation, reparations, prosecutions or measures aimed at reconciling old enemies, while others have confined themselves to uncovering and reporting the facts about human rights violations. Among the latter, some have made their reports fully public, while others have withheld details such as the names of perpetrators, or have published abbreviated versions of their findings.[10]

Despite these and other differences, it is possible to see the South African TRC as marking a new moment in the evolution of truth commissions. Before the South African case, truth commissions were created in contexts where the judiciary was seen as corrupt and unlikely to deliver any kind of justice. It was hoped that even if justice could not be achieved, the truth about the past might be uncovered, and so truth commissions emerged as ad hoc ways of securing the truth, broadly similar to commissions of enquiry in parliamentary systems of government. In the South African case, however, a much more deliberate project was launched, which took stock of earlier experiences of political transitions. The result was the creation of a truth commission with a uniquely public dimension, linked to an offer of conditional amnesty to perpetrators of human rights violations. Once key members of the African National Congress had been persuaded to support the TRC project rather than press for a war crimes tribunal, the institution was created by an act of parliament, and went into operation in 1995.

The TRC made an offer of amnesty from criminal and civil prosecution to perpetrators of human rights abuses, but it set several conditions for securing amnesty. Those seeking amnesty had to: apply before a cut-off date (subsequently extended); make full disclosure of their actions; demonstrate that those actions were performed in the service of a political movement or party; show that the actions in question were proportional to the political goal and not gratuitously cruel. These applications were reviewed by the TRC's Committee on Amnesty, staffed mainly by lawyers. In addition, a second committee, the Committee on Human Rights Violations, made decisions concerning the conferral of victim status on people who claimed that they had been the objects of violent abuse. The hearings held by this committee were fully public, reported daily on national television, and covered in detail on national radio. The hearings became a forum for victims to tell their stories, and are undoubtedly the feature of the TRC most familiar to people outside South Africa. Finally, the Committee on Reparation and Rehabilitation was charged with making recommendations to parliament concerning urgent interim financial relief for victims, as well as long-term reparations policy.

It should immediately be clear that the chief bone of contention concerning the TRC was its offer of conditional amnesty; critics charged that this entailed a morally unacceptable sacrifice of justice. Indeed, a case to this effect was brought before the South African Constitutional Court by the families of several mur-

10. See Hayner 2002. For two insiders' views of the TRC, see Boraine 2000 and Ntsebeza 2000.

dered anti-apartheid activists. An early reaction to this kind of challenge was to invoke considerations of practicality. Truth commissions, it was argued, were better equipped to reveal more about the past than trials. Trials would be more expensive, more selective, and would involve only cases seen as winnable by the prosecution. Truth commissions, operating with lower standards of evidence, would be cheaper and easier to run, would cover more cases, would be more likely to promote a broad public awareness of a wider range of past abuses, and would be less likely to jeopardise the new democracy by generating a backlash from threatened supporters of the old regime.[11]

THE IDEA OF TRUTH COMMISSIONS: THE 'SIMPLE SACRIFICE' ACCOUNT

Another kind of response presented a more recognisably moral argument. Here the argument conceded that the granting of amnesty involved a denial of legitimate claims for justice—but it continued by arguing that justice here was in competition with the claims of some other value or set of values, either of greater importance than justice, or not obviously inferior to it. Those who advanced this kind of argument identified the competing value differently—as truth, 'personal healing', social catharsis, 'closure', 'reconciliation' or even forgiveness. In my judgement, however, the most plausible candidate was 'reconciliation', understood as a synonym for a kind of social unity able to overcome the deep divisions of the past. Claims that the truth commission should seek to achieve personal healing, closure or social catharsis cannot serve as the central justification of the TRC, either because they appeal to too vague and contestable a value, or because the realisation of the value in question is dependent on too many variable factors beyond the control of any institution.[12] The idea that 'forgiveness' could form the purpose of the TRC is arguably dependent on religious beliefs not shared by all citizens, and seems a strange goal for any public institution to seek in any case.[13] Finally, although it is

---

11. A good survey of these arguments is provided in an unpublished paper by Du Toit (1996).

12. Individual victims' reactions to participation in the TRC hearings have varied greatly. Participants have predictably disagreed amongst themselves in their perceptions of the process, and in addition reactions within the same person have shifted over time, in part because of delays in securing parliamentary approval for reparations payments.

13. Spokesmen for the TRC have in fact repeatedly insisted that forgiveness was not one of its formal goals, though some critics have pointed out that victims were placed under informal pressure to grant forgiveness. For a discussion of this issue, see Wilson 2001, 119–20. Wilson's book is an indispensable point of reference on the TRC.

plausible to see one of the aims of the TRC as the compilation of an accurate or true record of past events, in practice this became harnessed to the wagon of reconciliation. It was necessary to make the dark truth of the past public, so the argument went, in order to move forward into the dawn of a new society.[14]

A number of public statements made during the early stages of the TRC's existence articulated the idea that it made a simple but defensible sacrifice of justice to the value of social unity. For example, in a legal case brought by the Azanian People's Organization and the Biko, Ribeira and Mxenge families, challenging the constitutionality of the TRC, Judge Ismail Mohamed found that a deliberate choice had been made in the Interim Constitution for reconciliation and democratic consolidation over prosecution and punishment (see Wilson 2001, 167–73). While this argument appealed simply to the issue of constitutionality, others argued along similar lines for the moral defensibility of the sacrifice. Thus, a working paper prominently displayed on the TRC's website for an extended period of time appealed to a kind of intuitive value pluralism. The dilemmas surrounding the TRC, the paper argued, are best seen as moral conflicts, conflicts among values in a plural moral universe. Though justice is clearly a very significant value, it is one among many values and thus does not enjoy automatic priority over them. In something of a *non sequitur*, the paper then assumes that it is legitimate to choose 'reconciliation', 'peace' and the 'common good' over justice in the case of the TRC. Thus, the paper suggests that while the choice may be difficult, the moral conflict between justice and social unity essentially challenges us to make a simple sacrifice of one value to the other.[15]

I believe that this argument, incomplete though it is, articulates a view of the TRC's moral purpose that was intuitively plausible to many of its defenders. For many people, while it would have been preferable in principle to honour the requirements of justice, the risk of exacerbating racial and other social divisions that this arguably entailed was too great, and might indeed jeopardise the existence of the new democracy, the only hope of securing justice for the victims of apartheid in the long run. Better, on this view, to choose social unity over justice, in the hope that in the long term this would prove the best guarantee of achieving an equitable justice system. This was not simply a judgement of expedience, but also involved the belief that the goal of reconciliation or social unity was itself morally valuable—a plausible view in any society marked by deep conflicts.

---

14. I am paraphrasing a public statement made by Kader Asmal, then Minister of Justice. For a fuller discussion, see Allen 1999, 324.

15. I do not wish to suggest that the claims made in this unpublished paper (Verwoerd 1997), whose author was at the time a researcher for the TRC, represent his considered views (he has indicated otherwise to me in person). However, I believe the paper presented a widespread view of the TRC, a view that requires discussion.

However, this 'simple sacrifice' account of the TRC's purposes is both politically problematic and vulnerable to the kinds of objections raised by Ronald
Dworkin against value pluralism in general. In the first place, the claim that it is
acceptable to sacrifice justice to social unity fails to break with a characteristic
feature of societies with an authoritarian or totalitarian past—viz., the tendency
to subordinate concerns of justice or rights to projects deemed socially important.
Most defenders of truth commissions argue that it is necessary to confront the
past in order to signal a break with predecessor regimes' disregard for, and active
violations of, the rights of individuals. Yet the 'simple sacrifice' defence of truth
commissions displays a similar willingness to jettison rights when they conflict
with a social project deemed to be important.

What is more, as Dworkin's objection suggests, the crude value pluralism of
the 'simple sacrifice' argument is too ready to assume that the conflict between justice and social unity is an all-or-nothing matter, and that therefore the only possible response is the sacrifice of one value *in toto* to another. There are several
assumptions here that are neither necessary nor particularly plausible. First, the
'simple sacrifice' defence offers no real arguments for preferring social unity over
justice, implying that this is simply a matter of fiat. However, while there may
indeed be cases of value conflict where the only available response is, as Berlin
says, simply to 'plump', this is not always the case (Berlin 1992, 103; see also IBLP
139). Berlin himself recognises that reasoned choice among values, guided by contextual considerations, is sometimes possible (see Berlin and Williams 1994). Value
pluralists may also consistently believe that it is sometimes feasible, in a particular
setting, to arrive at a defensible trade-off among values, without thereby committing themselves to belief in some overarching standard or decision-procedure.
Moreover, it will sometimes be possible to reconstruct our understandings of the
values in question to soften the conflict, provided that conceptual reconstruction
does not lose touch with the historical meanings that have become associated with
the values in question.[16]

Moreover, value pluralists have good reason to seek compromises where the
values in conflict are complex. In such cases, there is no reason to assume—as the
'simple sacrifice' defence does—that the whole of one value has entered into collision with the whole of another.[17] Rather, we may seek to secure as much of both
values as possible, though we accept that the outcome will involve some loss on
both sides of the conflict. This is in fact the best way of proceeding in the case of
the TRC, where the complex value of justice—a value with several domains of

---

16. See Bernard Williams, LIB 93–7. The point is not that conceptual reconstruction
is impossible, but that it is politically problematic when it becomes detached from the historical understandings of concepts, often simply displacing or disguising the real conflicts
that are occurring.

application, including distributive justice, punitive or criminal justice, and symbolic recognition—is in conflict with the complex and somewhat indeterminate good of social unity. Rather than sacrifice justice on the altar of social unity, we should look to secure as much justice as we can, consistent with promoting social unity—and we should allow our understanding of social unity to become inflected by considerations of justice. This goal of 'complex compromise' is more morally and politically ambitious than the assumption that a simple sacrifice of justice to social unity is appropriate, though it accepts that in some respects the outcomes are likely to be messy and imperfect, and will involve loss on the part of both values.

THE IDEA OF TRUTH COMMISSIONS: THE 'RESTORATIVE JUSTICE' ACCOUNT

If the 'simple sacrifice' account of the moral purpose of truth commissions is too pessimistic, too ready to accept that truth commissions sacrifice justice to social unity, the 'restorative justice' account suffers from the opposite vice—excessive ambition. While both the 'simple sacrifice' conception of the TRC and the 'complex compromise' view that I have begun to sketch accept that truth commissions are a non-ideal option, defenders of the 'restorative justice' account challenge this view by arguing that it rests on a flawed understanding of justice as necessarily involving punishment. A view of justice in which punishment is seen as at best a contingent feature permits us to view the goals of truth commissions very differently, and provides an alternative critical perspective on the TRC itself. Like the 'simple sacrifice' argument, the 'restorative justice' view did in fact influence the outlooks of many associated with the TRC—so much so that the TRC Final Report explicitly states that one of the institution's principal goals was to promote the 'restorative dimensions of justice' (Tutu 1998, 126; see also Tutu 1999). The report goes on to claim that perceptions that the TRC sacrificed justice were based on the mistaken assumption that justice necessarily involves retribution, and thus failed to grasp the importance of restorative justice.

The term 'restorative justice' used here first appeared as a label for a cluster of initiatives in Australia, New Zealand, Britain and the United States, aimed at reforming the criminal justice system. In practice, the distinguishing mark of

---

17. This question is distinct from that of whether sacrifices or trade-offs *in toto* may be rational or not. I do not deny that some sacrifices *in toto* are justifiable and rational. Rather, I simply wish to stress that when we are dealing with conflicts between complex or comprehensive values, with many domains of application, we should investigate whether the whole of both values is engaged in the conflict rather than assuming this from the outset.

these projects has been an emphasis on victim–offender reconciliation during the sentencing stage, typically promoted through voluntary encounters between victims, offenders and community representatives, regulated by mediators or judges. The aim of these 'restorative justice conferences' or 'reintegrative shaming rituals' is to get offenders to recognise the implications of their crimes for others and take responsibility for them, thereby repairing damaged relations of trust and communal bonds. When presented as a *theory* of criminal justice, restorative justice is distinguished by a core commitment to the idea that the moral purpose of criminal justice is not punishment, but rather the restoration of disturbed or damaged relations of trust and community. While punishment or 'penalties' may sometimes be necessary, this is seen only as a means to the end of moral transformation and the re-establishment of trust and community.[18]

It is easy to understand why this view appealed to many defenders of the TRC. First of all, the emphasis of the theory on the morally transforming quality of participation in restorative justice processes seemed to fit the experience of the public hearings held by the Human Rights Violations Committee, which produced a number of remarkable encounters between victims and perpetrators. The theory of restorative justice allowed defenders of the TRC to see these public hearings as analogues to victim–offender conferences, and to present them as the moral heart of the TRC. In this vein, some advocates of the 'restorative justice' interpretation then went on to criticise the designers of the TRC for not integrating the reparations process more closely with the victim–offender hearings, and for not supporting victim–offender reconciliation more effectively. Second, the idea that the goal of justice is the promotion of community and the restoration of social trust provided a robust defence against the claim that the TRC wrongly denied justice to victims. Defenders of the TRC could respond to such critics by arguing that they had simply misunderstood the requirements of justice, and that because punishment was not a necessary part of justice, the TRC was in fact promoting a higher or more authentic conception of justice. Finally, the focus on community and social trust seemed to provide content to the hazy talk of 'reconciliation', collective healing and catharsis that swirled around the TRC.[19]

---

18. On the history of 'restorative justice' reforms, see the articles collected in Wright and Galaway 1989. Proponents of the theory of restorative justice include Cragg 1992, Braithwaite 2000 and Zehr 1990. These theorists differ over the place of punishment within the framework of restorative justice. However, to the extent that restorative justice presents a distinctive theory of criminal justice (distinct from older theories of rehabilitation, for example), it is committed to the view that punishment is at best a means, not a central goal, of justice.

19. Advocates of the 'restorative justice' interpretation of the TRC include Llewellyn and Howse 1999, Kiss 2000 and, most notably, Tutu 1999.

The restorative justice interpretation of the TRC is nevertheless problematic in at least three respects. The first problem concerns the applicability of the theory of restorative justice to societies marked by deep conflicts. As noted above, in practice and in theory, participation in restorative justice conferences is voluntary, as is the agreement of the offender to abide by the decision reached concerning appropriate penalties or forms of restitution. The viability of the process depends heavily on the extent to which the offender cares about his or her standing with community representatives. In divided societies, however, it is likely that while many perpetrators of human rights violations may indeed care about the judgements of family members, friends, and members of their own racial or ethnic community, they may not be especially concerned about how other communities view them. In other words, without some enforcement mechanism besides 'reintegrative shaming', the theory of restorative justice will not be equipped to overcome the kinds of divisions all too frequently found in societies with a totalitarian or authoritarian past.

This practical flaw directs attention to problems more closely related to the redefinition of justice as social or communal reconciliation. Thus, second, if practices of restorative justice depend on voluntary participation, and if the role of social stigma in motivating participation is likely to be weak in divided societies, then some other mechanism is required to induce perpetrators to participate. In the case of the TRC, this was provided by the threat of criminal or civil prosecution. This should lead us to suspect, however, that the idea of restorative justice does not after all offer a comprehensive or sufficient theory of criminal justice, but is better thought of as a supplement to a system of justice whose purposes are not fully explicable along the lines of restorative justice.

Third, and most important, the idea that the principal goal of criminal justice is communal reconciliation or solidarity is not compelling. Advocates of restorative justice often understand community on the model of face-to-face personal relationships—a view reinforced by the religious themes of forgiveness and reconciliation and the language of conflict resolution that were applied to the TRC. With this *Gemeinschaft* model of community in mind, they tend either to be impatient concerning the legal side of the TRC or, more generally, to see the function of law and criminal justice as the peaceful resolution of disputes and the promotion of harmonious social relations. Yet while a criminal justice system should indeed aim to reduce violence and resolve conflicts, to think that these are its central functions is to neglect other crucially important aspects of justice, especially procedural fairness and the symbolic condemnation of crime. The tendency to see criminal justice simply as a matter of conflict resolution fails to distinguish it from processes of civil law (perhaps even from non-legal means of resolving disputes), and thus treats wrongs, which injure a person's moral standing, and are therefore significant for the public as a whole, in the same way as private harms.[20] Yet the TRC was an attempt to confront, in public and by public means, very grave wrongs—wrongs deeply offensive to the new democratic constitutional order adopted in South Africa. The challenge the TRC faced was to find an adequate way of combating the effects of a political culture in which casual brutality had become deeply lodged, and to establish a principle of basic moral equality for all citizens.

Although more could be said in criticism of the restorative justice defence of the TRC, I want to confine myself to two concluding observations. In the first place, this view avoids the undue willingness of the 'simple sacrifice' defence to jettison considerations of justice under the pressure of an important project of collective reconciliation—but only by redefining justice so that its meaning simply coincides with that project. Yet so much that is central to any adequate understanding of justice is lost in the process that we are entitled to regard this as a spurious resolution. The restorative justice account of the purposes of truth commissions thus provides a striking example of what I earlier referred to as the monistic tendency.

In the second place, the implication of this account is that those who call for justice—understood conventionally as requiring a public commitment to prosecute serious offences of individual rights, and, where appropriate, to subject offenders to severe penalties—should be told that they are simply mistaken about the requirements of justice.[21] This is not in itself a decisive objection against the restorative justice view—all accounts of justice must deny some claims made by victims. But where so many features necessary to the idea of justice seem to have been eliminated, to respond in this way is inappropriate. The restorative justice view of the TRC deprives victims of the right to demand, not reconciliation with offenders, but rather a public commitment to enforce laws that secure basic dignity for all. In my view, this 'reconstructs' the meaning of justice out of all recognition. Moreover, the moral and political value of doing so is highly questionable. Although some see the 'moral ambition' of the restorative justice view as a virtue, this ambition has largely met with failure—the TRC at best delivered moral transformation only in a handful of cases. This has resulted in an atmosphere of dissatisfaction with the TRC—though in fact most of its 'failures' are attributable to the conceptual flaws and lack of political realism displayed by the restorative justice view.[22]

---

20. For the distinction between 'wrongs' and 'harms', see Hampton 1992, 1662–7.

21. This is explicitly stated in Desmond Tutu's Foreword to Tutu 1998, 9.

22. This mood is reflected by several of the articles collected in James and Vijver 2001.

COMPLEX COMPROMISES
AND REMEDIAL LIBERALISM

I have been arguing that Berlin's conception of value pluralism has a clear relevance for reflection on the moral purposes of truth commissions. That relevance is chiefly negative, allowing us to avoid seeing truth commissions either as simple sacrifices of justice to social unity or as instruments of restorative justice. In this final section, I want to show that a more nuanced understanding of Berlin's liberal pluralism may help us to articulate an alternative and more constructive account of the purposes of truth commissions.

Berlin's liberalism, though closely related to his value pluralism, remains a distinct theme in his work. As I understand it, it is strikingly similar to the 'liberalism of fear' articulated by Judith Shklar, aimed at combating or avoiding 'extremes of suffering'.[23] However, unlike Shklar, who presents her version of liberalism as a kind of negative politics with no additional philosophical commitments, Berlin finds a moral basis for his liberalism in an appreciation for the complexity of individual human beings. His is thus an anti-Procrustean liberalism, whose central article of faith is the belief that 'To force people into the neat uniforms demanded by dogmatically believed-in schemes is almost always the road to inhumanity' (CTH 19). To some extent, this view complements the appreciation for the human capacity for choice and self-creation evident in value pluralism, but it is not to be equated with it, and in fact provides reasons for curbing our enthusiasm for human creativity when that produces a rigid and dehumanising politics, as in the case of Marxism and some forms of nationalism. Much of Berlin's historical work is aimed at providing lessons in the ethos of this anti-Procrustean liberalism. He does this either by pointing us to positive exemplars—political thinkers and actors who recognise and respect human complexity—or through considering the implications of political ideologies and theories that attempt to enforce rigid systems on political life.

Berlin's liberalism is a response to, and a diagnosis of, political evils—and as such can assist us to understand the condition of most societies undergoing transitions from totalitarian or authoritarian rule. But does it help us to reflect on how truth commissions might offer a constructive response to the spectacle of ideological shipwreck? I believe that Berlin's liberal pluralism offers essential general guidelines for this project. It does so, first, by suggesting that the negative task of avoiding the worst political evils should be prioritised, and second, by encouraging us to be content to live with some degree of messiness in our moral and political commitments. As Berlin memorably comments, 'The best that can be

---

23. See Shklar 1998. The phrase 'extremes of suffering' is taken from CTH 18.

done, as a general rule, is to maintain a precarious equilibrium that will prevent the occurrence of desperate situations, of intolerable choices—that is the first requirement for a decent society.'[24] But how may truth commissions, themselves the products of extremity, promote the idea of a decent society?

The short answer is that advocates of truth commissions must understand that their task is neither to license a wholesale sacrifice of justice to social unity nor to promote a redefined conception of restorative justice, but rather to achieve a *complex* compromise between justice and social unity. By 'complex compromise', I mean a set of arrangements that promote *both* justice and social unity as far as possible, and in which both values are affected by their juxtaposition.[25] As far as justice is concerned, truth commissions inevitably involve a considerable sacrifice of punitive justice in order to gain the participation of perpetrators of human rights violations. But they do not have to sacrifice *all* aspects of justice, and they do not even have to sacrifice punitive justice completely. As far as social unity is concerned, the proper aim for truth commissions is not to seek the kind of close-knit *Gemeinschaft* and 'communal healing' suggested by the theory of restorative justice, but rather a form of unity based primarily on a minimalist consensus about the unacceptability of political cruelty and injustice and about the importance of the rule of law. In practical terms, this means that truth commissions should work in tandem with a system of justice, and that those who fail to secure amnesty, or who never come forward, should confront the threat of prosecution for their offences.

In what ways may truth commissions actually promote justice? We should begin by remembering that justice is a multifaceted concept. Its root intuition is probably best defined by Justinian, as 'the constant and perpetual will to render everyone his due'.[26] This definition allows us to see that justice concerns not only

---

24. CTH 18. On the idea of a 'decent society', see Margalit 1996.

25. I now prefer the term 'complex compromise' to 'principled compromise', which I used in an earlier discussion of the TRC. Presumably some simple sacrifices of values may be made on principled grounds, so to imply that only complex compromises may be principled is misleading. For my earlier usage—and reservations about it—see Allen 1999, 325. See also Stuart Hampshire's charming distinction between 'shabby' and 'smart' compromises (2000, 32). I do not accept the claim that in compromises the goods in question are necessarily understood as 'strategic ends', which may be 'traded off' on the basis of instrumental considerations, as opposed to 'sacred values', whose central and intrinsic significance demands that we 'forsake' some value for another. It is precisely *because* the values of justice and social unity are of central significance in our collective lives that we should seek 'complex compromise' here. For the distinction between 'trade-offs' and 'sacrifices' see Lukes 1997.

26. 'Iustitia est constans et perpetua voluntas ius suum cuique tribuens' (Justinian 533, 1. 1. 1).

the material functions of rectification, distribution and punishment, but also expressive and ethical functions.

At the material level, truth commissions may facilitate the function of compensation or reparation for past injury, by ascertaining the facts and making recommendations for relief. Moreover, there is no reason why they cannot work together with land claims courts or other institutions whose functions are explicitly compensatory or redistributive.[27] On the other hand, if truth commissions are to provide an incentive to perpetrators of human rights violations to participate in the process, some form of amnesty has to be offered. But, first, this need not simply sacrifice punitive justice. Failed amnesty applicants and those who decide not to participate should be liable to normal criminal sanctions. The obverse of an official commitment to a truth commission must be a genuine commitment to the prosecution of offenders—an area that currently constitutes the most glaring flaw of the South African TRC.

Second, even if it is not possible for truth commissions to honour the full requirements of punitive justice, they may still promote many of its expressive and ethical aspects. In this respect, the public hearings held by the South African TRC are of crucial importance. In the first place, by making the distortions of law, injustices and brutalities of the past public, such hearings may sensitise present and future generations to the need to combat injustice, to prevent such intolerable situations from arising. Moreover, the stories of abuse provide an object lesson in the importance of respect for central aspects of the rule of law— especially equality before the law and basic individual rights—by showing the damage done to a society when that is absent. By providing an occasion for public education concerning the importance of the rule of law, truth commissions may promote an ethos of justice, aimed at combating the corruption of law and of the sense of injustice evident in the recent past.

Perhaps most important of all, public hearings serve as rituals of belated recognition of the dignity of individual victims of injustice. While advocates of the idea of restorative justice sometimes claim that their account of justice emphasises the needs of victims, in fact the most serious flaw of this view is that it does so little to focus our attention on the crime itself and on the need for public vindication of the dignity of victims. In contrast, expressivist theories of retributive justice remind us that serious crimes or human rights violations wrong victims not only by harming them, but by demeaning them—by conveying the message that the victims are insignificant or unworthy of moral concern. Such acts, whether they are intended to or not, make a claim of moral superiority on behalf of the perpetrator by signalling that his victims need not be treated with

---

27. This has in fact happened in the South African case.

respect but may simply be used for his purposes.[28] The hearings of the TRC counter this symbolic claim by deliberately presenting victims on the centre of the public stage, by recognising the importance of their stories, and by affirming their dignity. This task of recognising the dignity of victims is the most distinctive function of truth commissions. It amounts to a public commitment to avoiding the abuses of the past and a public vindication of the dignity of members of society whose rights were unjustly violated and who were excluded from equal respect—though this commitment remains incomplete unless it is expressed not only at the symbolic level, but also through reparations, compensation and the prosecution of failed amnesty applicants and non-participants. It is not enough simply to issue a public statement vindicating the dignity of victims; the denigration of that dignity and the assertion of their own mastery by perpetrators of human rights violations must be defeated, and for such a defeat to be convincing to onlookers, public action as well as statement is required.[29] Observers must not be able to conclude that the state's unwillingness to act against perpetrators confirms the claim of superiority they made over their victims. Such a perception would be deeply subversive of a constitutional order ostensibly based on the moral equality of all.[30]

The expressive vindication of victims' dignity at the same time promotes a distinctive vision of social unity—a vision of a society united by a principle of respect for the basic dignity of all its members, and mediated by the rule of law. This is neither the model of harmonious community nor that of morally transformed personal relationships advocated by some defenders of truth commissions, and it may seem unappealing or unexciting to those who believe that truth commissions should aim to effect profound moral changes. Yet the superficially humdrum goal of a decent society, unified by respect for the rule of law and by a consensus concerning the intolerable, seems both to offer a more realistic view of the purpose of truth commissions, and to be more capable of challenging the disregard for individual rights typically displayed by authoritarian and totalitarian societies. Truth commissions can and should serve as vivid reminders of the moral importance of this kind of remedial liberalism.

As I indicated at the outset, Isaiah Berlin's work is not noted for displaying a sustained interest in political institutions. Indeed, one commentator has argued

---

28. I am drawing here on the accounts of crime as an 'expressive act' offered by Murphy and Hampton. See Hampton 1990.

29. For a discussion of this point, see Hampton 1992, 1678–85. Hampton takes her inspiration from Hegel's claim that crime involves an infringement of *right*, understood as the equal sovereignty of individual wills. See Hegel 1821, 69 and 331 note. There is an illuminating discussion of Hegel's views in Reiman 1995, 281–2, 284.

30. For a more extensive argument on this issue, see Allen 2001, 35–9.

that the kind of value pluralism articulated by Berlin has little significance for questions of 'political design' (Newey 1998). Yet in the case of truth commissions, where the purpose of these institutions remains controversial, I believe this claim to be misleading. Berlin's value pluralism may, first, assist us negatively, helping us to elude the pitfalls into which some advocates of truth commissions have fallen. Thus, a nuanced understanding of value pluralism allows us to avoid an excessive willingness to see the goal of truth commissions as the promotion of national unity at the expense of justice—a view that is insufficiently impressed by the importance of law in its vision of a new national community. On the other hand, we can avoid the error of denying that no real moral loss is involved in the decision to hold a truth commission—an error committed by those who argue that truth commissions should promote a 'higher' non-punitive form of justice. Indeed, it is one of the strengths of Berlin's liberal pluralism that it does *not* respond to those who complain that truth commissions sacrifice their claim to justice by telling them that they have *misunderstood* the meaning of justice. As Bernard Williams warns, such a response is neither respectful nor politically prudent (LIB 102).

Berlin's theory of value pluralism serves to remind us of the nature of an adequate response to moral conflict. Such a response should recognise the importance of the values at stake in truth commissions, and should not attempt to deny the seriousness of the conflict between justice and social unity by redefining justice as social reconciliation. On the constructive side, Berlin's anti-Procrustean liberalism encourages us to seek the compromise best equipped, in the circumstances of transition, to protect individuals from 'extremes of suffering' by putting in place the building-blocks of a 'decent society'. These include respect for the rule of law, a vindication of the equal dignity of individual citizens, and the reinvigoration of a sense of justice in the political culture of the new society. In practical terms, liberal pluralism promotes the idea that truth commissions constitute not fully coherent 'models' of 'transitional justice' but unavoidably messy compromises—institutions that should work in partnership with conventional institutions of justice, to promote a minimalist social consensus on the importance of avoiding a politics of intolerable cruelty and injustice.

11

Must Value Pluralism and Religious Belief Collide?

WILLIAM A. GALSTON

Must liberalism be secular? As is typically the case, the answer depends on how we parse the question. Must liberal theory rely on secular premisses only? No: some forms of religion imply a recognisably liberal stance towards the political world. Must liberalism exclude religious practices from the public square? No, despite what French authorities say and do. Must liberal polities practice strict 'separationism'? No, regardless of never-ending efforts to transform Jeffersonian metaphor into constitutional doctrine. Must liberal polities exclude religion from public policy discourse? No, *pace* many contemporary proponents of 'public reason'. On the other hand: May liberal polities have an established Church? No, unless the establishment is all but vacuous. Consistent with what I take to be core liberal commitments, liberal polities cannot tax their citizens to fund sectarian teaching or indoctrination,[1] cannot coerce their citizens to engage in specific religious practices or adhere to specific religious laws, and cannot use public policy to promote the salvation (however understood) of souls.

Thus far I have spoken as though 'liberalism' is a single homogeneous body of thought and practice. But of course it is not, and this variety may subtly inflect

---

1. This should not be taken to mean that liberalism cannot accept vouchers redeemable at religious schools or public funding of social services conducted by faith-based institutions. I believe it can, under suitable conditions. But saying why would divert us from the topic at hand.

views on the relation between liberalism and religion. In recent years (2002, 2004), I have offered a revisionist account of liberalism—liberal pluralism—that relies on the moral theory of value pluralism as one of its core animating ideas. Those who cannot accept value pluralism will of course stumble at the threshold of liberal pluralism, but even those who do accept value pluralism may question the inferences I draw from it.

In the remarks that follow, I examine two objections to the liberal pluralist theory of politics that value pluralism helps justify. The first is that resting political theory on *any* general comprehensive theory has the consequence of denying legitimate diversity and justifying intrusive government enforcement of that theory, a result that is dangerous in practice and fatal for any liberal theory. The second is that value pluralism is deeply exclusionary because it rules out claims at the core of every revealed religion.

COMPREHENSIVE THEORY AND THE SCOPE OF LIBERTY

The relation between value pluralism and liberal politics is complex. In my view, which resembles Isaiah Berlin's, value pluralism offers the firmest foundation for a politics that accommodates a wide (though not unlimited) range of moral, cultural and religious diversity.[2] On the other hand, as Berlin rightly insisted, one can be a monist, secular or religious, without ceasing to be a liberal—as long as one believes that truth cannot rightly use oppression or coercion to overcome peaceful error (UD 72, 213). So it would be mistaken in theory, not just in practice, for liberal pluralists to marginalise liberal monists as less authentically liberal. This does not mean that value pluralists should cease exploring, or publicly declaring, the political consequences of their moral understanding.

If value pluralism is used as a basis for social theory, which is what my account of liberal pluralism does, that theory is (in the terms John Rawls made familiar) 'comprehensive' rather than 'political'. It makes sense, I believe, to connect what one believes to be the best account of public life with comparably persuasive accounts of morality, human psychology and the natural world. As a practical matter, of course, it makes sense to seek overlapping consensus. Politics as we know it would come to a halt if cooperation required agreement, not only on conclusions, but on premises as well. But philosophical argument, even concerning politics, need not mirror the structure of public life. A political philosopher may assert that X is true, and foundational for a particular understanding of a good,

---

2. For a representative statement to this effect, see UD 216–17.

decent or just society, without demanding that all citizens affirm and live according to the truth of X.

Indeed, the founders of a political regime may publicly proclaim what they take to be moral, metaphysical or religious truths as the basis of that regime without insisting that all citizens assent to those truths. In the United States, individuals assuming the privileges and obligations of citizenship affirm their loyalty to the Constitution, not to the Declaration of Independence, and all citizens pledge allegiance to the republic for which the flag stands, not to John Locke or Francis Hutcheson.

For this reason, I disagree with Martha Nussbaum (2001) when she suggests that making public claims about foundational truths somehow signals disrespect for those who dissent. Disrespect requires something more—namely, the use of coercive State power to silence and repress dissenters. Respect requires, not parsimony in declaring truth, but rather restraint in the exercise of power. By limiting the scope of legitimate public power, liberal pluralism does all that is necessary to secure the theoretical and institutional bases of respect.

Nicholas Meriwether is unconvinced, arguing that a political theory based on value pluralism is more likely to invade the liberties of differing ways of life than are those guided by some forms of monism. He points out, quite correctly, that both secular and religious monists can arrive at principled defences of liberty. But he takes an additional step, charging that to use value pluralism as the public foundation for liberty would be '*every bit as emphatic and invasive as any theologically based political regime*' (2002, 13, his emphasis).

Here I must disagree, on grounds that apply to Rawls's political liberalism as well. My argument is not that liberal citizens must acknowledge value pluralism as the community's official public creed. It is rather that, as a philosophical matter, pluralism gives a more accurate account of our moral universe than do its competitors. Yes, an overlapping consensus may exist in the realm of public opinion, and it may be more politically prudent to rely on that consensus that on any single religious, metaphysical or moral doctrine. But that does not imply that these foundational doctrines are irrelevant to political philosophy. There is no guarantee that what is philosophically defensible will coincide with what is publicly and politically desirable. To read the practical requirements of consensus back into the practice of philosophy is to distort and disfigure the process of rational enquiry.

Beyond these general considerations, value pluralism offers specific support for the theory and practice of individual liberty and government restraint. The reason is this: Within a wide range demarcated by basic goods and decency, value pluralism denies claims of the form 'We can know that way of life X is best for all individuals.' It follows that the State cannot justify paternalistic, homogenising or normalising interventions that rest on such claims (as many do).

Thus far I have addressed the concern that a 'comprehensive' value-pluralist defence of liberalism must insufficiently respect and accommodate ways of life that rest on monistic accounts of the moral world. But my position is exposed as well to the opposite criticism—namely, that it is excessively hospitable to monistic views. In a paper that deserves to be better known, Henry Hardy advances an argument that implies this criticism. To take pluralism seriously, he suggests, is to acknowledge that monistic approaches to life are fundamentally flawed. Of course we must tolerate the adherents of such views, as long as they do not seek to impose their ways on others. On a deeper level, however, it is not consistent for pluralists to regard 'ineradicably' non-pluralist views as 'straightforward contributions to the diversity of human value-systems'. Monisms, Hardy concludes, 'are not suitable long-term components of a plurality, and while we must not suppress them, it is right for pluralists to hope that they will wither away' (288 below).

As a threshold matter, Hardy is surely right to suggest that if pluralism is true, then all monisms are false. But while this definitional point strikes a blow for intellectual probity, it does not entirely resolve the issue he poses. We must always recall that value pluralism is a philosophical account of morality, locked in battle with other accounts. However strong the reasons for preferring value pluralism may be, probity requires us to acknowledge that its justification falls well short of certainty.

Value pluralism is the mirror-image of monistic consequentialism. Its comparative strength lies in a depiction of heterogeneity that seems truer to the facts of moral experience; its comparative weakness is an account of moral decision-making that has wavered thus far between existentialist, traditionalist and intuitionist. The existentialist variant, to which Berlin sometimes inclined, led towards a view of ultimately ungrounded 'radical' choice. At other moments, Berlin saw human beings as embedded in moral, cultural or religious traditions, each of which puts values in at least partial order and creates communities of moral discourse that shape choices without quite determining them. The intuitionist option, to which I incline,[3] is a variant of particularism with links to the Aristotelian tradition: deliberative closure is often possible, even when decision-makers cannot adduce general principles as the reasons for choosing as they do.

This option does not fully resolve the difficulty, however. It is easier to describe the process of particularist choice than to say why it ends, or should end, where it does. Along with other forms of intuitionism, intuitionist value pluralism lacks a compelling account of decision under circumstances of radical heterogeneity—that is, a non-aggregative and non-deductive strategy for judging when

---

3. My reasons for this preference are roughly those offered by George Crowder in his LVP, chapters 3 and 8.

moral deliberation has adduced considerations sufficient to determine the intellect and guide the will. If this is a fair account of our intellectual situation, then it seems to me that all of John Stuart Mill's familiar arguments about the advantages of contestation among rival views come into play, and on not only practical but also intellectual grounds we have reason to hope that monistic views do not wither away any time soon.

Another consideration points in the same direction. As an empirical-philosophical account of morality, value pluralism cannot prove that every (or any particular) religion is mistaken. Philosophy cannot prove that God does not exist or that miracles cannot occur. If so, the miraculous event we call revelation may happen in principle, and may already have happened in practice. Secular reason may speak with authority about the domain of non-miraculous events and non-revealed truths. But after two millennia of contestation between faith and reason, we have reason to conclude that neither combatant can score a decisive victory over the other. If so, intellectual probity requires those of us who seek to base politics on a secular moral theory to do so in full awareness of its incompleteness. Hoping for the demise of doctrines we believe but cannot know to be false seems inconsistent with the modesty that reason's limits should impose upon us.

VALUE PLURALISM AND THE THEOLOGICAL SUMMUM BONUM

My argument thus far has done little more than raise the question of the relation between value pluralism and religion. We must dig deeper. Hardy quotes Stuart Hampshire as asserting, 'Obviously, if one God, only one morality—His law and the falsity of moral pluralism therefore' (280 below, note 4). I find this alleged entailment less obvious than Hampshire did.

In the first place, unadorned monotheism is compatible with a wide range of moral views. Consistent with their core premises, deists have embraced views ranging from deterministic naturalism to post-medieval natural law to forms of conventionalism. The God of the deists seems not to require anything in particular of human beings; deist moral codes rest on competing accounts of Creation, the nature of which is open to rational inspection, rather than on the will or even the nature of the Creator.

This does not dispose of Hampshire's position, however, because unadorned monotheism is not what he has in mind. His full position not only rejects all supernatural sources of moral authority but 'denies, more specifically, that there exists a God, the Creator, who has communicated to humanity his plans for humanity and hence has supplied a set of moral prescriptions flowing from these plans'. Those who accept monotheism, thus understood, will believe that 'all mankind is subject to the same moral constraints, and that only one conception of the good is finally acceptable' (1999, 51).

With great respect, I would suggest that Hampshire did not enquire into revealed religion with the sympathy and care he devoted even to secular accounts of morality with which he disagreed fundamentally. If he had probed a bit more deeply, he would have noticed that, for example, only Jews are said to be subject to the laws of the Torah, and that because of a specific covenantal event, demonstrating that a revealed religion can bind particularistically rather than universally. As the British Commonwealth's Chief Rabbi, Jonathan Sacks, has observed, 'there is no equivalent in Judaism to the doctrine that *extra ecclesiam non est salus*, "outside the Church there is no salvation"'. Indeed, a classic Talmudic passage declares that 'the pious of the nations [that is, of non-Jewish communities] have a share in the world to come' (2003, 52–3). In light of these facts, one might conjecture that Hampshire's thesis reflects the particular history of Christian Europe, and of the Catholic Church at the peak of its triumphalist phase, rather than a truth about monotheism as such.

This raises the broader question of the status of human plurality and difference within monotheistic faiths. The Torah, Sacks argues, teaches that plurality is divinely ordained. When mankind is united, as it was before Babel, it is prone to hubris. The division of the human race into different nations and faiths reminds us of our human limitations and teaches us to make space for difference. This human wisdom has theological implications; as Sacks puts it, it shows that *'the unity of God is to be found in the diversity of creation'*.[4]

This stance is not confined to Judaism. If Hampshire had considered Islam, he might might well have run across an important passage in the Koran, which runs as follows:

> Unto every one of you We have appointed a [different] law and way of life. And if God had so willed, He could surely have made you all one single community, but [He willed it otherwise] in order to rest you by means of what he has given you. Vie, then, with one another in doing good works! Unto God you all must return, and then He will make you truly understand all that on which you were wont to differ. (Koran 5:48)

Not only is this passage consistent with Sacks's interpretation of the Babel story; it also offers an interesting gloss on Hampshire's contention that for the faithful

---

4. Sacks 2003, 51–3 (his italics). In the Jewish tradition, pre-Babel humanity is understood as enforced unity, as the first instance of totalitarianism. For a compilation of classic texts illustrating the stance of traditional Judaism towards religious diversity, see Sacks n.d.

only one conception of the good is finally acceptable. If by 'finally' one means in heaven, or at the Last Judgement, then the Koran supports Hampshire's claim. But if we are talking about living and acting on earth, then it does not. Human beings cannot pretend to know God's will and must therefore peaceably cultivate their own moral and religious gardens. Surely, from Hampshire's perspective, it is this mundane reality that counts.[5]

In fairness, to say that only Jews are subject to Torah laws is not to deny all aspects of divinely ordained moral universality. In the Jewish tradition, God's covenant with Noah, which prescribes a minimal moral code, is said to be binding on all human beings. Adherence to this code defines the border between decent human beings and those who are, morally speaking, beyond the pale.

But to affirm this kind of minimal universality is not to deny value pluralism. As Hampshire, following Berlin, makes clear, pluralism is not relativism. Pluralists affirm the existence of unmitigated evils—genocide, tyranny, pandemics, mass starvation, among others—the abatement of which is a great aim of politics. As Hampshire puts it, there are 'always and everywhere considerations that count for evil in striking the balance between good and evil. There are obvious limits set by common human needs to the conditions under which human beings flourish and human societies flourish. History records many ways of life that have crossed these limits' (1983, 155).

Indeed, as we look across a number of moral traditions, secular and religious, we see isomorphic structures. There is a common core, based affirmatively on intuitions about decent social life and negatively on an understanding of the great evils of the human condition. Above this common sphere of 'thin' morality is 'thick' morality, which reflects the diverse experiences and histories of different communities.[6] Pluralism is held to be legitimate above the line that separates thick and thin moralities. While there may be boundary disputes concerning what is below, and what above, the line of universality, value pluralists and advocates of universal human rights can agree with one another, and with most adherents of the great religions, on this basic moral structure.

In this respect among many others, Rabbi Sacks argues, biblical morality points towards the duality of the human situation. On the one hand, we are members of the 'universal human family' and obligated to treat our fellow human beings with basic decency and respect. On the other hand, we are also members of particular families and communities, and our ties give rise to particular obligations we do not

---

5. As everyone knows, Islamic practice has often diverged from the course this passage appears to support. But judging any faith, polytheist or monotheist, by its historical excesses rather than its innermost possibilities is bound to lead to despairing conclusions.

6. For the best brief discussions of this distinction that I know, see Walzer 1987, chapter 1, and Walzer 1994.

owe to the generalised 'Other'. Because Jews were strangers in Egypt, they are required to treat the strangers among them as every human being should be treated. But because Jews share the memory of a specific communal experience—the exodus from Egypt—they form a separate and distinct community with distinctive responsibilities towards one another and towards God (2003, 57–9).

The structural similarity between biblical morality and value pluralism should relieve the anxiety of many liberals (pluralist and otherwise) that monotheistic religion *as such* is intolerant of deep differences. Indeed, many faiths offer a principled defence of tolerance: one may never use coercion to spread the faith one believes to be true. Tolerance does not require us to set aside our convictions or espouse religious relativism; it asks only that, in our interactions with others in our society who do not share our faith, we confine ourselves to recognised means of persuasion. We find endorsements of tolerance, so understood, in sources as diverse as the Koran and John Locke's *Letter on Toleration*. While it is true that religious practice often diverges from this principle, the same may be said of secular liberal societies. Breach of morally demanding norms is a universal danger.

So far, so good. But these considerations address the relation between value pluralism and monotheism at the level of social and political practice. There is a deeper concern: whether value pluralism can make room for what might be termed the basic structure of revealed religion—a hierarchical account of the cosmos that culminates in divinity. Many believers fear that it cannot, and they reject it for that reason. Consider the views of Nicholas Wolterstorff, one of the most philosophically sophisticated theologians of our time:

> A dominant strand in Judaism, Christianity and Islam alike holds that there is in fact a highest good for all human beings in all circumstances, that highest good consisting in being related rightly to God. Those within these three religions who hold this thesis specify somewhat differently what exactly that right relationship is; but that there is a highest good for everyone in all circumstances, and that that consists in being related to God in a certain way, is, as I say, the conviction of a dominant strand in each of these Abrahamic religions. Now I assume that [...] the value pluralist means to deny this claim. Accordingly, those who hold this theistic view concerning the highest good will not accept the premiss of Galston's [value-pluralist] argument. In our present-day American society, that's a large number of people; it might well be the majority. (2002, 8–9)

Let me respond, first politically, then theologically. When Americans are asked to choose between two propositions, 'My religion is the one true faith leading to eternal life' and 'Many religions lead to eternal life', 75 per cent endorse the latter proposition and only 18 per cent the former. Remarkably, commitment to this ecumenicism is seen across all faiths and backgrounds (Pew Forum 2002, 11–12, 60). In light of this, the prevailing sentiment among America's faithful might be described roughly as follows: While one mountain in the range of human goods is the highest, there are many ways (perhaps an indefinitely large number) of scaling that peak, and there is no compelling reason to prefer one of these paths to the others, let alone to prevent others from following their preferred paths.[7]

Now to theology. While Wolterstorff is obviously right that the Abrahamic faiths endorse the general *concept* of the highest good as right relation to God, they disagree, not only among one another, but also internally, as to the specific *conception* of that right relation. A transcendent God is not only inexhaustibly infinite, beyond the capacity of finite speech to describe (let alone circumscribe), but also substantially hidden. To quote Rabbi Sacks once more, 'the truth at the beating heart of monotheism is that God transcends the particularities of culture and the limits of human understanding. [...] [such a God is] greater not only than the natural universe but also than the spiritual universe capable of being comprehended in any human language, from any single point of view' (2003, 65).

Not surprisingly, as the Abrahamic faiths have developed over time, each has undergone a process of internal pluralisation. Depending on how a specific religious community specifies and orders God's attributes and interprets God's word, there may be an endless variety of orientations—towards faith as opposed to works, the heart as opposed to the law, inner spirituality as opposed to external observance, self-improvement as opposed to social reform, retreat from the world as opposed to immersion in the world, contemplation as opposed to action, political innocence as opposed to worldliness, and so forth.

My point, briefly, is this: for the Abrahamic faiths, the unknowable inexhaustibility of God's nature recapitulates, at the level of theology, the diversity that value pluralists observe on the plane of the mundane, and also the pluralist view that no single culture or conception of the good can encompass all worthy goods and values. So to endorse the concept of right relation to God as the highest good is to leave room for much the same variation in conceptions of that right relation, and in corresponding ways of life, that we observe in secular thought.

To be sure, those who believe that God has been fully, finally and unequivocally revealed through a specific act must reject this theological pluralism as well as philosophical value pluralism. But this belief is certainly not required by faith in the Abrahamic God. So while some traditional Jews believe that the Torah is the literal word of God, which Moses simply wrote down or recited, other Jews equally rooted in the tradition believe that the Torah represents a human

---

7. For much more evidence along these lines, see Wolfe 1998, chapter 2.

response to, or interpretation of, the encounter between the Israelites and God at Sinai. Even the most traditional Jews believe that while the Torah is *from* heaven, it is not *in* heaven: its interpretation and application to specific circumstances is the exclusive responsibility of human beings, not God. And when human beings disagree, as they almost always do, it is the majority of competent interpreters that decides the matter, not a heavenly intervention.[8]

This diversity of views is not confined to Judaism. Indeed, it appears that the sacred text of every faith community is not the end, but rather the source, of diversity. As F. F. Bruce notes, 'The possession of a common holy book [...] does not guarantee religious unity. The interpretation of the holy book [...] is important; and divergent interpretations tend to produce religious divisions' (1968, 70).

Within every faith tradition of which I am aware, there are competing methods of interpretation; within every tradition that takes the form of law, there are competing modes of legal reasoning. (Within Sunni Islam alone, there are four schools of jurisprudence.) And more than that: typically there are disagreements about the relative weight to be accorded to the original text versus accumulated traditions of interpretation. Within Judaism, a split developed between those who believed in the oral as well as the written law—in the tradition of rabbinic exegesis as well as the Torah—and those who rejected rabbinic authority in the name of the written text. Within Islam, some hold that traditions concerning the customs of the Prophet enjoy authority as originary texts along with the Koran, while others wish to return to the Koran as the sole source of doctrine and law. And Protestants, notoriously, rejected the Church's tradition of institutionalised interpretation in the name of *sola scriptura*, the scriptures alone (Levinson 1988, 18–22), a strategy that guaranteed an efflorescence of competing interpretations. (Interpretive unity of a sacred text can persist only when there is an institutional authority to enforce it.)

In the book of Exodus we read the familiar story of the Golden Calf, which leads a wrathful Moses to dash to the ground, and break, the tablets of the law he carried down from Sinai. These tablets were said to be entirely divine in their origin, hewn by God and inscribed by the finger of God. As Moses prepares to ascend the mountain once more, he receives a new set of instructions: rather than God providing tablets, Moses himself is to hew them out of the rock. And in the ensuing encounter with God, it is Moses, not God, who ends up inscribing the commandments on the tablets.

An interpretation: the divine words that endure are those that embody the efforts of human mediators. But then these mediators are more than automata, dictation machines, passive transparent mediums for the transmission of God's

---

8. For citations of the classic Talmudic sources on these points, see Walzer 1987, 30–2.

words. Rather, they are active mediators, infusing the experience of God's presence with the powers of perception, reason and emotion that characterise human existence. As mediators, the prophets are of necessity interpreters. Not even Moses can encounter God 'face to face'. The transmitted word of God cannot but reflect human limits and human diversity.

We must grant Hampshire this much: there can be, and are, faith traditions whose members (1) agree on the texts that enjoy ultimate authority, (2) espouse the same method of interpretation, (3) recognise a single authority as the legitimate and final arbiter of interpretative disagreements, and (4) make claims held to be binding on all human beings, not just members of their particular community. Such monistic traditions are indeed incompatible, in principle, with value pluralism. (Whether a pluralist polity should suppress them is a different matter.)

But most faith communities, I have argued, are not of this type. Because they reject one or more of the premises that constitute religious monism, they allow for a continuing process of internal development and disagreement. This is especially true of the Abrahamic faiths, for a reason that goes to their core: the more seriously one takes the idea of God as transcendent, the less inclined one will be to see the mediated word of God as literally expressing the nature or will of God.

Still, one may object, this line of argument reframes the difficulty without quite resolving it. Even at the most general level of right relation to God, faith traditions differ: for example, Judaism emphasises law and justice, Christianity faith and forgiveness. And within each tradition, specific denominations or tendencies are often exclusionary vis-à-vis one another. So, one might argue, the religious pluralism I emphasise is on the plane of abstract generality, while the lived experience of individuals encountering real-world faiths is more monistic.

While I have no knock-down response to these objections, there are some considerations that seem to me to blunt their force. In the first place, familiar gross differences among traditions often amount to stereotypes. 'Love thy neighbour as thyself' is a verse from the Hebrew Bible, not an original saying of Jesus, and while Catholic canon law differs substantively from Judaism's Torah-based Talmudic law, it is no less developed or important. Second, history suggests that, over time, the experience of plurality within specific faith traditions tends toward coexistence as denominations cease to regard their distinguishing characteristics as necessarily binding on the tradition as a whole. No doubt this process is farther advanced within some traditions than others, and it is incomplete everywhere. But when denominations lack the power to extirpate one another, the experience of coexistence, I suggest, takes the edges off their differences and promotes awareness of underlying commonalities. Relatively few Americans can even describe the differences of doctrine and ritual that once divided Protestants; official Protestant anti-Catholicism, once ubiquitous, is now a fringe phenomenon; fewer and fewer Christians believe that 'God Almighty does not hear the prayers of a Jew' (Smith 1980); the President of the United States has affirmed that Christians and Muslims pray to the same God. It is when political adversaries deploy religious differences for strategic advantage that coexistence comes to seem unbearable.

Shortly before he died, Berlin asked Rabbi Sacks to officiate at his funeral. On that occasion, Sacks quoted a famous Talmudic parable about Mercy, Righteousness and Truth quarrelling before God about the wisdom of creating human beings, a dispute that God can resolve only by 'throwing truth to the ground'. Sacks commented that this story seemed to him to say what Berlin had spent his life teaching: 'for life to be liveable, truth on earth cannot be what it is in heaven. Truth in heaven may be platonic—eternal, harmonious, radiant. But man cannot aspire to such truth, and if he does, he will create conflict not peace' (2003, 63–4). The understanding of God as infinite and unknowable, and the negative theology to which the divide between human beings and God gives rise, points in the same direction.[9] So value pluralism is consistent after all with the principal thrust of monotheism in its most familiar forms, and with the self-understanding of many communities that orient themselves monotheistically. And thus, *pace* Hardy, taking Berlin's value pluralism seriously does not compel us to hope for the disappearance of monotheistic religions.

---

9. This tendency is manifest in the cases of Judaism and Islam. One might think that the centrality of incarnation for Christianity creates a different dynamic, but as the example of Karl Barth demonstrates, Christian theology can embrace the conception of God as radically Other and criticise the religious humanism that views the infinite God through finite human categories. Conversely, both Judaism and Islam have produced reformers who endeavour to purify their respective faiths of what they regard as impious humanisms and spurious mediations between human beings and God.

12

Pluralism and Religious Faith

Michael Jinkins

MAKING THE WORLD SAFE FOR DISAGREEMENT

Jonathan Sacks, in *The Dignity of Difference*, counters an argument popular among many religious leaders today, that peace can be achieved if only everyone will share *their* beliefs and *their* sacred texts. Sacks observes: 'Tragically, that path does not lead to peace.' We need, instead, 'a way of living with, and acknowledging the integrity of, those who are not of our faith' (2002, 9, 5).

In his study of the virtue of reverence, Paul Woodruff seems to agree. 'If you desire peace in the world, do not pray that everyone share your beliefs. Pray instead that all may be reverent.' Woodruff explains: 'without reverence, things fall apart. People do not know how to respect each other and themselves' (2001, 15, 13).

Sensible arguments from two sensible scholars: Woodruff reasons from a wealth of classical wisdom, Rabbi Sacks from a deep grounding in Judaism. Both articulate the possibility that a life of faith need not lead to irrationality, obscurantism, violence and exclusion. Both describe a reverence for God that remains incomplete without a corresponding respect for humankind. But while such voices of sanity reason together, the newspaper headlines mount a disturbing counterpoint, arguing that the possibility for reverence and mutual respect is little more than a humanistic sentiment or a pious dream. To many, the Huntingtonian 'clash of civilisations' appears to be in full swing.[1] Apparently intractable conflicts rage between competing versions of 'religious totalitarianism', to borrow Thomas Friedman's phrase (2001).

As Isaiah Berlin recognised, if there can be only one right answer to any real question of faith and values, and if peace is conditional on all people sharing this one answer, there can be no realistic hope for peace. If peaceful coexistence among people of faith depends on agreement in beliefs and conformity in practices, then the prospect looms ever larger for continued coercion and violence in the name of God.[2]

Are there alternatives to this religious and cultural 'uniformitarianism', whether this drive to sameness is expressed in Christian, Islamic, Hindu, Jewish or secular versions? Are there alternatives to the compulsion for conformity that threatens contemporary society at its most intimate *and* international levels?[3]

I believe there are. And while these alternatives will never capture the hearts and minds of some, there is at least a chance for a measure of peace wherever people of faith and good will (including those who eschew religious faith altogether) are willing to grant respect to the humanity of others and entertain the possibility that reality is ultimately deeper and larger than the experience of any single people. Our task, Nicholas Rescher has said, is to strive 'to make the world safe for disagreement' (1993, 5). This essay seeks to explore certain theological aspects of this task.

A note of caution should be sounded from the outset of this essay. As a theologian much of whose work has been devoted to practical ecclesiology, I am principally interested in probing the theological dimensions of this task in relation to faith communities.[4] While I hope this essay can contribute to a broader inter- (and extra-) faith conversation, my reflections proceed from a specifically Christian perspective and are grounded in a particular theological, historical and cultural location. I would argue, indeed, that recognition of one's own particularity and limitations is essential to an appropriately modest, respectful and reverent approach to human axiological diversity.[5]

---

1. Huntington 1993. Huntington's influential book (1996) builds on the argument originally advanced in 1993.

2. Isaiah Berlin states this core monistic assumption in a variety of contexts, with slightly different emphases. See for example CTH 5–6, 24–25, 53, 209.

3. The term 'uniformitarianism' was coined by Arthur Lovejoy, and is cited by Isaiah Berlin at CTH 85.

4. I have explored these themes in considerably greater detail in Jinkins 2004.

5. Rabbi Abraham Heschel observed that 'the first and most important prerequisite of interfaith is faith'. Cited in Coffin 2004, 85.

THE PRACTICALITY OF THEORY

A few years ago, in an address to a conference of North American religious scholars and Church leaders, I observed that my own faith tradition, Protestant Christianity, does not yet possess an adequate theoretical framework to account for diversity. My faith tradition is by no means unique in this.

The tendency among many people of faith is either (1) to absolutise their beliefs, rejecting diversity out of hand, scorning inclusivity as a merely 'humanistic' value (or as an expression of 'political correctness'), and excluding from their fellowship or society those persons whose beliefs, values and aspirations differ significantly from their own; or (2) to relativise all beliefs and values as matters of subjective, individual preference or taste. I would argue that neither absolutism nor relativism represents an adequate response to diversity. Absolutism tends to dismiss the faith of others. Relativism tends to trivialise it. Neither can escape from essentially the same monistic continuum.

A colleague in the audience that day strongly contested my assessment. 'The problems we are facing aren't theoretical,' he said, 'they are practical. We certainly don't need more theories.' As I explained then, there are few things more practical than theory, especially a useful theory that allows us to reframe reality. A theory is, after all, simply a model to explain reality. A good theoretical model is not only descriptive, it is heuristic. It invites us to expand, even to transform, our understanding.

The most promising theoretical model I have found to account for human diversity and to counter the soul-stultifying enforcement of 'uniformitarianism' emerges from Isaiah Berlin's analysis of pluralism. One of the most valuable of Berlin's contributions is the way he distinguished between monism, relativism and pluralism. His definitions cut across conventional usages of these terms, offering a fresh perspective on the place of pluralism in communities of faith.

MONISM

Berlin describes monism as that view which holds the truth to be one and indivisible, identical for all people in all places at all times. For the monist, every real question has one and only one right answer. Every real problem has a single solution. Whether one discovers these answers and solutions in sacred texts, prophetic utterances or ecstatic religious experiences, through a process of carefully regulated scientific methodology, on the lips of primitive people unsullied by civilisation, or in the voice of democratic majorities, the truth can, at least in theory, be discovered. If discovered, the truth will be consistent and will harmonise with all other established truths, because every truth, be it in the world of science or of human values or of religious faith, must be consistent with all other truths (CTH 24–5).

In the history of Christian theology the great representatives of monism have emerged from streams of faith influenced by Plato and Aristotle. This history includes some of the Church's most influential thinkers, such as Origen, Augustine and Aquinas. Though the Protestant Reformation, especially in its first and most dynamic generation in the sixteenth century, tested the theological boundaries of the monism it inherited, particularly the assumption that there is one single universal natural law, and the corresponding tendency to discount particularity in taking account of human life, values and commitments, the currents of monism were generally too strong to resist, especially for the successors to the earliest Protestant reformers.[6]

Christian theology has struggled for centuries with the doctrinal, liturgical and ecclesiastical implications of monism. Undoubtedly the message of the Church has all too often been dominated by absolutist and exclusivist claims within this monistic framework. However, the faith discourses and the communal practices of the Church in particular communities, in various cultural contexts and historical moments, has exhibited a startling pluralism made all the more striking in contrast to the doctrinal, ecclesiastical-political and liturgical attempts to affirm and sometimes enforce uniformity in the name of Christian unity and catholicity. In one way or another, the Church has striven within its soul between two alternatives, the first expressed by Cyprian's 'Extra ecclesiam nulla salus' ('Outside the Church there is no salvation'), and the second a fundamental openness to the diversity and plurality implicit in the Christian doctrines of creation, incarnation, revelation and inspiration. Despite the discomfort of the dominant voices in Christian history and the general inability among them to account for even its own diversity, the pluralism practiced by the Church has been sustained. Indeed, it flourishes.

It is also true that for many Christians the persistence of pluralism, the stunning variety of ways of human living across the great span of history and in whatever age one finds oneself, is an embarrassment and a problem. Among many Christians, however, diversity in creation and in human history can be a matter of celebration more than of lamentation, and deserves careful description and theological reflection. While they have never represented the dominant stream in Christendom, there are many Christians, Christian scholars and communities of

---

6. Berlin himself notes the contribution the Protestant Reformation nevertheless made to the development of historicism and the engagement with pluralism. See CTH 32, 83; AC 3.

faith that have rejected or called into question a monistic perspective. Some have been influenced by various streams of romanticism and existentialism, others by the liberal progressivism of figures such as Horace Bushnell and, more recently, William Sloane Coffin and James Forbes; some influenced by the pragmatism of William James, or by postmodernism, as exemplified by John D. Caputo or Mark C. Taylor, or by the philosophical and political communitarianism of Charles Taylor and Michael Walzer; and still others elevate Christian practices and acts of service (e.g. the Society of Friends) over the enforcement of dogma, including many communities of faith that would be classified in Avery Dulles's ecclesiological model as 'the Church as servant'.[7]

Berlin discerns in all forms of monism a levelling tendency toward sameness, a fear of the many in favour of the one, and an anxiety in the face of the Other. Largely because of the terrible repressions and persecutions he witnessed at the hands of Communists and Fascists, Berlin remained throughout his life deeply opposed to the social forces within monism that enforce uniformity and unanimity, and that vilify those who do not conform, those whose otherness cannot or will not be reduced to uniform expectations, harmony and consensus. In contrast to those who favor monism (especially in its absolutist and exclusivist forms), he believed that variety is, in and of itself, a good and viable end of human life, and that a society is fundamentally enriched by the diversity of its members.

RELATIVISM

While Berlin apparently found monism relatively easy to describe, relativism proved more difficult. For Berlin, the best way to determine the meaning of a word is to observe its usages; and in his writings the term 'relativism' is generally used to designate a personal, primarily individualistic, preference for one thing over another on the basis of subjective, often private, experience. Berlin attempts to express relativism's atomistic, quasi-aesthetic character by describing it as a 'taste'. According to Berlin, a relativist says: ' "I prefer coffee, you prefer champagne. We have different tastes. There is no more to be said." That is relativism' (CTH 11).

While appearing to leave room for other persons to experience life on their own terms, this socially agnostic relativism (i.e. agnostic at the most basic human level, which says 'I cannot know your humanity, nor you mine') locks others out of our individual subjective experience of the world, and us out of theirs. It restricts

---

7. For example: Bushnell 1887; Coffin 2004; James 1902, 1909; Caputo 1997; Taylor 1984; Johnson 1997; Taylor 1992; Dulles 1987, 96–100; Walzer 1997.

any real empathetic understanding of our relationships to the most superficial level, and tends to deny the possibility of a community of common experience.

The Christian theologian John Hick expressed this form of relativism when he equated the confession of a Christian with romantic infatuation: 'That Jesus is my Lord and Saviour is language like that of a lover, for whom his Helen is the sweetest girl in the world' (1974, 18). Relativism is a position which many Christians and non-Christians find objectionable, a position in which matters of real importance, matters of life and death, of conscience and faith, are trivialised into matters of mere preference, private opinion and personal taste.

There is another aspect of relativism, however, which Berlin's usage of the term describes—and rejects. Berlin finds in at least some expressions of relativism a deterministic posture toward human intellectual and moral agency, according to which the thoughts, convictions and actions of individuals are not simply *influenced* by various factors in a historical, cultural and social context, but are inevitably, one might even say fatalistically, *determined* by these factors. Berlin defended Giambattista Vico and Johann Gottfried Herder against such charges (CTH 76–7). This sort of relativism says, in effect: 'I cannot help believing as I do. I am programmed this way.' According to this kind of relativism, one is a product—or, as contemporary culture implies, a victim—of circumstance.

Berlin takes his critique of the determinism in such expressions of relativism one step further, however, demonstrating a common thread running through some expressions of relativism:

> Relativism, in its modern form, tends to spring from the view that men's outlooks are unavoidably determined by forces of which they are often unaware— Schopenhauer's irrational cosmic force; Marx's class-bound morality; Freud's unconscious drives; the social anthropologists' panorama of the irreconcilable variety of customs and beliefs conditioned by circumstances largely uncontrolled by men. (CTH 78)

Relativism ('in its modern form') brings one to stand before 'the Other' and to say: 'I cannot know you. I cannot understand your world of experiences. I cannot begin to imagine who you are, or what motivates you, or what you care about. I do not know what you mean when you say that you are human.' And sometimes 'the other' before whom one stands as a stranger is oneself staring back from the mirror. Each of us, in this expression of relativism, is so much a product of largely unconscious forces that we remain alienated from and essentially unknowable even to ourselves. Such is the auto-da-fé of this form of relativism.

The point that Berlin makes in distinguishing his concept of pluralism from relativism is this: 'Relativism is not the only alternative to universalism [...] nor does incommensurability entail relativism. There are many worlds, some of which overlap' (CTH 85). The variety of human experiences and perspectives does not necessitate alienation either from one another or from our selves.

There is another point about relativism which is crucial for a theological appropriation of Berlin's thought. For Berlin, monism, with its claim to absolute knowledge of the single universal truth, is in some sense the other side of the coin of that form of relativism which claims, either implicitly or explicitly, to be able to evaluate the various moral and axiological systems of humanity and to judge them in relation to one another, either as equally mistaken or as equally valid. Indeed, both absolutism and relativism assume that one (either the religiously or the culturally 'enlightened' one) can somehow assume a trans-historical (or, even, an a-historical) position from which to make judgements, and that one can from this position appeal to certain criteria of valuation against which human systems of values and beliefs can be comparatively assessed. Berlin's thought, at this point, bears certain similarities to that of Ludwig Wittgenstein and, more recently, Jacques Derrida. No one possesses a ladder to crawl up out of history, from which to gain a trans-historical viewpoint. And even if one did possess a ladder from which to view any number of other historical and cultural contexts, the ladder must still stand somewhere, on some patch of historical and cultural particularity. Everything that is human is historically and culturally grounded, and every judgement we make is historically conditioned, in that we must make it from some historical perspective.[8]

To put this idea into specifically religious terms, one might argue that God has the capacity to transcend history. But humanity does not. God's judgement may be eternal. But human judgements cannot be. And, as Paul Woodruff has observed, the hubris that leads creatures to believe that they share the divine perspective is the very opposite of reverence (2001, 4–5, 90–91).

Some of the most insightful theological critiques of 'pluralism', those, for example, of Alan Torrance and Gavin D'Costa, are more appropriately seen as criticisms of forms of relativism, and not of pluralism, at least not as Berlin uses the term. 'Pluralism', Torrance writes, 'suggests that all religions and philosophies contain elements of truth and true revelations, but that no religion can "claim final and definitive truth". This leads to the conclusion that the main religious traditions share more or less equal degrees of validity.' Such a 'pluralism' demands that its adherents hold to this central theological truth claim, 'that truth is found in various "fragmentary and incomplete" forms within the claims of other religions' (1997, 114–5).

This demand for faith adherence represents not an inclusion of all others; rather, as D'Costa perceptively observes, it represents 'a form of exclusivism'

---

8. Though this lies well beyond the scope of this essay, fruitful scholarly enquiry could focus on Berlin's relationship to postmodern thought, along the lines of Staten 1984.

(1996, 225, cited by Torrance, 115). Pluralism is frequently characterised in these terms. However, and despite the application of the name 'pluralism' to this position, this is not the pluralism for which Berlin argues, but is a form of relativism, just another attempt to account for diversity (in this case, religious diversity) within a monistic framework, specifically a framework grounded in and determined by 'the Enlightenment project' (see D'Costa 2000, 2–13, 19–52). The confusion proceeds, at least in part, because some philosophers of religion persist in describing their work as pluralistic when it remains relativistic.

PLURALISTIC ALTERNATIVES

Isaiah Berlin was a renowned champion of pluralism. What is less widely understood is that Berlin described at least two distinct forms of pluralism: the first, the kind of teleologically conditioned pluralism one discerns in Hamann, Vico and Herder, and the second, Berlin's own thoroughgoing pluralism. The first form of pluralism would not be problematic for many faith traditions, though the second form, Berlin's own more thoroughgoing approach, would.

Pluralism 1: The Pluralism of Hamann, Vico and Herder

J. G. Hamann's thought is robust and far-reaching. What might be described today as his pluralism is grounded in his historicism and a deep respect for the variety of human cultures. It represents a theological *Weltanschauung* that attempts to account both for the revelatory rationale of a God who communicates with humanity through a vast array of means, and for the unpredictable, the suprarational and irrational elements in creation that resist the superficialities of those who would reduce all reality to the terms of a rationalistic ideology.

Hamann believed that truth is concrete and particular, never general. If one wishes to understand anything, one must attend to the variable specificities of historical context, to the local, even provincial, the historically, linguistically and culturally embedded ways of a people. Hamann rejected attempts to construct systems of thought that divert one's attention from the complex and sometimes contradictory realities of existence. As Berlin says of Hamann: 'History alone yields concrete truth, and in particular the poets describe their world in the language of passion and inspired imagination' (AC 9). Hamann believed that attention to the messy and diverse character of historical existence and the passionate language and imagination of poetry were the best ways to gain access to truth because 'God is a poet, not a mathematician' (AC 8).

Hamann resisted the attempts of strict rationalism to ignore and despise history, and of certain representatives of the French Enlightenment to reject the folkways of the provincial and the primitive in the name of a higher, truer culture—i.e. their own. Hamann, sometimes like an ecstatic Hebrew prophet, at other times like certain philosophical empiricists, and always with a profound respect for the way 'the various features of our experience—ourselves, others, language, the world, ultimately God—are all inextricably related' (Dickson 1995, 16), demands that we become attentive to the world that surrounds us, rather than the mental abstractions we are tempted to substitute for complex and concrete realities. According to Hamann, God speaks through every aspect of creation. God speaks in the intractable and hidden mystery of humanity as well as through the open book of the universe itself and the written text of the Christian Bible. God wills to draw humanity by faith into a participation in God's ultimate purposes.

Hamann draws together his sense of the immediacy of God the divine communicator and revealer with that of God the purposeful creator. His pluralism, while taking account of the variety of ways human cultures have sought to answer the most important questions pressed upon them by their existence, finds a point of unity in God's purpose for creation, a purpose God speaks in and through the universe and invites human beings to share, wherever they find themselves.

Vico and Herder, in effect, simply raised the stakes in the game, increasing the tension between, on one hand, a pluralism that takes seriously the historically specific diversity of humanity and, on the other, a fundamental belief that the plurality of human cultures, religions, values and ends ultimately serve God's purposes (CTH 76). While the cultures of the world afford a plurality of values, beliefs and aspirations, for Vico and Herder as for Hamann, there remains a fundamental teleological orientation grounded in the conviction that God works through all of the cultures of the world to achieve God's own *telos*. While pluralism reigns supreme across human history and throughout human cultures, they posited singularity in the hidden heart of God. The God whom they revere is a God who loves diversity for its own sake, who has woven plurality into the very fabric of creation, who delights in this variety, but, at the same time, who is working through the staggering diversity of creation to accomplish final purposes known ultimately to God alone. These affirmations are irreducible faith claims for these distinctive Christian thinkers.

Despite the debt he acknowledges to Hamann, Vico and Herder, Berlin resists their version of pluralism specifically because of its teleology. John Gray observes that, according to Berlin, it is appropriate to speak teleologically of individual persons, to affirm that they are 'purposive creatures', that they work towards ends, and that they construct meaning from and for their lives. But to speak in this manner of history as a whole is to introduce into the discussion a 'historical theodicy' that inevitably favors the values and ends of some cultures over others and that undercuts the import of pluralism as an end in itself (JG 84).

Gray's usage of the phrase 'historical theodicy' with reference to Berlin merits closer investigation, because it is both apt in describing Berlin and theologically significant. Normally, in Christian theology, the term 'theodicy' is reserved to describe 'the vindication of divine providence in view of the existence of evil' (Pearsall 1999, 1486). What Gray conveys in adapting the term to describe Berlin's rejection of a teleological interpretation of history is this: Berlin resists *any* attempt, religious or secular, to try to justify the evils and misdeeds of the present by appealing to a larger purpose, to a great and glorious goal beyond the horizon of the present. For Berlin, no grand abstractions, no castles in the air, no promised land, no chosen people, no eschatological kingdom, no heaven on earth, no State purged of counter-revolutionaries or of the spectre of terrorism, no utopian omelette of any sort can justify the breaking of any number of eggs (AC 196). This protest lies at the heart of Berlin's rejection of every 'historical theodicy'. Berlin witnessed too often the cynical and the idealistic, the callous politicians, the dreamy-eyed utopians and the ruthless tyrants from Hitler to Stalin, from Mao to Pol Pot (and, we might add, any number of false messiahs and charismatic religious leaders as well), marching down the same terrible path provisionally rationalising and justifying the most appalling injustices, repressions, cruelties, murders and mass suicides by invoking some teleological interpretation of history. While the perfect future for which so many have died remains temporally deferred, the habit of breaking eggs only grows (CTH 15–16). Many philosophers and theologians have raised concerns similar to Berlin's, and no one can remain insensitive to this issue in the wake of the ideologically inspired atrocities witnessed by the twentieth century and the religiously motivated terrorism which has become a daily threat.

For Berlin, there are no answers in the back of the textbook of history. In his estimation, therefore, despite the tremendous contributions of Hamann, Vico and Herder, in the end they do not take us far enough, because of their profound and essentially religious commitment to a teleological view of history (CTH 79).

Pluralism 2: Berlin's thoroughgoing pluralism

One might be tempted to describe Berlin's pluralism by saying that it is similar to that of Hamann, Vico and Herder provided one omits their teleological interpretation of history. But this would not account for the positive force, the originality and importance of Berlin's own contribution:

> I do believe that there is a plurality of values which men can and do seek, and that these values differ. There is not an infinity of them: the number of human

values, of values which I can pursue while maintaining my human semblance, my human character, is finite [...] if a man pursues one of these values, I, who do not, am able to understand why he pursues it or what it would be like, in his circumstances, for me to be induced to pursue it. Hence the possibility of human understanding. (POI 12)

Here there is no undisclosed monistic conception of metaphysical purpose, no divine providence 'according to which everything conspires towards a final harmonious resolution' (CTH 57). There is, as Berlin observed, no Archimedean point outside of human history and values from which (whether one is an absolutist or a relativist) one can evaluate all human values and beliefs. Various cultures at different historical moments have defined truth, good and beauty in particular ways, and their cultures have expressed and pursued those ends—ultimate and objective for their cultures—which they believed were appropriate and right. And, yet, as different as cultures are, and as diverse as their values and ends may be, it is possible for a human being living in Oxford in the latter half of the twentieth century, by diligent effort and imagination, to understand something of what it would mean to live in, and to value and work towards the ends pursued by, a human society such as the one in which Homer performed his epic poems.

The fact that I can understand as human the values and ends of another society does not mean that I am bound to endorse them, however, as Berlin himself frequently makes clear. From within our own historical and cultural particularity it is possible, and inevitable and necessary, that we should form judgements based on our understanding of the good, the true and the beautiful. As Berlin writes, 'if I pursue one set of values I may detest another, and may think it is damaging to the only form of life that I am able to live or tolerate for myself and others; in which case I may attack it, I may even—in extreme cases—have to go to war against it. But I still recognise it as a human pursuit' (POI 12).

The recognition of a plurality of values and ends which function in various cultural and historical contexts does not imply that one must accept these values and ends as valid. But it does mean that one must recognise the diverse ways of being human and of living together in human society that have been historically pursued, and the irreducible incommensurability of many of the values and ends that human societies have pursued. It also means that we recognise that our critique of other human judgements is grounded in our own cultural and historical context, in the context of our own pursuit of values and ends, and that we do not occupy a privileged position outside of all culture and history from which to make our assessments.

This, of course, was the crucial point that Berlin discovered in Niccolò Machiavelli. The Florentine diplomat and political thinker has stumped his critics for centuries, but what Machiavelli discerned, according to Berlin, is simply this: Christian morality, which, for example, in Jesus's Sermon on the Mount, values charity, for-giveness of enemies, self-sacrifice, self-abnegation and otherworldliness, represents a completely different set of values and ends from the *antiqua virtus* of Republican Rome which Machiavelli advocated for those who assume public leadership. The latter, devoted to public-spirited strength and courage, the assertion of self and devotion to worldly ambition, power and the willingness to take vengeance on one's enemies, represents another way of living in a society altogether, indeed another society altogether, the values and ends of which are no less ultimate and no less objective than various Christian ways (and there are, indeed, many Christian ways other than that represented in the Sermon on the Mount).[9] Machiavelli's critical insight, according to Berlin, was not that public leadership demands unscrupulous behaviour or political shady dealings. His insight was altogether more profound than this. In fact, Berlin's Machiavelli was a moralist arguing for another moral code, a pagan code of public virtue (AC 69–71).

In Berlin's view, there are in various cultures, and frequently in the same cul-ture, and sometimes in the same individual, conflicting and incommensurable values and ends that remain ultimate and objective. The axiological conflicts we endure within and among us are as unavoidable as they are intractable. There is no place outside of time and space, outside of our own axiological worlds, where we can stand to make our choices between them. We must, in a manner appro-priate to our own historical, cultural and social understandings and commitments, make our choices. And as we choose we must do so in the knowledge that to choose certain worthwhile values and ends may necessarily mean that we are rejecting others no less important to us, and that our choices frequently entail losses that are irremediable and irretrievable (Galipeau 1994, 59).

Perhaps most radically, according to Berlin, the various values and ends of life which emerge from various historical and cultural contexts cannot simply be com-bined without loss. Irreparable loss is an essential feature of historicism. Whatever the combination of particular historical and cultural factors, of personal factors (including the very unpredictable factor of personal genius), of social, familial and economic factors which gave us, for example, Shakespeare's plays and Mozart's operas, they come together only fleetingly, and are then lost to history for ever.

Even closer to home, the values that many in our Western popular culture of personal autonomy and psychological self-improvement hold most precious, values such as self-examination and self-knowledge, of mental health and psycho-logical well-being, may actually work against other things that we value just as highly, such as artistic genius. Even the most important values of human life stand in conflict with one another. Berlin understood this as few others have, but he also

---

9. See Niebuhr 1932 and Bonhoeffer 1949.

understood something more, that conflicts between our values are neither rare nor exceptional, but are typical of human social existence.

Believing, as Berlin does, that human values are a human creation, not a creation simply of individuals, but of entire human societies, then the central 'problems' of pluralism have to do, not with trying to harmonise the diverse perspectives and claims of life, but with negotiating our lives through the complex tangle of often incommensurable values and ends that compete for our allegiance, affection and time. This negotiation of incommensurable values may take a form as personal as the choice one makes between a celibate calling and the vocation of marriage, or a form as public as an entire society's wrestling with the value it places on freedom of expression against its maintenance of national security. Berlin's pluralism of values is an attempt to describe the concrete complexities of human social existence in a manner that takes seriously the moral agency, the freedom and the responsibility of persons.

PLURALISM AND CHRISTIAN FAITH

In concluding, I shall reflect briefly on the issue of pluralism explicitly from a Christian perspective. One question that emerges for me is fairly straightforward: Can a Christian share the kind of thoroughgoing pluralism we find in Isaiah Berlin? The key to answering this question lies in determining whether, or to what degree, a Christian believes (1) Christianity necessarily entails a monistic claim to a single, universal, absolute and exclusive standard by which good, truth and beauty are judged; (2) Christian faith provides us with a place to stand outside of history and culture from which to judge values and ends; and (3) Christianity requires a teleological view of history.

Clearly the modesty and humility of Berlin's pluralism, which rejects the idea that we as human beings can transcend our historical and cultural contexts and can claim for ourselves a privileged position above history and culture from which to judge the values and ends of others, is not altogether without parallel in religious thought, including Christianity. Judgement belongs to God, Christians are taught, not to humanity. Jesus of Nazareth told at least one audience: 'Do not judge, so that you may not be judged. For with the judgement you make you will be judged, and the measure you give will be the measure you get' (Matthew 7:1–2). This teaching was viewed as so typically 'Christian' that versions of it entered into the writings of a variety of early Christian communities, as is attested by the canonical texts they produced. The Pauline Church taught: 'Therefore you have no excuse, whoever you are, when you judge others; for in passing judgement on another you condemn yourself' (Romans 2:1). And in this at least the Jerusalem community seems to have been in agreement with Paul: 'There is one lawgiver and judge who is able to save and to destroy. So who, then, are you to judge your neighbour?' (James 4:12).

Though some Christians assert the claim that our faith grants us a trans-historical or a-historical ground from which to make ultimate judgements on the values and ends of others, there is perhaps nothing as certain as the fact that this is the one thing Christians cannot possess. Christian theologians, such as Karl Barth and Dietrich Bonhoeffer, have sternly warned against the temptation to equate human endeavours (including religion, theology and morality) with God.[10] And some Christian theologians, for example, Ernst Troeltsch, Rowan Williams, Reinhold Bernhardt, Kathryn Tanner, Eugene March and Shirley Guthrie, Jr, find in Christian scripture and theology explicit theological grounds for pluralism.[11]

Berlin's caution against trans-historical arrogance is crucial for Christians to remember in the face of those who suppose that because they are Christians they now share a God's-eye view of the world. Berlin's warning is no less crucial for relativists (religious and secular), however, who believe that a particular philosophical perspective or historical consciousness gives them access to a privileged position and to privileged information from which they can judge all religions in relation to one another. There is a healthy scepticism within various texts of the New Testament (representing faith and practices in particular Christian communities) that resists religious humbug and theologically fuelled hubris, though many Christians gloss over this in their desire to find in the Bible a confirmation of their own parochial views and values. Other canonical texts from these same ancient communities also make absolutist and exclusive claims in the name of Christ. This fact cannot be denied.

Irremediable loss, which emerges in making inevitable and necessary choices between competing values, another aspect of Berlin's thought, is also implicit in Christian scripture. Generally speaking, the variety of Christian religious experiences and practices of faith, though historically well attested, creates an uneasy tension in certain Christian texts which, from the time of the very earliest Churches, have often demonstrated a deep commitment to singularity. But, even within the New Testament, the most important collection of explicitly Christian texts (many of which in one way or another seem to wish to enforce unanimity in religious experience and doctrine), there is considerable and conscious intertextual conflict and incongruity. The Christian canon, as a whole, holds these tensions between texts permanently within itself, ensuring that Christianity is enriched by a plurality of Christian ways.

---

10. Barth 1919, 107–287; Bonhoeffer 1952, 278–82, and 294–300, 357–61.

11. Troeltsch trans. 1991, 343–59; Coakley 1988; Bernhardt 1990; Tanner 1997; Williams 2000, 167–80; Guthrie 1986; March 2005; Irvin 1998; and Rhoads 1996.

As David Kelsey explains, the ways in which Christians attempt to understand God and to live faithfully are 'present in concrete reality *in and as various Christian congregations or worshiping communities in all their radical pluralism*' (1992, 110). This has always been true. It was the case among the earliest Christian communities, including those that gave rise to and are represented in the New Testament itself, and has been in every historical era since. The way of St Paul (and, I hasten to add, there is considerable diversity of faith and practice even in the Pauline 'way'), just to note one biblical example, is not simply synonymous with—is, indeed, often in profound conflict with—the way of St James. But these very different ways (and the same can be said of many other Christian ways) are enshrined and blessed by their inclusion in the Christian canon (Dunn 2001; Park 2003).

Choosing to live one's life according to the teachings of one Christian way may result in the loss of worthwhile aspects of the values of another way. Protestants, for example, have historically framed the difference between a Pauline way and the way advocated in the Epistle of James as a contrast between faith and works. If we minimise, attempt to harmonise, or deny the differences between these two Christian ways we cut ourselves off from much of the creative power of the message of Jesus of Nazareth; and yet, as Martin Luther understood (though his solution was classically monistic), the ways of both cannot be fully and consistently honoured in a single human life. Choices must be made. These choices between Christian ways entail irreparable losses. And, it should be noted, there are many authentically Christian ways represented in all sorts of Christian communities historically and contemporaneously, from monastic communities held together by the Rule of St Benedict, and thoroughly non-monastic communities of faith bound together in their common commitment to eradicating poverty and social injustice, to congregations that are united by nothing so much as their appreciation of diversity. Some Christian denominations—my own, for example —have explicitly endorsed this rich diversity in their confessions and forms of polity, recognising that the variety reflects the extravagant multiversity of God's creation, which can only be experienced in the particular.[12]

Finally, Berlin's exclusion of historical purposefulness runs counter to various understandings of divine providence one finds in Christian scripture, dependent as the New Testament is and building as it does on a Hebrew understanding of God's involvement in human history, specifically God's working out of God's purposes in and through the people of Israel. For many Christians, facing and making sense of the ordinary discomforts and losses of existence, and attempting to rationalise the problem of evil and human suffering, the thoroughgoing pluralism of Berlin remains unacceptable. But, it must also be said that there are biblical texts that

---

12. In my own religious tradition this is enshrined in Presbyterian Church 1999, xi–xx.

resist the yearning to find teleological meaning in the movements of history. The books of Job and Ecclesiastes do not stand alone, though they come to mind most immediately in this context. It would not, therefore, be easy even for Christians with a robust belief in divine providence to dismiss the rejection of historical theodicy in Berlin's pluralism, and especially his unwillingness to accept rational-isations for the evil that humanity does in the name of a perfect future. Indeed, there are significant points of resonance between Berlin's thought and the resurgence of interest in the theological category of lamentation in Christian scholarship (Inbody 1997; Hall 1986; Zenger 1994).

TWO CHEERS FOR PLURALISM, BUT THREE FOR HUMILITY

Isaiah Berlin once observed that the best we can do in living together as human beings is 'to maintain a precarious equilibrium that will prevent the occurrence of desperate situations, of intolerable choices [...] in the light of the limited range of our knowledge and even of our imperfect understanding of individuals and societies'. Berlin adds, 'A certain humility in these matters is very necessary' (CTH 17–18).

If it does require 'a certain humility' to embrace a life that denies neither the faith one holds precious nor scorns the faith (or faithlessness) of another, then it behoves Christians to practice humility, since our founder promised that the meek, the merciful, the pure of heart and the makers of peace are blessed (Matthew 5:5–9). This is intellectually honest and spiritually sane. This is also appropriate to the 'deep understanding of human limitations', the 'capacity for awe' toward God, or whatever it is that transcends the self, and the respect for other people that Woodruff speaks of, without which 'things fall apart' (2001, 3, 13).

While I find that Berlin's interpretation of pluralism offers a compelling framework for taking account of diversity, I recognise that within that diversity there are many who see the world through a monistic lens. These various monistic value and belief systems do not necessarily represent a threat to the larger society. It is when a system exerts the claim of a totalitarian ideology that it may threaten the common good by seeking to displace or eradicate all other value and belief systems. Certainly pluralism itself need not become such a totalitarian ideology. The world would be infinitely poorer if it lost any number of expressions of faith that, though explicitly monistic, have contributed vital new insights and social benefits to the common good.[13]

---

13. I am especially instructed at this point by William A. Galston's response to Henry Hardy's stimulating essay, 'Taking Pluralism Seriously', in 'Must Value Pluralism and Religious Belief Collide?' Both essays are in this volume.

13

Taking Pluralism Seriously

HENRY HARDY

What a loathsome malady it is to believe that you are so right that you convince yourself that nobody can think the opposite.

Michel de Montaigne[1]

Not only are the varieties of morality innumerable, but some of them are conflicting with each other.

James Fitzjames Stephen[2]

[T]he ultimately possible attitudes towards life are irreconcilable, and hence their struggle can never be brought to a final conclusion.

Max Weber[3]

PREFACE

The article that follows was written in the early 1990s, and first published in Dutch (1995). It still seems to me, over a decade later, to make a point

---

1. Montaigne ed. Screech 1991, book 1, chapter 56, 'On Prayer', 358.
2. Stephen 1873, 141.
3. Weber 1918, 152.

that has, oddly, hardly been addressed in the literature[4]—perhaps partly because of understandable religious sensibilities. My purpose in writing it was to draw out from Isaiah Berlin's pluralist ideas a consequence that seemed to me clearly to follow from them, though he had not made this consequence explicit in his own published writings.[5] However, as I explain below, he read and largely endorsed what I had to say, which seems to me to make this article a useful addition to the material available for the interpretation of his thought, quite apart from whatever intrinsic plausibility my observations may possess.

Although I should not write the same piece if I were to start again from scratch, I have deliberately left it substantially unaltered, partly because it entered Frege's 'third realm' (Popper's 'World 3')—that is, was given an independent public existence of its own—in 1995, and I wanted the original English text to be available as it was written. My attempts to publish it in English in the conventional manner when I wrote it were unsuccessful,[6] though a greatly condensed version (2002) has appeared in the faculty journal of the Austin Presbyterian Theological Seminary, Texas. The other main reason for leaving the text as it was is that I find, to my slight surprise, that there is nothing of importance that I wish to withdraw.

Nevertheless, I have naturally learned from the contributions to this volume by William Galston and Michael Jinkins, and from my discussions with them and with George Crowder about their arguments. One thing that these other essays bring out is the great plurality of belief and practice within nominally unitary religious traditions. I am not sure, though, that this radically affects my central contention, which I might now express in terms of the defining aspirations of at any rate some key religions, rather than in terms of their achievements. Some of the most widespread and historically influential religions, I should say, especially

---

4. Though Stuart Hampshire (1999, 47) subsequently wrote something that chimes in with my argument: 'Obviously, if one God, only one morality—His law and the falsity of moral pluralism therefore.'

5. Though in notes written for a friend in 1981 he took the first step towards it: 'Few things have done more harm than the belief on the part of individuals or groups (or tribes or states or nations or churches) that he or she or they are in *sole* possession of the truth: especially about how to live, what to be & do—& that those who differ from them are not merely mistaken, but wicked or mad: & need restraining or suppressing. It is a terrible and dangerous arrogance to believe that you alone are right: have a magical eye which sees *the* truth: & that others cannot be right if they disagree' (L 345).

6. I particularly relished the judgement of one referee for a leading UK politics journal: 'The paper is not [...] scholarly, since it makes no reference to any writer in the field except Berlin' (not quite true, but no matter). So much for a good deal of philosophy's shamefully unscholarly past. I am further encouraged by the outright rejection of Allen 2003, a far better contribution than this.

mainstream variants of Christianity and Islam, aspire to a monism that they may not in practice achieve. The particular kind of religious impulse that their doctrines express is essentially monistic, even if such monistic ambitions are frustrated by the exigencies of reality, especially our own quarrelsome and partially-sighted nature. But this failure is a temporary matter of human imperfection, not reflected (according to believers) in the reality that we fail properly to comprehend: God's transcendent reality does not manifest the value-plurality of our world of experience, which is therefore no guide to the former. (On this point I agree with Berlin, who said that, if values cohere in another world, then they are not our values; from which it follows that no persuasive escape from earthly plurality can be made by appealing to heavenly unity.)[7]

Comments by George Crowder have made me realise that I might have made something else clearer, too: namely, that the link from (especially religious) monism to intolerance and violence is sustained by the fanaticism of some believers rather than by the inexorable logic of monist belief itself; it is a psychological fact about the sensibility of many monists rather than a conceptual matter, as is the link between pluralism and liberalism, at any rate on Berlin's view (UD 226). To that extent, fanaticism in general rather than potentially fanatical monisms might have been my target. To be against fanaticism, however, is hardly controversial, and in any case there is also a reason why religious monism, at least when espoused with evangelical fervour,[8] is a particularly dangerous customer. This is its conviction of its rectitude about ultimate matters, especially our fate in the eternal hereafter. If you know how to save people's souls, what may you not do to achieve this outcome?[9] The belief that licenses fanaticism is, in the case of evangelical religious monism, a

---

7. CTH 13: 'collisions of values are of the essence of what they are and what we are. If we are told that these contradictions will be solved in some perfect world in which all good things can be harmonised in principle, then we must answer, to those who say this, that the meanings they attach to the names which for us denote the conflicting values are not ours. [...] the world in which what we see as incompatible values are not in conflict is a world altogether beyond our ken [...] it is on earth that we live, and it is here that we must believe and act.' The notion of a God who by some form of transcendent conjuring-trick turns the base metal of human pluralism into the pure gold of divine monism was mooted by William James (1891, 353): 'It would seem [...] that the stable and systematic moral universe for which the ethical philosopher asks is fully possible only in a world where there is a divine thinker with all-enveloping demands. If such a thinker existed, his way of subordinating the demands to each other would be the finally valid casuistic scale.'
8. George Crowder reasonably points out that there are some religions that are/were not tarred with this brush, e.g. Buddhism, Hinduism and Greek and Roman polytheism.
9. Cf. CTH 16: 'If your desire to save mankind is serious, you must harden your heart, and not reckon the cost.'

greater spur to the fanatic precisely because it treats of salvation for all eternity. The same cannot be said for secular sources of fanaticism.

A useful metaphor from the literature that I might have used in this connection is that of 'thin' and 'thick' principles: a thin principle might be that one should not cause gratuitous pain to others, a much thicker one, that the Sabbath must be observed, and an even thicker, that one should wear black at a funeral. For a pluralist, the thicker, the more plural; so that religions are more likely to be objectionable to the pluralist to the extent that their monist commitments are thicker. Moreover, thicker commitments are likely to provoke more disagreement, and those who are determined to proselytise may attempt to overcome that disagreement by force. It might be more difficult to argue that a religion without a fairly definite list of thick commitments isn't really a paradigmatic case of a religion, but my instinct is to say that religious belief has a permanent inbuilt tendency to sponsor thick certitude beyond its proper boundaries—which can lead (albeit, once again, as a matter of psychology rather than of logic) to fundamentalist intolerance. As I formulated it in a subsequent piece: 'It is an essential characteristic of the great monistic religions and political ideologies to claim that there is only one way to salvation, one right way to live, one true value-structure. This is the claim which, when it is given fanatical expression, leads to fundamentalism, persecution and intolerance.'[10]

One series of events took place after the Dutch translation was published which it is relevant to record. In 1996 I showed the piece to a philosopher who asked me if I had written anything in this area, and received a somewhat negative response. This came to Berlin's notice, and he asked to see what I had written. I sent him the piece, and he wrote me a letter, dated 21 January 1997, which I reproduce below. It would be entirely characteristic of him if this letter is more generous than just, but I do not believe that he would have written as he did if he had seriously disagreed with me.

> I have read your piece on Taking Pluralism Seriously with great interest, and indeed admiration. I think it is a splendid piece, you need not be too modest about it—I am glad it was published, even if only in Dutch—and I think I agree with almost every word you say. There are points where I might deviate from you, or think you hadn't got it quite right, but they are so minor that I am not going to list them; if you really want me to do that, I'll read it again and then we can go through them when we next meet—but honestly, they are so small that it's not worth doing. The only point that struck me at all was that you give the impression (without positively saying so—you deny it to begin with, but then give the opposite impression) that all ultimate values collide: as you know, they do not: there is nothing wrong

---

10. L x.

with happiness and liberty, knowledge and equality, etc. That is the only place where I think you slightly mislead the reader about your own view. Anyway, I congratulate you on it, I think it is a fine piece, I really do.

In my reply I said that I should be interested to know where he thought there were mistakes, but in the event we did not discuss the piece further.

Taking Pluralism Seriously

The word 'pluralist' appears increasingly in the press in a weak sense that underuses its capacity to describe a distinctive ethical viewpoint. Journalists who write of a 'pluralist society' usually appear to mean little more than a tolerant, liberal society which respects different interests and accepts its cultural heterogeneity—as opposed, presumably, to a culturally homogeneous society which can be regarded as pulling together in the same direction. In this usage no particular view is implied about the comparative status of the diverse components of this social plurality. Noel Annan puts the point well:

> Pluralism is a dingy word. Most people accept that there are many groups and interests in society and a good society arranges for them to tolerate each other's existence: indeed the most powerful of all institutions in society, the State, should make a special effort to give these minority interests as much scope as possible. Most people think pluralism is a pragmatic compromise. It does not compel us to abandon our belief in socialism, or in the beneficence of the inequality produced by the market economy, or our belief that there is a rule, could we but act upon it, that should govern all our lives. (1990, 375)

In the tougher sense in which it is used today by moral philosophers—largely, perhaps, as a result of the work of Isaiah Berlin, who has done more than anyone to bring the notion into the limelight, to enrich it, and thus enable others to enrich it further—'pluralism' means the 'more disturbing' view, as Annan calls it (ibid.), that ultimate human values are irreducibly many; that they cannot be translated into a single super-value; and that they are sometimes (or often) incommensurable, that is, cannot be measured against one another in such a way that rationally compelling preferences between them can always be arrived at. Liberty and equality, for instance, or truth and mercy, or knowledge and happiness, or efficiency and spontaneity, are all distinct values whose requirements sometimes conflict; and when they do conflict, there is no superior criterion to which reference can be made in order to discover a resolution that ought to be accepted by every reasonable person. Sometimes a decision must be made, for life must go on;

and there can be reasons for such a decision, but it must not be represented as a uniquely rational solution of the problem when it is not. A different decision might have been no less rational.

If values are plural in this way, so are the more complex structures in which they are constituents: conceptions of life, cultures, ethical traditions, moral codes. Indeed, the plurality of the systems of values exhibited by these structures is one of the most striking ways in which the plurality of individual values is displayed. Both pluralities are made possible by the hospitable flexibility of human nature, which not only allows us to pursue a multiplicity of goals, but also enables us to order our lives in terms of a multiplicity of traditions. If by nature men had as comparatively invariant a way of life as non-human animals, then anthropological plurality, at any rate on the scale on which it has actually existed, could not have developed. As things are, though, both anthropological variety, and thus the role it plays in displaying ethical pluralism, reflect a central fact about human beings: that although there is a shared core of common humanity across people and times and places (and it is this which provides the common ground that enables us to avoid complete social and moral anarchy), nevertheless human nature is also essentially flexible and self-transforming, and can accommodate a large variety of substantively distinct approaches to life without suffering violation. Indeed, it is a central characteristic of human nature, on this view, that it is open-ended, able to develop in unpredictable directions, and not confinable, without arbitrarily restricting its essential indeterminacy, within any single detailed specification of how life is to be lived.

It is because of this indeterminacy, then, that there exist, through time and across the world of today, a large variety of markedly different cultural traditions. These differ not merely in matters of convention, or custom, or 'lifestyle' (in the usual modern sense, in which this is principally a matter of externals); these matters, it may be thought, being to some degree arbitrary and superficial, do not touch the question of the variability of human nature at the level of life-forming values. Cultures also differ, more importantly, in their deeper conceptions of how life should be lived, what human goals should be, what is worth pursuing, how different values should be ranked, how society should be structured, what an individual's rights and responsibilities are, and so forth. The values of the world of Odysseus are not those of the Victorian age; coming of age in Samoa is not a differently costumed version of Tom Brown's schooldays. The contrast with the case of non-human animals is obvious.

If values could be arranged in a fixed hierarchy, so that no two reasonable people ever disagreed about how to reconcile the inconsistent requirements of two values, the scope for variation in human life would be far more restricted than it actually is. It would not be eliminated, because there are many other dimensions of cultural variation besides the ethical; but that part of human variation that stems from the plurality of values, and the pluralism of their relations to one another, is central.

To recapitulate: if ultimate values are incomparably distinct and incommensurable, then it follows—not only in the case of divergences between cultures, but also in disagreements between members of a shared culture, as well as when values clash for an individual—that no unique resolution of conflicts of values, no single preference as between different traditions, can necessarily be arrived at and justified at the expense of all alternatives. Pluralism is the untidy view that there may be more than one 'correct' decision, more than one way forward, more than one way of living life, and that to view this as a matter of regret or as a reflection of human infirmity or ignorance is mistaken. We should not misrepresent our predicament in spuriously simple terms. As J. L. Austin once wrote: 'Why, if there are nineteen of anything, is it not philosophy?' (1950, xi/48).

It is worth stressing at this point that we may be unhesitatingly devoted to our own cultural tradition, prepared to defend it perhaps to the death, and yet recognise that it is not mandatory for all members of the human race—not necessarily even the best option, in any useful sense. It is sometimes thought that unless a way of life is sanctioned by some supernatural authority, or underpinned by some invariant and immutable aspect of reality, so that it is enjoined on everyone, it cannot be pursued with conviction. But this, although it satisfies an understandable and deep-seated wish for security, is not the only route to a firmly grounded sense of direction. This point has been memorably expressed in these words, used for a somewhat different purpose by Joseph Schumpeter: 'To realise the relative validity of one's convictions and yet stand for them unflinchingly is what distinguishes a civilised man from a barbarian.'[11]

---

11. Schumpeter 1943, 243. His remark was given currency by Isaiah Berlin, who quotes it at L 217. This sentence is the last in a section in which Schumpeter makes the point that support for democracy is context-dependent: one cannot simply give democracy one's universal support in all circumstances; it is the best system only when the conditions are right. It is worth being aware of this setting, since if the remark is taken out of context the reference to 'relative validity' might be taken to connote a relativistic conception of values, whereby values are arbitrary, subjective, impenetrable to those who adopt different ones—a view quite at odds with pluralism. Clearly, though, this thought was not in Schumpeter's mind. When read in isolation, but not understood in this relativist way, the sentence works well as a pluralist slogan. The point is now rather that the convictions in question are not compulsory for all men. They are not subjective, as relativism perhaps implies, but their objectivity is not such as to make them universal. Nevertheless the civilised person will find no difficulty in standing by them. Taken in isolation, Schumpeter's remark also contains an ambiguity which it is worth making explicit. It can be taken as a general denial of the need for any form of a priori validation of moral principles that

If individuals and groups, cultures and peoples, while all drawing on a basic common humanity, are seen as properly manifesting a wide range of more fully developed notions of what they are, or ought to be, or would wish to be, then the question arises, naturally, of how people or groups with differing visions of life should relate to each other. This is not the problem of balancing the claims of different interest-groups (though this is a not unrelated issue)—of classes, generations, or competitors for any kind of limited resource. It is the deeper problem of multiculturalism, both inter- and intra-national (the latter being sometimes posed with special force when immigration has occurred): that is, the problem of the proper attitude towards those from whom we differ—even within our own culture and age-group—in our overall approach to the living of life.

At a practical level this can be an extremely difficult problem, requiring complex accommodations that may be hard to negotiate and implement.[12] But at a theoretical level the natural basis for its solution is, prima facie, entirely straightforward. It is simply this: differences in conduct that do not flout the basic general ground-rules of interpersonal human behaviour should not be suppressed or discriminated against, and should as far as possible be treated equitably. Let a hundred flowers bloom. This is why pluralism is often taken to provide support for liberalism. Though it would be possible, instead, to advocate a fight for supremacy between competing outlooks, this does not seem a sensible option. Who would prefer strife, followed by a dominance based on strength, to peaceable coexistence, where this is possible? Nevertheless, perhaps it cannot be claimed that pluralism strictly entails a liberal attitude to rival outlooks. (What extra ingredient would be required to yield that conclusion?)

Two qualifications should immediately be entered. First, it is certainly a very difficult matter to establish exactly what the basic rules I refer to are, at any rate at the edges. No final agreement on this can reasonably be expected. But we can still make use of the notion that there are such rules, without being able to draw up a complete, definitive list; just as we use the notions of night and day without being able to specify non-arbitrarily exactly when one succeeds the other.

The second qualification is that it is not sensible, despite the stipulations of political correctness, to regard all bona fide cultures (whatever the qualifications may be for membership of that class) as automatically of equal merit, simply in

---

are held to be binding on all men (an important denial in other contexts); or, as here, it can be seen as a defence of commitment to 'particularist' values, as they are sometimes called—values acknowledged to be specific to the outlook of an individual or group, and yet defended with complete firmness.

12. A stark recent [in 1995] example is provided by the case of a child of a Christian mother and a Muslim father. The mother organised a baptism, and the father was granted an injunction to prevent it.

virtue of their status as cultures. One can dispense equitable treatment without implying that there can be no respects in which one culture is preferable to another, however unrealistic it may be to hope to secure agreement to any such inter-cultural preferences, let alone to expect many changes to occur as a consequence. (An analogous point might be made about the equitable treatment of individuals.) This is an important qualification, because it is sometimes maintained that different cultures, like ultimate values, are inevitably and in all respects incommensurable. In many of their manifestations they may well be,[13] but not perhaps in all.

However this may be, there is one kind of candidate for equitable treatment under this rubric which differs from all the others: the kind which believes in its own unique claim to truth.

'A TERRIBLE AND DANGEROUS ARROGANCE'

It often seems to be assumed that there can, or should, be an unqualified welcome in a mature, civilised world order for monistic, universalistic ideologies: for creeds, whether or not they are explicitly religious, part of whose essence is that they are held by their adherents to be uniquely true, for all men, everywhere; whereas all rival creeds, at least to the extent that they conflict with the favoured one, are held to be false. The clash between such creeds has of course been loud and bloody through history. Wars have been fought over differing conceptions of the truth about man's relation to a (supposed) deity, and more recently over rival views of the best political order for mankind. Remarkably, though, despite this historical background, and despite the obvious potential for intolerance[14] in such creeds, there seems to exist an unspoken consensus that conflict of this kind need not be reproduced in the future, or can at least be expected gradually to diminish,

---

13. A *reductio ad absurdum* of the thesis that all ways of life are necessarily of equal value would be that there is nothing to choose between the culture of a caveman and the culture of a modern European (even leaving aside advances in science and technology—especially medicine). To take a less extreme example, is it plausible to say that traditional African tribal music is incommensurable with the music of Mozart? There is room for both, certainly, but is there not a clear sense in which the latter is genuinely richer than the former?

14. The tolerance exhibited by monists is quite different from that required of pluralists towards other pluralists. A monist tolerates, patronisingly, views he regards as mistaken, hoping that one day they will be discarded in favour of the truth. A pluralist tolerates, open-endedly, the pursuit of values whose claims he recognises, at least in some cases, to be no less strong than those of his own values. If one wanted a label, one might call the latter variety of tolerance 'radical tolerance', to mark the fact that it calls on deeper reserves of flexibility, and does not see itself as ideally temporary.

presumably because the different ideologies in question, while retaining their central characteristics, can learn to live together peaceably, and not to waste their energies in futile combat.

This, though, is surely an unrealistic expectation, which places the blame in the wrong place—not on the beliefs which are of their nature mutually antagonistic, but on the way in which their adherents manage this antagonism. Members of different traditions should agree to differ, it may be urged; they should learn tolerance; they should respect the convictions of others, just as they expect others to respect their own. They should accept the principle of self-determination, and not seek to impose their own beliefs, however deeply held, where they are not welcome.

I do not wish to be misunderstood: injunctions of this kind are of course not necessarily pointless or ineffectual. But if they are thought to be the only proper response to problems caused by conflicting ideologies, this shows that the deeper cause of such problems has not been identified. What I want to suggest is that the whole convention of being acquiescent in the face of excessive claims to exclusive certainty, of any kind, needs to be challenged. This does not, I hasten to add, amount to a plea for intolerance of those who wish to make such claims. I fully accept the principle that tolerance[15] should be extended towards all those who hold views different from one's own, subject to the usual proviso that such tolerance should be withheld from intolerance or the forcible imposition of one's views on others. (The boundaries of this last category, incidentally, are very difficult to define: how, for example, does one distinguish indoctrination from education in the upbringing of children?) My point is rather that it is not consistent for a pluralist to regard as straightforward contributions to the diversity of human value-systems that he acknowledges—and perhaps welcomes—approaches to life which are ineradicably non-pluralist in their central thrust. Monisms, in a word, are not suitable long-term components of a plurality,[16] and while we must not suppress them, it is right for pluralists to hope that they will wither away.

---

15. The tolerance extended by the pluralist to the monist is not 'radical' in the sense defined in the previous note. Just as the monist hopes that the pluralist will see the light and embrace the unique truth, the pluralist looks for the abandonment by the monist of his overweening and exclusive certainty. There is this much truth—and no more—in the gibe that pluralism is just another form of monist intolerance: as a second-order, meta-ethical view pluralism does not exemplify the same restrictiveness as a monism claiming that all men should subscribe to a particular, definite morality. Indeed it is only if some form of pluralism is true that monisms are bound to be unduly restrictive as such.

16. Because the rejection of variety is not a way of contributing to it. Karl Popper might have called this 'the paradox of pluralism', by analogy with the other paradoxes—for example, of democracy, freedom, tolerance and sovereignty—to which he draws attention in *The Open Society and Its Enemies* (1945).

MONISM AND MULTICULTURALISM

The idea of the peaceful co-existence of different approaches to life is in one way, by now, commonplace. 'It takes all sorts to make a world' could be said of cultures as well as of individuals, without attracting much disagreement. The history of ideas may show that this acceptance of cultural heterogeneity is comparatively recent: contrast the attitudes that produced the Crusades, or paternalist imperial expansion, or nineteenth-century missionary activity (which all have their modern descendants). Nevertheless, at any rate in the West, the notion that no one culture has automatic pride of place is no longer startling. But there is a corollary of this new broadmindedness that remains to be absorbed: namely, that if the world is to be hospitable to a range of cultural forms, any candidates for such hospitality that do not reciprocate this attitude cannot be regarded as on all fours with candidates that do.

Once again, this is not a plea for selective intolerance. Freedom of belief remains a vital, unrestricted human right, for reasons that are well understood in the liberal tradition. Rather it is to insist that, if part of the basis of a moral and political order is to be the pluralist conception that claims to uniquely valid, privileged access to fully fledged, organised systems of moral, religious or political truth not only go beyond the information available to us, but are inconsistent with an understanding of the open-endedness of human nature, then we cannot look on those who sponsor such closed systems with the same impartial eyes as we look on those who, however different the culture they inhabit, share our own pluralist meta-ethical view.

Here a crude analogy is provided by the nursery rhyme 'Tinker, tailor, soldier, sailor, rich man, poor man, beggar man, thief': the last one in the list, the thief, is the odd one out, because he is the only one who necessarily trespasses on the private territory of the others. Just as robbery is not regarded as a profession on a par with those that begin the rhyme, so adherents of a monist creed are not on a par with other participants in a multicultural order.

I come to my central contention. However tolerant we may decide to be in social and political terms, no intellectual quarter should be given by pluralists to adherents of monist creeds, especially those who maintain that their view can co-exist, without tension, either with the views of pluralists or, even more absurdly, with the incompatible views of other monists. If pluralism is true, all monisms are false, and it is not honest to pretend otherwise. To be consistent, the pluralist must look forward to the time—even though it may very well never come—when the holding of monist beliefs is regarded as just as strange as the belief in the propriety of slavery, or in the divine right of kings.

Why is this an issue of any importance? It is because the potential perniciousness of those who believe they have the only answer is needlessly encouraged by the pretence that they need pose no threat, or by the failure to acknowledge the damage they already do or may do in the future. For example, religious monism has played a role (along with other factors, certainly, especially nationalism) in a number of contemporary political conflicts—in Northern Ireland and Bosnia, to name only two of the most obvious examples. And yet in all the miles and hours of media coverage of such conflicts, it is rarely if ever roundly declared that any blame attaches to the notion that a particular religious tradition can acceptably claim a privileged access to transcendent truth: almost any other factor is blamed sooner than this one. One natural conclusion to draw from this is that politicians and journalists, astonishingly, do not believe that there is anything intrinsically antagonistic or destabilising in belief-systems of this kind. (It may be, rather, that they inwardly know that this problem exists, but are debarred from expressing it for reasons of political correctness: if so, here is another powerful reason for eschewing the malign influence of this modern intellectual disease, which prefers a spurious equitableness to plain speaking.)

Whether we are concerned with Christianity or Islam, Judaism or any other religion or pseudo-religion which takes monist or fundamentalist forms, anyone convinced of the truth of pluralism must in consistency hold that, unless such creeds can accommodate themselves to pluralism without a denial of their essential natures, they cannot be regarded as full participants in the pluralist enterprise of tolerant co-existence between differing cultural traditions.[17] To my mind such an accommodation is indeed impossible, since it is such a deeply ingrained assumption of the world religions that they offer a definitive answer, a uniquely true vision of God and man's proper relationship to him: indeed, this is a central purpose of the whole exercise. In this context the increasingly frequent attempts by members of these faiths to portray themselves and their rivals as somehow jointly embarked on the same venture can seem somewhat ludicrous. Of course, the claims of one faith can be watered down to the point at which they do become compatible with the similarly watered-down claims of another, but a few minutes spent reading the Bible or the Koran, for example, makes clear that a reconcilia-

---

17. The addition of 'tolerant' is significant. Co-existence between cultures which are not aware of one another—or, if aware, not in a position to come into conflict—is hardly pluralist in character, except in the descriptive sense that might be adopted by the observing social anthropologist: if he describes 'primitive' or 'pre-contact' cultures in a spirit that approves their variousness he might be described as having a pluralist attitude to these cultures; but the pluralism is in him, not in the cultures, at any rate as far as their own view of themselves is concerned. A self-consciously pluralistic attitude to one's own cultural imperatives is a late flower of civilisation (some would regard it, wrongly in my view, as the first intimation of decadence); and since it cannot be entertained by a monist, it is not neutral with regard to the cultures that actually exist today.

tion of this kind can only be achieved by effectively abandoning the central tenets of both faiths.[18]

It is not only religions that fail the pluralist test. Authoritarian political systems such as Communism and Fascism are equally culpable. Even democratic systems are not innocent. The way in which rival political parties conduct themselves, at any rate in Britain, has many of the hallmarks of monist narrow-mindedness. The wearisome convention that a political party must always present itself as right on every issue, and its opponents as always wrong, may be explained as a necessary piece of play-acting in an adversarial parliamentary democracy; but it is a small step to taking the play seriously, and even if the consciousness that it is a play remains, this is a mode of political life which militates against the pooling of good ideas, against a co-operative approach to the serious and difficult problems of government. (The same might be said about the relationship between an adversarial system of justice and the search for the truth; and about those individuals, known to all of us, who have a constitutional reluctance ever to admit error or uncertainty, or to seek compromise or consensus, least of all in connection with fundamental moral issues, especially when they themselves are directly implicated.)

In all these cases, and in many others, the same duty falls upon the pluralist who wishes to face up to the consequences of what he believes to be true: the duty to reject, intellectually, any monist philosophy or creed as an acceptable option in the search for an honest understanding of man and his place in the world. This is not to say that he is entitled to pour scorn on such philosophies; nor should he deny that they bring comfort, or make possible great human achievements which may not be accessible by another route, or incorporate profound insights into human nature. He cannot even, perhaps, assert categorically that he knows for certain that they are false, however deep he feels their implausibility to be. But he must not pretend that, in the garden of many flowers, the invasive weeds are to be treated as equal partners in the display.

One small example may illustrate the change of attitude that results from acceptance of the thesis I have urged. Consider the visible badges, of membership or office, that are often adopted by monists: dog-collars, crucifixes, yarmulkes, Muslim scarves, monastic habits and hairstyles, uniforms priestly and political. The list could be extended, and individual items on it could be the subject of dispute. Some of the badges emphasise a role within a larger institution rather than stressing plain membership of it. Nevertheless, part of what many badges of this

---

18. Cf. Hardy 1993, where I go into this point a little more fully. (Of course, some of the claims made by religions are factual rather than ethical, and the problem of adjudicating between different factual claims is not the same as the problem of reconciling different moralities; nor, however, is it entirely different.)

kind convey, more or less vociferously, is not only 'I am different' or 'I am committed'—which are indeed important aspects of their message—but 'I know and accept the unique truth (and you do not).' In this respect they differ from a vast assemblage of other sources of outfitters' revenues: dinner jackets, school ties, policemen's helmets, naval uniforms, three-piece suits, *et hoc genus omne*. These may still mark difference and commitment, and the differences marked may in some cases be invidious and offensive—but not in the important way I have just specified in connection with the monist badges. A nurse's uniform does not enjoin others to become nurses, or reprove them for not doing so. Nursing is one of many options, and claims no special status. The same cannot be said, from the point of view of the faithful, for the affirmation of a monist creed.

This is where the change of attitude comes in. Conventionally the wearing of such badges is regarded by outsiders with indifference or indulgence—even with approval, because of the strength of the implied commitment. Commitment, like sincerity and integrity, is seen as good in itself, whatever its object. But if we recognise that these symbols are in part a way of rubbing in the existence and claims of belief-systems that are potentially if not actually inimical to a plural society, they take on a more sinister aspect. Why should we endorse the attitude of intellectual ostriches? I have found that, when I mention this viewpoint out of context, it is immediately derided as intolerant and narrow-minded. But I hope I have explained how it is possible to view it in a different light.

If it is true, as it is increasingly suggested, that fundamentalism is today one of the major threats to world stability, it is surely worth being on one's guard against the first signs of a condition that can develop in that direction. Religious monism is to fundamentalism as being HIV-positive is thought to be to AIDS: some do not succumb to the full-blown condition, but there is always the danger. Believing that your truth is the only truth can be the first step (especially if salvation is held to be dependent on its acceptance) on the path to believing that you must impose it on others, by means however barbarous, because nothing can be more important than spreading the truth. No one supposes that benign English country vicars are going to become fire-breathing terrorists enforcing world Christianity, but they are the more acceptable face of an enterprise which in other contexts abets political violence and hatred. Islamic fundamentalism may show as much about the state of the societies in which it flourishes as it does about the intrinsic properties of Islam, but again the religious contribution is real and to be regretted. One cannot pick and choose: benign or otherwise, monism is the enemy of pluralism; which is to say, if pluralism is true, the enemy of truth.

Appendix

BERLIN'S UNIVERSAL VALUES—CORE OR HORIZON?

GEORGE CROWDER AND HENRY HARDY

That which is really immutable in morality can be reduced to such generalities
that almost everything personal in them is lost.

Alexander Herzen (1855, 141)

In the last decade or so of Berlin's life Henry Hardy wrote and talked to him
from time to time in an attempt to clarify in his own mind Berlin's views on
various aspects of value pluralism. Berlin had not written a systematic account of
this topic, central though it was to his thought, and his scattered remarks were
tantalisingly incomplete and, at times, frustratingly unclear or even (it seemed)
contradictory. At one point Hardy showed Berlin the Euler diagram on 294, and
asked him whether it fairly represented his views on the topics it attempted to
illustrate. Berlin agreed that it did.

A little explanation may help to make sense of the diagram. 'Moral core' is
Hardy's term for the minimum requirements common to the vast majority of
moralities. (What the members, if any, of this class are, and whether they are the
right basic moral requirements, are different questions, not raised in this context.)
In this connection Berlin standardly used the formulation due to St Vincent of
Lérins, 'What is believed everywhere, always, by everyone.'[1]

---

1. 'Quod ubique, quod semper, quod ab omnibus creditum est.' Vincent 434, 2. 3.

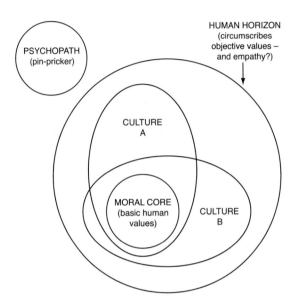

The psychopath or 'pin-pricker' is the figure Berlin often used to illustrate what he meant by attitudes and/or behaviour that would fall outside the 'human horizon'. Here is one version of this recurrent example:

Supposing a man comes along and he pushes pins into people, and I say to him: 'Why do you do this?' The man says: 'Because I enjoy it.' I say: 'Are you enjoying giving pain to people?' 'No, not particularly.' That would be an intelligible aim. Sadism I understand. Then I ask him: 'But why do you do it?' And he says: 'Because I rather like it.' 'But you realise that it causes them great pain?'; and he says: 'Yes, I do.' 'But then, they might do it to you.' 'No they wouldn't, because I am stronger than they are, and I would stop them.' So far so good. But then I say: 'But why do you do it?' And he answers: 'But I like doing it. I like pushing pins into resilient surfaces.' 'If I give you a tennis ball, would that be just as good?' 'Of course, just as good', he replies, 'as human skin.' At this point I stop understanding him. To talk to a man for whom inflicting pain is something of no importance, doesn't make any difference, is totally puzzling. I repeat: 'You are inflicting pain'; and he says: 'So what? Why do you mention it?' This 'So what?' means that we do not live in the same world. I call him mad. People in his kind of mental condition are locked up in asylums, not prisons. (1992, 104–5)

The human horizon, then, is the outer limit of what counts as human or sane, the limit beyond which empathy cannot penetrate. The values that fall within it are called 'objective' by Berlin because they are not merely subjective, arbitrary, varying from person to person (as some relativists hold), but stable features of the world based in human nature, open to empirical view like the world's other contents. Because we are human, we can understand what other humans are up to even if they are pursuing values different from our own: we can imagine ourselves in their shoes, and see the world from where they are standing. Berlin also regards these values as 'ultimate', non-instrumental: 'There is a world of objective values. By this I mean those ends that men pursue for their own sakes, to which other things are means' (CTH 11).

To this explanation of the terminology used in the diagram it may be helpful to add excerpts from the exchange between Hardy and Berlin about what the diagram attempts to depict. On Friday 13 March 1992 Hardy wrote to Berlin:

[W]hat is it, for you, that plays the principal (exclusive?) role in rebutting relativism? Is it the 'moral core', the fact that all known value-systems share a minimal conception of the demands of common humanity? Or is it the capacity for empathy with values we don't share? Is it perhaps sometimes one, sometimes the other, depending on which values are claimed to be relative? I could expand the question, but won't at this stage, in case your answer takes the wind out of my sails.

You may say that my two candidates are different aspects of the same phenomenon, so that it is artificial to prise them apart. Perhaps you believe that our common humanity *both* gives rise to a shared core of basic values, *and* enables us to empathise with the unshared values at the periphery of this core. Relativism, then, is false as it is ordinarily understood because it is true in a wider sense— i.e. because our values are relative to our humanity—rather than because our values are prescribed by some supra-human edict.

I attach a diagrammatic representation of your view, drawn up in an attempt to clarify my own thoughts, and I should be interested to know how wide of the mark this is.

Berlin replied on 13 April:

The basic reason for rejecting relativism is the 'moral core', but the reason for pluralism, which is also incompatible with relativism but a separate doctrine, is, as you say, empathy with values which we may or may not share but which belong to other cultures. I do not see why this answer takes any wind out of any of your sails. You are right to say that I believe relativism to be false on both grounds; on the other hand, it is also true that without the first ground—i.e. the common ground between the vast majority of systems of values in different cultures or among different persons—the second ground would not work. Is this confused? I do hope not.

Your diagram is excellent, and I think does represent my views.

The relationship of the diagram to this exchange should now be clear.

Although the diagram seemed to Hardy at the time to capture what Berlin was saying, and although Berlin endorsed it, it is possible to doubt whether it represents either Berlin's view, or the true state of affairs, as perspicuously as it might. George Crowder suggests that it does not fit a plausible alternative understanding of moral universals, according to which what really differentiates one culture from another is not that it endorses a different subset of human values, but that it interprets the same, universal, 'thin' values in different 'thick' ways.[2] On this understanding, the 'moral core' in the diagram would be much wider, perhaps coextensive with the human horizon, but at any rate containing, rather than contained by, the different cultures. Such a view takes Martha Nussbaum's theory of human capabilities as its model. It has the general advantage of emphasising, as the diagram does not, that the shared values of the 'moral core' must be very thin, or highly generic, compared with the thicker, more specific, values of particular cultures. Nussbaum's view also makes a connection between thin and thick values, the latter being interpretations of the former, thus providing the framework for a unified explanation of both universality and particularity in ethics.

The alternative view also has advantages for interpreting Berlin's position. In particular, it helps to answer two questions. First, how can we empathise with the values of other cultures without sharing those values? Berlin's answer is the human horizon. But what this means (for Crowder) is that we are identified as human by the fact that there are certain generic ends that are pursued by all human beings. It is because we have 'values in common with these distant figures' that we can understand them (CTH 11).[3] This is essentially the same idea as

---

2. Hardy wonders whether these two accounts may not be topologically equivalent, as it were, if we regard the individuation of values as to some degree a matter of convention: whether we say that culture A pursues value X and culture B value Y, or that cultures A and B both pursue value P, though in the different forms Pa and Pb, may boil down to the same. Even if this is right, one account may fit the facts more snugly than the other.

3. Hardy disagrees with this characterisation of Berlin's 'human horizon', which (in Berlin's usage) circumscribes not the values we all pursue, but the values that make sense to us all. As Berlin says, we don't all actually pursue all the values that are comprehensible to us: 'There is a finite variety of values and attitudes, some of which one society, some another, have made their own' (CTH 79); 'all human beings must have some common values or they cease to be human, and also some different values else they cease to differ, as in fact they do' (POI 12). If this is right, the proposed near-equivalence between core and horizon fails. Crowder's response is that values we understand but don't pursue are in fact just different thick versions of thin values we pursue in other forms: which returns us to the question, broached in the previous note, of whether there is in fact a substantive difference between our two views. For a useful discussion that favours Crowder's interpretation, see Shweder 2003, 39–43.

Nussbaum's thin universals. On this reading, the shared 'moral core' is approximately coextensive with the human horizon; if the overlap were complete, indeed, one or other metaphor might simply be dropped.

A second question, conversely, is this: How is our capacity to empathise with other cultures whose particular values we do not share evidence (as Berlin thinks it is) of universal values that we share or ought to share?[4] Crowder's answer is that we are able to empathise with the values of other cultures because they are specific interpretations of more generic values that we do share—that is, even in the most alien practices we can recognise, if only dimly, our own most fundamental purposes. For example, the Aztec practice of human sacrifice can be understood as a particular expression, however wrongheaded, of a universal concern with fertility and regeneration.[5] Again, this interpretation of Berlin's position aligns the shared moral core with a broad set of generic goods linked closely to the human horizon.

It may be that not all values can be accounted for in this way—as either thin human values or particular expressions of these—but this is at any rate a possible hypothesis for future investigation. Crowder believes that Berlin might have been attracted to it, despite his approval of Hardy's diagram. Such thoughts remain speculative because Berlin's actual comments in this area are so scattered, unsystematic and lacking in examples. Here as elsewhere, however, he has left us with clues that are well worth following up.

---

4. This seems to Crowder to be the general thrust of Berlin's 'Alleged Relativism in Eighteenth-Century European Thought' (in CTH). There he argues that pluralists, such as Vico and Herder, should be distinguished from relativists. While relativists are confined within the 'windowless boxes' of particular perspectives, we pluralists 'insist on our need and ability to transcend the values of our own culture or nation or class' (CTH 85), and to evaluate other cultures—presumably by reference to non-relative, i.e. universal, values. What makes this possible is the ability to ' "feel oneself into" the mentality of remote societies' (CTH 82). The capacity for cross-cultural empathy is thus evidence of the universality of value that underwrites that capacity and points to the truth of pluralism rather than relativism.

5. See Edward Westermarck's description of human sacrifice: 'it is as a rule a method of life-insurance—absurd, no doubt, according to our ideas, but not an act of wanton cruelty' (Westermarck 1932, 188–9).

Bibliography

Henry Hardy

T his bibliography serves two purposes. The first of these is to provide a brief overview of Berlin's own writing, and of the principal studies of it that have appeared in English in volume form. The second is to list the publications referred to by the contributors to this volume.

BERLIN'S WORK

Much of Isaiah Berlin's published work takes the form of essays, which often originated in lectures, and often appeared in somewhat inaccessible places in the first instance. Over the last thirty years I have brought most of these essays together in a series of thematic volumes,[1] and have also edited a number of volumes of material that had not previously been published in any form. In the following lists of Berlin's books (which appear in the chronological order of their first publication), the titles of separate essays appear under the titles of the collections that they comprise.

Readers who wish to explore the many pieces not collected in volume form should consult my complete bibliography of Berlin's writings. This appears in its

---

1. Jointly edited, in the case of *Russian Thinkers*, with Aileen Kelly; in the case of the *Proper Study of Mankind*, with Roger Hausheer.

currently most up-to-date printed form in the Princeton University Press edition (2001) of *Against the Current*, and a continuously updated version is available as part of *The Isaiah Berlin Virtual Library* (IBVL), the official website of the Isaiah Berlin Literary Trust, whose URL is <http://berlin.wolf.ox.ac.uk/>. This site also contains full lists of interviews with and writing about Berlin, in all languages.

There are in addition several recordings of Berlin's lectures and broadcasts, including his 1965 A. W. Mellon Lectures on romanticism,[2] in the British Library Sound Archive in London: the experience of listening to him speaking is highly recommended. In cases where these items are unpublished, transcripts are available in the IBVL.

Books published by Berlin in his lifetime

The books listed in this section and the next are referred to in this volume by the abbreviations listed at 15–16 above. Most of these books have been published by more than one publisher, typically being reissued in paperback under a different imprint; the publishers specified below are those of the editions that are in print at the time of writing (June 2006).

The following list does not include independent entries for individual essays or lectures initially published separately in volume form. One such essay, *The Hedgehog and the Fox* (1951–3) is still in print in such a format (Phoenix/Ivan R. Dee). Asterisked essays are included in *The Proper Study of Mankind*, an anthology of essays drawn from the other collections; this appeared in early 1997, the year of Berlin's death (on 5 November).

Karl Marx: His Life and Environment first appeared in 1939 in Thornton Butterworth's Home University Library series; further editions were published by Oxford University Press (who took over the series) in 1948,[3] 1963 and 1978, and the latest, fourth, edition was reissued, with a new introduction by Alan Ryan and a revised guide to further reading by Terrell Carver, by Fontana in London in 1995, and by Oxford University Press in New York in 1996. After the Fontana edition went out of print, the OUP edition was made available worldwide.

The Age of Enlightenment: The Eighteenth-Century Philosophers, 1956 (out of print), is a selection, with commentary, from these philosophers' works. The introduction appears in POI as 'The Philosophers of the Enlightenment'.

---

2. These lectures can also be heard at the National Gallery of Art in Washington, DC, where they were delivered.

3. Substantial additions were also made to the fourth impression (1960) of the second edition. See <http://berlin.wolf.ox.ac.uk/published_works/km/marxconcordance.html>.

Four Essays on Liberty, 1969: incorporated in *Liberty* (see 305 below)

Vico and Herder: Two Studies in the History of Ideas, 1976: incorporated in *Three Critics of the Enlightenment* (see 304 below)

Russian Thinkers, 1978 (Penguin):
    Introduction by Aileen Kelly
    Russia and 1848
   * The Hedgehog and the Fox
    Herzen and Bakunin on Individual Liberty
    A Remarkable Decade [1838–48]
        I   The Birth of the Russian Intelligentsia
        II   German Romanticism in Petersburg and Moscow
        III   Vissarion Belinsky
        IV   Alexander Herzen
    Russian Populism
    Tolstoy and Enlightenment
    Fathers and Children: Turgenev and the Liberal Predicament

Concepts and Categories: Philosophical Essays, 1978 (Pimlico/Princeton University Press):
    Introduction by Bernard Williams
    The Purpose of Philosophy
    Verification
    Empirical Propositions and Hypothetical Statements
    Logical Translation
    Equality
   * The Concept of Scientific History
   * Does Political Theory Still Exist?
   * From Hope and Fear Set Free

Against the Current: Essays in the History of Ideas, 1979 (Pimlico/Princeton University Press):
    Introduction by Roger Hausheer
   * The Counter-Enlightenment
   * The Originality of Machiavelli
   * The Divorce between the Sciences and the Humanities
    Vico's Concept of Knowledge
    Vico and the Ideal of the Enlightenment
    Montesquieu
    Hume and the Sources of German Anti-Rationalism [Hume and Hamann]
   * Herzen and His Memoirs
    The Life and Opinions of Moses Hess
    Benjamin Disraeli, Karl Marx and the Search for Identity
    The '*Naïveté*' of Verdi

Georges Sorel
* Nationalism: Past Neglect and Present Power

Personal Impressions, 1980; 2nd ed. 1998 (Pimlico/Princeton University Press; † = added in 2nd ed.):
Introduction by Noel Annan
* Winston Churchill in 1940
* President Franklin Delano Roosevelt
Chaim Weizmann
Einstein and Israel
† Yitzhak Sadeh
L. B. Namier
Felix Frankfurter at Oxford
Richard Pares
Hubert Henderson at All Souls
J. L. Austin and the Early Beginnings of Oxford Philosophy
John Petrov Plamenatz
Maurice Bowra
† David Cecil
† Memories of Virginia Woolf
† Edmund Wilson at Oxford
Auberon Herbert
Aldous Huxley
Meetings with Russian Writers in 1945 and 1956
† Epilogue: The Three Strands in My Life

The Crooked Timber of Humanity: Chapters in the History of Ideas, 1990 (Pimlico/Princeton University Press):
* The Pursuit of the Ideal
The Decline of Utopian Ideas in the West
Giambattista Vico and Cultural History
Alleged Relativism in Eighteenth-Century European Thought
Joseph de Maistre and the Origins of Fascism
European Unity and Its Vicissitudes
* The Apotheosis of the Romantic Will: The Revolt against the Myth of an Ideal World
The Bent Twig: On the Rise of Nationalism

The contents of the next two volumes were written during earlier decades, but (with one exception)[4] had not previously been published:

---

4. An earlier version of 'Socialism and Socialist Theories'.

The Magus of the North: J. G. Hamann and the Origins of Modern Irrationalism (1965), 1993: incorporated in *Three Critics of the Enlightenment* (see 305 below)

The Sense of Reality: Studies in Ideas and Their History, 1996 (Pimlico/Farrar, Straus and Giroux):
    Introduction by Patrick Gardiner
    The Sense of Reality
    Political Judgement
    Philosophy and Government Repression
    Socialism and Socialist Theories
    Marxism and the International in the Nineteenth Century
    The Romantic Revolution: A Crisis in the History of Modern Thought
    Artistic Commitment: A Russian Legacy
    Kant as an Unfamiliar Source of Nationalism
    Rabindranath Tagore and the Consciousness of Nationality

The Proper Study of Mankind: An Anthology of Essays, 1997 (Pimlico/Farrar, Straus and Giroux):
    Foreword by Noel Annan
    Introduction by Roger Hausheer
    The Pursuit of the Ideal
    The Concept of Scientific History
    Does Political Theory Still Exist?
    From Hope and Fear Set Free
    Historical Inevitability
    Two Concepts of Liberty
    The Counter-Enlightenment
    The Originality of Machiavelli
    The Divorce between the Sciences and the Humanities
    Herder and the Enlightenment
    The Hedgehog and the Fox
    Herzen and his Memoirs
    Conversations with Akhmatova and Pasternak
    The Apotheosis of the Romantic Will
    Nationalism: Past Neglect and Present Power
    Winston Churchill in 1940
    President Franklin Delano Roosevelt
    Concise Bibliography of Isaiah Berlin's Writings

Books published posthumously

The First and the Last (New York/London, 1999: New York Review of Books/Granta)
    The Purpose Justifies the Ways

My Intellectual Path
Tributes by Noel Annan, Stuart Hampshire, Avishai Margalit, Bernard Williams and Aileen Kelly

The Roots of Romanticism (the A. W. Mellon Lectures in the Fine Arts, 1965), 1999 (Pimlico/Princeton University Press), an edited transcript

The Power of Ideas, 2000 (Pimlico/Princeton University Press), a collection of shorter essays:
My Intellectual Path
The Purpose of Philosophy
The Philosophers of the Enlightenment
One of the Boldest Innovators in the History of Human Thought [Vico]
Russian Intellectual History
The Man Who Became a Myth [Belinsky]
A Revolutionary without Fanaticism [Herzen]
The Role of the Intelligentsia
Liberty
The Philosophy of Karl Marx
The Father of Russian Marxism [Plekhanov]
Realism in Politics
The Origins of Israel
Jewish Slavery and Emancipation
Chaim Weizmann's Leadership
The Search for Status
The Essence of European Romanticism
Meinecke and Historicism
General Education

Three Critics of the Enlightenment: Vico, Hamann, Herder, 2000 (Pimlico/Princeton University Press), incorporating *Vico and Herder* and *The Magus of the North*:
Vico and Herder
Introduction
The Philosophical Ideas of Giambattista Vico
Vico's Theory of Knowledge and Its Sources
* Herder and the Enlightenment
The Magus of the North

Freedom and Its Betrayal: Six Enemies of Human Liberty (1952), 2002 (Chatto and Windus/Princeton University Press) an edited transcript of lectures delivered on the Third Programme of the BBC

Liberty, 2002 (Oxford University Press), a revised and expanded edition of *Four Essays on Liberty*.

> The Editor's Tale *Henry Hardy*
> Five Essays on Liberty (second edition of *Four Essays on Liberty*)
>> Introduction
>> Political Ideas in the Twentieth Century
>> * Historical Inevitability
>> * Two Concepts of Liberty
>> John Stuart Mill and the Ends of Life
>> * From Hope and Fear Set Free
> Liberty
> The Birth of Greek Individualism
> Final Retrospect [excerpts from 'My Intellectual Path']
> The Purpose Justifies the Ways
> A Letter to George Kennan
> Notes on Prejudice
> Berlin and his Critics *Ian Harris*

The Soviet Mind: Russian Culture under Communism, 2004 (Brookings Institution Press)

> Foreword by Strobe Talbott
> The Arts in Russia under Stalin
> A Visit to Leningrad
> A Great Russian Writer [Mandel'shtam]
> Conversations with Akhmatova and Pasternak
> Boris Pasternak
> Why the Soviet Union Chooses to Insulate Itself
> The Artificial Dialectic: Generalissimo Stalin and the Art of Government
> Four Weeks in the Soviet Union
> Soviet Russian Culture
> The Survival of the Russian Intelligentsia
> Glossary of Names *Helen Rappaport*

Political Ideas in the Romantic Age: Their Rise and Influence on Modern Thought (early 1950s), 2006 (Chatto and Windus/Princeton University Press)

INTERVIEWS AND CORRESPONDENCE

The items in the remaining sections of the bibliography (listed where relevant in alphabetical order of author's surnames) are referred to by the name-date system (e.g. 'Berlin 1939'), except that some of the books in this section and the next, like Berlin's own books, are referred to so often that they too have been allocated abbreviations at 15–16 above.

Berlin, Isaiah (1964) (with A. J. Ayer and J. B. Priestley), 'Conversations for Tomorrow', BBC Television, 25 April, IBVL, <http://berlin.wolf.ox.ac.uk/lists/nachlass/conversa.pdf>

—— (1992), 'In Conversation with Steven Lukes' (first published in Italian in 1992), *Salmagundi* 120 (Fall 1998), 52–134

—— (1993), 'Fragebogen', *Frankfurter Allgemeine Magazin*, 22 January, 27

—— (2004), *Flourishing: Letters 1928–1946*, ed. Henry Hardy (London: Chatto and Windus; paperback, Pimlico, 2005), published in the USA by Cambridge University Press as *Letters 1928–1946*

—— (2005), letters to Andrzej Walicki in Andrzej Walicki (ed.), *Russia, Poland and Marxism: Isaiah Berlin to Andrzej Walicki 1962–1996* [*Dialogue and Universalism* 15: 9–10], 53–173

—— (2006) (with Beata Polanowska-Sygulska), *Unfinished Dialogue* (Amherst, NY: Prometheus Books)

—— and Stuart Hampshire (1972), 'I'm Going to Tamper with Your Beliefs a Little' (dialogue); film available online through the British Film and Video Council, at <http://www.emol.ac.uk/>; transcript in the IBVL, <http://berlin.wolf.ox.ac.uk/lists/nachlass/imgoing.pdf>

Gardels, Nathan (1991), 'Two Concepts of Nationalism: An Interview with Isaiah Berlin', *New York Review of Books*, 21 November, 19–23

Jahanbegloo, Ramin (1992), *Conversations with Isaiah Berlin* (London: Peter Halban)

Magee, Bryan (1972), 'The Problem of Nationalism', discussion with Isaiah Berlin and Stuart Hampshire broadcast on Thames Television, 30 November, IBVL, <http://berlin. wolf.ox.ac.uk/lists/nachlass/probnat.pdf>

—— (1978), 'An Introduction to Philosophy', interview with Isaiah Berlin in Bryan Magee, *Men of Ideas: Some Creators of Contemporary Philosophy* (London: British Broadcasting Corporation)

—— (1992), 'Nationalism: The Melting-Pot Myth', discussion with Isaiah Berlin broadcast on BBC Radio 3, 19 February, IBVL, <http://berlin.wolf.ox.ac.uk/lists/nachlass/bigidea. pdf>

Tamir-Rafaeli, Yael (1987), 'Israel Must Be a Liberal Democracy', interview with Isaiah Berlin, *Israeli Democracy*, February, 10–14

A full list of individual interviews is provided in the IBVL at <http://berlin.wolf.ox.ac.uk/lists/interviews/interviews.htm>.

BOOKS ON BERLIN

Aarsbergen-Ligtvoet, Connie (2006), *Isaiah Berlin: A Value Pluralist and Humanist View of Human Nature and the Meaning of Life* (Amsterdam/New York: Rodopi)

Burtonwood, Neil (2006), *Cultural Diversity, Liberal Pluralism, and Schools: Isaiah Berlin and Education* (London: Routledge)

Coles, Norman (2004), *Human Nature and Human Values: Interpreting Isaiah Berlin* (Bexhill on Sea: Egerton House)

Crowder, George (2004), *Isaiah Berlin: Liberty and Pluralism* (Cambridge: Polity)

Dalos, György (1998), *The Guest from the Future: Anna Akhmatova and Isaiah Berlin* (London: Murray; New York, 2000: Farrar, Straus and Giroux)

Galipeau, Claude J. (1994), *Isaiah Berlin's Liberalism* (Oxford: Clarendon Press)

Gray, John (1995), *Isaiah Berlin* (London: HarperCollins; New York, 1996: Princeton University Press; paperback, retitled *Berlin*, London, 1995: Fontana Modern Masters)

Ignatieff, Michael (1998), *Isaiah Berlin: A Life* (London: Chatto and Windus; New York: Metropolitan)

Jinkins, Michael (2004), *Christianity, Tolerance and Pluralism: A Theological Engagement with Isaiah Berlin's Social Theory* (London/New York: Routledge)

Kocis, Robert (1989), *A Critical Appraisal of Sir Isaiah Berlin's Political Philosophy* (Lewiston, NY, etc.: Edwin Mellen Press)

COLLECTIONS OF ESSAYS ON BERLIN

Crowder, George, and Henry Hardy (2007) (eds), *The One and the Many: Reading Isaiah Berlin* (Amherst, NY: Prometheus)

Lilla, Mark, Ronald Dworkin and Robert B. Silvers (2001) (eds), *The Legacy of Isaiah Berlin* (New York: New York Review of Books; London: Granta)

Mali, Joseph, and Robert Wokler (eds), *Isaiah Berlin's Counter-Enlightenment* [*Transactions of the American Philosophical Society* 93: 3] (Philadelphia: American Philosophical Society, 2003)

Margalit, Avishai, and others (1990), *On the Thought of Isaiah Berlin: Papers Presented in Honour of Professor Sir Isaiah Berlin on the Occasion of His Eightieth Birthday* (Jerusalem, 1990: Israel Academy of Sciences and Humanities)

Margalit, Edna, and Avishai Margalit (1991) (eds), *Isaiah Berlin: A Celebration* (London: Hogarth Press; Chicago: University of Chicago Press)

Ryan, Alan (1979) (ed.), *The Idea of Freedom: Essays in Honour of Isaiah Berlin* (Oxford and New York: Oxford University Press)

UNCOLLECTED WORK BY BERLIN CITED IN THIS VOLUME

Berlin, Isaiah (1930), 'Some Procrustations', *Oxford Outlook* 10, 491–502

—— (1935a), 'Literature and the Crisis'; published as 'A Sense of Impending Doom' in the *Times Literary Supplement*, 27 July 2001, 11–12

—— (1935b), Letter to Mendel Berlin, Autumn, MSB 292/121–2, IBVL, <http://berlin.wolf.ox.ac.uk/published_works/f/l1supp.pdf> (accessed 7 June 2006), 4

—— (1937), Review of Julius Weinberg, *An Examination of Logical Positivism*, *Criterion* 17, 174–82

—— (1949a), 'Democracy, Communism and the Individual', IBVL, <http://berlin.wolf
.ox.ac.uk/lists/nachlass/demcomind.pdf>

—— (1949b), Contribution to 'Notes on the Way', *Time and Tide* 30, 1133–4, 1157–8, 1187–8

—— (late 1940s), Untitled and undated talk, IBVL, <http://berlin.wolf.ox.ac.uk/lists/
nachlass/speech.pdf>

—— (1950a), 'The Trends of Culture', contribution to 'The Year 1949 in Historical Perspective', in *1950 Britannica Book of the Year* (Chicago etc.: Encyclopaedia Britannica)

—— (1950b), 'Soviet Beginnings', review of E. H. Carr, *A History of Soviet Russia*, vol. 1: *The
Bolshevik Revolution 1917–1923*, *Sunday Times*, 10 December 1950, 3

—— (1951), 'Nineteen Fifty: A Survey of Politico-Cultural Trends of the Year', in *1951
Britannica Book of the Year* (Chicago etc.: Encyclopaedia Britannica)

—— (1951b), Review of E. H. Carr, *Studies in Revolution*, *International Affairs* 27, 470–1

—— (1952), 'Nineteen Fifty-One: A Survey of Cultural Trends of the Year', in *Britannica
Book of the Year 1952* (Chicago etc.: Encyclopaedia Britannica)

—— (1954), *Historical Inevitability* (London: Oxford University Press)

—— (1962), 'Mr Carr's Big Battalions', review of E. H. Carr, *What is History?*, *New Statesman*
63 (January–June), 15–16

—— (1971), 'The Assault on the French Enlightenment, 1: Herder and Historical Criticism', IBVL, <http://berlin.wolf.ox.ac.uk/lists/nachlass/assault1.pdf>

—— (1973), 'The Origins of Cultural History', IBVL, <http://berlin.wolf.ox.ac.uk/
lists/nachlass/origins1.pdf> and the same URL with '2' and '3' in place of '1'

—— (1975), 'The Achievement of Zionism', lecture delivered as part of a symposium at
the Institute of Jewish Affairs in London on 1 June, IBVL, <http://berlin.wolf.ox
.ac.uk/lists/nachlass/achiezio.pdf>

—— (1980), 'A Tribute to my Friend' (on Jacob Talmon), *Forum* No 38 (Summer)

—— (1981a), 'Russian Thought and the Slavophile Controversy', review of Walicki 1980
and Andrzej Walicki, *The Slavophile Controversy*, *Slavonic and East European Review* 59: 4
(October), 572–86

—— (1981b), reply to Hans Aarsleff, 'Vico and Berlin', *London Review of Books*, 5–18
November, 7–8

—— (1992), 'Reply to Ronald H. McKinney, "Towards a Postmodern Ethics: Sir Isaiah
Berlin and John Caputo"', *Journal of Value Inquiry* 26, 557–60

—— (1993), 'A Reply to David West [West 1993]', *Political Studies* 41, 297–8

—— (1996) 'Berlin', in Thomas Mautner (ed.), *A Dictionary of Philosophy* (Oxford: Blackwell), reissued with revisions as *The Penguin Dictionary of Philosophy* (London etc.,
1997: Penguin), 51–2 (Penguin, 67–9)

—— and Bernard Williams (1994), 'Pluralism and Liberalism: A Reply' (to Crowder
1994), *Political Studies* 42, 306–9

OTHER PUBLICATIONS CITED IN THIS VOLUME

The number of publications on Berlin, or on topics treated by him, is now so large, and increasing at such a rate, that a complete list cannot be provided here, even if it could be compiled. See the IBVL, <http://berlin.wolf.ox.ac.uk/lists/onib/onib .htm>, for the fullest list currently known to the editors. The list that follows includes only those publications cited in this book; many of these discuss Berlin's ideas. (A number of the articles critical of 'Historical Inevitability' and 'Two Concepts of Liberty' are discussed in Berlin's introduction to 'Five Essays on Liberty', in *Liberty*, which also includes an invaluable survey by Ian Harris, 'Berlin and his Critics'.)

Note that, in order (*a*) to avoid anachronisms such as 'Aristotle 2006', and (*b*) to display the chronology of ideas more perspicuously, the date of original publication of older works is cited first (and used in references), followed by details of the modern edition to which page references are given. For example, a page reference to 'Constant 1815' is to the 1997 Gallimard edition of *Principes de politique*, first published in 1815, listed thus:

> Constant, Benjamin (1815), *Principes de politique*, in *Écrits politiques*, ed. Marcel Gauchet (Paris, 1997: Gallimard)

Allen, Jonathan (1998), review of SR, *South African Journal of Philosophy* 17, 173–7
—— (1999), 'Balancing Justice and Social Unity: Political Theory and the Idea of a Truth and Reconciliation Commission', *University of Toronto Law Journal* 49, 315–53
—— (2001), 'Between Retribution and Restoration: Justice and the TRC', *South African Journal of Philosophy* 20, 22–41
—— (2003), 'Anti-Procrustean Liberalism: Isaiah Berlin on Political Judgement and the Protean Individual', prepared for presentation at the annual meeting of the American Political Science Association (28–31 August 2003, Philadelphia, Pennsylvania), IBVL, <http://berlin.wolf.ox.ac.uk/lists/onib/allen2003.pdf>
Annan, Noel (1990), *Our Age* (London: Weidenfeld and Nicolson)
Arblaster, Anthony (1984), *The Rise and Decline of Western Liberalism* (Oxford: Blackwell)
Auerbach, Eric (1968), *Mimesis: The Representation of Reality in Western Literature*, trans. Willard R. Trask (Princeton: Princeton University Press)
Austin, J. L. (1950), review of Gilbert Ryle, *The Concept of Mind*, *The Times Literary Supplement*, 7 April, Religious Books Section [*sic*], xi; repr. in Oscar P. Wood and George Pitcher (eds), *Ryle* (London etc., 1971: Macmillan)
Barrett, William (1949), 'Art, Aristocracy and Reason', *Partisan Review* 16, 658–65
—— (1958), *Irrational Man* (New York: Doubleday)
Barth, Karl (1919), *Epistle to the Romans*, trans. Edwyn C. Hoskyns (Oxford, 1933: Oxford University Press)
Benner, Erica (1997), 'Nationality without Nationalism', *Journal of Political Ideologies* 2, 189–206

Ben-Rafael, Eliezer (2002) (ed.), *Jewish Identities: Fifty Intellectuals Answer Ben Gurion* (Leiden/Boston: Brill)

Berdyaev, N. A., S. N. Bulgakov, M. O. Gershenzon, A. S. Izgoev, B. A. Kistyakovsky, P. B. Struve and S. L. Frank (1909), *Vekhi* ['Signposts'] (Moscow: Tipografiya V. M. Sablina)

Berlin, Isaiah: see previous section

Bernhardt, Reinhold (1990), *Der Absolutheitsanspruch des Christentums* (Gütersloh: Gütersloher Verlagshaus, Gerd Mohn)

Bonhoeffer, Dietrich (1949), *Ethics*, trans. Reinhard Krauss, Charles C. West and Douglas W. Stott (Minneapolis, 2005: Fortress Press)

—— (1952), *Letters and Papers from Prison*, ed Eberhard Bethge, enlarged ed. (New York, 1971: Macmillan)

Boraine, Alex (2000), 'Truth and Reconciliation in South Africa: the Third Way', in Rotberg and Thompson 2000

Bosanquet, Bernard (1899), *The Philosophical Theory of the State* (London: Macmillan)

Bowra, C. M. (1966), *Memories: 1898–1939* (London: Weidenfeld and Nicolson)

Braithwaite, John (2000), 'Repentance Rituals and Restorative Justice', *Journal of Political Philosophy* 8, 115–31

Brighouse, Harry (1998), 'Against Nationalism', in Jocelyne Couture, Kai Nielsen and Michel Seymour (eds), *Rethinking Nationalism* (Calgary: University of Calgary Press) (*Canadian Journal of Philosophy*, supplementary vol. 22), 365–405

—— (2000), *School Choice and Social Justice* (Oxford: Oxford University Press)

Brodsky, Joseph (1989), 'Isaiah Berlin at Eighty', *New York Review of Books*, 17 August, 44–5

Brogan, A. P. (1931), 'Objective Pluralism in the Theory of Value', *International Journal of Ethics* 41, 287–95

Bruce, F. F. (1968), 'Scripture and Tradition in the New Testament', in id. and E. G. Rupp (eds), *Holy Book and Holy Tradition: International Colloquium Held in the Faculty of Theology, University of Manchester* (Manchester: Manchester University Press)

Bulgakov, S. N. (1903), *Ot marksizma k idiealizmu: sbornik statei (1896–1903)* (St Petersburg: Obshchestvennaya Polza)

Bull, Martin (1993), 'God, Creation and the Genitals', *Guardian*, 26 October, 15

Burke, Edmund (1790), *Reflections on the Revolution in France*, in *The Writings and Speeches of Edmund Burke*, General Editor Paul Langford (Oxford, 1981– : Clarendon Press), vol. 8, *The French Revolution 1790–1794*, L. G. Mitchell (ed.) (1989)

Bushnell, Horace (1887), 'Sermon XVIII: The Outside Saints', in *Sermons on Living Subjects* (New York: Scribner)

Butler, Joseph (1726), *Fifteen Sermons Preached at the Rolls Chapel* (London, 1726)

Caputo, John D. (1997), *The Prayers and Tears of Jacques Derrida: Religion without Religion* (Bloomington: Indiana University Press)

Carr, E. H. (1945), *Democracy in International Affairs* (Nottingham: University College Nottingham)

—— (1946), *The Soviet Impact on the Western World* (London: Macmillan)

Carpenter, Humphrey (1996), *The Envy of the World: Fifty Years of the BBC Third Programme and Radio 3, 1946–1996* (London: Weidenfeld and Nicolson)

Carr, E. H. (1961), *What Is History?* (London/New York: Macmillan/St Martin's Press)

Carter, Ian (1995), 'The Independent Value of Freedom', *Ethics* 105, 819–45

—— (1999), *A Measure of Freedom* (Oxford: Oxford University Press)

Carver, Terrell (1983), *Marx and Engels: The Intellectual Relationship* (Brighton: Harvester/ Wheatsheaf)

Chamberlain, Lesley (2004), *Motherland: A Philosophical History of Russia* (London: Atlantic)

Chang, Ruth (1997) (ed.), *Incommensurability, Incomparability, and Practical Reason* (Cambridge, Mass., and London: Harvard University Press)

Cherniss, Joshua L., and Henry Hardy (2005), 'Berlin, Isaiah', *Stanford Encyclopedia of Philosophy*, online at <http://plato.stanford.edu/entries/berlin/>

—— (2006), 'Isaiah Berlin's Political Ideas: From the Twentieth Century to the Romantic Age', introduction to PIRA

Chernyshevsky, N. G. (1858), 'The Struggle of the Parties in the France of Louis XVIII and Charles X', *Polnoe sobranie sochinenii* (Moscow, 1939–53: Khudozhestvennaya Literatura), vol. 5

Coakley, Sarah (1988), *Christ without Absolutes: A Study of the Christology of Ernst Troeltsch* (Oxford: Clarendon Press)

Cocks, Joan (2002), *Passion and Paradox: Intellectuals Confront the National Question* (Princeton and Oxford: Princeton University Press)

Coffin, William Sloane (2004), *Credo* (Louisville: Westminster/John Knox)

Cohen, G. A. (1978) *Karl Marx's Theory of History: A Defence* (Oxford: Clarendon Press)

—— (2003), 'Freedom and Money', <http://www.fiu.edu/~henleyk/Cohen, Freedom and Money.htm > (accessed 21 November 2006)

Collingwood, R. G. (1939), *An Autobiography* (London: Oxford University Press)

—— (1940), *An Essay on Metaphysics*, revised ed., Rex Martin (ed.) (Oxford, 1998: Clarendon Press)

Confino, M. (1974) (ed.), *Daughter of a Revolutionary: Natalie Herzen and the Bakunin–Nechaev Circle* (London: Alcove Press)

Constant, Benjamin (1815), *Principes de politique*, in *Écrits politiques*, Marcel Gauchet (ed.) (Paris, 1997: Gallimard)

Cracraft, James (2002), 'A Berlin for Historians', *History and Theory* 41, 277–300

Cragg, Wesley (1992), *The Practice of Punishment: Towards a Theory of Restorative Justice* (London: Routledge)

Crowder, George (1994), 'Pluralism and Liberalism', *Political Studies* 42, 293–305 (see also Berlin and Williams 1994)

—— (2002), *Liberalism and Value Pluralism* (London and New York: Continuum)

—— (2006), 'Gray and the Politics of Pluralism', *Critical Review of International Social and Political Philosophy* 9, 171–88

—— (2007), 'Two Concepts of Liberal Pluralism', *Political Theory*, forthcoming

Danto, Arthur C. (1999), 'In Their Own Voice: Philosophical Writing and Actual Experience', in id., *The Body/Body Problem: Selected Essays* (Berkeley: University of California Press)

Dawson, Christopher (1957), review of Berlin 1954, *Harvard Law Review* 70, 584–8

Day, J. P. (1970), 'On Liberty and the Real Will', *Philosophy* 45, 177–92

D'Costa, Gavin (1996), 'The Impossibility of a Pluralist View of Religions', *Religious Studies* 32, 223–32

—— (2000), *The Meeting of Religions and the Trinity* (Maryknoll: Orbis)

Dickson, Gwen Griffith (1995), *Johann Georg Hamann's Relational Metacriticism* (Berlin/New York: Walter de Gruyter)

Disraeli, Benjamin (1847), *Tancred, or, The New Crusade*, vol. 10 of the Bradenham Edition of the Novels and Tales of Benjamin Disraeli, 1st Earl of Beaconsfield (London, 1926–7: P. Davies)

Dulles, Avery (1987), *Models of the Church*, expanded ed. (New York: Doubleday)

Duncan, Graeme (1973), *Marx and Mill: Two Views of Social Conflict and Social Harmony* (Cambridge: Cambridge University Press)

Dunn, James D. G. (2001), 'Diversity in Paul', in Dan Cohn-Sherbok and John M. Court (eds), *Religious Diversity in the Graeco-Roman World: A Survey of Recent Scholarship* (Sheffield: Sheffield Academic Press)

Du Toit, André (1996), 'Philosophical Perspectives on the Truth Commission? Some Preliminary Notes and Fragments' (presented at the Annual Meeting of the Philosophical Society of Southern Africa, Stellenbosch, South Africa)

Dworkin, Ronald (1977), 'What Rights Do We Have?', in id., *Taking Rights Seriously* (London: Duckworth)

Elster, Jon (2004), *Closing the Books: Transitional Justice in Historical Perspective* (Cambridge: Cambridge University Press)

Engstrom, Stephen (2002), 'The Inner Freedom of Virtue', in Mark Timmons (ed.), *Kant's Metaphysics of Morals: Interpretive Essays* (Oxford: Oxford University Press)

Ferguson, Adam (1767), *An Essay on the History of Civil Society*, ed Fania Oz-Salzburger (Cambridge, 1995: Cambridge University Press)

Franco, Paul (2003), 'The Shapes of Liberal Thought: Oakeshott, Berlin, and Liberalism', *Political Theory* 31, 484–507

Friedman, Thomas L. (2001), 'The Real War', *New York Times*, 27 November, A21

Frisch, Morton J. (1998), 'A Critical Appraisal of Isaiah Berlin's Philosophy of Pluralism', *Review of Politics* 60, 421–33

Furet, François (1995), *Le passé d'une illusion: Essai sur l'idée communiste au XXᵉ siècle* (Paris: Calmann-Lévy); English trans. by Deborah Furet, *The Passing of an Illusion: The Idea of Communism in the Twentieth Century* (Chicago and London, 1999: University of Chicago Press)

Galston, William A. (2002), *Liberal Pluralism* (Cambridge: Cambridge University Press)

—— (2004), *The Practice of Liberal Pluralism* (New York: Cambridge University Press)

Garrard, Graeme (2003), *Rousseau's Counter-Enlightenment: A Republican Critique of the Philosophes* (Albany, NY: SUNY Press)

—— (2006), *Counter-Enlightenments: From the Eighteenth Century to the Present* (London and New York: Routledge)

Gelderen, Martin van, and Quentin Skinner (2002) (eds), *Republicanism: A Shared European Heritage* (Cambridge: Cambridge University Press)

Gellner, Ernest (1997), *Nationalism* (London: Weidenfeld and Nicolson)

Gerth, H. H., and C. Wright Mills (1946) (eds and trans.), *From Max Weber: Essays in Sociology* (New York: Oxford University Press)

Geyl, Pieter (1955), *Debates With Historians* (Groningen/The Hague/London: J. B. Wolters/Martinus Nijhoff/Batsford)

Gray, John N. (1980), 'On Negative and Positive Liberty', *Political Studies* 28, 507–26

—— (1993), *Post-Liberalism: Studies in Political Thought* (New York and London: Routledge)

—— (1995), *Enlightenment's Wake: Politics and Culture at the Close of the Modern Age* (New York and London: Routledge)

—— (2000), *Two Faces of Liberalism* (Cambridge: Polity)

—— (2006), 'Reply to Critics', *Critical Review of International Social and Political Philosophy* 9, 323–47

Green, T. H. (1895), *Lectures on the Principles of Political Obligation* (London: Longmans, Green)

Guthrie, Shirley C., Jr (1986), *Diversity in Faith, Unity in Christ* (Philadelphia: The Westminster Press)

Gutmann, Amy (1999), 'Liberty and Pluralism in Pursuit of the Non-Ideal', *Social Research* 66, 1039–62

—— and Dennis Thompson (2006) (eds), *Ethics and Politics: Cases and Comments*, 4th ed (Belmont, CA: Wadsworth)

Ha-'am, Ahad (1891), 'Avdut be-toch herut' ['Slavery in Freedom'], in *Selected Essays*, ed. and trans. Leon Simon (Cleveland/New York and Philadelphia, 1962: The World Publishing Company and The Jewish Publication Society of America)

Hacohen, Malachi Haim (2000) *Karl Popper—The Formative Years, 1902–1945: Politics and Philosophy in Interwar Vienna* (Cambridge: Cambridge University Press)

Hall, Douglas John (1986), *God and Human Suffering* (Minneapolis: Augsburg)

Hampshire, Stuart (1983), *Morality and Conflict* (Cambridge, MA: Harvard University Press)

—— (1999), *Justice Is Conflict* (London/Princeton: Duckworth/Princeton University Press)

Hampton, Jean (1990), 'The Retributive Idea', in Jeffrie G. Murphy and Jean Hampton, *Forgiveness and Mercy* (Cambridge: Cambridge University Press)

—— (1992), 'Correcting Harms versus Righting Wrongs: The Goal of Retribution', *UCLA Law Review* 39: 6 (August), 1659–1702

Hanley, Ryan Patrick (2004), 'Political Science and Political Understanding: Isaiah Berlin on the Nature of Political Inquiry', *American Political Science Review* 98, 327–39

Hardy, Henry (1993), 'The Compatibility of Incompatibles', *Independent*, 20 February, 33

—— (1995), 'Het ware pluralisme' (Dutch translation of 'Taking Pluralism Seriously', in this volume), *Nexus* No 13, 74–86; a Spanish translation, 'Tomándose el pluralismo en serio', appeared in Pablo Badillo O'Farrell and Enrique Bocardo Crespo (eds), *Isaiah Berlin: La mirada despierta de la historia* (Madrid, 1999: Tecnos)

—— (2000–) (ed.), *The Isaiah Berlin Virtual Library*, <http://berlin.wolf.ox.ac.uk> (Oxford: Wolfson College)

—— (2002), 'Pluralism and Radical Tolerance', *Insights* 118: 1 (Fall), 21–3, also available in the IBVL at <http://berlin.wolf.ox.ac.uk/writings_on_ib/hhonib/plurradtol.html>

Hart, H. L. A. (1979), 'Between Utility and Rights', in Ryan 1979

Hayner, Priscilla B. (2002), *Unspeakable Truths: Facing the Challenge of Truth Commissions* (New York and London: Routledge)

Hegel, G. W. F. (1821), *Philosophy of Right*, trans. and ed T. M. Knox (Oxford, 1942: Clarendon Press)

Herder, J. G. (1774), 'Auch eine Philosophie der Geschichte zur Bildung der Menschheit', in *Herder's sämmtliche Werke*, ed Bernhard Suphan (Berlin, 1877–1913: Weidmann), vol. 5

Herzen, Alexander (1855), *From the Other Shore*, trans. Moura Budberg, and *The Russian People and Socialism*, trans. Richard Wollheim, introduced by Isaiah Berlin (London, 1956: Weidenfeld and Nicolson)

Hess, Moses (1962): M. Heß, *Rom und Jerusalem: die letzte Nationalitätsfrage, Briefe und Noten* (Leipzig: Eduard Wengler)

Hick, John (1974), 'Christ's Uniqueness', *Reform*, October, 18–19

Hitchens, Christopher (1998), 'Moderation or Death', review of Ignatieff 1998, *London Review of Books*, 26 November, 3–11

Holmes, Stephen (1989), 'The Lion of Illiberalism', *New Republic*, 30 October, 32–7

Huntington, Samuel (1993), 'The Clash of Civilizations', *Foreign Affairs* 72, 22–49

—— (1996), *The Clash of Civilizations and the Remaking of World Order* (New York: Simon and Schuster)

Ignatieff, Michael (1993), *Blood and Belonging: Journeys into the New Nationalism* (London: BBC Books/Chatto and Windus)

—— and others (2002), *Human Rights as Politics and Idolatry*, ed Amy Gutmann (Princeton: Princeton University Press)

—— (2004), *The Lesser Evil: Political Ethics in an Age of Terror* (Princeton: Princeton University Press)

Inbody, Tyron L. (1997), *The Transforming God: An Interpretation of Suffering and Evil* (Louisville: Westminster/John Knox)

Irvin, Dale T. (1998), *Christian Histories, Christian Traditioning: Rendering Accounts* (Maryknoll: Orbis Books)

Ivanov-Razumnik (1907), *Istoriya russkoi obshchestvennoi mysli* (St Petersburg: Tipografiya M. M. Stasyulevicha)

—— (1908), *O smysle zhizni* (St Petersburg: Tipografiya M. M. Stasyulevicha)

James, Clive (2004), 'Guest from the Future', review of L1 and SM, *Times Literary Supplement*, 3 September, 3–8

James, William (1890), *The Principles of Psychology*, 2 vols (New York/London: Henry Holt/Macmillan)

—— (1891), 'The Moral Philosopher and the Moral Life', *International Journal of Ethics* 1, 330–54

—— (1902), *The Varieties of Religious Experience: A Study in Human Nature* (New York, London etc.: Longmans, Green)

—— (1909), *A Pluralistic Universe* (London: Longmans, Green)

James, Wilmot, and Linda van de Vijver (2000) (eds), *After the TRC: Reflections on Truth and Reconciliation in South Africa* (Cape Town/Athens, Ohio: David Philip/Ohio University Press)

Johnson, William Stacy (1997), *The Mystery of God: Karl Barth and the Postmodern Foundations of Theology* (Louisville: Westminster/John Knox Press)

Justinian (533), *Institutiones*, ed Paul Krüger, in *Corpus Iuris Civilis*, 16th ed., vol. 1 (Berlin, 1954: Weidmann)

Kahler, Erich (1964), *The Meaning of History* (London: Chapman and Hall)

Kant, Immanuel (1784), 'Idea for a Universal History with a Cosmopolitan Purpose', in *Kant's gesammelte Schriften* (Berlin, 1900–), vol. 8

Kekes, John (1993), *The Morality of Pluralism* (Princeton: Princeton University Press)

—— (1997), *Against Liberalism* (Ithaca: Cornell University Press)

—— (1998), *A Case for Conservatism* (Ithaca: Cornell University Press)

Kelly, Aileen (1998), *Toward Another Shore: Russian Thinkers between Necessity and Chance* (New Haven and London: Yale University Press)

Kelly, Paul (1999), 'Contextual and Non-Contextual Histories of Political Thought', in Jack Hayward, Brian Barry and Archie Brown (eds), *The British Study of Politics in the Twentieth Century* (Oxford: Oxford University Press)

Kelsey, David H. (1992), *To Understand God Truly: What's Theological about a Theological School* (Louisville: Westminster/John Knox Press)

Kenny, Michael (2000), 'Isaiah Berlin's Contribution to Modern Political Theory', *Political Studies* 48, 1026–39

Kiss, Elizabeth (2000), 'Moral Ambition within and beyond Political Constraints: Reflections on Restorative Justice', in Rotberg and Thompson 2000

Kohn, Hans (1944), *The Idea of Nationalism: A Study in Its Origins and Background* (New York: Macmillan)

Kritz, Neil J. (1995) (ed.), *Transitional Justice: How Emerging Democracies Reckon with Former Regimes* (Washington, DC: United States Institute of Peace Press)

Kymlicka, Will (1989), *Liberalism, Community, and Culture* (Oxford: Clarendon Press)

—— (1995), *Multicultural Citizenship* (Oxford: Clarendon Press)

—— (2001), 'From Enlightenment Cosmopolitanism to Liberal Nationalism', in id., *Politics in the Vernacular: Nationalism, Multiculturalism and Citizenship* (Oxford: Oxford University Press)

Lampert, E. (1965), *Sons against Fathers: Studies in Russian Radicalism and Revolution* (Oxford: Clarendon Press)

Lamprecht, Sterling P. (1920), 'The Need for a Pluralistic Emphasis in Ethics', *Journal of Philosophy, Psychology and Scientific Methods* 17, 561–72

—— (1921), 'Some Political Implications of Ethical Pluralism', *Journal of Philosophy* 18, 225–44

Larmore, Charles (1996), *The Morals of Modernity* (Cambridge: Cambridge University Press)

Laslett, Peter (1956) (ed.), *Philosophy Politics and Society: A Collection* (Oxford: Blackwell)

Lenin, V. I. (1915), 'Karl Marx: A Brief Biographical Sketch with an Exposition of Marxism', in *Collected Works*, 4th ed., vol. 21, *August 1914–December 1915* (London/ Moscow, 1964: Lawrence & Wishart/Progress Publishers), 43–91

—— (1937) *What Is to Be Done?* (London: Lawrence and Wishart)

Levinson, Sanford (1988), *Constitutional Faith* (Princeton: Princeton University Press)

Libelt, Karol (1844), *On the Love of the Fatherland*, in id., *Samowladztwo rozumu i objawy filozofii slowianskiej* (Warsaw, 1967: Panstwowe Wydawnictwo Naukowe)

Lichtheim, George (1961), *Marxism: An Historical and Critical Study* (London: Routledge and Kegan Paul)

Lilla, Mark (1994), 'The Trouble with the Enlightenment', *London Review of Books*, 6 January, 12–13

Llewellyn, Jennifer, and Robert Howse (1999), 'Institutions for Restorative Justice: The South African Truth and Reconciliation Commission', *University of Toronto Law Journal* 49, 355–88

Locke, John (1689), 'A Letter concerning Toleration', Isaac Kramnick (ed.), in *The Portable Enlightenment Reader* (New York etc., 1995: Penguin)

Lukes, Steven (1994), 'The Singular and the Plural: On the Distinctive Liberalism of Isaiah Berlin', *Social Research* 61: 3 (Fall), 687–717

—— (1995), 'Pluralism Is Not Enough', *The Times Literary Supplement*, 10 February, 5

—— (1997) 'Comparing the Incomparable: Trade-Offs and Sacrifices', in Chang 1997

Machiavelli, Niccolò (1531), *Discourses on Livy*, trans. Harvey C. Mansfield and Nathan Tarcov (Chicago and London, 1996: University of Chicago Press)

MacCallum, Gerald C., Jr (1967), 'Negative and Positive Freedom', *Philosophical Review* 76, 312–34

McKinney, Ronald J. (1992), 'Towards a Postmodern Ethics: Sir Isaiah Berlin and John Caputo', *Journal of Value Inquiry* 26, 395–407

MacCormick, Neil (1982), 'Nation and Nationalism', in id., *Legal Right and Social Democracy: Essays in Legal and Political Philosophy* (Oxford: Clarendon Press)

Macdonald, Margaret (1951), 'The Language of Political Theory', in Antony Flew (ed.), *Essays on Logic and Language* (Oxford: Blackwell)

—— (1956), 'Natural Rights', in Laslett 1956

Macfarlane, L. J. (1966), 'On Two Concepts of Liberty', *Political Studies* 14, 77–81

McLellan, David (1969), *The Young Hegelians and Karl Marx* (London: Macmillan)

—— (1970), *Marx before Marxism* (London: Macmillan)

—— (1971a) (ed. and trans.), Karl Marx, *Early Texts* (Oxford: Blackwell)

—— (1971b), *The Thought of Karl Marx: An Introduction* (London: Macmillan)

—— (1973), *Karl Marx: His Life and Thought* (London: Macmillan)

Maistre, Joseph de (1797), *Considerations on France*, trans. and ed Richard A. Lebrun (Cambridge, 1994: Cambridge University Press)

—— (1821), *Les Soirées de Saint-Pétersbourg*, in *Œuvres complètes de J. de Maistre* (Lyon/Paris, 1884–7: E. Vitte), vol. 5

March, W. Eugene (2005), *The Wide, Wide Circle of Divine Love: A Biblical Case for Religious Diversity* (Louisville: Westminster/John Knox Press)

Margalit, Avishai (1996), *The Decent Society* (Cambridge, Mass., and London: Harvard University Press)

—— and Joseph Raz (1995), 'National Self-Determination', in Will Kymlicka (ed.), *The Rights of Minority Cultures* (Oxford: Oxford University Press)

Mazurek, Kas (1979), 'Isaiah Berlin's Philosophy of History: Structure; Method; Implications', *Philosophy and Social Criticism* 6, 391–406

Mazzini, Giuseppe (1861), open letter to Messrs Rodbertus, Von Berg and L. Bucher, 30 March, in Giuseppe Mazzini, *Lettere aperte*, ed Giuseppe Tramarollo (Pisa, 1978: Pacini); trans. in part as 'Reply to the German Nationalists' in Ignazio Silone (ed.), *The Living Thoughts of Mazzini* (London etc., 1939: Cassell)

Meriwether, Nicholas (2002), 'The Irrelevance of Value Pluralism for Political Theory', unpublished MS

Merleau-Ponty, Maurice (1969), *Humanism and Terror: An Essay on the Communist Problem*, trans. J. O'Neill (Boston: Beacon Press)

Mikhailovsky, N. K. (1869), *Polnoe sobranie sochinenii* (St Petersburg, 1896: Tipografiya B. M. Vol'fa)

Mill, John Stuart (1859), *On Liberty*, in Robson and others (1977), vol. 18

—— (1861), *Considerations on Representative Government*, in Robson and others (1977), vol. 19

Miller, David (1983), 'Constraints on Freedom', *Ethics* 94, 66–86

—— (1995), *On Nationality* (Oxford: Clarendon Press)

—— (2004), review of Cocks 2002, *History of Political Thought* 25 (2004), 365–7

—— (2005), 'Reasonable Partiality Towards Compatriots', *Ethical Theory and Moral Practice* 8, 63–81

—— and Cécile Fabre (2003), 'Justice and Culture: Rawls, Sen, Nussbaum and O'Neill', *Political Studies Review* 1, 4–17

Montaigne, Michel de (1588), *Essais*, book 3, chapter 3, 'De trois commerces'

—— ed. Screech (1991): *The Essays of Michel de Montaigne*, trans. and ed M. A. Screech (London: Allen Lane, the Penguin Press)

Murphy, Jeffrie (2003), *Getting Even: Forgiveness and Its Limits* (Oxford and New York: Oxford University Press)

Nagel, Ernest (1960), 'Determinism in History', *Philosophy and Phenomenological Research* 20, 291–317

Naiman, Anatoly (2002), *Ser: Roman* (Moscow: Eksmo)

Newey, Glen (1998), 'Value-Pluralism in Contemporary Liberalism', *Dialogue* 37, 493–522

Niebuhr, Reinhold (1932), *Moral Man and Immoral Society* (New York: Scribner)

Nietzsche, Friedrich (1877), *Nachgelassene Fragmente*, in Nietzsche, *Werke: Kritische Gesamtausgabe*, Giorgio Colli and Mazzino Montinari (eds) (Berlin, 1967– : Walter de Gruyter), part 8, vol. 2

Nordau, Max (1897), 'Address at the First Zionist Congress, Basle, August 29, 1897', in *Max Nordau to his People: A Summons and a Challenge* (New York, 1941: Scopus)

Ntsebeza, Dumisa (2000), 'The Uses of Truth Commissions: Lessons for the World', in Rotberg and Thompson 2000

Nussbaum, Martha (2000), *Women and Human Development: The Capabilities Approach* (Cambridge: Cambridge University Press)

—— (2001), 'Political Objectivity', *New Literary History* 32, 883–906

—— (2003), 'Political Liberalism and Respect: A Response to Linda Barclay', *Sats* 4: 2, 25–44

—— (2006), *Frontiers of Justice: Disability, Nationality, Species Membership*, The Tanner Lectures on Human Values 2002 (Cambridge, Mass.: Belknap)

Oakeshott, Michael (1962), 'The Voice of Poetry in the Conversation of Mankind', in id., *Rationalism in Politics and Other Essays* (London: Methuen)

Oppenheim, Felix E. (1961), *Dimensions of Freedom: An Analysis* (New York/London: St Martin's Press/Macmillan)

Orlova, Raisa (1982), *Poslednii god zhizni Gertsena* (New York: Chalidze)

O'Sullivan, Noël (2004), *European Political Thought since 1945* (London: Palgrave Macmillan)

Pearsall, Judy (1999) (ed.), *The Concise Oxford Dictionary*, 10th ed. (Oxford: Oxford University Press)

Pew Forum (2002), 'American Views on Religion, Politics, and Public Policy', The Pew Forum on Religion and Public Life and the Pew Research Center for the People and the Press, Washington DC, April

Plaw, Avery (2004), 'Why Monist Critiques Feed Value Pluralism: Ronald Dworkin's Critique of Isaiah Berlin', *Social Theory and Practice* 30, 105–26

Park, Eung Chun (2003), *Either Jew or Gentile: Paul's Unfolding Theology of Inclusivity* (Louisville: Westminster/John Knox)

Passmore, John (1959), 'History, the Individual, and Inevitability', *Philosophical Review* 68, 93–102

Plamenatz, John (1938), *Consent, Freedom and Political Obligation* (London: Oxford University Press)

Plamenatz, John (1973), 'Two Types of Nationalism', in Eugene Kamenka (ed.), *Nationalism: The Nature and Evolution of an Idea* (Canberra: Australian National University Press)

Plekhanov, G. V. (1896), *Essays in the History of Materialism*, trans. Ralph Fox (London, 1934: John Lane The Bodley Head)

Pocock, J. G. A. (1999), 'Enlightenment and Counter-Enlightenment, Revolution and Counter-Revolution: A Eurosceptical Enquiry', *History of Political Thought* 20, 125–39

Popper, Karl (1945), *The Open Society and Its Enemies* (London: Routledge and Kegan Paul)

Presbyterian Church (1999), The Constitution of the Presbyterian Church (USA), Part I: *The Book of Confessions* (Louisville: The Office of the General Assembly)

Rathenau, Walter (1816), letter to Wilhelm Schwaner of 18 August, in Walther Rathenau, *Ein preussischer Europäer: Briefe*, ed Margarete von Eynern (Berlin, 1955: Käthe Vogt)

Rawls, John (1971), *A Theory of Justice* (Cambridge, Mass.: Belknap Press)

—— (1993), *Political Liberalism* (New York: Columbia University Press)

Raz, Joseph (1995) 'Multiculturalism: A Liberal Perspective', in id., *Ethics in the Public Domain: Essays in the Morality of Law and Politics* (Oxford: Clarendon Press)

Reich, Rob (2002), *Bridging Liberalism and Multiculturalism in American Education* (Chicago: University of Chicago Press)

Reiman, Jeffrey (1995), 'Justice, Civilization and the Death Penalty: Answering van den Haag', in A. John Simmons and others (eds), *Punishment* (Princeton: Princeton University Press)

Rescher, Nicholas (1993), *Pluralism: Against the Demand for Consensus* (Oxford: Oxford University Press/Clarendon Press)

Rhoads, David (1996), *The Challenge of Diversity: The Witness of Paul and the Gospels* (Minneapolis: Fortress Press)

Robson, J. M., and others (1977), *Collected Works of John Stuart Mill* (Toronto/London, 1963–91: University of Toronto Press/Routledge and Kegan Paul), vols 18–19, *Essays on Politics and Society*

Rorty, Richard (1989), *Contingency, Irony, and Solidarity* (Cambridge etc.: Cambridge University Press)

Rosen, Michael (1993), 'The First Romantic? J. G. Hamann's Passionate Critique of the Enlightenment', review of MN, *The Times Literary Supplement*, 8 October, 3–4

Rosenblum, Nancy L. (1987), *Another Liberalism: Romanticism and the Reconstruction of Liberal Thought* (Cambridge, Mass., and London: Harvard University Press)

Rotberg, Robert I. (2000), 'Truth Commissions and the Provision of Truth, Justice, and Reconciliation', in Rotberg and Thompson 2000

—— and Dennis Thompson (eds) (2000), *Truth v. Justice: The Morality of Truth Commissions* (Princeton: Princeton University Press)

Rotenstreich, Nathan (1963), 'Historical Inevitability and Human Responsibility', *Philosophy and Phenomenological Research* 23, 380–96

Rousseau, Jean-Jacques (1762), *On the Social Contract*, in *The Collected Writings of Rousseau*, vol. 4, ed Roger D. Masters and Christopher Kelly, trans. Judith R. Bush, Roger D. Masters and Christopher Kelly (Hanover and London, 1994: University Press of New England)

Ruggiero, Guido de (1925), *Storia del liberalismo europeo* (Bari: Laterza), trans. R. G. Collingwood as *The History of European Liberalism* (London, 1927: Oxford University Press)

Ryan, Alan (2005), 'Isaiah Berlin, 1909–1997', *Proceedings of the British Academy* 130, 3–20

Schmidt, James (2000), 'What Enlightenment Project?', *Political Theory* 28, 734–57

Sacks, Jonathan (2002), *The Dignity of Difference: How to Avoid the Clash of Civilizations* (London: Continuum)

—— (n.d.), 'A Clash of Civilizations? Judaic Sources on Co-existence in a World of Difference', <http://www.chiefrabbi.org/dd/titlecontents.html> (accessed 21 November 2006)

Schumpeter, Joseph A. (1943), *Capitalism, Socialism and Democracy* (London: Allen and Unwin)

Sen, Amartya (1988), 'Freedom of Choice: Concept and Content', *European Economic Review* 32, 269–94

Shestov, Lev (1903), *Dostoevskii i Nitshe: filosofiya tragedii* (St Petersburg: Tipografiya M. M. Stasyulevicha)

—— (1905), *Apofeoz bezpochvennosti: opyt adogmaticheskogo myshleniya* (St Petersburg: Tipografiya Tovarishchestva 'Obshchestvennaya Pol´sa')

Shklar, Judith N. (1957), *After Utopia* (Princeton: Princeton University Press)

—— (1989), 'The Liberalism of Fear', in Nancy L. Rosenblum (ed.), *Liberalism and the Moral Life* (Cambridge, Mass., and London: Harvard University Press)

—— (1996), 'A Life of Learning', in Bernard Yack (ed.), *Liberalism without Illusions* (Chicago: University of Chicago Press)

Shweder, Richard A. (2003), 'The Idea of Moral Progress: Bush versus Posner versus Berlin', in the yearbook of the Philosophy of Education Society (USA), *Philosophy of*

Education 2003, 29–56; the article, and a series of replies, is available online at <http://www.ed.uiuc.edu/EPS/PES-yearbook/2003/2003toc.htm> (accessed 21 November 2006)

Siedentop, L. A. (1994), 'The Ionian Fallacy: Isaiah Berlin's Attack on Singlemindedness', *The Times Literary Supplement*, 23 September

Skagestad, Peter (2005), 'Collingwood and Berlin: A Comparison', *Journal of the History of Ideas* 66, 99–112

Skinner, Quentin (1984), 'The Idea of Negative Liberty: Philosophical and Historical Perspectives', in Richard Rorty, J. B. Schneewind and Quentin Skinner (eds), *Philosophy in History* (Cambridge: Cambridge University Press)

—— (1998), *Liberty before Liberalism* (Cambridge: Cambridge University Press)

—— (2002a), 'A Third Concept of Liberty', *Proceedings of the British Academy* 117, 237–68

—— (2002b), *Visions of Politics*, vol. 1, *Regarding Method* (Cambridge: Cambridge University Press)

Smith, Adam (1759), *The Theory of Moral Sentiments*, ed D. D. Raphael and A. L. Macfie (Oxford, 1976: Clarendon Press)

Smith, Anthony D. (1991), *National Identity* (London: Penguin)

Smith, Revd Bailey (1980), Religious Roundtable national affairs briefing, Dallas, Texas, July

Smith, Steven B. (2006), *Reading Leo Strauss: Politics, Philosophy, Judaism* (Chicago: University of Chicago Press)

Spender, Stephen (1950) Contribution to Arthur Koestler and others, *The God That Failed: Six Studies in Communism* (London: Hamish Hamilton)

Staten, Henry (1984), *Wittgenstein and Derrida* (Lincoln: University of Nebraska Press)

Steiner, Hillel (1975), 'Individual Liberty', *Proceedings of the Aristotelian Society* 75, 35–50

Stephen, James Fitzjames (1873), *Liberty, Equality, Fraternity*, ed Stuart D. Warner (Indianapolis, 1993: Liberty Fund)

Sternhell, Zeev (2006), *Les anti-Lumières: Du XVIIIe siècle à la guerre froide* (Paris: Fayard)

Strauss, Leo (1952), *Persecution and the Art of Writing* (Glencoe, Ill.: Free Press)

—— (1961) ' "Relativism" ', in Helmut Schoeck and James W. Wiggins (eds), *Relativism and the Study of Man* (Princeton: Van Nostrand)

Swift, Adam (2001), *Political Philosophy: A Beginners' Guide for Students and Politicians* (Cambridge: Polity)

Talmon, J. L. (1952), *The Origins of Totalitarian Democracy* (London: Secker and Warburg)

Tamir, Yael (1993), *Liberal Nationalism* (Princeton: Princeton University Press)

Tanner, Kathryn (1997), *Theories of Culture: A New Agenda for Theology* (Minneapolis: Fortress Press)

Taylor, Charles (1979), 'What's Wrong with Negative Liberty', in Ryan 1979

—— (1985), 'Neutrality in Political Science', in *Philosophy and the Human Sciences: Philosophical Papers 2* (Cambridge etc.: Cambridge University Press)

—— (1992), *Multiculturalism and 'The Politics of Recognition'* (Princeton: Princeton University Press)

Taylor, Mark C. (1984), *Erring: A Postmodern A/theology* (Chicago: University of Chicago Press)

Teitel, Ruti G. (2000), *Transitional Justice* (Oxford and New York: Oxford University Press)

Thomas, Paul (1991), 'Critical Reception: Marx Then and Now', in Terrell Carver (ed.), *The Cambridge Companion to Marx* (Cambridge: Cambridge University Press)

Torrance, Alan J. (1997), 'Theology and Political Correctness', in Lawrence Osborn and Andrew Walker (eds), *Harmful Religion: An Exploration of Religious Abuse* (London: SPCK)

Troeltsch, Ernst (trans. 1991), *Religion in History*, trans. James Luther Adams and Walter F. Bense (Minneapolis, 1991: Fortress Press)

Turgenev, Ivan (1860), *Hamlet and Don Quixote: An Essay*, trans. Robert Nichols (London, 1930: Hendersons)

Tutu, Desmond (chairman) (1998), *Truth and Reconciliation Commission of South Africa: Report*, vol. 1 (Cape Town: Juta)

—— (1999), *No Future without Forgiveness* (London: Rider)

Valls, Andrew (2003), 'Racial Justice as Transitional Justice', *Polity* 36, 53–71

Verwoerd, Wilhelm (1997), 'Justice after Apartheid? Reflections on the South African Truth and Reconciliation Commission' (presented at the Fifth International Conference on Ethics and Development, Madras, India)

Vincent, A. (1997), 'Liberal Nationalism: An Irresponsible Compound?', *Political Studies* 45, 275–95

Vincent, Saint, of Lérins (434), *The Commonitorium of Vincentius of Lérins*, ed Reginald Stewart Moxon (Cambridge, 1915: Cambridge University Press)

Waismann, Friedrich (1945), 'Verifiability', in Waismann ed Harré 1968, 39–66

—— (1946), 'Language Strata', part 1, in Waismann ed Harré 1968, 91–102

—— ed Harré (1968), *How I See Philosophy*, ed R. Harré (London: Macmillan)

Waldron, Jeremy (1995), 'Minority Cultures and the Cosmopolitan Alternative', in Will Kymlicka (ed.), *The Rights of Minority Cultures* (Oxford: Oxford University Press)

Walicki, Andrzej (1959), 'Materializm "antropologiczny" Nikołaja Czernyszewskiego', *Studia Filozficzne* 4 (13), 149–81; trans. into Russian by Galina Mileikovskaya as '"Antropologicheskii" materializm N. G. Chernyshevskogo', *Studia Filozoficzne: izbrannye stat'i/ Selected Articles/Articles choisis/Ausgewählte Aufsätze*, vol. 1, *1957–1960* (1962), 181–99

—— (1962), 'Turgenev and Schopenhauer', *Oxford Slavonic Papers* 10, 1–17

—— (1980), *A History of Russian Thought from the Enlightenment to Marxism* (Oxford: Clarendon Press)

—— (1982), *Philosophy and Romantic Nationalism: The Case of Poland* (Oxford: Clarendon Press)

—— (1990), ' "The Captive Mind" Revisited: Intellectuals and Communist Totalitarianism in Poland', in Ellen Frankel Paul (ed.), *Totalitarianism at the Crossroads* (New Brunswick and London: Transaction Books)

—— (1993), *Zniewolony umysł po latach* (Warsaw: Czytelnik)

—— (1994), 'Russian Philosophers of the Silver Age as Critics of Marxism', in James P. Scanlan (ed.), *Russian Thought after Communism: The Recovery of a Philosophical Heritage* (Armonk, NY: M. E. Sharpe)

—— (2005), *Russia, Poland and Marxism: Isaiah Berlin to Andrzej Walicki 1962–1996* [*Dialogue and Universalism* 15: 9–10]

Walzer, Michael (1987), *Interpretation and Social Criticism* (Cambridge, Mass.: Harvard University Press)

—— (1990), 'Nation and Universe', in Grethe B. Peterson (ed.), *The Tanner Lectures on Human Values* 11 (Salt Lake City: University of Utah Press)

—— (1994), *Thick and Thin: Moral Argument at Home and Abroad* (Notre Dame: University of Notre Dame Press)

—— (1997), *On Toleration* (New Haven and London: Yale University Press)

Weber, Max (1917), 'The Meaning of "Ethical Neutrality" in Sociology and Economics', in id., *The Methodology of the Social Sciences*, ed and trans. Edward A. Shils and Henry A. Finch (Glencoe, Ill., 1949: Free Press)

—— (1918a), 'Politics as a Vocation', in Gerth and Mills 1946

—— (1918b), 'Science as a Vocation', in Gerth and Mills 1946

West, David (2003), 'Spinoza on Positive Freedom', *Political Studies* 41, 284–96 (see also Berlin 1993)

Westermarck, Edward (1932), *Ethical Relativity* (London: Routledge and Kegan Paul)

Wheen, Francis (1999), *Karl Marx* (London: Fourth Estate)

White, Morton (1999), *A Philosopher's Story* (University Park: Pennsylvania State University Press)

Williams, Bernard (2001), 'From Freedom to Liberty: The Construction of a Political Value', repr. in id., *In the Beginning Was the Deed* (Princeton, 2005: Princeton University Press)

Williams, Rowan (2000), *On Christian Theology* (Oxford: Blackwell)

Wilson, Richard A. (2001), *The Politics of Truth and Reconciliation in South Africa: Legitimizing the Post-Apartheid State* (Cambridge: Cambridge University Press)

Wokler, Robert (1995), 'Singular Praise for a Pluralist', *The Times Higher Education Supplement*, 3 March, 22

Wolfe, Alan (1998), *One Nation, After All* (New York: Viking)

[Wollheim, Richard] (1959), 'A Hundred Years After', review (unattributed) of Berlin 1958, *The Times Literary Supplement*, 20 February, 89–90

Wolterstorff, Nicholas (2002), 'Comments on William A. Galston's *Liberal Pluralism*', prepared for delivery at The Pew Forum on Religion and Public Life, Washington DC, 20 June

Woodruff, Paul (2001), *Reverence: Renewing a Forgotten Virtue* (Oxford/New York: Oxford University Press)

Wright, M., and B. Galaway (1989) (eds), *Mediation and Criminal Justice: Victims, Offenders and Community* (London: Sage)

Zakaras, Alex (2004), 'Isaiah Berlin's Cosmopolitan Ethics', *Political Theory* 32, 495–518

Zehr, Howard (1990), *Changing Lenses: A New Focus for Crime and Justice* (Scottdale, Penn.: Herald Press)

Zenger, Erich (1994), *Ein Gott der Rache: Feindpsalmen verstehen* (Freiburg im Breisgau: Herder)

Zuckert, Catherine, and Michael Zuckert (2006), *The Truth about Leo Strauss: Political Philosophy and American Democracy* (Chicago: University of Chicago Press)

Index

Douglas Matthews

Works by Isaiah Berlin (IB) appear under their titles; works by others under the author's name